文化与经典
Cultures and Classics

丛书主编：申相会　杨　斌　李潇珂
本册主编：申相会　张发强　杨华佳

高三
Senior Three

重庆市巴蜀中学校英语教研室
渝中区杨斌名师工作室
重庆市高中英语多维听说课程创新基地

SWUP 西南大学出版社

图书在版编目(CIP)数据

文化与经典. 高三 / 申相会, 张发强, 杨华佳主编
. -- 重庆 : 西南大学出版社, 2024.4
ISBN 978-7-5697-2358-8

Ⅰ. ①文… Ⅱ. ①申… ②张… ③杨… Ⅲ. ①英语课
- 高中 - 教学参考资料 Ⅳ. ①G634.413

中国国家版本馆CIP数据核字(2024)第086765号

文化与经典(高三)
WENHUA YU JINGDIAN
本册主编　申相会　张发强　杨华佳

责任编辑　张　琳
责任校对　王玉竹
排　　版　黄金红
出版发行　西南大学出版社(原西南师范大学出版社)
网址　www.xdcbs.com
地址　重庆市北碚区天生路2号
邮编　400715
经　　销　全国新华书店
印　　刷　重庆新荟雅科技有限公司
成品尺寸　185 mm×260 mm
印　　张　30.25
字　　数　712千字
版　　次　2024年4月 第1版
印　　次　2024年4月 第1次印刷
书　　号　ISBN 978-7-5697-2358-8
定　　价　58.00元

《文化与经典》(高三)编委会

出版说明

本丛书的目的是为学生提供一个全面了解英美文化和经典文学的平台。通过精选的文化短文和经典作品，激发学生对英语学习的兴趣，并提升他们的文化理解能力和文学素养。每个单元的文章都经过精心挑选和审校，确保文章的原汁原味，同时也易于学生理解。

本册(高三)内容包括:

Section A: Cultures(编者:申相会 杨华佳)

Unit One: Health(编者:徐薇 杨华佳)

Unit Two: Technology(编者:郭若仙 杨华佳)

Unit Three: Culture(编者:邓维 杨诗晗)

Unit Four: The Media(编者:申相会 傅钰)

Unit Five: Geography(编者:王晓佳 唐旭地)

Section B: Classics(编者:张发强 杨斌 李潇珂)

Anne of Green Gables(编者:张发强 杨斌 李潇珂)

特别说明:

1.本丛书是阅读类书籍，仅限于巴蜀中学和所属分部、分校师生使用，该书编写无任何商业目的，不面向社会发行。

2.由于选材途径广泛(网络、书刊等)，“文化”部分有些美文的作者未能署名或出处不明，在这里深表歉意。如涉及版权问题，烦请原作者联系以下邮箱:(wwsxh2@gmail.com)，方便支付稿酬。我们编写组特别尊重每一位作者的知识产权，选择您的作品只因喜欢、欣赏，深感值得将其推荐给我们的学生去阅读。

3.本丛书生词音标既有英式音标，也有美式音标。《普通高中英语课程标准(2017年版2020年修订)》在语音知识要求中提道:与不同地域的人进行交流时，可以识别出其发音和语调的不同。可见，教学中让学生熟悉英式语音和美式语音的差异是必要的。另外，部分生词重复出现，可加深学生对生词的印象。

编写团队

2024年4月

前言

作为一名从教三十余载的中学英语教师，我与同龄同事一道见证了我们国家近35年以来的教育改革和教材版本的变更，使用过的教材有20世纪80年代初期的川教版，之后的人教版（试用本）、人教版（正式本），英国教材*Look Ahead*，现在的外研版、人教版、北师大版、牛津版、重大版等。每一个版本的教材都有其时代的烙印和独特的优势，但在使用过程中，我总是想起自己上学的时候，除了精读教材，还有泛读教材以及多种课外阅读材料。我们徜徉在卷帙浩繁的书海里，不仅增长了语言文化知识，同时还获得了身心的愉悦。于是我便有了这个想法：阅读不仅是为了提高理解能力和答题能力，更是让我们在获取知识的同时愉悦身心。因此，我要为我的学生提供广博涉猎的阅读机会，为他们编一套阅读类书籍。这个梦想一直根植于我心中。

2014年，在带我校英语骨干教师申相会去海南参加全国赛课时，我将这一想法分享给她，我俩竟一拍即合。2015年春，在巴蜀中学微课题申报之际，我心中埋藏多年的这个夙愿终于迎来了第一缕阳光。作为英语教师，我想带领我的团队为学生提供一套能让他们既增长英语国家文化知识又提升文学素养的阅读类书籍。美好的初衷、研究的热忱、专家的指导、踏实的团队、充分的准备工作赢得了学校专家团队的认可，我们的“高中英语课外阅读——文化与经典校本教材研究编写”微课题顺利通过。

之后，重庆市教育学会第八届（2015—2017年）基础教育科研立项课题申报工作启动，我带领团队积极申报，并获准立项，于是该课题由校级微课题成长为市级课题。2015年12月29日，学校举行了开题报告会，将课题题目小幅调整为“高中英语课外阅读——文化与经典校本教材编写研究”。本丛书包括高一上至高三，一共五册，每册都包含“文化”与“经典”两个部分。“文化”部分收集英美国家有关生活、信念、艺术、道德法则、法律、风俗等方面的中短篇美文。“经典”部分收集具有典范性，经过历史沉淀下来的“最有价值的、最具代表性的”作品。

在编写过程中，老师们力求做到材料地道、原味。教材的编排充分考虑学生水平的差异，有效地预测学生在阅读过程中可能会遇到的阅读障碍。版面分为左右两栏，左边为文本主体，着重标出生词和难点，右边为对应注释。两部分难易层次分明,“文化”部分(Section A)难度较低,趣味性强,适合所有学生阅读;经典部分(Section B)则深入探讨文学经典,鼓励学生通过批判性思维来解读和评价文学作品。

随着本丛书的逐步深入,我们迎来了新的编纂团队成员,我由衷地为本丛书的不断精进与完备感到欣喜。在编纂本丛书的过程中,各领域专家的悉心指导和宝贵建议起到了举足轻重的作用,进一步充实了阅读内容并提升了其教育意义。

在此,我要向所有为本丛书倾注心血的编者和专家表达由衷的感谢。正是他们的不懈努力与深厚的专业素养,为本丛书的成功编纂提供了坚实的基石。同时,我也要感谢巴蜀中学及其分部、分校的师生们,他们的诚恳反馈与宝贵建议,使得本丛书更加契合实际教学的需要。愿这套精心编纂的丛书能成为学生学习路上的得力助手,帮助他们在掌握英语的同时,更好地理解和欣赏不同的文化和文学经典。

左文珍

2024年4月

目 录
Contents

Section A: Cultures

Section B: Classics

Section C: Answer Key

Section A

Cultures

Unit One Health

Text 1 Science Shows Watching Cute Animals Is Good for Your Health

You knew watching videos of puppies and kittens felt good but now there's data to back that feeling.

A study conducted by the University of Leeds in the United Kingdom, in partnership with Western Australia Tourism, has found evidence to suggest that watching cute animals may contribute to a reduction in stress and anxiety.

The study examined how watching images and videos of cute animals for 30 minutes affects blood pressure, heart rate and anxiety.

Dr. Andrea Utley, an associate professor at the University of Leeds, put together the 30-minute **montage** of the cute **critters**.

"There were some kittens, there was puppies, there were baby **gorillas**. There were **quokkas**. You know—the usual stuff that you would expect," Utley told CNN.

The quokka, an adorable creature found in Western Australia, is often referred to as "the world's happiest animal".

The sessions, conducted in December 2019, involved 19 subjects—15 students and four staff—and were intentionally timed

montage [ˌmɒnˈtɑːʒ] *n.* 蒙太奇;剪辑
critter [ˈkrɪtər] *n.* 生物
gorilla [gəˈrɪlə] *n.* 大猩猩
quokka [ˈkwɒkə] *n.* 短尾小袋鼠

during winter exams, a time when stress is at a significantly high level, particularly for medical students, according to Utley.

In all cases, the study saw blood pressure, heart rate and anxiety go down in participants, 30 minutes after watching the video.

The study recorded that average blood pressure dropped from 136/88 to 115/71—which the study pointed out is "within ideal blood pressure range". Average heart rates were lowered to 67.4 bpm, a reduction of 6.5%.

Anxiety rates also went down by 35%, measured using the State-Trait Anxiety Inventory, a self-assessment method often used in clinical settings to diagnose anxiety, according to the American Psychological Association.

"I was quite pleasantly surprised that during the session, every single measure for every single participant dropped—some heart rate reduced, blood pressure reduced," Utley said, "When they left, they filled the questionnaire in again and indicated that they were feeling less anxious."

When questioning the participants, the study found that most preferred video clips over still images, particularly of animals interacting with humans.

Utley hoped to conducted eight sessions in total but was forced to postpone due to **coronavirus** restrictions. She acknowledges it' ll likely not be until next year that more sessions can be conducted in person. Until then, she' s exploring online options to keep the study going.

By Joe Bagliere

coronavirus [kəˈrəʊnəvaɪrəs] *n.* 冠状病毒

Exercises

I. Read the following statements and decide whether they are true (T) or false (F) according to the text.

1.Watching cute animals may contribute to a reduction in stress and anxiety. T □ F □

2.The quokka is often referred to as "the world's happiest animal". T □ F □

3.A blood pressure of 136/88 is "within ideal blood pressure range". T □ F □

4.Most participants preferred video clips over still images. T □ F □

5.Utley has conducted a total of eight sessions on the relationship between watching cute animals and human health. T □ F □

II. Read the text and find answers to the following questions.

1.What did the research investigate?

____

2.What is the content of the video intended for the reseach subjects?

____

3. What arrangements did Utley make to increase the pressure of the participants before watching the video?

____

4.How can we scientifically measure our anxiety level?

____

III. Question for consideration.

If you wanted to continue to study the relationship between watching cute animals and human health, how would you conduct the research?

Text 2 Middle School Student Shares Story to Encourage Others Fighting Cancer

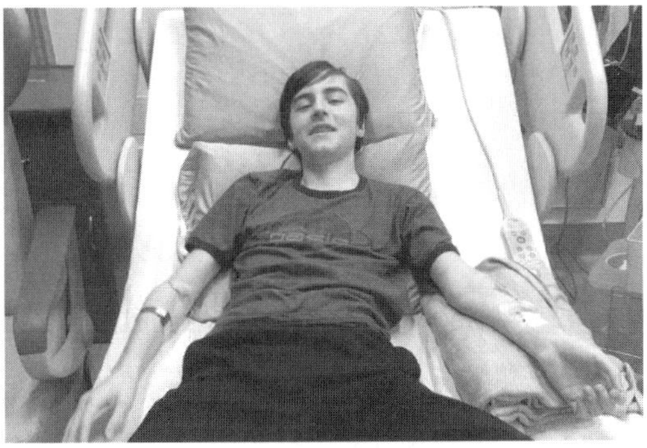

Like most 12-year-olds, Jaxon Starling loves sports, animals and hanging out with his family.

Starling has a **guinea pig** named Moon, and when he's not taking care of her, he's out running. Last year he was on the track team and also played soccer.

guinea pig [ˈɡɪni pɪɡ] *n.* 天竺鼠，豚鼠

"When he first started complaining about his leg hurting, we were thinking it was from him running track," said Shay Roberts, Starling's mother. She said over time the pain got worse, to the point where her son was limping and having problems walking. After a visit to the doctor and some tests, in December Starling was diagnosed with stage 4 **osteosarcoma**, a type of bone cancer that ended up spreading to his lungs.

osteosarcoma [ˌɒstɪəʊsɑːˈkəʊmə] *n.* 骨肉瘤

"Scared, fear, concerned—as a mom, that's one of the worst things you can hear about your child, and so I had a million thoughts run through my head at once. I think, for me, first off, it was just 'What do I need to do to make sure my child is okay? Who do I need to take him to? What do we need to do?' Let's put together a plan," Roberts explained.

Jaxon immediately started his journey in battling the disease and began **chemotherapy** at the Pauline Allen Gill Center for Cancer and Blood Disorders at Children's Health.

He also had his right knee replaced and a left lung transplanted this year.

Despite what he's gone through, Starling's attitude remains positive and his spirit continues to **soar**.

"I want to share my story with other kids," Starling said.

He said he wants to give kids in the hospital hope and let them know that they're not alone. He uses pipe cleaners to make **figurines** he calls "stick men" to hand out to other kids so that they're not alone.

"He is such a humble, humble kid; he doesn't think about himself, he thinks about others all the time. He always says, 'Ms. Sharon, you know, I'm going to help them, I'm going to talk to them,' and gives encouraging words and say 'they're going to be okay,' and he's just so sweet all the way around, I love him," said Sharon Stewart Walton, Starling's **phlebotomist** at Children's Health.

She, along with his family and faith are what help motivate him to keep pushing.

Walton understands what Starling and the other kids are going through, she too is battling cancer.

"I wanted the kids to know that they're not in it alone and that I'm fighting their battle with them," she said.

The relationship that she and Starling have is something Roberts appreciates for her son and finds comforting. They even have matching T-shirts that they wear, which says, "His fight is our fight, Jax the great."

"The conversation that we've had, she was like, 'As much as I'm going through and I'm battling, I have to be an example for these children to show. Hey, if they can go through this and they're going

chemotherapy [ˌkiːməʊˈθerəpi] *n.* 化疗

soar [sɔːr] *v.* 急升；升空

figurine [ˌfɪɡəˈriːn] *n.*（人、动物的）小雕像，小塑像

phlebotomist [fləˈbɒtəmɪst] *n.* 采血员；刺络医师

through this situation, I know that I need to push through and show them an example and to be here just as well.' So that means so much to me and to so many others," Roberts said.

Between their bond with staff and the family's faith, Roberts said they take it one day at a time and are making it through.

"Things in life happen, and we know that God will never put more on us that we can't bear, so we started saying 'trust the process', and we have trusted this process. God has taken through and has allowed us to see the end of this journey," Roberts said.

On Wednesday they learned Starling only has two more weeks of chemo and a final lung surgery in October.

"Literally that is it! So as long as the scans look good, Jaxon can say that he beat cancer," Roberts said.

The 12-year-old is pushing for support from the community to help other kids who are battling diseases too. North Texas Giving Day is on Sept. 17 and Children's Medical Center Foundation is one of the thousands of non-profits that benefit from donations from the community.

"North Texas Giving Day is critically important to all non-profits across the region, it's especially powerful here at Children's Health," said Brent Christopher, the President of Children's Medical Center Foundation. "It's the one day out of the year that the entire community **rallies** together and wrap their arms around the non-profits that mean so much to the quality of life that we enjoy."

rally['ræli] *v.* 集合

Children's Health is a not-for-profit health care system.

"We depend on community support to put some wind beneath wings of the physicians and all the caregivers here as they take care of patients and families all year long and make life better for children," Christopher said.

He said the money benefits the care of patients like Starling and also helps fund research.

"Jaxon is such an incredible trooper, what an incredible story and young man he is. He's got an **infectious** smile and everything he does to make people feel good around him really covers such powerful and personal stories that he's been through," Christopher said.

"He would be the first to tell you that it means the world to him and patients like him to know that people all across Dallas Fort Worth are stepping up on North Texas Giving Day to let him know that they care about him and they want to help ensure that places like Children's Health can meet his needs, provide the best care available for him and do it in world-class facilities with incredible physicians and caretakers," Christopher said.

By Sophia Beausoleil

infectious [ɪnˈfekʃəs] *adj.* 传染性的，感染的（尤指通过空气或水传染的）；患有传染病；有传染力

Exercises

I. Read the text and find answers to the following questions.

1.How was the disease of Jaxon Starling found out?

____

2.What did Starling do for kids in the hospital like him?

____

3.When is the North Texas Giving Day?

____

4.What does Christopher think of Jaxon?

____

II. Translate the following sentences into English, using the words given below.

1. 尽管她竭尽全力控制自己，但声音仍然在颤抖。(despite)

____

2. 如果你有伞，让我们合用吧。(share sth. with)

____

3. 人们做事情就是不肯停下来想想后果。(think about)

____

4. 他是一个总为他人考虑的人。(定语从句)

____

III. Questions for consideration.

What do you think touches you the most about Jaxon Starling? What do you want to say to those who are fighting cancer?

Text 3 Why Riding a Bike Isn't Just Good for Your Health But for Your Career

A SANDAG report published in *The San Diego Vnion-Tribune* on September 10 shows a 42 percent increase in bicycle ridership during the first five months of the stay-at-home order.

No question, those two-wheelers are everywhere. Personally, I ride a road bike, once per week, approximately 28 miles. I ride alone because I like to talk to myself out loud. I use it as a talking therapy session. I know who the other guy is sitting in the chair opposite me, so I **banter** back and forth in an effort to approach tough issues and refine my own personal rational man behavior. (After all, I **purport** to teach this stuff.)

banter [ˈbæntə(r)]
v.（和某人）开玩笑；逗乐
purport [pəˈpɔːt]
v. 自称；标榜

Riding a bike provides a quasi-therapy session to work out issues. It is a simple repetitive motion that does not require massive mental effort. (You can't do this while playing golf, way too much frustration.) Look, I'm not crazy (OK, jury's still out on that one), but this is not a case of Sybil. Freud argues that pedaling a bike "automatically without attention" is one method to allow the unconscious to bubble up to the surface.

I wanted to understand if this model of riding and talking was effective in a larger context. So, since I like data, I contacted my long-time psychoanalyst, who sent me multiple studies on the subject. For example, "The effect of cycling on **cognitive** function and well-being in older adults," authored by Louise-Ann Leyland in the journal *PLOS One*. As you might expect, the data showed that bicycle riding resulted in "increased psychological well-being". And it matters whether you are moving or **stationary**. Apparently, the Peloton is not as effective as when the wind whips through your helmet. "The Eriksen flanker task measure" showed large improvements in "**executive** function", while psychological mood improvement was demonstrated in the "Stroop and Letter Updating task". Don't ask.

I read another scientific report with 21 contributors who reached the conclusion that "bicycling is associated with several positive health effects". I wonder what that study cost. But, the real research scientists are confirming that riding a bike is good for you.

And now to the core of the puzzle. Recently, I had a disagreement with some folks, who wanted to reintroduce me to Litigation Louie. So, on a particular ride, I spent almost an hour in a mental **court-room**. I interviewed the jury, I cross-examined the **plaintiffs**, I argued all sides of the case. And I was able to absolutely prove that I was in the right, with an **unassailable** position. And then I reached the correct decision, which was to settle and move on. I figure that first hour on the bike saved me $100,000.

What about other kinds of activity? No surprise again. It turns out that being in motion (swimming or walking for example), creates a mental and physical environment that is **conducive** to better health. But the bike still rules. "Results suggest that the use of a bicycle as a transport mode could help improve social **cohesion** with reduced feelings of loneliness." It is hard to find many positives to the virus, but maybe riding a bike outdoors is one of them. So, when you see an old

cognitive [ˈkɒɡnətɪv]
adj. 认知的

stationary [ˈsteɪʃənri]
adj. 静止的

executive [ɪɡˈzekjətɪv]
adj. 有执行权的；行政的

courtroom [ˈkɔːtruːm]
n. 法庭；审判室

plaintiff [ˈpleɪntɪf]
n. 原告

unassailable [ˌʌnəˈseɪləbl]
adj. 不可战胜的；不容置疑的

conducive [kənˈdjuːsɪv]
adj. 有助于

cohesion [kəʊˈhiːʒn]
n. 黏合；凝聚性

man on a bike talking to himself, just wave.

In these Zoom times, venture **capitalists** are still taking meetings, but the duration has been compressed. Some are booking in 15-minute **increments**, but most no more than 30 minutes. So, as they say, every minute counts. A client of mine recently got the infamous good news, bad news assessment. They said his deck was spectacular, great technology, etc., but the "story" that he told and the way he told it would not get him out of second grade. Learning how to tell a great story is a unique skill. It is a combination of crisp and focused, delivered with a touch of a song and dance Broadway performance. You are the actor in your own play.

You think it's about your technology, your vision and the market, but the truth is you're selling soap. And you need to grab me around the throat and convince me that I am not leaving that room alive until I shower with that bar of soap.

Storytelling can be learned. Try practicing it out loud while riding your bike.

By Neil Senturia

capitalist [ˈkæpɪtəlɪst] *n.* 资本主义者;资本家

increment [ˈɪŋkrəmənt] *n.* 增加

Exercises

I. Fill in the blanks with correct words according to the text.

1.I know who the other guy is sitting in the chair _______ me, so I banter back and forth in an effort _______ approach tough issues and refine my own personal rational man behavior.

2.Riding a bike provides a quasi-therapy session to work _______ issues.

3.“The Eriksen flanker task measure” showed large improvements in “executive function”, _______ psychological mood improvement was demonstrated in the “Stroop and Letter

Updating task".

4.Recently, I had a disagreement with some folks, who wanted to reintroduce me _______ Litigation Louie.

5. It turns _______ that being in motion (swimming or walking for example), creates a mental and physical environment that is conducive to better health.

II. Translate the phrases into English according to the text.

自言自语 _______________ 浮出水面 _______________

孤独感 _______________ 讲故事 _______________

III. Question for consideration.

In what way do you think riding a bicycle benefits you? How does the author illustrate the benefits of cycling?

Text 4 5 Things to Look for on a College Campus that Benefit Mental Health

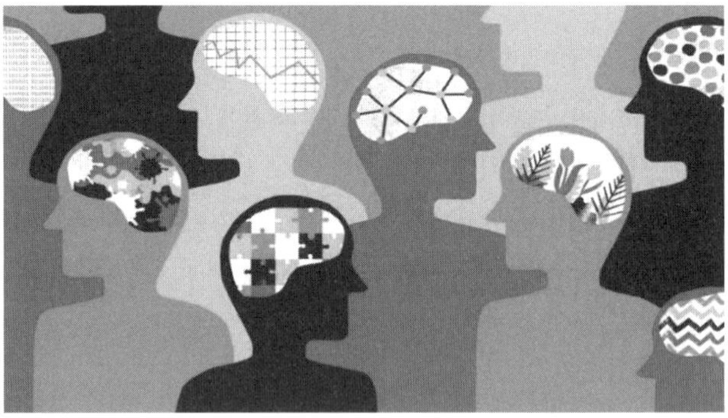

Researchers have studied college students' mental health for decades. Even in the 1920s, it was clear that the many stresses of higher education—like academic demands, post-graduation plans and financial concerns—wear on students. This stress can **incite** new mental health concerns and worsen existing ones, such as anxiety and depression. Sleep disturbances, restlessness, **irritability** and even feelings of hopelessness can make college feel harder than it already is.

incite [ɪnˈsaɪt]
v. 煽动

irritability [ˌɪrɪtəˈbɪlətɪ]
n. 易怒；暴躁

For all of these reasons, it pays to take campus design into consideration when selecting a school. Campus design affects the college experience, and students can choose a campus or change their existing routines to support their mental health. Such consideration is especially important during the COVID-19 **pandemic**, when new rules and norms have left many students more anxious and depressed than normal.

pandemic [pænˈdemɪk]
n. 流行病

As researchers and administrators who focus on the student experience, we've analyzed research on how people interact with their environments. Below are five things that we believe students should look for in a college to help them stay as healthy as possible.

1. A quiet sleeping space

Getting a good night's sleep is a building block for staying mentally well. Sleep-**deprived** students are more sensitive to disruptions in their day, have trouble staying awake, and have trouble completing tasks. They may also be irritable or easily angered. Significant and frequent sleep disturbances are linked to depression.

deprive [dɪˈpraɪv]
v. 剥夺；使丧失；使不能享有

The physical environment can influence sleep. Most colleges require students to have at least one roommate, depending on the **amenities** available. However, roommates' nighttime conversation or lighting can be disruptive. Students who live alone have better nighttime routines that allow them to get more sleep, but the room where a student sleeps is also important. A room with a comfortable temperature can improve sleep, thereby lowering depressive symptoms, so make sure you can change the temperature in your room. The eco-friendly Dialynas Hall at Pomona College has air conditioning that turns off when the windows open, while nearby Sontag Hall has a rooftop garden for some pre-bedtime fresh air.

amenity [əˈmiːnəti]
n. 生活设施；便利设施

Some colleges, like Georgia Tech, are encouraging students to move into single dorms in an attempt to prevent the spread of COVID-19. Still, it may remain difficult to social distance in residence halls that are designed to encourage social interaction through features like shared **lounges**.

lounge [laʊndʒ]
n. 休息室

2. Places to socialize

Students seek a supportive campus that makes them feel wanted and accepted, which is possible partly through developing a social network. For those dealing with mental health concerns, though, the fear of social situations often interferes with daily routines, relationships and school work. Even for those without mental health challenges, crowded public spaces can increase stress.

While some students may be tempted to rely on alcohol to ease social anxiety, a healthier strategy is to purposefully find a friend who can provide some positivity in daily life. "Third places", like coffee shops, are neither home nor classroom, and may offer the opportunity for social support to those lacking connection. University programming, like the University of Utah's student **entrepreneurship** residential group, can create support networks among strangers.

COVID-19 restrictions will, no doubt, limit the **spontaneous** in-person interactions that can make a campus **vibrant** for some time to come. School-**sanctioned** social or educational events, like virtual movie nights or skill-building workshops, may provide a social **outlet** when regular social life doesn't come easily.

3. Green space and natural light

Natural light—the kind that streams in through a window on a sunny day—offers vitamin D. This free pick-me-up can enhance students' concentration and productivity, while improving mental health and emotional well-being.

Spending time in nature is just one way to enjoy natural light. Green spaces, such as parks and playing fields, allow students to escape daily stress. Those who regularly connect with nature are generally happier than those who do not. One study connects campus "greenness" to students' satisfaction with their college experience, as well as graduation rates.

There are plenty of schools to choose from if outdoor space is a priority. Colorado College is **nestled** in the Rocky Mountain foothills, making it a haven for hikers and climbers, while North Central College is an **accredited arboretum**. For a change of pace, Florida Gulf Coast University is located a few steps away from sunny beaches in Fort Myers.

entrepreneurship [ˌɒntrəprəˈnɜːʃɪp] *n.* 企业家的身份(或活动)

spontaneous [spɒnˈteɪniəs] *adj.* 自发的,自然的

vibrant [ˈvaɪbrənt] *adj.* 充满生机的;生气勃勃的;精力充沛的

sanction [ˈsæŋkʃn] *v.* 认可,准许

outlet [ˈaʊtlet] *n.* 出路

nestle [ˈnesl] *v.* 坐落,位处

accredited [əˈkredɪtɪd] *adj.* 官方认可的

arboretum [ˌɑːbəˈriːtəm] *n.* 树木园,植物园

It's easy to take advantage of green space in good weather, but students should create a plan for getting vitamin D in the colder months as well. During this time, light therapy—which can involve sitting under a lamp emitting light that **mimics** natural light—may be a welcome escape from the winter blues.

mimic ['mɪmɪk] *v.* 模仿(某人的言行举止)

4. Nearby services and amenities

College students don't just study and sleep while they're getting their degrees. Student services, and access to off-campus amenities, can improve any student's experience. Campuses that follow this principle are part of a trend in which colleges—often historically located on isolated plots of land—purposefully integrate with their broader communities and cities, planning campuses with students' daily needs in mind.

For students trying to stay on top of their mental health care, on-campus counseling can be great, but these services are often underfunded and under-staffed. Students' use of community facilities can positively affect their college experience. While New York City—home to institutions like New York University and Columbia University —is ranked as the number-one "most walkable" city in the United States, Fayetteville, Arkansas, which hosts the University of Arkansas, holds the lowest rank for 2020.

Since some parts of campuses are either shut down or facing higher demand during the pandemic, creating a **roster** of off-campus resources and emergency service providers can prepare students for any mid-semester surprises.

roster ['rɒstə(r)] *n.* 候选名单

5. Mood-boosting design

Studies in education show that, from a young age, students' moods and behaviors are responsive to their learning environments, which affects both their mental health and how they fare in school. A building's design can affect how people act, feel and make sense of their environments. The colors used in the design of campus buildings can make people feel warm, cool, calm, invited or excluded. For example, while red can be energizing, green can be relaxing, which can affect the functionality of a space for college students.

Beyond paint choices, students' learning environments should include views that allow their minds and eyes to take a break. Something as simple as a landscape art poster hung indoors can offer stress relief. Many universities, such as Loyola University Chicago, have art galleries that can break up otherwise office-heavy and classroom-heavy views, offering **respite** from a morning of PowerPoint presentations.

respite [ˈrespaɪt]
n. 暂停

If the campus or local art gallery is closed, students might consider making their own galleries. Many websites **curate** collections of prints and original works that won't break the bank, and craft stores stock canvas, paint and other supplies to help them bring out their inner Monet.

curate [ˈkjʊəˈreɪt]
vt. 管理(博物馆或美术馆的藏品);策展

By Naomi Schalit

Exercises

I. Read the text and find answers to the following questions.

1. According to paragraph 1, why do we need to take campus design into consideration when selecting a school?

____

2. What negative effects will inadequate sleep have on students?

____

3.What does Georgia Tech do to prevent the spread of COVID-19?

____

4.In what ways can students get vitamin D?

____

II. Translate the following sentences into English, using the words given below.

1. 我辨认她的笔迹有困难。(have trouble doing)

____

2. 万物靠太阳生长。(depend on)

____

3. 他飞快地翻了一下邮件,但一封也没有打开。(without)

____

4. 他趁着天气好,出去散散步。(take advantage of)

____

III. Question for consideration.

After reading the text, what do you think your school can do to help students stay as healthy as possible?

Text 5　If I Had Three Days to See (Excerpt)

If, by some miracle, I were granted three seeing days, to be followed by a **relapse** into darkness, I should divide the period into three parts.

relapse [ˈriːlæps]
n. 旧病复发

The First Day

On the first day, I should want to see the people whose kindness and gentleness and companionship have made my life worth living. First I should like to gaze long upon the face of my dear teacher, Mrs. Anne Sullivan Macy, who came to me when I was a child and opened the outer world to me. I should want not merely to see the outline of her face, so that I could cherish it in my memory, but to study that face and find in it the living evidence of the sympathetic **tenderness** and patience with which she accomplished the difficult task of my education. I should like to see in her eyes that strength of character which has enabled her to stand firm in the face of difficulties, and that compassion for all humanity which she has revealed to me so often.

tenderness [ˈtendənɪs]
n. 温柔；柔情

I do not know what it is to see into the heart of a friend through that "window of the soul", the eye. I can only "see" through my finger tips the outline of a face. I can detect laughter, sorrow, and many other obvious emotions. I know my friends from the feel of their faces. But I cannot really picture their personalities by touch. I know their personalities, of course, through other means, through the thoughts they express to me, through whatever of their actions are revealed to me. But I am denied that deeper understanding of them which I am sure would come through sight of them, through watching their reactions to various expressed thoughts and circumstances, through noting the immediate and fleeting reactions of their eyes and **countenance**.

countenance [ˈkaʊntənəns]
n. 面容；脸色

Friends who are near to me I know well, because through the months and years they reveal themselves to me in all their phases; but of casual friends I have only an incomplete impression, an impression gained from a handclasp, from spoken words which I take from their lips with my finger tips, or which they tap into the palm of my hand.

How much easier, how much more satisfying it is for you who can see to grasp quickly the essential qualities of another person by watching the **subtleties** of expression, the **quiver** of a muscle, the **flutter** of a hand. But does it ever occur to you to use your sight to see into the inner nature of a friends or acquaintance? Do not most of you seeing people grasp casually the outward features of a face and let it go at that?

subtlety [ˈsʌtlti]
n. 细微；微妙之处
quiver [ˈkwɪvə(r)]
n. 轻微抖动
flutter [ˈflʌtə(r)]
n. 飘动；挥动；颤动

For instance can you describe accurately the faces of five good friends? Some of you can, but many cannot. As an experiment, I have questioned husbands of long standing about the color of their wives' eyes, and often they express embarrassed confusion and admit that they do not know. And, incidentally, it is a **chronic** complaint of wives that their husbands do not notice new dresses, new hats, and changes in household arrangements.

chronic [ˈkrɒnɪk]
adj. 长期的；慢性的

The eyes of seeing persons soon become accustomed to the routine of their surroundings, and they actually see only the **startling** and spectacular. But even in viewing the most spectacular sights the eyes

startling [ˈstɑːtlɪŋ]
adj. 惊人的；让人震惊的；极鲜亮的

are lazy. Court records reveal every day how inaccurately "eyewitnesses" see. A given event will be "seen" in several different ways by as many witnesses. Some see more than others, but few see everything that is within the range of their vision.

Oh, the things that I should see if I had the power of sight for just three days!

The first day would be a busy one. I should call to me all my dear friends and look long into their faces, imprinting upon my mind the outward evidences of the beauty that is within them. I should let my eyes rest, too, on the face of a baby, so that I could catch a vision of the eager, innocent beauty which **precedes** the individual' s consciousness of the conflicts which life develops.

precede [prɪ'siːd]
v. 在……之前发生(或出现)

And I should like to look into the loyal, trusting eyes of my dogs—the grave, canny little Scottie, Darkie, and the stalwart, understanding Great Dane, Helga, whose warm, tender, and playful friendships are so comforting to me.

On that busy first day I should also view the small simple things of my home. I want to see the warm colors in the **rugs** under my feet, the pictures on the walls, the **intimate trifles** that transform a house into home. My eyes would rest respectfully on the books in raised type which I have read, but they would be more eagerly interested in the printed books which seeing people can read, for during the long night of my life the books I have read and those which have been read to me have built themselves into a great shining lighthouse, revealing to me the deepest channels of human life and the human spirit.

rug [rʌg]
n. 小地毯；垫子
intimate ['ɪntɪmət]
adj. 亲密的；密切的
trifle ['traɪfl]
n. 小事；琐事；不值钱的东西

In the afternoon of that first seeing day, I should take a long walk in the woods and **intoxicate** my eyes on the beauties of the world of Nature, trying desperately to absorb in a few hours the vast **splendor** which is constantly unfolding itself to those who can see. On the way

intoxicate [ɪn'tɒksɪkeɪt]
v.(酒)使陶醉
splendor ['splendə(r)]
n. 华丽；壮丽；雄伟；豪华

home from my woodland **jaunt** my path would lie near a farm so that I might see the patient horses ploughing in the field (perhaps I should see only a tractor!) and the serene content of men living close to the soil. And I should pray for the glory of a colorful sunset.

When dusk had fallen, I should experience the double delight of being able to see by artificial light which the genius of man has created to extend the power of his sight when Nature **decrees** darkness.

In the night of that first day of sight, I should not be able to sleep, so full would be my mind of the memories of the day.

The Second Day

The next day—the second day of sight—I should arise with the dawn and see the thrilling miracle by which night is transformed into day. I should **behold** with awe the magnificent **panorama** of light with which the sun awakens the sleeping earth.

This day I should devote to a hasty glimpse of the world, past and present. I should want to see the **pageant** of man' s progress, the **kaleidoscope** of the ages. How can so much be **compressed** into one day? Through the museums, of course. Often I have visited the New York Museum of Natural History to touch with my hands many of the objects there exhibited, but I have longed to see with my eyes the **condensed** history of the earth and its inhabitants displayed there—animals and the races of men pictured in their native environment; gigantic **carcasses** of dinosaurs and **mastodons** which **roamed** the earth long before man appeared, with his tiny stature and powerful brain, to conquer the animal kingdom; realistic presentations of the processes of development in animals, in man, and in the **implements** which man has used to fashion for himself a secure home on this planet; and a thousand and one other aspects of natural history.

jaunt [dʒɔːnt]
n. (短途)游览,旅行

decree [dɪˈkriː]
v. 裁定;判决;颁布

behold [bɪˈhəʊld]
v. 看;看见

panorama [ˌpænəˈrɑːmə]
n. 全景; 全景画卷

pageant [ˈpædʒənt]
n. 盛大华丽的情景

kaleidoscope [kəˈlaɪdəskəʊp]
n. 万花筒

compress [kəmˈpres]
v. 压缩

condensed [kənˈdenst]
adj. 压缩的,精简的;浓缩的

carcass [ˈkɑːkəs]
n. 动物尸体

mastodon [ˈmæstədɒn]
n. 柱牙象; 乳齿象

roam [rəʊm]
v. 徜徉;漫步

implement [ˈɪmplɪment]
n. 工具; 器具

I wonder how many readers of this article have viewed this panorama of the face of living things as pictured in that inspiring museum. Many, of course, have not had the opportunity, but I am sure that many who have had the opportunity have not made use of it. There, indeed, is a place to use your eyes. You who see can spend many fruitful days there, but I with my imaginary three days of sight, could only take a hasty glimpse, and pass on.

My next stop would be the Metropolitan Museum of Art, for just as the Museum of Natural History reveals the material aspects of the world, so does the Metropolitan show the **myriad facets** of the human spirit. Throughout the history of humanity the urge to artistic expression has been almost as powerful as the urge for food, shelter, and **procreation**. And here, in the vast chambers of the Metropolitan Museum, is unfolded before me the spirit of Egypt, Greece, and Rome, as expressed in their art. I know well through my hands the sculptured gods and goddesses of the ancient Nile-land. I have felt copies of Parthenon friezes, and I have sensed the rhythmic beauty of charging Athenian warriors. Apollos and Venuses and the Winged Victory of Samothrace are friends of my finger tips. The **gnarled**, bearded features of Homer are dear to me, for he, too, knew blindness.

My hands have lingered upon the living marble of Roman sculpture as well as that of later generations. I have passed my hands over a **plaster** cast of Michelangelo's inspiring and heroic Moses; I have sensed the power of Rodin; I have been awed by the devoted spirit of Gothic wood carving. These arts which can be touched have meaning for me, but even they were meant to be seen rather than felt, and I can only guess at the beauty which remains hidden from me. I can admire the simple lines of a Greek vase, but its figured decorations are lost to me.

myriad [ˈmɪriəd]
adj. 无数的；大量的

facet [ˈfæsɪt]
n. (事物的)部分，方面

procreation [ˌprəʊkrɪˈeɪʃən]
n. 生殖；繁殖；生育；繁衍后代；生育或生产

gnarled [nɑːld]
adj. 扭曲的；(因年老或疾病)弯曲的

plaster [ˈplɑːstə]
n. 灰泥

So on this, my second day of sight, I should try to **probe** into the soul of man through this art. The things I knew through touch I should now see. More splendid still, the whole magnificent world of painting would be opened to me, from the Italian Primitives, with their **serene** religious devotion, to the Moderns, with their **feverish** visions. I should look deep into the canvases of Raphael, Leonardo da Vinci, Titian, Rembrandt. I should want to feast my eyes upon the warm colors of Veronese, study the mysteries of E1 Greco, catch a new vision of Nature from Corot. Oh, there is so much rich meaning and beauty in the art of the ages for you who have eyes to see!

probe [prəʊb]
v. 详尽调查

serene [sə'riːn]
adj. 平静的；宁静的；安详的

feverish ['fiːvərɪʃ]
adj. 激动的；焦虑不安的

Upon my short visit to this temple of art I should not be able to review a fraction of that great world of art which is open to you. I should be able to get only a superficial impression. Artists tell me that for deep and true appreciation of art one must educate the eye. One must learn through experience to weigh the merits of line, of composition, of form and color. If I had eyes, how happily would I embark upon so fascinating a study! Yet I am told that, to many of you who have eyes to see, the world of art is a dark night, unexplored and unilluminated.

It would be with extreme reluctance that I should leave the Metropolitan Museum, which contains the key to beauty—a beauty so neglected. Seeing persons, however, do not need a metropolitan to find this key to beauty. The same key lies waiting in smaller museums, and in books on the shelves of even small libraries. But naturally, in my limited time of imaginary sight, I should choose the place where the key unlocks the greatest treasures in the shortest time.

The evening of my second day of sight I should spend at a theatre or at the movies. Even now I often attend theatrical performances of all sorts, but the action of the play must be spelled into my hand by a companion. But how I should like to see with my own eyes the fascinating figure of Hamlet, or the **gusty** Falstaff amid colorful Elizabethan trappings! How I should like to follow each movement of the graceful Hamlet, each strut of the hearty Falstaff! And since I could see only one play, I should be confronted by a many-horned dilemma, for there are scores of plays I should want to see. You who have eyes can see any you like. How many of you, I wonder, when you gaze at a play, a movie, or any spectacle, realize and give thanks for the miracle of sight which enables you to enjoy its color , grace, and movement?

gusty [ˈgʌsti]
adj. 有阵风在吹的；刮风的

I cannot enjoy the beauty of rhythmic movement except in a sphere restricted to the touch of my hands. I can vision only dimly the grace of a Pavlowa, although I know something of the delight of rhythm, for often I can sense the beat of music as it vibrates through the floor. I can well imagine that **cadenced** motion must be one of the most pleasing sights in the world. I have been able to gather something of this by tracing with my fingers the lines in sculptured marble; if this **static** grace can be so lovely, how much more acute must be the thrill of seeing grace in motion.

cadenced [ˈkeɪdənst]
adj. 韵律的；有节奏的

static [ˈstætɪk]
adj. 静止的，停滞的

One of my dearest memories is of the time when Joseph Jefferson allowed me to touch his face and hands as he went through some of the gestures and speeches of his beloved Rip Van Winkle. I was able to catch thus a **meager** glimpse of the world of drama, and I shall never forget the delight of that moment. But, oh, how much I must miss, and how much pleasure you seeing ones can derive from watching and hearing the interplay of speech and movement in the unfolding of a dramatic performance! If I could see only one play, I should know how to picture in my mind the action of a hundred plays which I have read or had transferred to me through the medium of the manual alphabet.

meager [ˈmiːgə(r)]
adj. 少量且劣质的

So, through the evening of my second imaginary day of sight, the great fingers of dramatic literature would crowd sleep from my eyes.

The Third Day

The following morning, I should again greet the dawn, anxious to discover new delights, for I am sure that, for those who have eyes which really see, the dawn of each day must be a **perpetually** new **revelation** of beauty.

This, according to the terms of my imagined miracle, is to be my third and last day of sight. I shall have no time to waste in regrets or longings; there is too much to see. The first day I devoted to my friends, **animate** and **inanimate**. The second revealed to me the history of man and Nature. Today I shall spend in the **workaday** world of the present, amid the **haunts** of men going about the business of life. And where can one find so many activities and conditions of men as in New York? So the city becomes my destination.

I start from my home in the quiet little suburb of Forest Hills, Long Island. Here, surrounded by green lawns, trees, and flowers, are neat little houses, happy with the voices and movements of wives and children, **havens** of peaceful rest for men who **toil** in the city. I drive across the **lacy** structure of steel which spans the East River, and I get a new and startling vision of the power and **ingenuity** of the mind of man. Busy boats **chug** and **scurry** about the river—racy speed boat, **stolid**, **snorting tugs**. If I had long days of sight ahead, I should spend many of them watching the delightful activity upon the river.

I look ahead, and before me rise the fantastic towers of New York, a city that seems to have stepped from the pages of a fairy story. What an **awe-inspiring** sight, these glittering **spires**. These vast banks of stone and steel-structures such as the gods might build for themselves! This animated picture is a part of the lives of millions of people every day. How many, I wonder, give it so much as a second's

perpetually [pə'petʃuəli] *adv.* 永久地
revelation [ˌrevə'leɪʃn] *n.* 披露；揭露
animate ['ænɪmət] *adj.* 有生命的
inanimate [ɪn'ænɪmət] *adj.* 无生命的
workaday ['wɜːkədeɪ] *adj.* 工作日的
haunt [hɔːnt] *n.* 常去的地方
haven ['heɪvn] *n.* 安全地
toil [tɔɪl] *v.* 辛勤劳作
lacy ['leɪsi] *adj.* 带花边的
ingenuity [ˌɪndʒə'njuːəti] *n.* 才智
chug [tʃʌg] *v.* 发出轧轧声
scurry ['skʌri] *v.* 疾跑
stolid ['stɒlɪd] *adj.* 迟钝的
snort [snɔːt] *v.* 喷出蒸汽声
tug [tʌg] *n.* 拖船
awe-inspiring ['ɔːɪnspaɪərɪŋ] *adj.* 令人惊叹的
spire ['spaɪə(r)] *n.* 尖顶

glance? Very few, I fear. Their eyes are blind to this magnificent sight because it is so familiar to them.

I hurry to the top of one of those gigantic structures, the **Empire** State Building, for there, a short time ago, I "saw" the city below through the eyes of my secretary. I am anxious to compare my fancy with reality. I am sure I should not be disappointed in the panorama spread out before me, for to me it would be a vision of another world.

Now I begin my rounds of the city. First, I stand at a busy corner, merely looking at people, trying by sight of them to understand something of their live. I see smiles, and I am happy. I see serious determination, and I am proud, I see suffering, and I am **compassionate**.

I **stroll** down Fifth **Avenue**. I throw my eyes out of focus, so that I see no particular object but only a **seething** kaleidoscope of colors. I am certain that the colors of women' s dresses moving in a **throng** must be a gorgeous spectacle of which I should never tire. But perhaps if I had sight I should be like most other women—too interested in styles and the cut of individual dresses to give much attention to the splendor of color in the mass. And I am convinced, too, that I should become an **inveterate** window shopper, for it must be a delight to the eye to view the **myriad** articles of beauty on display.

From Fifth Avenue I make a tour of the city—to Park Avenue, to the **slums**, to factories, to parks where children play. I take a stay-at-home trip abroad by visiting the foreign quarters. Always my eyes are open wide to all the sights of both happiness and misery so that I may probe deep and add to my understanding of how people work and live. My heart is full of the images of people and things. My eye passes lightly over no single trifle; it **strives** to touch and hold closely each thing its gaze rests upon. Some sights are pleasant, filling the heart with happiness; but some are miserably **pathetic**. To these latter I do

empire [ˈempaɪə(r)]
n. 帝国

compassionate
[kəmˈpæʃənət]
adj. 有同情心的
stroll [strəʊl]
v. 散步，闲逛
avenue [ˈævənjuː]
n. 大街
seething [ˈsiːðɪŋ]
adj. 火热的
throng [θrɒŋ]
n. 一大群

inveterate [ɪnˈvetərət]
adj. 成癖的
myriad [ˈmɪriəd]
adj. 无数的

slum [slʌm]
n. 贫民窟

strive [straɪv]
v. 努力，力争

pathetic [pəˈθetɪk]
adj. 令人怜悯的

not shut my eyes, for they, too, are part of life. To close the eye on them is to close the heart and mind.

My third day of sight is drawing to an end. Perhaps there are many serious pursuits to which I should devote the few remaining hours, but I am afraid that on the evening of that last day I should again run away to the theater, to a **hilariously** funny play, so that I might appreciate the **overtones** of comedy in the human spirit.

At midnight my temporary **respite** from blindness would cease, and permanent night would close in on me again. Naturally in those three short days I should not have seen all I wanted to see. Only when darkness had again **descended** upon me should I realize how much I had left unseen. But my mind would be so crowded with glorious memories that I should have little time for regrets. **Thereafter** the touch of every object would bring a glowing memory of how that object looked.

Perhaps this short outline of how I should spend three days of sight does not agree with the program you would set for yourself if you knew that you were about to be stricken blind. I am, however, sure that if you actually faced that fate your eyes would open to things you had never seen before, storing up memories for the long night ahead. You would use your eyes as never before. Everything you saw would become dear to you. Your eyes would touch and embrace every object that came within your range of vision. Then, at last, you would really see, and a new world of beauty would open itself before you.

I who am blind can give one hint to those who see—one **admonition** to those who would make full use of the gift of sight: Use your eyes as if tomorrow you would be stricken blind. And the same method can be applied to the other senses. Hear the music of voices, the song of a bird, the mighty **strains** of an orchestra, as if you would

hilariously [hɪˈleriəsli] *adv.* 引人发笑地

overtone [ˈəʊvətəʊn] *n.* 暗示，寓意

respite [ˈrespaɪt] *n.* 暂缓，暂延

descend [dɪˈsend] *v.* 下来，下降

thereafter [ˌðeərˈɑːftə(r)] *adv.* 其后，此后

admonition [ˌædməˈnɪʃn] *n.* 警告

strain [streɪn] *n.* 旋律，曲调

be stricken deaf tomorrow. Touch each object you want to touch as if tomorrow your **tactile** sense would fail. Smell the perfume of flowers, taste with **relish** each **morsel**, as if tomorrow you could never smell and taste again. Make the most of every sense: glory in all the facets of pleasure and beauty which the world reveals to you through the several means of contact which Nature provides. But of all the senses, I am sure that sight must be the most delightful.

By Hellen Keller

tactile [ˈtæktaɪl] *adj.* 触觉的
relish [ˈrelɪʃ] *n.* 享受，乐趣
morsel [ˈmɔːsl] *n.* 一口

About the author

Helen Adams Keller (June 27, 1880—June 1, 1968) was an American author, disability rights advocate, political activist and lecturer. Born in West Tuscumbia, Alabama, she lost her sight and her hearing after a bout of illness when she was 19 months old. She then communicated primarily using home signs until the age of seven, when she met her first teacher and lifelong companion Anne Sullivan. Sullivan taught Keller language, including reading and writing. After an education at both specialist and mainstream schools, Keller attended Radcliffe College of Harvard University and became the first deafblind person in the United States to earn a Bachelor of Arts degree.

She was named one of *Time Magazine*'s 100 Most Important People of the 20th Century.

Keller worked for the American Foundation for the Blind (AFB) from 1924 until 1968. During this time, she toured the United States and traveled to 35 countries around the globe advocating for those with vision loss.

Keller was also a prolific author, writing 14 books and hundreds of speeches and essays on topics ranging from animals to Mahatma Gandhi. Keller campaigned for those with disabilities, for women's suffrage, labor rights, and world peace. In 1909, she joined the Socialist Party of America. She was a founding member of the American Civil Liberties Union.

Keller's autobiography, *The Story of My Life* (1903), publicized her education and life with Sullivan. It was adapted as a play by William Gibson, and this was also adapted as a film under the same title, *The Miracle Worker*. Her birthplace has been designated and preserved as a

National Historic Landmark. Since 1954 it has been operated as a house museum and sponsors an annual "Helen Keller Day".

Keller was inducted into the Alabama Women's Hall of Fame in 1971. She was one of twelve inaugural inductees to the Alabama Writers Hall of Fame on June 8, 2015.

Exercises

I. Read the following statements and decide whether they are true (T) or false (F) according to the text.

1.Mrs. Anne Sullivan once showed great kindness to the author. T□ F□

2.On the busy first day, the author wanted to go outside home and enjoy natural scenery. T□ F□

3.On the second day the author wanted to catch a hasty glimpse of the world by traveling around. T□ F□

4. Metropolitan Museum of Art displays artworks from different parts of the world. T□ F□

5.The author was also interested in drama. T□ F□

II. Translate the following sentences into English, using the words given below.

1. 很多人来到动物园为的就是一睹熊猫的风采。(glimpse)

____

2. 昨天晚上我看了电影之后,这个问题就一直在我的脑海里萦绕。(linger)

____

3. 如果我们早意识到这个问题的话,我们的做法就会完全不同。(虚拟语气)

____

4. 我们着手一项紧急任务,目的是要实现一个雄心勃勃的目标。(embark on)

____

5. 这篇论文探讨了一系列的问题,包括语言表现、文学修养、文体风格等。(probe into)

____

III. Question for consideration.

If you had three days to see, what would you do?

Cultural Notes

The World Health Organization

The World Health Organization (WHO) is a specialized agency of the United Nations responsible for international public health. It is headquartered in Geneva, Switzerland, and has six regional offices and 150 field offices worldwide.

The WHO was established on April 7, 1948, and convened its first meeting on July 24 of that year. It incorporated the assets, personnel, and duties of the League of Nations' Health Organization and the Paris-based Office International d'Hygiène Publique, including the International Classification of Diseases (ICD). The agency's work began in earnest in 1951 after a significant infusion of financial and technical resources.

The WHO's official mandate is to promote health and safety while helping the vulnerable worldwide. It provides technical assistance to countries, sets international health standards, collects data on global health issues, and serves as a forum for scientific or policy discussions related to health. Its official publication, the World Health Report, provides assessments of worldwide health topics.

The WHO has played a leading role in several public health achievements, most notably the eradication of smallpox, the near-eradication of polio, and the development of an Ebola vaccine. Its current priorities include communicable diseases, such as HIV/AIDS, Ebola, malaria and tuberculosis; non-communicable diseases such as heart disease and cancer; healthy diet, nutrition, and food security; occupational health; and substance abuse. The agency advocates for universal health care coverage, engagement with the monitoring of public health risks, coordinating responses to health emergencies, and promoting health and well-being generally.

The WHO is governed by the World Health Assembly (WHA), which is composed of its 194 member states. The WHA elects and advises an executive board made up of 34 health specialists; selects the WHO's chief administrator, the director-general; sets goals and priorities; and approves the budget and activities. The WHO is funded primarily by contributions from member states, followed by private donors. Its total approved budget for 2020—2021 is over $7.2 billion, while the approved budget for 2022—2023 is over $6.2 billion. The budget is $6.83 billion for 2024—2025.

Unit Two　Technology

Text 1　Future of Travel May Be in Hands of This Female Teen Scientist

Finding inspiration in Elon Musk's Hyperloop, at the age of 13, Caroline Crouchley created a new concept for a cheaper and more **sustainable** train and became a **finalist** at the Discovery Education and 3M Young Scientist Challenge.

Two years have passed since her invention made the headlines and Caroline keeps proving she deserves to **be on the radar** for young talents in science. She has shared with us her **aspirations** and latest projects that could change the world for future generations.

As part of the International Women's Day 2021 celebration of women, we look closely at Caroline's scientific successes and **en-deavuors** that inspire girls to pursue science.

Now 15, Caroline's goal is to become an engineer and a scientist one day. Aspiring to study STEM (science, technology, engineering, and mathematics) fields at MIT and Harvard, she wants to be "known for solving large problems facing our world, leaving the planet a better place and improving the lives of all people".

With the dream of answering "some of the greatest mysteries of

sustainable [səˈsteɪnəbl] *adj.* 可持续的

finalist [ˈfaɪnəlɪst] *n.* 参加决赛者

be on the radar 受人关注

aspiration [ˌæspəˈreɪʃn] *n.* 抱负；志向

endeavour [ɪnˈdevə(r)] *n.* 努力，尝试

our time", Caroline hasn't **ceased** pushing forward in science. When she isn't at school, she is working on engineering better **irrigation** systems for watering plants. Her research includes plant growth, root caps, stages of mitosis, and root development with the hopes to lower the levels of carbon dioxide in the atmosphere.

cease [siːs]
v. 停止
irrigation [ˌɪrɪˈgeɪʃn]
n. 灌溉

She is also working on a **filter** to limit the amount of salt, **nitrates**, and other chemicals found in water.

filter [ˈfɪltə(r)]
n. 过滤器
nitrate [ˈnaɪtreɪt]
n. 硝酸盐

"I feel a sense of responsibility to **undo** the damage that has been created for the next generation. Ideas to design our world are limitless so why don't we design a world that is sustainable for 100% of the world's population," said Caroline.

undo [ʌnˈduː]
v. 消除

When Caroline introduced her train concept, she was the only girl in her entire school to sign up for a science fair. With science still being highly male-**dominated** today, it was refreshing to meet other girls there that also enjoyed science.

dominate [ˈdɒmɪneɪt]
v. 控制；支配

"In order to solve the global challenges we face today we have to use the talent and creativity of all people. Girls have their own unique qualities and **attributes** that can greatly contribute to science. Most girls are very curious about the world but they are put into **stereotypes** at a young age," said Caroline.

attribute [ˈætrɪbjuːt]
n. 特征；性质
stereotype [ˈsteriətaɪp]
n. 刻板印象；老一套

The passion with which Caroline describes the necessity to have more young women in science proves that it's an important topic for her and her family. Her mom introduced her to Marie Curie whose determination and **resilience** have served as an inspiration to her ever since. In turn, Caroline is becoming a role model for many young girls, and with her efforts, she is creating a domino effect for the next generations of women to encourage others to think big.

resilience [rɪˈzɪliəns]
n. 适应能力

Her recent recognition as a Children's Climate Prize Finalist in Sweden and mentions in the American Girl Book called *Love the*

Earth and *Diversity in Action Magazine* have been encouraging girls to get involved in STEM fields.

Besides her scientific projects, Caroline is working on Girl Scout Gold Award that's creating STEM awareness for girls in elementary and middle schools. She talks with them about her journey and participation in 12 science fairs over the last three years and strives to educate them with real project examples, such as the one that explores the use of dome house designs in hurricane-**prone** areas to limit possible **devastation** to **infrastructure**.

But above all, Caroline is setting an example for all girls and minorities not only in her school district but globally and she does it by staying true to her scientific pursuit. In spite of her young age, she has a clear vision of the world she wants to leave behind and won't let her gender **dictate** her future.

By Jana Brnáková

-prone [prəʊn] (构成形容词)易于遭受……的

devastation [ˌdevəˈsteɪʃn] *n.* 毁坏,破坏

infrastructure [ˈɪnfrəstrʌktʃə(r)] *n.* 基础设施,基础建设

dictate [dɪkˈteɪt] *v.* 支配;摆布

Exercises

I. Read the text and find answers to the following questions.

1.Why does Caroline deserve to be on the radar for young talents in science?

____

2.Why does Caroline aspire to study STEM fields?

____

3.Which one of the girls' unique qualities and attributes that greatly contribute to science is mentioned?

____

4.How is Caroline setting an example for all girls and minorities?

____

II. Fill in the blanks with the words or phrases given below. Change the form where necessary.

take control of	endeavor	aspire to
undo the damage	a sense of responsibility	serve as
be curious about	contribute to	

1.The manager is expected to use his best _________ to promote the artist's career.

2.You need to _________ your feelings and stop getting angry so easily.

3.They _________ be gentlemen, though they fell far short of the ideal.

4.Doing chores can put _________ into students' minds and teach them the spirit of rules as well as teamwork.

5.The judge said the punishment would _________ a warning to others.

6.She knew it would be difficult to _________ that had been done.

7.I was intensely _________ the world I came from.

8.Several factors, including changes in diet and lifestyle, have _________ the increase in childhood obesity.

III. Question for consideration.

What stereotypes are girls put into at a young age?

Text 2 These Revolutionary Science-Tech Fields Will Make the World a Safer Place

We live in an era of misinformation, mistrust and science **skepticism**. Yet, to **resolve** the challenges we face, we must drive **innovative** science-based solutions forward and emphasize science as a **nonpartisan** issue.

As leader of one of the world's largest scientific R&D organizations, a big **perk** of my job is getting an insider's view of solutions to tomorrow's challenges. **Subsequently**, I've identified three science-driven fields that I believe will enable us to **carve out** a better and brighter future by protecting people and the planet.

No. 1: Biotechnology will protect us from future health threats

No one can argue that even the tiniest virus can make a worldwide impact. As we contend with COVID-19 **mutations** and administer **vaccinations**, we still have much to learn. For example, we must conduct an in-depth study of **immunity** to determine the **longevity** of protection and assess the potential need for **booster** vaccinations.

The incredible amount of data that has been generated and collected over the course of the pandemic will provide vital insights that aid the development of better **diagnostics** and treatments.

skepticism [ˈskeptɪsɪzəm]
n. 怀疑态度
resolve [rɪˈzɒlv]
v. 解决(问题或困难)
innovative [ˈɪnəvətɪv]
adj. 创新的
nonpartisan [ˌnɒnpɑːtɪˈzæn]
adj. 中立的
perk [pɜːk]
n. 额外待遇
subsequently [ˈsʌbsɪkwəntli]
adv. 随后
carve out
开创
mutation [mjuːˈteɪʃn]
n. 突变
vaccination [ˌvæksɪˈneɪʃn]
n. 接种
immunity [ɪˈmjuːnəti]
n. 免疫(力)
longevity [lɒnˈdʒevəti]
n. 持久
booster [ˈbuːstə(r)]
n. (疫苗)加强剂
diagnostics [ˌdaɪəgˈnɒstɪks]
n. 诊断

Biotechnology also has a **pivotal** role to play in **proactively** protecting us. Research by the Defense Advanced Research Projects Agency (DARPA), a division of the U. S. Department of Defense, paved the way for **expedited** development of COVID-19 vaccines, as well as **countermeasures** that **sequence** a **pathogen**'s DNA and the host's **physiological** response.

This enables scientists to catch and stop the next virus before it gains **momentum**. Countermeasures to both natural and weaponized threats are also in the works, including technologies that will predict viral evolution and spread.

pivotal [ˈpɪvətl] *adj.* 关键性的
proactively [prəʊˈæktɪvli] *adv.* 积极主动地
expedite [ˈekspədaɪt] *v.* 加快
countermeasure [ˈkaʊntəmeʒə(r)] *n.* 对策
sequence [ˈsiːkwəns] *v.* 序列
pathogen [ˈpæθədʒən] *n.* 病原体
physiological [ˌfɪzɪəˈlɒdʒɪkl] *adj.* 生理学；生理学(上)的
momentum [məˈmentəm] *n.* 动力

No. 2: Neurotechnology will unlock new capabilities

In the rapidly evolving field of neurotechnology, scientists and engineers are redrawing the boundaries of what the brain can do to help people overcome a range of health conditions—from sleep issues and depression to devastating neurological damage and disorders.

With revolutionary Brain-Computer Interface (BCI) technology, people will one day be able to use their thoughts to expand physical capabilities. A wearable, portable version of Battelle's NeuroLife technology that enabled a **paralyzed** man to use his thoughts to move his fingers will allow people with **spinal cord** injuries and **paralysis** to regain immediate, impactful hand movements and connect to the Internet of Things (IoT) to control a wide range of smart devices in their home.

paralyzed [ˈpærəlaɪzd] *adj.* 瘫痪的
spinal cord 脊髓
paralysis [pəˈræləsɪs] *n.* 瘫痪

Scientists are also developing **noninvasive** Next-Generation Nonsurgical Neurotechnology (N3) devices. One likely approach will be to inject tiny magnetoelectric nanotransducers into the **circulatory** system and then use a magnet to guide them to the targeted area of the brain. This technology can revolutionize manufacturing, health care and national security capabilities.

noninvasive [ˌnɒnɪnˈveɪsɪv] *adj.* 无创的
circulatory [ˌsɜːkjəˈleztəri] *adj.* 血液循环的

No. 3: Ecotechnology will help safeguard people and the planet

The pandemic temporarily **eclipsed** our global environmental concerns, but they still **loom large**. Scientists widely recognize that controlling greenhouse gas emissions is critical to slowing, and ultimately **reversing**, global warming. In addition to increasing renewable energy, geoscience and engineering experts have been designing and managing economically **viable** carbon capture, **utilization** and storage (CCUS) technologies that stop carbon dioxide from entering the atmosphere.

At a local level, awareness of per-and poly-fluoroalkyl substances (PFAS) has raised concerns about **contamination** and environmental and human health risks. PFAS chemicals can be found in food, household products, workplace facilities, drinking water and living organisms, and because they don't break down, they accumulate in the environment and the human body over time. It's essential that we **leverage** ecotechnology to pioneer solutions that enable us to remove and **eradicate** these persistent manmade chemicals.

Humanity needs innovative solutions more than ever. As we **forge** ahead, I believe science is our best path forward.

By Lewis Von Thaer

eclipse [ɪ'klɪps]
v. 使失色

loom large
(尤指问题或忧虑)挥之不去

reverse [rɪ'vɜːs]
v. 颠倒;使反转

viable ['vaɪəbl]
adj. 切实可行的

utilization [ˌjuːtəlaɪ'zeɪʃn]
n. 利用

contamination [kənˌtæmɪneɪʃn]
n. 污染

leverage ['liːvərɪdʒ]
v. 充分利用

eradicate [ɪ'rædɪkeɪt]
v. 根除

forge [fɔːdʒ]
v. 稳步前进

Exercises

I. Read the following statements and decide whether they are true (T) or false (F) according to the text.

1.Misinformation, mistrust and science skepticism are irresolvable. T □ F □

2.No amount of data will provide vital insights that aid the development of better diagnostics and treatments. T □ F □

3. Neurotechnology enables scientists to catch and stop the next virus before it gains momentum. T☐ F☐

4. The pandemic temporarily put our global environmental concerns in the shade. T☐ F☐

5. It's essential that we make use of ecotechnology to pioneer solutions that enable us to remove the manmade chemicals. T☐ F☐

II. Translate the following sentences into English, using the words given below.

1. 学习另一种语言除了可以提升儿童未来的职业前景，还可以增强他们的自尊心。(in addition to)

____

2. 这个美术馆有一系列的现代艺术作品，可以满足各种各样的参观者。(a range of)

____

3. 在时尚界很难创出一席之地。(carve out)

____

4. 人们担心的其中一个问题是治疗的副作用。(concern)

____

III. Question for consideration.

Why does humanity need innovative solutions more than ever?

Text 3 This High Schooler Invented Color-Changing Sutures to Detect Infection

Dasia Taylor has juiced about three dozen **beets** in the last 18 months. The root vegetables, she's found, provide the perfect **dye** for her invention: **suture thread** that changes color, from bright red to dark purple, when a surgical wound becomes infected.

The 17-year-old student at Iowa City West High School in Iowa City, Iowa, began working on the project in October 2019, after her chemistry teacher shared information about state-wide science fairs with the class. As she developed her sutures, she **nabbed** awards at several regional science fairs, before advancing to the national stage. This January, Taylor was named one of 40 finalists in the Regeneron Science Talent Search, the country's oldest and most prestigious science and math competition for high school seniors.

As any science fair **veteran** knows, at the core of a successful project is a problem in need of solving. Taylor had read about sutures coated with a **conductive** material that can sense the status of a wound by changes in electrical **resistance**, and **relay** that information to the smartphones or computers of patients and doctors. While these "smart" sutures could help in the United States, the expensive tool might be less applicable to people in developing countries, where

beet [biːt]
n. 甜菜
dye [daɪ]
n. 染料
suture ['suːtʃə(r)]
n. 缝合
thread [θred]
n. 线

nab [næb]
v. 获得

veteran ['vetərən]
n. 老手

conductive [kən'dʌktɪv]
adj. 能传导(电、热等)的
resistance [rɪ'zɪstəns]
n. 电阻
relay ['riːleɪ]
v. 转发(信息、消息等)

internet access and mobile technology is sometimes lacking. And yet the need is there; on average, 11 percent of surgical wounds develop an infection in low- and middle-incoming countries, according to the World Health Organization, compared to between 2 and 4 percent of surgeries in the U.S.

Infections after Cesarean sections particularly caught Taylor's attention. In some African nations, up to 20 percent of women who give birth by C-section then develop surgical site infections. Research has also shown that health centers in Sierra Leone, the Democratic Republic of the Congo and Burundi have similar or lower rates of infection, at between 2 and 10 percent, following C-sections than the U. S., where rates range from 8 to 10 percent.

But smartphone access is markedly different. A BBC survey published in 2016 found that in Sierra Leone, about 53 percent of people own mobile phones, and about three-quarters of those owned basic cell phones, not smartphones.

"I've done a lot of racial **equity** work in my community, I've been a guest speaker at several conferences," says Taylor. "So when I was presented with this opportunity to do research, I couldn't help but go at it with an equity lens."

equity [ˈekwəti] *n.* 公正

Before the Covid-19 pandemic, Taylor spent most of her time after school in the Black History Game Show, a club she's been a member of since eighth grade, and attending weekly school board and district meetings to advocate for an anti-racist curriculum. For the four months leading up to her first regional science fair in February 2020, Taylor committed Friday afternoons to research under the guidance of her chemistry teacher, Carolyn Walling.

Healthy human skin is naturally **acidic**, with a pH around five. But when a wound becomes infected, its pH goes up to about nine.

acidic [əˈsɪdɪk] *adj.* 酸性的

Changes in pH can be detected without electronics; many fruits and vegetables are natural indicators that change color at different pH levels.

"I found that beets changed color at the perfect pH point," says Taylor. Bright red beet juice turns dark purple at a pH of nine. "That's perfect for an infected wound. And so, I was like, 'Oh, okay. So beets is where it's at.'"

Next, Taylor had to find a suture thread that would hold onto the dye. She tested ten different materials, including standard suture thread, for how well they picked up and held the dye, whether the dye changed color when its pH changed, and how their thickness compared to standard suture thread. After her school transitioned to remote learning, she could spend four or five hours in the lab on an **asynchronous** lesson day, running experiments.

A cotton-**polyester blend** checked all the boxes. After five minutes under an infection-like pH, the cotton-polyester thread changes from bright red to dark purple. After three days, the purple fades to light gray.

Working with an eye on equity in global health, she hopes that the color-changing sutures will someday help patients detect surgical site infections as early as possible so that they can seek medical care when it has the most impact. Taylor plans to patent her invention. In the meantime, she's waiting for her final college admissions results.

"To get to the Top 40, this is like **post-doctoral** work that these kids are doing," says Maya Ajmera, the president and CEO of the Society for Science, which runs the Science Talent Search. This year's top prizes went to a matching **algorithm** that can find pairs in an **infinite pool** of options, a computer model that can help identify useful compounds for **pharmaceutical** research and a sustainable drinking water **filtration** system. The finalists also voted to grant Taylor the Sea-

asynchronous [eɪˈsɪŋkrənəs] *adj.* 不同时存在(或发生)的
polyester [ˌpɒliˈestə(r)] *n.* 聚酯(纤维)
blend [blend] *n.* 混合物

post-doctoral [pəʊstˈdɒktərəl] *adj.* 博士后(的)
algorithm [ˈælgərɪðəm] *n.* 算法
infinite [ˈɪnfɪnət] *adj.* 无限的
pool [puːl] *n.* 共用的资源(或资金)
pharmaceutical [ˌfɑːməˈsjuːtɪkl] *adj.* 制药的
filtration [fɪlˈtreɪʃn] *n.* 过滤

borg Award, making her a spokesperson for their cohort.

Kathryn Chu, the director of the Center for Global Surgery at Stellenbosch University in South Africa, focuses on improving **equitable** access to surgical care. "I think it is amazing that this young high school scientist was inspired to work on a solution to address this problem," the surgeon writes in an email. "A product that could detect early (surgical site infections) would be extremely valuable."

However, she adds, "how this concept could translate from the bench to the bedside needs further testing."

Current suture threads are good at their job: they're affordable, they're not **irritating** on the skin, and they are strong enough to hold a wound together. The beet juice-dyed thread will need to be competitive on all of these attributes. Surgical site infections can also occur below the surface of a wound—a C-section involves cutting through, and then repairing, not just the skin but also the muscle underneath. As it stands, the color-changing suture thread wouldn't help detect an infection below the skin, and "if the infection **oozes** through the skin, or involves the skin, the infection has already reached later stages," writes Chu.

Lastly, the same non-**absorbency** that makes standard suture thread hard to dye with beet juice also keeps bacteria out, and **vice versa**. While cotton thread's **braided** structure gives it the ability to pick up the beet dye, it also provides a hiding place for bacteria that cause infections.

Taylor has been pursuing a line of research since the beginning of her project that might **counteract** the risks posed by using cotton.

"I read some studies that said beet juice was antibacterial. And although I want to take their word, I wanted to try it for myself. I wanted to reproduce their results," says Taylor.

equitable [ˈekwɪtəbl] *adj.* 公正的

irritate [ˈɪrɪteɪt] *v.* 刺激

ooze [uːz] *v.* (浓液体)渗出

absorbency [əbˈzɔːbənsi] *n.* 吸收性

vice versa [ˌvaɪs ˈvɜːsə] 反之亦然

braided [breɪdid] *adj.* (衣服)用穗带装饰的

counteract [kaʊntərˈ ækt] *v.* 抵消

But studying bacteria requires specific, **sterile** practices that neither Taylor, nor her **mentors** Walling and Michelle Wikner, both chemistry teachers, were initially familiar with. In the months leading up to the Science Talent Search competition, Taylor connected with microbiologist Theresa Ho at University of Iowa to create a research plan **incorporating** the proper techniques, and that work is ongoing.

sterile [ˈsteraɪl]
adj. 无菌的
mentor [ˈmentɔː(r)]
n. 导师

incorporate
[ɪnˈkɔːpəreɪt]
v. 包含

Reflecting on the science fair experience, Taylor most wants to thank Carolyn Walling for encouraging her to participate. "We're kind of **basking in** all of this together," she says, especially because it's her first year doing independent research. She's also thankful for the support of her community.

bask in 沉浸

"I have so much school pride because when somebody in our school does something great, they're celebrated to its fullest extent," says Taylor. "And being able to be one of those kids has been so amazing."

After graduation, Taylor hopes to attend Howard University, study political science and eventually become a lawyer.

"I am looking forward to seeing how Dasia uses this project moving forward," says Ajmera. "And on a long-term scale, I'm really interested in watching what problems she is going to continue to solve, to make the world a better place."

By Theresa Machemer

Exercises

I. Translate the following sentences from the text into Chinese.

1.While these "smart" sutures could help in the United States, the expensive tool might be less applicable to people in developing countries, where internet access and mobile technology is sometimes lacking.

____

2. Working with an eye on equity in global health, she hopes that the color-changing sutures will someday help patients detect surgical site infections as early as possible so that they can seek medical care when it has the most impact.

____

3. I think it is amazing that this young high school scientist was inspired to work on a solution to address this problem.

____

4. Reflecting on the science fair experience, Taylor most wants to thank Carolyn Walling for encouraging her to participate.

____

II. Match the words with the best meanings on the right.

1.infect	a.to publicly say that something should be done
2.advance	b.the right to use something
3.advocate	c.to give someone a disease
4.detect	d.to develop and improve
5.access	e.to try to achieve sth. over a period of time
6.pursue	f.to notice or discover something

III. Question for consideration.

What contributes to the success of Dasia Taylor?

Text 4 Robots Are Proving Themselves Now More Than Ever

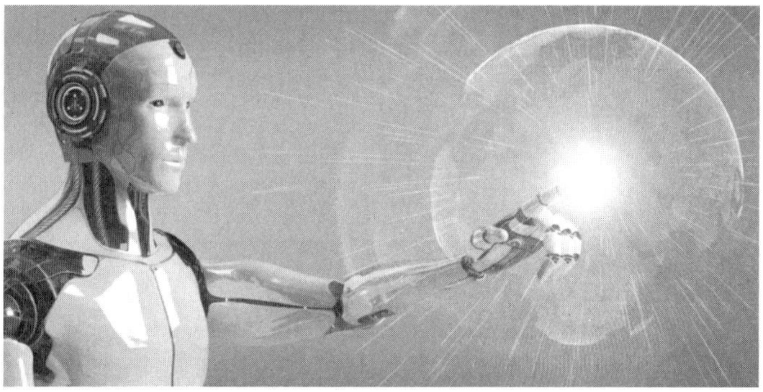

The year was 1923. Forty-two thousand people in Cincinnati signed a **petition** to force all cars in the city to have governing devices that would shut off the engine at 25 miles per hour.

The proposal was defeated in an election **referendum**, but it illustrates the anxiety and suspicion that the automobile ran into around the world soon after its introduction. Some people just thought horses were better and safer.

History **is littered with** examples of initial skepticism around **radically** new technologies. When the operatorless elevator was invented in the late 19th century, many people were terrified. People in the 1930s worried telephones would **electrocute** them.

So it comes as no surprise that one of today's game-changing innovations—robots—have faced the same kind of fear.

Whether it is movies like *The Terminator*, *The Matrix*, and *2001: A Space Odyssey* that feature **malevolent** machines bent on world domination, or studies finding that a substantial number of people are **paranoid** about robots taking over their jobs, it sometimes seems that robot technology has advanced faster than our minds can get comfortable with it.

An interesting thing about new technologies, though: The most

petition [pə'tɪʃn]
n. 请愿书

referendum [ˌrefə'rendəm]
n. 全民公投

be littered with
充满

radically ['rædɪkli]
adv. 根本地

electrocute [ɪ'lektrəkjuːt]
v. 使触电受伤(或死亡)

malevolent [mə'levələnt]
adj. 有恶意的

paranoid ['pærənɔɪd]
adj. 多疑的

important ones soon prove themselves to be useful and valuable in **myriad** ways, the **trepidation dissipates**, and we end up taking them for granted as **integral** parts of our everyday lives.

This is a trend that has repeated itself over and over again through the centuries, and I am confident we are witnessing this **progression** now with robotics.

As I write this, robots have already become an indispensable part of the manufacturing industry and are quickly moving into other environments such as healthcare, hospitality, energy, agriculture, and **warehousing**.

And two crises in the last 20 years, in particular, have served to accelerate the development and adoption of robots in powerful ways.

First—9/11. Small, portable robots were used in the disaster response after 9/11. It was a relatively new application that showed the world what the technology was capable of under practical **constraints**, and this **galvanized** new **entrepreneurial** and academic activity to expand the horizons of robots as real-world problem solvers.

9/11 **spawned** other innovations as well—most designed to make us safer—but robotics may be the best example of one that spread in new directions because of the crisis.

Think **drones**, that is, robots that fly. You' d be hard pressed to find a reference to them pre-9/11, yet here we are today with drones delivering books at our doorstep and supplying life-saving medicines around the world.

Second—there' s Covid-19. Robots have been used to automate laboratory research, disinfect hospitals, and even protect healthcare workers from the virus.

They' ve delivered **medication** and test supplies to Ghana and other remote regions. Singapore deployed a Boston Dynamics' popu-

myriad [ˈmɪrɪəd]
adj. 无数的
trepidation [ˌtrepɪˈdeɪʃn]
n. 不安
dissipate [ˈdɪsɪpeɪt]
v. 消失
integral [ˈɪntɪgrəl]
adj. 必需的
progression [prəˈgreʃn]
n. 发展；前进
warehousing [ˈweəhaʊzɪŋ]
n. 仓储
constraint [kənˈstreɪnt]
n. 限制
galvanized [ˈgælvənaɪzd]
adj. 电镀的
entrepreneurial [ˌɒntrəprəˈnɜːriəl]
adj. 企业家的
spawn [spɔːn]
v. 引发；引起
drone [drəʊn]
n. 无人机
medication [medɪˈkeɪʃn]
n. 药物

lar robot dog Spot to **patrol** public parks and broadcast messages to people in an effort to enforce social distancing.

Beyond pandemic-related applications, robots have helped reduce **strain** on the supply chain by automating and **streamlining** order fulfillment. Amazon has kept up with its tight delivery commitments in large part due to the integration of robots in its warehouses.

Covid-19 has brought a different scary movie genre into the **limelight**—the one with epidemics and the fight to save the future of humanity.

Fortunately, in this run of real-life Hollywood, robots have been our friends. It is impossible not to wonder what else robots could be capable of were society to go all in on their use.

Business leaders are asking what role robots can play in future—proofing against another health emergency or some other **upheaval** that prevents employees from physically accessing the workplace.

How can increased **reliance** on robots safeguard and streamline our businesses on an ongoing basis for **mechanically-oriented** tasks? Robots, after all, don't need social distancing.

Global crises tend to spawn new technological approaches. Some of the best innovations that advance mankind are born out of **sheer** discomfort rather than a time of comfort. Emergencies force us to change our perspectives and open up to new ideas and ways of doing things.

Necessity, after all, is the mother of invention.

Look at how many people thought a totally remote workforce couldn't be successful. After it became a sudden reality for so many companies, most found strength to adapt that they may not have known they had and invented new processes to maintain and encourage **collaboration**. As a result, employees have maintained or even

patrol [pəˈtrəʊl]
v. 巡逻

strain [streɪn]
n. 压力
streamline [ˈstriːmlaɪn]
v. 使(系统、机构等)效率更高

limelight [ˈlaɪmlaɪt]
n. 公众注意的中心

upheaval [ʌpˈhiːvl]
n. 动乱

reliance [rɪˈlaɪəns]
n. 依赖
mechanically [məˈkænɪkli]
adv. 机械地
-oriented [ˈɔːrientɪd]
adj. 以……为导向的
sheer [ʃɪə(r)]
adj. 十足的 完全的

collaboration [kəˌlæbəˈreɪʃn]
n. 合作

improved their productivity.

Again, all this demonstrates how psychology rather than technology readiness often is the primary barrier to new technology adoption. Robot technology is getting smarter all the time.

The question is, how can we most effectively take advantage of it?

And I'll answer the question I know you're about to ask: What about people's jobs? The fact is, robots have already gone **mainstream** in some far-reaching industries.

mainstream [ˈmeɪnstriːm] *n.* 主流思想

The next time you receive your speedy Amazon shipment, remember that the company has 200,000 mobile robots working in its warehouses, alongside hundreds of thousands of human employees.

Increasing the use of robots doesn't necessarily have to mean that jobs disappear. Instead, it means a **redeployment** of human workers to the intellectual rather than mechanical tasks that humans excel at.

redeployment [ˌriːdɪˈplɔɪmənt] *n.* 重新部署

Robotics is one of the most exciting fields in **cutting-edge** technology at this point, whose potential we're only now just starting to realize. So there's that to be thankful about, given the state of our times.

cutting-edge [ˌkʌtɪŋˈedʒ] *adj.* 最前沿的

Exercises

I. Read the text and find answers to the following questions.

1.Why are examples of initial skepticism around new technologies mentioned at the beginning?

____

2. What are the two crises serving to accelerate the development and adoption of robots in powerful ways?

____

3. What is the mother of invention?

____

4. What will happen to human jobs with the increasing use of robots?

____

II. Translate the following sentences into English, using the words given below.

1. 最近的商业新闻都是公司倒闭的消息。(litter)

____

2. 骑自行车可以锻炼腿部力量应是意料中的事。(surprise)

____

3. 他似乎想当然地认为他应该以代表的身份发言。(take for granted)

____

4. 得了这种病不一定就活不长。(necessarily)

____

III. Question for consideration.

Do you think robots will replace humans in the future? Why or why not?

Text 5 Frankenstein Chapter IV

It was on a dreary night of November that I **beheld** the accomplishment of my **toils**. With an anxiety that almost amounted to **agony**, I collected the instruments of life around me, that I might **infuse** a spark of being into the lifeless thing that lay at my feet. It was already one in the morning; the rain pattered **dismally** against the **panes**, and my candle was nearly burnt out, when, by the glimmer of the half-extinguished light, I saw the dull yellow eye of the creature open; it breathed hard, and a **convulsive** motion **agitated** its limbs.

How can I describe my emotions at this catastrophe, or how **delineate** the **wretch** whom with such infinite pains and care I had endeavoured to form? His limbs were in proportion, and I had selected his features as beautiful. Beautiful! —Great God! His yellow skin scarcely covered the work of muscles and **arteries** beneath; his hair was of a **lustrous** black, and flowing; his teeth of a **pearly** whiteness; but these **luxuriances** only formed a more horrid contrast with his watery eyes, that seemed almost of the same colour as the dun-white **sockets** in which they were set, his **shrivelled** complexion and straight black lips.

The different accidents of life are not so changeable as the feelings of human nature. I had worked hard for nearly two years, for the

behold [bɪ'həʊld]
v. 看;看见
toil [tɔɪl]
n. 苦工;劳累的工作
agony ['æɡəni]
n. 精神或肉体的极度痛苦
infuse [ɪn'fjuːz]
v. 使具有
dismal ['dɪzməl]
adj. 凄凉的,惨淡的
pane [peɪn]
n. (一片)窗玻璃
convulsive [kən'vʌlsɪv]
adj. 突然而无法控制的
agitate ['ædʒɪteɪt]
v. 煽动,鼓动
delineate [dɪ'lɪnieɪt]
v. (详细地)描述,解释
wretch [retʃ]
n. 可怜的人
artery ['ɑːtəri]
n. 动脉
lustrous ['lʌstrəs]
adj. 柔软光亮的
pearly ['pɜːli]
adj. 珍珠色的
luxuriance [lʌɡ'ʒʊəriəns]
n. 华丽
socket ['sɒkɪt]
n. 插座;插口
shrivel ['ʃrɪvl]
v. (使)皱缩

sole purpose of infusing life into an **inanimate** body. For this I had deprived myself of rest and health. I had desired it with an **ardour** that far exceeded **moderation**; but now that I had finished, the beauty of the dream vanished, and breathless horror and disgust filled my heart. Unable to endure the aspect of the being I had created, I rushed out of the room and continued a long time **traversing** my bed-chamber, unable to compose my mind to sleep. At length **lassitude** succeeded to the **tumult** I had before endured; and I threw myself on the bed in my clothes, endeavouring to seek a few moments of forgetfulness. But it was in vain: I slept, indeed, but I was disturbed by the wildest dreams. I thought I saw Elizabeth, in the **bloom** of health, walking in the streets of Ingolstadt. Delighted and surprised, I embraced her; but as I imprinted the first kiss on her lips, they became **livid** with the **hue** of death; her features appeared to change, and I thought that I held the corpse of my dead mother in my arms; a **shroud** enveloped her form, and I saw the grave-worms crawling in the folds of the **flannel**. I started from my sleep with horror; a cold dew covered my forehead, my teeth chattered, and every limb became **convulsed**; when, by the dim and yellow light of the moon, as it forced its way through the window shutters, I beheld the wretch—the miserable monster whom I had created. He held up the curtain of the bed; and his eyes, if eyes they may be called, were fixed on me. His jaws opened, and he muttered some inarticulate sounds, while a grin wrinkled his cheeks. He might have spoken, but I did not hear; one hand was stretched out, seemingly to **detain** me, but I escaped and rushed down stairs. I took refuge in the courtyard belonging to the house which I inhabited; where I remained during the rest of the night, walking up and down in the greatest agitation, listening attentively, catching and fearing each sound as if it were to announce the approach

inanimate [ɪnˈænɪmət]
adj. 无生命的
ardour [ˈɑːdə(r)]
n. 激情，热情
moderation [ˌmɒdəˈreɪʃən]
n. 适度；适中；合理

traverse [trəˈvɜːs]
v. 横过；穿过
lassitude [ˈlæsɪtjuːd]
n. 倦怠；疲乏
tumult [ˈtjuːmʌlt]
n. 混乱

bloom [bluːm]
n. 健康，有精神的面貌

livid [ˈlɪvɪd]
adj. 乌青色的
hue [hjuː]
n. 颜色；色调
shroud [ʃraʊd]
adj. 裹尸布
flannel [ˈflænl]
n. 法兰绒
convulse [kənˈvʌls]
v. 使痉挛（或抽筋）；（身体）震动（或抖动）

detain [dɪˈteɪn]
v. 耽搁；阻留

of the **demoniacal** corpse to which I had so miserably given life.

Oh! No mortal could support the horror of that **countenance**. A mummy again **endued** with animation could not be so **hideous** as that wretch. I had gazed on him while unfinished; he was ugly then, but when those muscles and joints were **rendered** capable of motion, it became a thing such as even Dante could not have **conceived**.

I passed the night **wretchedly**. Sometimes my pulse beat so quickly and hardly that I felt the **palpitation** of every artery; at others, I nearly sank to the ground through **languor** and extreme weakness. Mingled with this horror, I felt the bitterness of disappointment: dreams that had been my food and pleasant rest for so long a space, were now become a hell to me; and the change was so rapid, the overthrow so complete!

Morning, dismal and wet, at length dawned, and discovered to my sleepless and aching eyes the church of Ingolstadt, its white **steeple** and clock, which indicated the sixth hour. The **porter** opened the gates of the court, which had that night been my **asylum**, and I issued into the streets, pacing them with quick steps, as if I sought to avoid the wretch whom I feared every turning of the street would present to my view. I did not dare return to the apartment which I inhabited, but felt **impelled** to hurry on, although wetted by the rain, which poured from a black and comfortless sky.

I continued walking in this manner for some time, endeavouring by bodily exercise to ease the load that weighed upon my mind. I traversed the streets without any clear conception of where I was or what I was doing. My heart palpitated in the sickness of fear, and I hurried on with irregular steps, not daring to look about me:

Like one who, on a lonely road,
Doth walk in fear and dread,

demoniacal [diːˈmɒnɪkl]
adj. 狂野的，邪恶的
countenance [ˈkaʊntənəns]
n. 面容；面部表情
endue [ɪnˈdjuː]
v. 赋予
hideous [ˈhɪdiəs]
adj. 十分丑陋的；令人厌恶的
render [ˈrendə(r)]
v. 使变得；使处于某种状态
conceive [kənˈsiːv]
v. 设想；构想
wretched [ˈretʃɪd]
adj. 不适的；难受的
palpitate [ˈpælpɪteɪt]
v. （心脏）急速跳动，悸动（尤指因恐惧或兴奋）
languor [ˈlæŋgə(r)]
n. 慵懒，懒洋洋

steeple [ˈstiːpl]
n. 〔教堂的〕尖塔
porter [ˈpɔːtə(r)]
n. 门卫
asylum [əˈsaɪləm]
n. （政治）避难，（政治）庇护

impel [ɪmˈpel]
v. 促使；驱策

And, having once turned round, walks on,
And turns no more his head;
Because he knows a frightful **fiend**
Doth close behind him tread.

Continuing thus, I came at length opposite to the inn at which the various diligences and carriages usually stopped. Here I paused, I knew not why; but I remained some minutes with my eyes fixed on a coach that was coming towards me from the other end of the street. As it drew nearer I observed that it was the Swiss diligence; it stopped just where I was standing, and on the door being opened, I **perceived** Henry Clerval, who, on seeing me, instantly sprung out. "My dear Frankenstein," exclaimed he, "how glad I am to see you! How fortunate that you should be here at the very moment of my **alighting**!"

Nothing could equal my delight on seeing Clerval; his presence brought back to my thoughts my father, Elizabeth, and all those scenes of home so dear to my recollection. I grasped his hand, and in a moment forgot my horror and misfortune; I felt suddenly, and for the first time during many months, calm and **serene** joy. I welcomed my friend, therefore, in the most **cordial** manner, and we walked towards my college. Clerval continued talking for some time about our mutual friends and his own good fortune in being permitted to come to Ingolstadt. "You may easily believe," said he, "how great was the difficulty to persuade my father that all necessary knowledge was not comprised in the noble art of book-keeping; and, indeed, I believe I left him **incredulous** to the last, for his constant answer to my unwearied **entreaties** was the same as that of the Dutch school-master in *The Vicar of Wakefield*: 'I have ten thousand **florins** a year without Greek, I eat heartily without Greek.' But his affection for me at length overcame his dislike of learning, and he has permitted me to undertake a voyage

fiend [fiːnd]
n. 残忍的人；恶魔般的人

perceive [pə'siːv]
v. 注意到；意识到

alight [ə'laɪt]
adj. 容光焕发；兴奋

serene [sə'riːn]
adj. 宁静的

cordial ['kɔːdiəl]
adj. 热情友好的

incredulous [ɪn'kredʒələs]
adj. 不能相信的；不肯相信的

entreaty [ɪn'triːti]
n. 恳求；乞求

florin ['flɒrɪn]
n. 弗罗林（英国1971年以前使用的硬币，约等于10便士）

of discovery to the land of knowledge."

"It gives me the greatest delight to see you; but tell me how you left my father, brothers, and Elizabeth."

"Very well, and very happy, only a little uneasy that they hear from you so seldom. By the by, I mean to lecture you a little upon their account myself. But, my dear Frankenstein," continued he, stopping short and gazing full in my face, "I did not before remark how very ill you appear; so thin and pale; you look as if you had been watching for several nights."

"You have guessed right; I have lately been so deeply engaged in one occupation, that I have not allowed myself sufficient rest, as you see; but I hope, I sincerely hope, that all these employments are now at an end and that I am at length free."

I trembled excessively; I could not endure to think of, and far less to **allude** to, the occurrences of the **preceding** night. I walked with a quick pace, and we soon arrived at my college. I then reflected, and the thought made me shiver, that the creature whom I had left in my apartment might still be there, alive and walking about. I dreaded to behold this monster, but I feared still more that Henry should see him. Entreating him therefore, to remain a few minutes at the bottom of the stairs, I **darted** up towards my own room. My hand was already on the lock of the door before I recollected myself. I then paused, and a cold shivering came over me. I threw the door forcibly open, as children are accustomed to do when they expect a **spectre** to stand in waiting for them on the other side; but nothing appeared. I stepped fearfully in: the apartment was empty; and my bedroom was also freed from its hideous guest. I could hardly believe that so great a good-fortune could have **befallen** me, but when I became assured that my enemy had indeed fled, I clapped my hands for joy, and ran down to Clerval.

allude [əˈluːd]
v. 影射，暗指

preceding [prɪˈsiːdɪŋ]
adj. 前一个的

dart [dɑːt]
v. 猛冲；飞奔

spectre [ˈspektə(r)]
n. 恐惧

befall [bɪˈfɔːl]
v. （令人不快的事）降临到（某人）的头上；发生在（某人）身上

We **ascended** into my room, and the servant presently brought breakfast; but I was unable to contain myself. It was not joy only that possessed me; I felt my flesh tingle with excess of sensitiveness, and my pulse beat rapidly. I was unable to remain for a single instant in the same place; I jumped over the chairs, clapped my hands, and laughed aloud. Clerval at first attributed my unusual spirits to joy on his arrival; but when he observed me more attentively, he saw a wildness in my eyes for which he could not account; and my loud, unrestrained, heartless laughter frightened and astonished him.

ascend [ə'send]
v. 上升，登高

"My dear Victor," cried he, "what, for God's sake, is the matter? Do not laugh in that manner. How ill you are! What is the cause of all this?"

"Do not ask me," cried I, putting my hands before my eyes, for I thought I saw the dreaded spectre **glide** into the room; "He can tell. Oh, save me! Save me!" I imagined that the monster seized me; I struggled **furiously** and fell down in a fit.

glide [glaɪd]
v. 滑行；滑动

furious ['fjʊəriəs]
adj. 狂怒的，暴怒的

Poor Clerval! What must have been his feelings? A meeting, which he anticipated with such joy, so strangely turned to bitterness. But I was not the witness of his grief; for I was lifeless and did not recover my senses for a long, long time.

This was the commencement of a nervous fever which **confined** me for several months. During all that time Henry was my only nurse. I afterwards learned that, knowing my father's advanced age and unfitness for so long a journey, and how wretched my sickness would make Elizabeth, he spared them this grief by concealing the extent of my disorder. He knew that I could not have a more kind and attentive nurse than himself; and, firm in the hope he felt of my recovery, he did not doubt that, instead of doing harm, he performed the kindest action that he could towards them.

confine [kən'faɪn]
v. 监禁；禁闭

But I was in reality very ill, and surely nothing but the unbounded and **unremitting** attentions of my friend could have restored me to life. The form of the monster on whom I had **bestowed** existence was forever before my eyes, and I raved incessantly concerning him. Doubtless my words surprised Henry; he at first believed them to be the wanderings of my disturbed imagination, but the **pertinacity** with which I continually recurred to the same subject persuaded him that my disorder indeed owed its origin to some uncommon and terrible event.

unremitting [ˌʌnrɪˈmɪtɪŋ] *adj.* 持续不断的
bestow [bɪˈstəʊ] *v.* (将……)给予，授予
pertinacity [ˌpəːtɪˈnaszti] *n.* 固执

By very slow degrees, and with frequent **relapses** that alarmed and grieved my friend, I recovered. I remember the first time I became capable of observing outward objects with any kind of pleasure, I perceived that the fallen leaves had disappeared and that the young buds were shooting forth from the trees that shaded my window. It was a **divine** spring, and the season contributed greatly to my **convalescence**. I felt also sentiments of joy and affection **revive** in my bosom; my gloom disappeared, and in a short time I became as cheerful as before I was attacked by the fatal passion.

relapse [rɪˈlæps] *n.* 旧病复发
divine [dɪˈvaɪn] *adj.* 极美的；绝妙的
convalescence [ˌkɒnvəˈlesns] *n.* 康复期；恢复期
revive [rɪˈvaɪv] *v.* (使)苏醒，恢复

"Dearest Clerval," exclaimed I, "how kind, how very good you are to me. This whole winter, instead of being spent in study, as you promised yourself, has been consumed in my sick room. How shall I ever repay you? I feel the greatest **remorse** for the disappointment of which I have been the occasion, but you will forgive me."

remorse [rɪˈmɔːs] *n.* 懊悔，悔恨

"You will repay me entirely if you do not **discompose** yourself, but get well as fast as you can; and since you appear in such good spirits, I may speak to you on one subject, may I not?"

discompose [ˌdɪskəmˈpəʊz] *v.* 使焦虑，使不安

I trembled. One subject! What could it be? Could he allude to an object on whom I dared not even think? "Compose yourself," said Clerval, who observed my change of colour, "I will not mention it if it agitates you; but your father and cousin would be very happy if they received a letter from you in your own hand writing. They hardly know how ill you have been and are uneasy at your long silence."

"Is that all, my dear Henry? How could you suppose that my first thought would not fly towards those dear, dear friends whom I love and who are so deserving of my love?"

"If this is your present temper, my friend, you will perhaps be glad to see a letter that has been lying here some days for you; it is from your cousin, I believe."

About the book

Frankenstein or The Modern Prometheus is an 1818 novel written by English author Mary Shelley. It is a combination of Gothic horror story and science fiction. The book tells the story of Victor Frankenstein, a Swiss student of natural science who creates an artificial man from pieces of corpses and brings his creature to life. Though it initially seeks affection, the monster inspires loathing in everyone who meets it. Lonely and miserable, the monster turns upon its creator, who eventually loses his life.

Exercises

I. Translate the following sentences from the text into Chinese.

1.With an anxiety that almost amounted to agony, I collected the instruments of life around me, that I might infuse a spark of being into the lifeless thing that lay at my feet.

____

____

2.It was already one in the morning; the rain pattered dismally against the panes, and my candle was nearly burnt out, when, by the glimmer of the half-extinguished light, I saw the dull yellow eye of the creature open; it breathed hard, and a convulsive motion agitated its limbs.

3.I had desired it with an ardour that far exceeded moderation; but now that I had finished, the beauty of the dream vanished, and breathless horror and disgust filled my heart.

4.At length lassitude succeeded to the tumult I had before endured; and I threw myself on the bed in my clothes, endeavouring to seek a few moments of forgetfulness.

5.Delighted and surprised, I embraced her; but as I imprinted the first kiss on her lips, they became livid with the hue of death; her features appeared to change, and I thought that I held the corpse of my dead mother in my arms; a shroud enveloped her form, and I saw the grave-worms crawling in the folds of the flannel.

6. Nothing could equal my delight on seeing Clerval; his presence brought back to my thoughts my father, Elizabeth, and all those scenes of home so dear to my recollection. I grasped his hand, and in a moment forgot my horror and misfortune.

II. Translate the following sentences into English, using the words given below.

1.终于,玫瑰开花了,西红柿也成熟了。(at length)

2.有各种原因促使我得出那个结论。(impel)

3. 我们一直努力使车辆环保。(endeavour)

____

4. 科学研究让我踏上知识之国的探索之旅。(permit)

____

III. Question for consideration.

Will modern science bring more "monsters" to our society? Why or why not?

Cultural Notes

Technology is the application of conceptual knowledge for achieving practical goals, especially in a reproducible way. The word technology can also mean the products resulting from such efforts, including both tangible tools such as utensils or machines, and intangible ones such as software. Technology plays a critical role in science, engineering, and everyday life.

Technological advancements have led to significant changes in society. The earliest known technology is the stone tool, used during prehistoric times, followed by the control of fire, which contributed to the growth of the human brain and the development of language during the Ice Age. The invention of the wheel in the Bronze Age allowed greater travel and the creation of more complex machines. More recent technological inventions, including the printing press, telephone, and the Internet, have lowered barriers to communication and ushered in the knowledge economy.

Emerging technologies are novel technologies whose development or practical applications are still largely unrealized. They include nanotechnology, biotechnology, robotics, 3D printing, blockchains, and artificial intelligence.

Estimates on the advent of artificial general intelligence vary, but half of machine learning experts surveyed in 2018 believe that AI will "accomplish every task better and more cheaply" than humans by 2063, and automate all human jobs by 2140. This expected technological unemployment has led to calls for increased emphasis on computer science education and debates about universal basic income. Political science experts predict that this could lead to a rise in extremism, while others see it as an opportunity to usher in a post-scarcity economy.

While technology contributes to economic development and improves human prosperity, it can also have negative impacts like pollution and resource depletion, and can cause social harms like technological unemployment resulting from automation. As a result, there are ongoing philosophical and political debates about the role and use of technology, the ethics of technology, and ways to mitigate its downsides.

Unit Three Culture

Text 1 Tom and Jerry: 80 Years of Cat VS Mouse

A cartoon cat, sick of the annoying mouse living in his home, devises a plot to take him out with a trap loaded with cheese. The mouse, wise to his plan, safely removes the snack and **saunters** away with a full belly.

You can probably guess what happens next. The story ends as it almost always does: with the cat yelling out in pain as yet another plan backfires.

The **duo** was dreamt up from a place of desperation. MGM's **animation** department, where creators Bill Hanna and Joe Barbera worked, had struggled to **emulate** the success of other studios who had hit characters like Porky Pig and Mickey Mouse.

Out of boredom, the animators, both aged under 30, began thinking up their own ideas. Barbera said he loved the simple concept of a cat and mouse cartoon, with conflict and chase, even though it had been done countless times before.

Puss Gets the Boot was the first they released, in 1940. The **debut** was a hit and won the studio an Oscar nomination for best animated short.

saunter [ˈsɔːntə(r)] *v.* 漫步

duo [ˈdjuːəʊ] *n.* 一对表演搭档

animation [ænɪˈmeɪʃn] *n.* 动画片

emulate [ˈemjuleɪt] *v.* 模仿

debut [ˈdeɪbjuː] *n.* (演员、运动员的)初次登台(或上场)

According to Barbera there was no real discussion about the characters not speaking, but having grown up with silent films starring Charlie Chaplin, the creators knew they could be funny without dialogue. Music composed by Scott Bradley underscored the action and Tom's trademark human-like scream was voiced by Hanna himself.

For the best part of the next two decades, Hanna and Barbera oversaw the production of more than 100 of these shorts. Each took weeks to make and cost up to $50,000 to produce, so only a handful could be made every year.

These Toms and Jerrys are almost universally considered the best, with rich hand-drawn animation and detailed backdrops helping win them seven Academy Awards and **cameos** in Hollywood feature films.

Tom and Jerry, with its **slapstick** violence and dark comedy, remains extremely popular around the world today.

In the 80 years since their creation, the cat and mouse have appeared in everything from a "kids" version to a 1992 musical movie where they sang and spoke.

Warner Brothers, who now own the rights to *Tom and Jerry*, will release a new live-action film just before Christmas this year.

By Kelly-Leigh Cooper

cameo [ˈkæmiəʊ]
n. (电影、戏剧中)名演员演的配角
slapstick [ˈslæpstɪk]
n. 粗俗滑稽剧

Exercises

I. Choose the correct answer according to the text.

1.What is the function of the first two paragraphs?

A.To introduce the topic.

B.To illustrate a concept.

C.To clarify a view.

2.Why did Barbera create the mouse and cat characters?

A.Because he hated them a lot.

B.Because they were his favourite animals.

C.Because he loved the concept of the animals' conflict.

3.What were the original names of the characters?

A.Porky and Mickey.　　B.Puss and Boot.

C.Hanna and Barbera.　　D.Tom and Jerry.

4.How did the public respond to the silent cartoon?

A.They gave it high praise.

B.They refused to watch it.

C.They made negative comments on it.

II. Match the words with their meanings on the right.

1.devise	a.different form of something
2.hit	b.to emphasize
3.backfire	c.to have the opposite results
4.underscore	d.a typical feature
5.trademark	e.to design
6.oversee	f.to watch sb. to make sth. done
7.version	g.sth. popular and successful

III. Question for consideration.

What is your favorite animated character? How did it come into existence?

Text 2 God's Story: Easter

You might know Easter as the Sunday when a **ginormous** bunny hides chocolate inside plastic eggs, but Easter is really all about how much Jesus loves us, and how God sent him to rescue us.

ginormous [dʒaɪ'nɔːməs] *adj.* 极大的

Remember how the Jews—God's special family—were waiting for a king to come to rescue them? Well, Jesus was the King, and this rescue was the whole reason he came to Earth. God had already rescued the Jews once before, but this time it was going to include everyone.

So one night, Jesus told his friends about the rescue. Exciting, right? But talking about this rescue was sad. That's because Jesus was going to rescue the world by dying.

Kids, every mean or bad thing we do deserves punishment. By dying, Jesus took our punishment. Lots of things in life have good parts and bad parts. And just like candy bars are mostly good, as long as you brush your teeth after you eat one, this story is a really good one.

Anyway, talking about the rescue made Jesus sad since he didn't really want to die. Thankfully, we can talk to God when we're sad, so Jesus took a few friends into a garden to pray. In the garden, a guy named Judas, who people thought was Jesus's friend, came with some people to help arrest Jesus.

Peter, one of Jesus' true friends, was so mad he cut off a servant's ear with his sword, but Jesus didn't want his friends to hurt others, so Jesus healed the ear, and let them arrest him.

Then Jesus was taken to trial. One of the most powerful men in the city, Pontius Pilate, wanted to let Jesus go. But many of the people wanted Jesus to die. They didn't believe he was the son of God or any kind of king. Even after all the miracles Jesus did like healing sick people and making blind people see, they didn't believe in him. The people were so mad they started yelling, "Kill him!" So Pontius Pilate let the soldiers take Jesus.

The soldiers made fun of the idea that Jesus was a king. They put a **crown of thorns** on his head and then nailed him to a cross. Many people watched, but not all of them wanted Jesus to die. His mother and close friends were there, too. Just imagine how they must have felt.

crown [kraʊn] *n.* 王冠
thorn [θɔːn] *n.* 荆棘

Once Jesus was up on the cross, the sun stopped shining for three whole hours in the middle of the day. But those soldiers kept right on making fun of him. They said, if you're really God's son, why don't you just call on some angels to save you? Jesus could have called on angels to save him, but he loved us so much that he wanted to rescue us. So instead, he prayed to God, "Father, I place my life into your hands." At that moment, Jesus died. And when he died, the soldiers who had just killed him realized he really was the son of God.

Later, Jesus was put into a tomb and a big rock blocked the entrance. Jesus's friends thought that was the end, but three days later, God sent an angel to roll the stone away. "Don't worry, Jesus could get out on his own." The angel moved the rock so everybody else could see the tomb was empty. Jesus's friends were the first to stop by the tomb. The angel said, "He has risen!" Which is another way of saying, "Jesus is alive!" Nobody could believe it. Jesus took our punishment and then proved he really is the son of God by coming back to life.

Now, if we choose to follow Jesus, God forgives us for all the wrong things we do, because Jesus already took our punishment. And that's the story of Easter. But that's not all there is. Here's a quick version of what happened after the angel told the good news. Jesus's friends got scared. Jesus appeared to them. They saw his scars. It was really him. Now they could share the good news, too. Jesus appeared to more than 500 people. He went back up to heaven. And the best part, he promised to come back someday for everybody who follows him. And all that is a part of God's story.

Exercises

I. Read the text and find answers to the following questions.

1.How was Jesus going to rescue the world?

____

2.What was Pontius Pilate's initial attitude to Jesus's being taken to trial?

____

3.How did the soldiers treat Jesus?

____

4.Why does God forgive us for all the wrong things we do according to the story?

____

II. Translate the following sentences into English, using the words given below.

1.Tom不敢在公众场合讲话，因为他怕受到别人的嘲笑。(fun)

____

2.任何违反校规的人都会受到惩罚。(deserve)

____

3.迈克是探险队里最先发现危险的人。(first)

____

4.在几位医生的共同努力下，他终于活了过来。(come)

____

III. Question for consideration.

Do you know any other stories of foreign festivals? If so, talk about them.

Text 3 How Coco Chanel Changed the Course of Women's Fashion

Gabrielle "Coco" Chanel was one of the 20th century's most influential **couturiers**. A **milliner** by training, she moved beyond hats to become a **rebel** and a pioneer of the fashion world, creating a new **sartorial** style that freed women from corsets and lace frills by offering them sailor shirts and wide-leg pants instead.

"Nothing is more beautiful than freedom of the body," she once said, and her designs lived by these words: Chanel's outlines were fluid and **androgynous**, her designs loose and—in the case of her iconic little black dress, or LBD—democratic. She wanted women to move and breathe in her clothes, just like men did in theirs. Her work was, in many ways, a form of female liberation.

Sunday marks 50 years since Chanel's death, aged 87, though her legacy endures. As well as revolutionizing how we dress, she helped form a new ideal of what a fashion brand could be: an **all-encompassing** force that could tend to all aspects of a woman's life, from formal clothes to holiday wardrobes and evening ones.

Chanel captured her vision in "Coco-isms" that read like **acerbic** pioneers of today's inspirational quotes—"a woman who doesn't wear perfume has no future", or "If you're sad, add more lipstick and attack".

couturier [kuˈtjʊərieɪ]
n.（尤指）女装设计师

milliner [ˈmɪlɪnə(r)]
n. 女帽制造商

rebel [ˈrebl]
n. 反抗权威者

sartorial [sɑːˈtɔːriəl]
adj. 服装的；（尤指）男装的

androgynous [ænˈdrɒdʒənəs]
adj. 中性的

all-encompassing [ˌɔːl ɪnˈkʌmpəsɪŋ]
adj. 包罗万象的

acerbic [əˈsɜːbɪk]
adj. 尖刻的

Here are some important style innovations from a designer who once famously said: "I don't do fashion. I am fashion."

Nautical tops

French sailors and fishermen had been sporting Breton tops—**striped** sweaters made from tightly knit wool to protect them from the elements—since the 19th century. Striped pieces appeared in Chanel's **boutique** in the 1910s. The nautical look was casual, and far less serious than the stiff **aesthetic** of the Belle Époque, quickly becoming a hit among stylish women both on and off the beach.

Nautical tops
n. 海军领

striped [straɪpt]
adj. 有条纹的

boutique [buː'tiːk]
n. 精品店

aesthetic [iːs'θetɪk]
n. 审美

The Chanel suit

The Chanel suit was a game-changer—not just for fashion but for women's sartorial liberation.

Coco Chanel introduced her first two-piece set in the 1920s, inspired by menswear and sportswear. Keen to free women from the restrictive **corsets** and long skirts of previous decades, Chanel crafted a slim skirt and collarless jacket made of tweed, a fabric then considered unglamorous.

corset ['kɔːsɪt]
n.(尤指旧时妇女束腰的)紧身内衣

Not only did she make "black" the black it is today, but she also created the wardrobe staple that none of us can live without—the little black dress!

Women's trousers

Chanel didn't invent women's pants—they had already entered wardrobes during World War I, when women started taking jobs traditionally carried out by men. But she undeniably popularized them as a fashion garment.

The designer liked wearing pants herself (she often borrowed them from her male lovers), and, as early as 1918, began sporting flowy "beach pajamas" while vacationing on the French Riviera. Drawing inspiration from the straight, wide cuts of sailor's pants, giving them a loose, comfortable shape, she matched them with oversized shirts or sleeveless tops.

The garment was considered **risqué** at the time, due to pajamas' association with the bedroom, but by the mid-1920s it had become a staple among wealthy ladies and a fixture of Chanel's collections.

risqué [ˈrɪskeɪ] *adj.* 有伤风化的

Here are some little-known facts about Coco Chanel:

1. She loved pockets

Coco Chanel was so enchanted with pockets that this would prove to be the main focus of her designs in handbags for women!

2. It started as a hobby

Chanel started her career by designing hats which later became a bit hit with **aristocratic** Parisians. It was her innovative and fancy hat designs that got her attention.

aristocratic [ˌærɪstəˈkrætɪk] *adj.* 贵族的

hosiery [ˈhəʊziəri] *n.*(尤用于商店的)袜类

3. **Hosiery** to high fashion

Did you know that before she became a fashion legend, Coco Chanel used to work as a clerk in a small hosiery shop? Legends do start small! From humble beginnings to grand achievements!

4. **Sun tan** was started by her

Sun tan 晒黑

If you thought tanning became fashionable by accident, think again! It was Coco Chanel who made it fashionable when she got burnt by sun rays way back in 1923 on a cruise towards Cannes!

5. 5 was her favorite number

Maybe there was something special in the number 5—enough to have Coco Chanel superstitious and in awe of it. Chanel No. 5 was introduced on 5th May 1921! No coincidence this!

6. She never got married

Coco Chanel might have dated and had affairs with plenty of men but she never got married. Maybe she thought it would take away from her dedication to the fashion world.

By Marianna Cerini

Exercises

I. Read the following statements and decide whether they are true (T) or false (F) according to the text.

1.Coco Chanel was born to a very wealthy family. T □ F □

2.Coco Chanel didn't like sun tanning. T □ F □

3.The Chanel suit was inspired by menswear and sportswear. T □ F □

4.The nautical tops look formal and serious. T □ F □

5.Coco Chanel believed freedom of the body was important. T □ F □

II. Match the words with their meanings on the right.

1.solitude	a.extremely interested
2.shackles	b.the important part
3.staple	c.the state of being alone
4.enchanted	d.believing some objects bring good or bad luck
5.superstitious	e.the limits put on your freedom or happiness

III. Question for consideration.

Do you like any of Coco Chanel's design? If so, list your reasons.

Text 4 US Woman **Sparks Transatlantic** Tea War with **Brutal** Online **Brew**

There have been more severe transatlantic arguments over a brew, such as the American Revolution, but few can have been quite so **twee**. Nearly 250 years after the Boston Tea Party, the British ambassador in Washington and her US **counterpart** in London are going at it over how to make a decent hot drink. And by Wednesday evening, the conflict was spilling over into mainland Europe.

Like many tense diplomatic **standoffs**, it began with a deliberate **provocation**. An American TikTok user going by the name of Michelle from North Carolina posted a video showing how to make what she describes as "hot tea", which needs mixing milk with powdered lemonade, **cinnamon**, **cloves** and sugar—a combination which turns out to be a soft drink.

As an afterthought she dipped a teabag, and then put the whole thing in the microwave. Her attempt at "British tea" involved cold water first. The British internet lost its marbles.

Michelle from North Carolina(a state of the US), who actually lives in Britain and has proven herself to be an effective wind-up merchant with follow-ups including her recipe for "UK eggs" —quickly accumulated 5 million TikTok likes. Meanwhile, the UK's powerful

spark [spɑːk]
v. 引发
transatlantic
[ˌtrænzətˈlæntɪk]
adj. 横渡大西洋的
brutal [ˈbruːtl]
adj. 残暴的;兽性的
brew [bruː]
n. 沏(茶)
twee[twiː]
adj. 矫揉造作的
counterpart
[ˈkaʊntəpɑːt]
n. 职务相当的人
standoff [ˈstændˈɒf]
n. 僵局
provocation
[ˌprɒvəˈkeɪʃn]
n. 挑衅
cinnamon[ˈsɪnəmən]
n. 肉桂
clove [kləʊv]
n. 丁香

ability to get on its high horse about **elevenses** kicked into gear.

Phillip Schofield, one of the most beloved British TV presenters, did a bit on *This Morning*. Davina McCall described it as a "call to war". **Inevitably**, Dame Karen Pierce, the British ambassador to Washington —who holds an MSc(Master of Science) in international strategy and diplomacy from the LSE, has served in the Foreign Office for 39 years and is a former president of the UN security council—was obliged to weigh in.

British ambassador to Washington calls in military for a tea-making demonstration video.

Karen Pierce posted a viral video of her own on Monday, explaining that "the **Anglo-American** relationship is defined by tea", a reference to the Boston Tea Party of 1773 that eventually led to US independence.

Then, in what Twitter enthusiasts viewed as a thrilling escalation, Pierce threw to three branches of the armed forces, who took it in turns to demonstrate how to make what one Royal Navy sailor called a "proper British cup of tea".

Christopher Hitchens, the late, great transatlantic writer who published a 2011 piece complaining about the impossibility of finding a decent brew in the US—"It's quite common to be served a cup or a pot of water, well off the boil, with the tea bags lying on a cold plate," he complained —would surely have approved. The war, Pierce must have assumed, was over.

However, the US ambassador to London, Woody Johnson, who recognised the impossibility of his position on the tea front, quickly shifted his forces to a classic British weakness: coffee.

"I'm going to make an American cup of coffee, the way I make it every day, responding to Ambassador Pierce's perfect cup of tea and

elevenses[ɪˈlevnzɪz] *n.* 午前茶点

inevitably [ɪnˈevɪtəbli] *adv.* 不可避免地

Anglo-American [ˌæŋgləu əˈmerɪkən] *adj.* 英美的

her instructions," he said in a serious voice, allowing his host nation's collective anxiety about not really understanding the difference between a cappuccino and a flat white to do its own work.

He proceeded to pour a bottle of water into a kettle, stick a spoon of instant coffee in a mug, splash in some milk and say "have a nice day". If he then told his social media assistant that no, he didn't have time for a second take, he had some chicken to sell, history did not record the interaction.

Johnson's **intervention** appears to have shocked his British counterpart into silence for the time being. But there may now be questions as to whether he had committed a serious strategic error, by making, to put it frankly, what looked like a terrible cup of coffee. On Wednesday evening, a source at the Italian embassy asked for a view on the US video replied: "What he made was American coffee. And I stress... American coffee." In winning one war, it appears that Johnson may have accidentally started another.

By Archie Bland

intervention
[ˌɪntəˈvenʃn]
n. 干涉行为

Exercises

I. Read the text and find answers to the following questions.

1.What caused a fierce war on the Internet at first?

____

2.How did Johnson respond to the tea-making demonstration video?

____

3.Do you think Johnson respond to the video properly? Why?

____

II. Match the underlined phrases with the best meanings on the right.

1.lose one's marbles	a.to go mad
2.get on its high horse	b.to put into effect
3.kick into gear	c.a worse situation
4.weigh in	d.to join in a fight or argument
5.a thrilling escalation	e.to show you are right in a rude way

III. Question for consideration.

Do you like tea or coffee? Do you make it in the way the text mentioned?

Text 5 An Adaptation of a Study in Scarlet (Excerpt)

We met next day as he had arranged, and inspected the rooms of No. 221B, Baker Street. We were both satisfied with the rooms, and agreed to take them there and then. We gradually began to settle down and get used to our new surroundings.

Holmes was certainly not a difficult man to live with. He was quiet in his ways, and his habits were regular. It was rare for him to be up after ten at night, and he had breakfast and was gone before I rose in the morning.

Sometimes he went to the laboratory, sometimes to the rooms where students would **dissect** dead bodies, sometimes to the most dangerous and criminal areas of the city.

dissect[dɪ'sekt] *v.* 解剖

I have never seen anyone so energetic as he was when he was hard at work, but now and again a reaction would take him, and for days on end he would lie upon the sofa in the sitting-room, hardly saying a word or moving a muscle from morning to night.

His appearance was such as to strike the attention of anyone who saw him. In height he was rather over six feet, and so excessively thin that he seemed to be considerably taller. His eyes were sharp and intense, and his thin nose gave his whole expression an air of alertness and decision.

I must confess that I was extremely curious about this man, and tried very hard to get him to tell me something about himself, which he seemed very reluctant to do.

I had no friends and my health prevented me from going out, so I welcomed this mystery and tried my best to solve it.

He was not studying medicine, nor did he appear to have followed any course of reading which might fit him for a degree in science. Yet his enthusiasm for certain studies was remarkable, and his knowledge of certain unusual subjects was so extremely full and detailed that his observations sometimes astonished me.

His ignorance was as remarkable as his knowledge. He appeared to know next to nothing of contemporary literature, philosophy and politics. Upon my quoting Thomas Carlyle, he asked the simplest questions such as who he might be and what he had done.

And my surprise reached a peak when I found that he was unaware of the Copernican Theory and of the composition of the Solar System.

"You appear to be astonished," he said, smiling at my expression of surprise.

"Now that I do know it, I will do my best to forget it."

"To forget it!"

"You see," he explained, "I consider that a man's brain originally is like a little empty room, and you have to stock it with such furniture as you choose.

A fool takes in all the junk he comes across, so that the knowledge which might be useful to him gets crowded out, or at best is mixed up with a lot of other things so that he has difficulty in finding it.

Now the expert worker is very careful indeed as to what he takes into his brain.

He will have nothing but the tools which may help him in doing his work, and he has a large collection of these tools, but all in the most perfect order.

The 'room' in one's brain is of fixed and limited size, so there comes a time when, for every addition of knowledge, you forget something that you knew before.

It is of the highest importance, therefore, not to have useless facts pushing out the useful ones."

"But the Solar System!" I protested.

"What is it to me?" he said impatiently, "You say that we go round the sun. If we went round the moon, it would make no difference to me or to my work."

I was on the point of asking him what that work might be, but something in his manner showed me that the question would be an unwelcome one.

During the first week or so we had no visitors, and I had begun to think that my companion was as friendless a man as I was myself.

Presently, however, I found that he had many acquaintances, and those in the most different classes of society.

There was one little pale rat-faced, dark eyed fellow who was introduced to me as Mr. Lestrade, and who came three or four times in a single week.

One morning a young girl called, fashionably dressed, and stayed for half an hour or more—closely followed by an elderly woman in dirty clothes. On another occasion an old white-haired gentleman had an interview with my companion, and another time, a railway porter in his uniform.

At such times Sherlock Holmes used to beg for the use of the sitting-room, and I would go back to my bed-room. He always apologized to me for putting me to this inconvenience.

"I have to use this room as a place of business," he said, "and these people are my clients."

Again I had an opportunity of asking him a point-blank question, and again my delicacy prevented me from forcing another man to **confide** in me.

confide [kən'faɪd]
v.（向某人）吐露（秘密、隐私等）

However, he soon told me himself. As I remember, it was on the 4th of March.

I rose somewhat earlier than usual, and found that Sherlock Holmes had not yet finished his breakfast.

I picked up a magazine from the table and attempted to pass the time with it, while my companion ate silently.

One of the articles had a pencil mark at the heading, and I naturally began to run my eye over it.

Its somewhat ambitious title was "The Book of Life", and it attempted to show how much an observant man might learn by an accurate and careful examination of all that came in his way.

The reasoning was close and intense, but the conclusions appeared to me to be far-fetched and exaggerated. The writer claimed by a temporary expression, a **twitch** of a muscle or a glance of an eye, to find out a man's inner thoughts.

twitch [twɪtʃ]
n. 痉挛；抽搐

According to him, it was impossible to fool a man who has been trained in such observation and analysis.

His conclusions were very definite.

To the untrained, his results would appear very surprising.

"From a drop of water," said the writer, "a logician could gather the possibility of an Atlantic or a Niagara without having seen or heard of one or the other.

So all life is a great chain, the nature of which is known whenever we are shown a single link of it.

By a man's finger nails, by his coat-sleeve, by his shoes, by his clothes, by his expression by each of these things a man's work is plainly revealed."

"What nonsense!" I cried, throwing the magazine down on the table, "I never read such rubbish in my life."

"What is it ?" asked Sherlock Holmes.

"This article," I said, pointing at it with my egg spoon as I sat down to my breakfast.

"I see that you have read it, since you have marked it.

I don't deny that it is cleverly written. It bothers me though. It is not practical. I should like to see him sit down in a third class carriage on the underground, and figure out the profession of all the travelers. I would lay a thousand to one against him."

"You would lose your money," Sherlock Holmes remarked calmly.

"As for the article, I wrote it myself."

"You!"

"Yes, I have a natural talent both for observation and for **deduction**. The theories which I have expressed there, and which appear to you to be so absurd, are extremely practical—so practical that I depend upon them for my bread and cheese."

deduction[dɪ'dʌkʃn] *n.* 演绎;推理

"And how?" I asked.

"Well, I have a trade of my own. I suppose I am the only one in the world. I'm a consulting detective, if you can understand what that is. Here in London we have lots of government detectives and lots of private ones. When these men are at fault they come to me, and I manage to put them on the right scent. They lay all the evidence before me, and I am generally able to give them the right idea, with the help of my knowledge of the history of crime. Lestrade is a well-known detective. He got himself into a mess recently over a case. That's what brought him here."

"But do you mean to say," I said, "that without leaving your room you can undo some knots which other men cannot figure out, although they have seen every detail for themselves?"

"Quite so. I have a kind of instinct about those things. Sometimes a case turns up which is a little more complex. Then I have to move about and see things with my own eyes. You see I have a lot of special knowledge which I apply to the problem, and which aids matters wonderfully. Those rules of deduction laid down in that article, which stirred your **contempt**, are precious to me in practical work. To me, observation is second nature. On our first meeting, you appeared to be surprised when I told you that you had come from Afghanistan."

contempt [kən'tempt] *n.* 蔑视

"You were told, no doubt."

"Nothing of the sort. I knew you came from Afghanistan. From long habit the sequence of thoughts ran so swiftly through my mind that I arrived at the conclusion without being aware of the **intermediate** steps. There were such steps, however. My thoughts went like this. Here is a gentleman of a medical type, but with the air of a military man. Clearly an army doctor, then. He has just come from the tropics, for his face is dark, and that is not the natural color of his skin, for his wrists are fair. He has experienced suffering and sickness, as his worn face says clearly. His left arm has been wounded. He holds it in a **stiff** and unnatural manner.

intermediate [ˌɪntə'miːdiət] *adj.* 中间的

stiff [stɪf] *adj.* 僵硬的

Where in the tropics could an English army doctor have seen much suffering and got his arm wounded? Clearly in Afghanistan.

The whole train of thought did not take a second.

I then remarked that you came from Afghanistan, and you were shocked."

"It is simple enough when you explain it," I said, smiling.

"No man lives, or has ever lived, who has brought the same amount of study and of natural talent to the detection of crime as I have done. And what is the result? There is no crime to detect, or, at most, some stupid crimes with a motive so obvious that even a Scotland Yard official can see through it." I was annoyed at his arrogant style of conversation.

I thought it best to change the topic. "I wonder what that fellow is looking for." I asked, pointing to a plainly-dressed man who was walking slowly down the other side of the street, looking anxiously at the numbers. He had a large blue envelope in his hand, and was evidently carrying a message to someone.

"You mean the retired sergeant of Marines," said Sherlock Holmes.

"Nonsense!" I thought to myself.

He knows that I cannot verify his guess.

The thought had hardly passed through my mind when the man whom we were watching caught sight of the number on our door, and ran rapidly across the road.

We heard a loud knock, a deep voice below, and heavy steps climbing the stair.

"For Mr. Sherlock Holmes," he said, stepping into the room and handing my friend the letter.

Here was an opportunity of taking the pride out of him.

He little thought of this when he made that random guess.

"May I ask, my man," I said, "what your job may be?"

"Messenger, sir," he said. "My uniform is away to be mended."

"And you were?" I asked.

"A sergeant, sir, Royal Marine Light Infantry, sir. No answer? Right, sir." He clicked his heels together, raised his hand in a salute, and was gone.

By Sir Arthur Conan Doyle

From *Sherlock Holmes*

About the book

Sherlock Holmes is a fictional detective created by British author Arthur Conan Doyle. Referring to himself as a "consulting detective" in the stories, Holmes is known for his proficiency with observation, deduction, forensic science and logical reasoning that borders on the fantastic, which he employs when investigating cases for a wide variety of clients, including Scotland Yard.

The character Sherlock Holmes first appeared in print in 1887's *A Study in Scarlet*. His popularity became widespread with the first series of short stories in *The Strand Magazine*, beginning with "A Scandal in Bohemia" in 1891; additional tales appeared from then until 1927, eventually totalling four novels and 56 short stories. All but one are set in the Victorian or Edwardian eras, between about 1880 and 1914. Most are narrated by the character of Holmes's friend and biographer Dr. John H. Watson, who usually accompanies Holmes during his investigations and often shares quarters with him at the address of 221B Baker Street, London, where many of the stories begin.

Though not the first fictional detective, Sherlock Holmes is arguably the best known. By the 1990s, there were already over 25,000 stage adaptations, films, television productions and publications featuring the detective, and Guinness World Records lists him as the most portrayed human literary character in film and television history. Holmes's popularity and fame are such that many have believed him to be not a fictional character but a real individual; numerous literary and fan societies have been founded on this pretence. Avid readers of the Holmes stories helped create the modern practice of fandom. The character and stories have had a profound and lasting effect on mystery writing and popular culture as a whole, with the original tales as well as thousands written by authors other than Conan Doyle being adapted into stage and radio plays, television, films, video games, and other media for over one hundred years.

Exercises

I. Choose the correct answer according to the text.

1.What did Dr. Watson think of Holmes?

A.He was always noisy.

B.He was difficult to deal with.

C.He was devoted to work with passion.

2.How did Holmes process knowledge not useful for him?

A.He tried to forget it.

B.He tried to remember it.

C.He tried to write it down.

3.What was the article *The Book of Life* about?

A.Music and art.

B.Literature and painting.

C.Observation and analysis.

4.What was Holmes's job?

A.He was a doctor.

B.He was a police officer.

C.He was a consulting detective.

5. What can we know about Dr. Watson?

A.He suffered in the war.

B.He was alert and decisive.

C.He was born in the tropics.

II. Match the underlined phrases with their meanings on the right.

1.on end	a.very little
2.next to nothing	b.to solve mysteries
3.crowd out	c.to make sb. discover sth.
4.at fault	d.happening without stopping
5.put them on the right scent	e.to force sb. out of a place or situation
6.undo some knots	f.be responsible for sth. bad that happened

III. Question for consideration.

Have you read any other works of *The Adventure of Sherlock Holmes* series? What do you know about Sherlock Holmes?

Cultural Notes

Culture, behaviour peculiar to Homo sapiens, together with material objects used as an integral part of this behaviour. Thus, culture includes language, ideas, beliefs, customs, codes, institutions, tools, techniques, works of art, rituals, and ceremonies, among other elements.

What has been termed the classic definition of culture was provided by the 19th-century English anthropologist Edward Burnett Tylor in the first paragraph of his *Primitive Culture* (1871):

Culture ... is that complex whole which includes knowledge, belief, art, morals, law, custom, and any other capabilities and habits acquired by man as a member of society.

In *Anthropology* (1881) Tylor made it clear that culture, so defined, is possessed by man alone. This conception of culture served anthropologists well for some 50 years. With the increasing maturity of anthropological science, further reflections upon the nature of their subject matter and concepts led to a multiplication and diversification of definitions of culture. In *Culture: A Critical Review of Concepts and Definitions* (1952), U.S. anthropologists A.L. Kroeber and Clyde Kluckhohn cited 164 definitions of culture, ranging from "learned behaviour" to "ideas in the mind," "a logical construct," "a statistical fiction," "a psychic defense mechanism," and so on. The definition—or the conception—of culture that is preferred by Kroeber and Kluckhohn and also by a great many other anthropologists is that culture is an abstraction or, more specifically, "an abstraction from behaviour".

These conceptions have defects or shortcomings. The existence of behavioral traditions — that is, patterns of behaviour transmitted by social rather than by biologic hereditary means— has definitely been established for nonhuman animals. "Ideas in the mind" become significant in society only as expressed in language, acts, and objects. "A logical construct" or "a statistical fiction" is not specific enough to be useful. The conception of culture as an abstraction led, first, to a questioning of the reality of culture (inasmuch as abstractions were regarded as imperceptible) and, second, to a denial of its existence; thus, the subject matter of nonbiological anthropology, "culture", was defined out of existence, and without real, objective things and events in the external world there can be no science.

Kroeber and Kluckhohn were led to their conclusion that culture is an abstraction by reasoning that if culture is behaviour, it becomes the subject matter of psychology; therefore, they concluded that culture "is an abstraction from concrete behavior but is not itself behavior". But what, one might ask, is an abstraction of a marriage ceremony or a pottery bowl, to use Kroeber and Kluckhohn's examples? This question poses difficulties that were not adequately met by these authors. A solution was perhaps provided by Leslie A. White in the essay "The Concept of Culture" (1959). The issue is not really whether culture is real or an abstraction, he reasoned; the issue is the context of the scientific interpretation.

When things and events are considered in the context of their relation to the human organism, they constitute behaviour; when they are considered not in terms of their relation to the human organism but in their relationship to one another, they become culture by definition. The mother-in-law taboo is a complex of concepts, attitudes, and acts. When one considers them in their relationship to the human organism—that is, as things that the organism does—they become behaviour by definition. When, however, one considers the mother-in-law taboo in its relationship to the place of residence of a newly married couple, to the customary division of labour between the sexes, to their respective roles in the society's mode of subsistence and offense and defense, and these in turn to the technology of the society, the mother-in-law taboo becomes, again by definition, culture. This distinction is precisely the one that students of words have made for many years. When words are considered in their relationship to the human organism—that is, as acts—they become behaviour. But when they are considered in terms of their relationship to one another—producing lexicon, grammar, syntax, and so forth—they become language, the subject matter not of psychology but of the science of linguistics. Culture, therefore, is the name given to a class of things and events dependent upon symboling (i.e., articulate speech) that are considered in a kind of extra-human context.

Unit Four The Media

Text 1 Why I'm grateful to be a journalist on World News Day

To mark World News Day today, I want to share one of the proudest moments I've experienced as a journalist.

In August, I was asked to write a story about what human **trafficking** looks like locally for a news series on crimes that are **thriving** in communities situated along major highways—specifically the trafficking of guns, drugs, and people.

I'm fortunate to have close connections with Const. Ann Collins of Grenville County OPP, as well as the **executive** director of Victim Services of Leeds and Grenville, Sonya Jodoin, who both contributed to my article with localized statistics and tips on how to identify a possible human trafficking victim.

That story has since **garnered** more than 22,000 views.

One week after the article was published, Victim Services shared it on their Facebook page, stating that they're looking into starting virtual public education on human trafficking this fall, given the interest in the topic and the amount of discussion that the article sparked on social media.

It made me feel like a superhero to have shined a light on an issue that truly needed it.

trafficking [ˈtræfɪkɪŋ]
n. 贩卖

thrive [θraɪv]
v. 兴旺发达

executive [ɪɡˈzekjətɪv]
adj. 有执行权的

garner [ˈɡɑːnə(r)]
v. 得到

The popularity of the article **prompting** additional efforts to raise awareness was awesome, too, but neither of these things were the true **highlight** for me.

prompt [prɒmpt]
v. 激起

highlight [ˈhaɪlaɪt]
n. 最精彩的部分

One of the 22,000 readers is a local grade 10 student at North Grenville District High School.

She reached out to me to let me know that she read my article, and she's been inspired to do what she can to raise awareness of the well-hidden global issue.

"I would like to address the issue and educate others about human trafficking and their safety because I believe the lack of acknowledgement and recognition on the topic is what's most harmful," she explained.

And she's right. The more the community knows about human trafficking, the better. But unfortunately, right now, we're still at the point where people are shocked to find out that it's happening here.

Having just been selected as a United Nations SDG **Ambassador** through a new program offered to Kemptville youth, this young woman chose the issue of human trafficking to campaign on.

ambassador
[æmˈbæsədə(r)]
n. 大使

Her intentions are to hold **seminars** focusing on children and youth, and the minority groups who are targeted the most. According to Victim Services, they're seeing a lot of girls under 18 being trafficked this year. Now, some of the most **vulnerable** are going to be educated on this issue by someone their own age.

seminar [ˈsemɪnɑː(r)]
n. 研讨会

vulnerable [ˈvʌlnərəbl]
adj. 易受……伤害的

I'm grateful to have my work inspire anyone, but I'm especially grateful to know who that person is, and to see them sharing their knowledge with others—that's much more valuable to me than any number of page views, comments, or shares.

by Paulina Hrebacka

Exercises

I. Read the text and find answers to the following questions.

1.What issue did the author write about in August?

______

2.What made the author feel like a superhero?

______

3.Who was selected as a United Nations SDG Ambassador?

______

4.What is the most valuable to the author?

______

II. Translate the following sentences into English, using the words given below.

1.我已经到达人生中可以自己做决定的时候。(point)

______

2.我的祖父激发了我对生活的热情和激情。(inspire)

______

3.这些提议预计会引起激烈的争论。(spark)

______

4.他不懈的努力是他事业成功的原因。(contribute)

______

III. Question for consideration.

What do you think makes a great journalist?

Text 2 Why We Need Media Reporting Guidelines for Road Safety

There's a problem with how we talk about our roads. From news reports on "accidents" to who gets blamed for road danger in comment pieces, our media sources sometimes **flip** the sources of death and injury on their head.

Language and accuracy matter, and too often reporting contributes to making the roads less safe. That's why the Active Travel Academy has drafted media reporting guidelines which we hope broadcasters and publishers will adopt, just as they have adopted guidelines for reporting on suicide or domestic violence.

There is excellent reporting out there, but there is also less thoughtful output. For example, the majority (61%) of **coverage** of cyclists is broadly negative, focusing on road danger, **criminality** or bad behaviour, although studies have shown cyclists are generally far more **law-abiding** than motorists.

Research has demonstrated that how journalists describe and discuss crashes affects how people see the causes of and solutions to road danger. Not only that, it influences how we treat others on the roads—with language that **dehumanizes** other road users, often cyclists, predicting aggression and violence between road users. Those who cycle regularly will tell you they **wince** when they see the latest article or

flip [flɪp]
v. 轻掷

coverage [ˈkʌvərɪdʒ]
n. 新闻报道
criminality
[ˌkrɪmɪˈnæləti]
n. 犯罪
law-abiding
[ˈlɔːəbaɪdɪŋ]
adj. 遵纪守法的

dehumanize
[ˌdiːˈhjuːmənaɪz]
v. 使(某人)丧失人性
wince [wɪns]
v. (因痛苦或尴尬)龇牙咧嘴,皱眉蹙额

TV programme about so-called "**lycra louts**".

It also affects how our legal system tackles law-breakers on the roads. Those working in the criminal justice system, from police, **magistrates** and **jurors** to **coroners** and judges, all read the news. When they read pieces that exaggerate the dangers presented by cyclists or pedestrians, it may affect their decision-making. **Conversely**, when they read that "a car", rather than "a driver", has caused injury or damage, it **trivializes** the dangers imposed on the most vulnerable road users by bad drivers.

One only has to read the comments under online news articles about motorists and cyclists to see how prejudices can be **reinforced** by ill-informed "keyboard warriors", most of whom will be **eligible** for jury service.

Media reporting has a direct influence on how safe we feel on our streets. Journalists can't be experts in all fields, so we want to help reporters, broadcasters and publishers be as accurate and fair as possible when reporting on road **collisions** and road safety.

We have written these guidelines with representatives from national roads policing, the National Union of Journalists' **ethics** council, road safety and legal experts, academics, and with advice from the independent journalism regulator Impress. Reporting guidelines already exist to protect the most vulnerable in society in other areas of life, and with road crashes claiming more than 1,700 lives a year and permanently altering thousands more, how we talk about the most vulnerable on our roads matters, too.

The four clauses each **align with** journalistic values that inform existing reporting guidelines. These are:

• Impartiality: publishers must not use the term "accident" when describing road collisions—"collision" or "crash" are more accurate,

lycra lout
n. 不守规矩的骑自行车的人

magistrate [ˈmædʒɪstreɪt]
n. 治安法官
juror [ˈdʒʊərə(r)]
n. 陪审员
coroner [ˈkɒrənə(r)]
n. 验尸官
conversely [kɒnvɜːsli]
adv. 相反地
trivialize [ˈtrɪvɪəlaɪz]
v. 使显得琐碎

reinforce [ˌriːɪnˈfɔːs]
v. 加强
eligible [ˈelɪdʒəbl]
adj. 有资格的

collision [kəˈlɪʒn]
n. 碰撞(或相撞)事故

ethics [ˈeθɪks]
n. 伦理学

align with
与……一致

especially when the facts of the incident are not known.

• Discrimination: publishers must avoid using negative generalisations of road users, and must not use dehumanising language or that which may **incite** violence or **hatred** against a road user.

• Accuracy: coverage of perceived risks on the roads should above all be accurate, based in fact and context. Publishers should make mention of human actors in a collision, and avoid reference to personal protective equipment, such as **hi-vis** and helmets, except when **demonstrably** relevant.

• Reporting on crime: publishers must avoid portraying dangerous or criminal behaviour on the roads, such as speeding, as acceptable, or those caught breaking the law as victims.

By Laura Laker and Martin Porter QC

incite [ɪnˈsaɪt] *v.* 煽动
hatred [ˈheɪtrɪd] *n.* 仇恨

hi-vis [ˌhaɪˈvɪz] *n.* 反光背心
demonstrably [dɪˈmɒnstrəbli] *adv.* 明显地

Exercises

I. Read the following statements and decide whether they are true (T) or false (F) according to the text.

1.Reporters of "accidents" on roads need to attach importance to language and accuracy.

T □ F □

2.Cyclists are less likely to observe laws than motorists. T □ F □

3.Our legal system that tackles law-breakers on the roads is also affected by biased reporting. T □ F □

4.When describing road collisions, many people prefer the term "accident" over others.

T □ F □

5.Accuracy based in fact and context must be involved in the coverage of perceived risks on the roads. T □ F □

II. Translate the following sentences into English, using the words given below.

1. 我在这次讲座中将集中讲解非常具体的问题。(focus on)

____

2. 无论是好是坏,科技都对我们的生活产生了巨大的影响。(have a/an ... influence on)

____

3. 最重要的是学生的身体健康和精神状态。(matter)

____

4. 当考试作弊被抓住时,他祈求老师原谅并试图逃避惩罚。(catch sb. doing...)

____

III. Question for consideration.

Can you give some more examples of how media coverage has changed our perception of the world?

Text 3 This Youth Generation: Media, Technology Take Influence from Parents

There was a time when parents were **concerned** about who their children were associating with, in fear of possible negative influences. If they were not in the physical presence of a person, then they were free from harm.

concerned [kən'sɜːnd] *adj.* 担心的

Parents today have much more to worry about in terms of negative influences.

The advancement of technology has made the task of **parenting** much more challenging than ever. I'm more concerned, as a father, about who my sons and daughter are listening to and watching. I **occasionally** hear a successful artist **refer to** who they were influenced by as a child. For me, it was Stevie Wonder, Aretha Franklin and Marvin Gaye. Why? Because it was what my parents and elders listened to.

parenting ['peərəntɪŋ] *n.* 养育

occasionally [ə'keɪʒnəli] *adv.* 偶然地

refer to 描述,提到

While I was in the house doing **chores**, there was James Brown playing in the background: "Say it Loud." You know! You could not have a family gathering without the O'Jays tune "For the Love of Money" or Marvin Gaye's "What's Going On".

chores [tʃɔː(r)] *n.* 日常事务

These artists were not only cultural **icons** but they were also making statements on the social-economic conditions of the urban society at the time, which in some ways **cultivated** critical thinking and in-

icon ['aɪkɒn] *n.* 标志;偶像

cultivate ['kʌltɪveɪt] *v.* 培育

spired consciousness. Aside from the **psychedelic**, diaper-wearing, weed-smoking **antics** of Parliament and George Clinton, this was an era of positive influence through music and entertainment. There were no **profanity-laced**, sexually **explicit** lyrics.

I know what you're thinking, but Prince didn't come on the scene until the 1980s.

How are today's artists and entertainers influencing the current youth generation? The media and entertainment industries are even more powerful today due to **overexposure** and constant repetition. Thanks to the digital world in which we live, your child could conveniently have 24 hours of nonstop ill-spirited messages **inculcated** into his or her mind on a daily basis.

Gone are the days you'd sit in the living room listening to a **vinyl** record with only eight songs. No 8-track tape or need to carry a 35-pound boom box with maybe an hour's worth of size D battery power.

Nah! Your children have unlimited access to all the sex and violence that can be stored on a 50-gigabyte multimedia device or smartphone the size of a credit card. And what's even more troubling is that you may never know what they are listening to because of the **discreet** tool of $150 earbuds.

This generation of youth will not be influenced by what their parents have passed on because we are **tuned out**.

We had to listen to what our parents were saying and playing because that was the only option. Not so for today's youth. Advanced technology has made it easy for them to disconnect and separate from their parents' influence. What happens eventually is that they become so disconnected until parents can't reach them emotionally or spiritually.

They can't hear us anymore because we **are foreign to** them.

They have YouTube, Instagram, Facebook and TikTok to ex-

psychedelic [ˌsaɪkəˈdelɪk]
adj. 引起幻觉的
antics [ˈæntɪks]
n. 荒唐的行为
profanity-laced
adj. 充满亵渎的
explicit [ɪkˈsplɪsɪt]
adj. 露骨的；明确的

overexposure [ˌəʊvərɪkˈspəʊʒə(r)]
n. 过度曝光
inculcate [ˈɪnkʌlkeɪt]
v. 谆谆教诲

vinyl [ˈvaɪnl]
n. 黑胶唱片

discreet [dɪˈskriːt]
adj. 谨慎的

tuned out
过时了

be foreign to
对……陌生

change thoughts and ideas that may not meet your approval. Parents don't have access to their social network. We don't even speak their language.

I have taken an active role to regain my power as the primary influence on my **offspring**. You can, too.

offspring [ˈɒfsprɪŋ] *n.* 后代

Rule No. 1: Family time is **mandatory**. That means we are all eating dinner at the same time at the table.

mandatory [ˈmændətəri] *adj.* 强制的;义务的

Rule No. 2: No cellphones or media during family time.

Rule No. 3: No headphones when we are in the car. Either share your music (and it better be appropriate) or you listen to whatever the driver (me) is playing. So if you can't appreciate the best of Mint Condition, then you can just walk.

Rule No. 4: Once-a-week mandatory family movie night and I am the program director. I decide what feature film to show. Spike Lee's *Do the Right Thing* or the classic *Lean On Me* starring Morgan Freeman.

Rule No. 5 ... and this is a **tough** one: No media in the kids' rooms. That means no laptop, desktop, iPhone, iPad, smartwatch, cellphone, Xbox, PlayStation. These devices must be controlled and distributed by me, the parent, to those who have earned the **privilege**. No video games during the week.

tough [tʌf] *adj.* 艰难的

privilege [ˈprɪvəlɪdʒ] *n.* 特权

Good luck. This will be a tough struggle to regain your rightful place as the primary influence of your child.

By Deon Price

Exercises

I. Read the text and decide the following statements are true or false?

1.It becomes easier to be parents with the development of technology. T☐ F☐

2.James Brown and O'Jays have positive influence on people's critical thinking. T☐ F☐

3.The young generation are influenced by what their parents have passed on. T☐ F☐

4.Advanced technology helps bridge the gap between children and parents. T☐ F☐

II. Paraphrase the following words.

1.offspring ______________________________

2.icon ______________________________

3.ill-spirited ______________________________

4.foreign ______________________________

III. Question for consideration.

Are you a big fan of a showman or entertainer? Do you think he or she has a positive or negative impact on you? Why?

Text 4 How Social Media Is Pushing Us Toward 1984

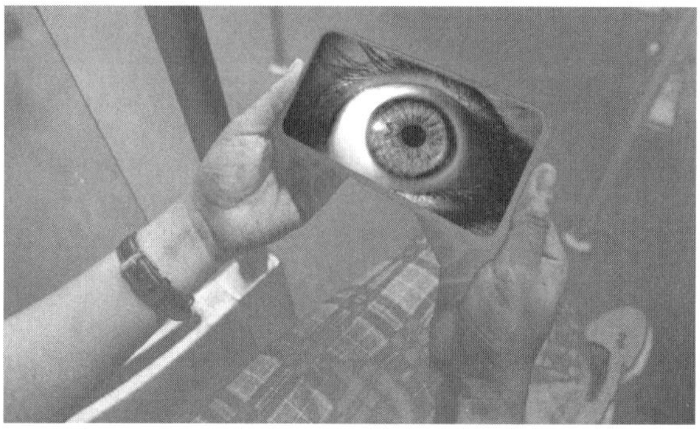

In his **dystopian** novel, *Nineteen Eighty-Four*, George Orwell created "Big Brother" and, with it, the perfect metaphor for Big Tech. Orwell's "telescreens", which can't be switched off and which record every conversation and monitor every movement of his characters, **bear a striking resemblance to** our smartphones. And just as telescreens automatically push programs on their viewers, social media's **algorithms** today decide what we see and shape our vision of the world. Orwell's heroes, under the Party's **surveillance**, try to ban certain ideas from their minds, in a way that resembles how we are starting to monitor our thoughts and actions under the influence of the internet.

While this metaphor is useful, as I reread the novel over the summer, I was struck by how Orwell seemed to anticipate our relationship with social media in other ways. With his concepts of Two Minutes Hate, a daily **ritual** of **outrage orchestrated** by the Party, and Newspeak, a deliberately ambiguous language that's designed to limit people's ability to communicate in **nuanced** ways, Orwell revealed how people's thoughts, emotions, and ultimately actions can be **manipulated**. The dynamics he describes **uncannily** reflect the way social networks now influence the lives of billions of people around the world.

dystopian [dɪsˈtəʊpiən] *adj.* 反乌托邦的

bear a striking resemblance to 和……极为相似

algorithm [ˈælɡərɪðəm] *n.* 算法

surveillance [sɜːˈveɪləns] *n.* 监视

ritual [ˈrɪtʃuəl] *n.* (尤指)宗教仪式;礼节

outrage [ˈaʊtreɪdʒ] *n.* 愤怒;愤慨

orchestrate [ˈɔːkɪstreɪt] *v.* 精心安排;策划

nuanced [ˈnjuːɑːnst] *adj.* 细微的;微妙的

manipulate [məˈnɪpjuleɪt] *v.* 操纵;操控

uncannily [ʌnˈkænɪli] *adv.* 惊异地

Two Minutes Hate

In Orwell's novel, people interrupt their activities each day and stand in front of their telescreens to **flame** enemies and celebrate Big Brother. The enemies change regularly, but the ritual, called the Two Minute Hate, doesn't:

The horrible thing about the Two Minutes Hate was not that one was obliged to act a part, but that it was impossible to avoid joining in. Within thirty seconds any **pretence** was always unnecessary. A hid - eous ecstasy of fear and vindictiveness, a desire to kill, to torture, to smash faces in with a sledge hammer, seemed to flow through the whole group of people like an electric current, turning one even against one's will into a grimacing, screaming **lunatic**. And yet the rage that one felt was an abstract, undirected emotion which could be switched from one object to another like the flame of a blowlamp.

This description sounds fantastical until you consider what's happening on our social networks. During the 2014 Gamergate **scandal**, a woman and her family became the target of a massive harassment campaign that included **leaking** her personal photos and threatening her with rape and death. Things have only gotten worse. Today, inflammatory hashtags and **hoaxes** are regularly promoted by fake accounts until they become official trends and are picked up by real people and even the mainstream media. The number of right-wing and **conspiracy**-spewing influencers propagating racist and misogynist memes to their followers is increasing. And all of this is not just enabled, but empowered and **compounded**, **by** social media platforms.

Beyond these highly organized hate campaigns, everyday harassment and bullying have also **spiked**. According to a report from the Pew Research Center, 59% of US teens have been bullied or harassed

flame [fleɪm]
v. 发送火药味电邮

pretene [prɪˈtens]
n. 假象；伪装

lunatic [ˈluːnətɪk]
n. 疯子

scandal [ˈskændl]
n. 丑闻

leak [liːk]
v. 泄露

hoax [həʊks]
n. 恶作剧

conspiracy
[kənˈspɪrəsi]
n. 阴谋

be compounded by...
因……而加剧

spike [spaɪk]
v. 急剧增值

online. In the **run-up** to December 2019's U.K. general election, an investigation by the BBC and the liberal think tank Demos found a surge in abuse and death threats on Twitter directed at parliamentary candidates. Around 7% of the tweets (i.e. 334,000) received by candidates were categorized as abusive.

run-up ['rʌn ʌp]
n. 准备阶段

Before you think "not me", consider whether you have ever participated in social media outrage, only to wake up the next day and think, "How could I have done that?" Have you ever realized that you didn't have all the facts and yet felt compelled to react? Have you ever posted, liked, or retweeted an article with a particularly incendiary title without actually reading it? If you have, you've participated in the social network **version** of Orwell's Two Minute Hate.

version ['vɜːʃn]
n. (电影、剧本、乐曲等的)版本

And while I wish we could all be a little more in control of our online urges, Orwell's dystopian novel reminded me that the real issue is that **viral** outrage is more than an accidental feature of social networks. It is the core of their products, of what they're aiming to create: a megaphone that continuously puts content in front of you that is so powerful, emotional, and extreme that, as Orwell's says, it's "impossible to avoid joining in". And as you keep **scrolling**, finding new topics for rage is easy: YouTube, Facebook, and Twitter's algorithms make sure of that.

viral ['vaɪrəl]
adj. 病毒的;快速传播的

scroll [skrəʊl]
v. 滚屏;滚动

The object of people's fury is as irrelevant to the Party in Orwell's novel as it is to social networks today. What matters is that people who are enraged are deeply engaged and more easy to manipulate.

Newspeak

Equally scary is how, in *Nineteen Eighty-Four*, the Party uses Newspeak to **strip meaning out of** language, making it impossible

strip...out of
把……剥离

for people to have certain thoughts. Reducing the number of words available to people prevents them from having proper feelings and ideas, and makes the world more difficult to process and comprehend. When language loses its meaning ("war is peace, freedom is slavery, ignorance is strength"), the Party is in control of what is considered reality. Facts and independent thought don't really exist anymore:

By 2050—earlier, probably—all real knowledge of Oldspeak will have disappeared. The whole literature of the past will have been destroyed. Chaucer, Shakespeare, Milton, Byron—they'll exist only in Newspeak versions, not merely changed into something different, but actually **contradictory** of what they used to be. Even the literature of the Party will change. Even the slogans will change. How could you have a slogan like Freedom is Slavery when the concept of freedom has been abolished? The whole climate of thought will be different. In fact, there will be no thought, as we understand it now. **Orthodoxy** means not thinking—not needing to think. Orthodoxy is unconsciousness.

contradictory [ˌkɒntrəˈdɪktəri] *adj.* 相互矛盾的

orthodoxy [ˈɔːθədɒksi] *n.* 正统观念

Our own language is becoming more reductive and simplistic, as a result of social media's character limits and use of hashtags to surface and promote catchy, easy-to-understand ideas, events, and trends. On these platforms, nuance is not rewarded. And by allowing any opinion (no matter how fringe) to take on the appearance of fact, social networks have made it harder for us to comprehend our reality.

Simple Solutions

Orwell's book concludes with the main character, Winston, totally accepting the Party's rule, fully participating in the ritualistic Two Minute Hate, and believing that two plus two equals five. We don't have to be Winston, but more importantly Big Tech doesn't have to behave like the Party.

What I find **disheartening** is that there are a few simple things that have been advocated for a long time that would, if not solve the problem entirely, at least help significantly:

disheartening [dɪsˈhɑːtnɪŋ] *adj.* 伤心欲绝的

·Add a warning message. Social media companies have tried to eliminate every friction point for users in order to maximize the volume of communication and engagement on their platforms. But what if they took a different approach? What if, when a user was about to post or tweet something inflammatory, social media companies interrupted with a pop-up message saying something **along the lines of**: "Are you sure?" Instagram **implemented** something similar in 2019 to limit damaging reactive communications. Though this approach won't prevent everyone from posting outrageous content, it will force a lot of us to pause and reflect before we do so.

along the lines of 类似于……样的话

implement [ˈɪmplɪment] *v.* 执行;实施

·Stop showing suggested posts or videos as a way to keep users scrolling / viewing even when they have seen everything that the people they follow have posted. YouTube launched AutoPlay in 2015, serving its viewers a series of continuously playing suggested videos. This feature is largely considered as the main driver for the **dissemination** of extreme content. Instagram, which had resisted until now, changed its policy in August and began including suggested posts in users' feeds.

dissemination [dɪˌsemɪˈneɪʃn] *n.* 传播

·Aggressively fights for facts. When someone writes that "two plus two equal five", make it your mission to at least stop **propagating** the lie, no matter how exciting it is for your users. This will be an incredibly difficult and likely never-ending battle. Mistakes will be made. But they're worth it. Efforts so far have been too timid; investments in robust fact checking teams and processes need to be **ramped up** dramatically. Researchers are still divided on whether placing warning messages alongside false information is effective in limiting

propagate [ˈprɒpəgeɪt] *v.* 宣传;传播

ramp up 增长

the sharing of it. Some have concluded that it could make users less likely to share; others have seen no impact. But it's worth trying.

· **Relentlessly** identify and shut down accounts, pages, and forums that promote hate. A study on the effects of a ban of two hate communities by Reddit in 2015 demonstrated that "by shutting down these echo chambers of hate, Reddit caused the people participating to either leave the site or dramatically change their linguistic behavior". In other words, the level of hate decreased altogether, even when the same users continued to use Reddit and joined other forums.

relentlessly [rɪˈlentləsli] *adv.* 无情地

All of these solutions **come down to** a simple idea: A truly human-centric business—one that wants to improve humanity—should support its users' strengths, rather than exploit our weaknesses. Though our world today may resemble *Nineteen Eighty-Four*, there's still time for us to write a different ending.

come down to 归根结底

By Maelle Gavet

Exercises

I. Paraphrase the following words and expressions.

1.monitor ______________________________

2.bear a striking resemblance to ______________________________

3.anticipate ______________________________

4.manipulate ______________________________

5.be obliged to ______________________________

6.Leak her personal photos ______________________________

7.be irrelevant to ______________________________

8.exploit our weaknesses ______________________________

II. Translate the following sentences into English.

1. 我们发现了那么古老的化石，与那棵树有惊人的相似之处。

____

2. 如果你不留心驾驶，我们将不得不没收你的驾照。

____

3. 假如这座岛屿的资源如食物、空气和水近乎零，那么所有的财富对他们的生存而言将是毫无相干的。

____

4. 除了力大无穷之外，他还有一种非同寻常的能力，那就是发现并利用对手的弱点。

____

III. Question for consideration.

In what ways does the simplification of language on social media platforms mirror Orwell's concept of Newspeak, and what are its effects on our ability to think critically?

Text 5 The Spectacular Adventures of Click and Bait

Chapter 1: The Curious Beginnings

In the **bustling** town of Viralia, everyone was always connected, glued to their screens, scrolling, tapping, and **swiping** away. No one could imagine a day without their precious digital devices. This was the world where two teenagers, Click and Bait, were inseparable. They spent their days browsing the web, consuming content faster than a **ravenous horde** of **piranhas**. If you ever needed a good meme or the latest trending video, these two were your go-to source.

One fateful day, they stumbled upon a curious website called "The Media Maestros." **Intrigued**, they clicked on the link and were greeted with a video message from a mysterious figure known as The Maestro. With his face **obscured** by shadows and wearing a top hat **adorned** with an **exclamation** mark, The Maestro extended a **tantalizing** invitation.

"Welcome to The Media Maestros, the ultimate test of your media **prowess**. Win the game, and you'll gain influence beyond your wildest dreams. The rules are simple—you'll be given media-related tasks. Complete them successfully and move on to the next level. Fail, and you'll be forgotten in the abyss of irrelevance. Are you ready to

bustling [ˈbʌslɪŋ]
adj. 繁忙的；熙熙攘攘的

swipe [swaɪp]
v. 滑动

ravenous [ˈrævənəs]
adj. 极其饥饿的；严重的

horde [hɔːd]
n. 人群

piranha [pɪˈrɑːnə]
n. 水虎鱼(南美的一种捕食动物的小淡水鱼)

intrigue [ɪnˈtriːg]
v. 激起……的兴趣；引发……的好奇心

obscure [əbˈskjʊə(r)]
v. 遮蔽

adorn [əˈdɔːn]
v. 装饰

exclamation [ˌekskləˈmeɪʃn]
n. 感叹

tantalize [ˈtæntəlaɪz]
v. 逗弄；使干着急

prowess [ˈpraʊəs]
n. 非凡的技能

play?" Without hesitation, Click and Bait accepted the challenge. They had always dreamed of becoming media **moguls** and shaping the digital landscape.

mogul ['məʊgl]
n. 大亨

Chapter 2: Going Viral

Their first task was simple: get a video to go viral in under 24 hours. Click and Bait brainstormed ideas, searching for something that would capture the attention of the masses. They decided on a high-stakes **prank**, one that would have people on the edge of their seats. They set up a fake **meteor** crash site in the heart of Viralia and filmed the chaos that **ensued**.

prank [præŋk]
n. 恶作剧;玩笑
meteor ['miːtiə(r)]
n. 流星
ensue [ɪn'sjuː]
v. 接着发生

Working tirelessly, they edited the footage into a dramatic and suspenseful video. With only a few hours left on the clock, they uploaded the video and watched as the view count **skyrocketed**. People were sharing it left, right, and center. News outlets picked up the story, and the video became an overnight **sensation**.

skyrocket ['skaɪrɒkɪt]
v. (价格)飞涨;猛涨
sensation [sen'seɪʃn]
n. 轰动

The Maestro appeared on their screens once more, applauding their success. "Impressive, Click and Bait. You've passed the first challenge. Let's see how you **fare** with the next task."

fare [feə(r)]
v. 成功(或不成功、更好等)

Chapter 3: The Art of **Manipulation**

manipulation [məˌnɪpju'leɪʃn]
n. (暗中)控制,操纵,影响

For their second challenge, Click and Bait were tasked with **swaying** public opinion on a controversial topic. They chose to focus on the age-old debate of pineapple on pizza. Half of Viralia loved it, while the other half despised it with a burning passion. It was a polarizing topic that seemed impossible to sway.

sway [sweɪ]
v. (使)摇摆,摆动;说服;使相信

The duo devised a cunning plan. They created a series of fake scientific studies claiming that pineapple on pizza improved cognitive function and mood. They even **fabricated** a quote from a renowned

fabricate ['fæbrɪkeɪt]
v. 制造;编造

chef, who **allegedly** said, "If you don't like pineapple on pizza, you just haven't had it prepared correctly."

They seeded their **concocted** stories on social media, and soon enough, people were changing their minds. The town was **abuzz** with pizza enthusiasts, and pineapple-topped pizza sales soared. The Maestro returned with a grin, congratulating them on their **triumph**.

allegedly [ə'ledʒɪdli]
adv. 据称

concoct [kən'kɒkt]
v. 编造;捏造
abuzz [ə'bʌz]
adj. 议论纷纷的;嘈杂的
triumph ['traɪʌmf]
n. 巨大成功;喜悦;狂喜

Chapter 4 : The Social Media Scandal

For their third challenge, The Maestro demanded something much more **sinister**: they had to create a social media **scandal** involving Viralia's beloved mayor, Mayor Goodwin. Click and Bait hesitated, not wanting to ruin the reputation of a genuinely good person. But their desire for influence was too strong, and they gave in.

sinister ['sɪnɪstə(r)]
adj. 邪恶的;不祥的
scandal ['skændl]
n. 丑行;丑闻

They concocted a fake story about Mayor Goodwin embezzling funds meant for a local animal shelter. They used photo manipulation to create convincing images and even made up quotes from **anonymous** sources. They hesitated for a moment before clicking "Post," but the thought of winning The Media Maestros pushed them forward.

anonymous
[ə'nɒnɪməs]
adj. 匿名的;不知姓名的;没有特色的

Within hours, the news spread like wildfire. Viralians were outraged, and Mayor Goodwin's reputation was **in tatters**. The Maestro appeared, pleased with their efforts, but there was something different about his **demeanour** this time. He seemed more sinister, his smile colder.

in tatters
破烂不堪

demeanour
[dɪ'miːnə(r)]
n. 风度;举止;行为

"Congratulations, Click and Bait. You're moving on to the final task. It's time to put your skills to the ultimate test."

Chapter 5: The Final Task

The final challenge was unlike anything Click and Bait had done before. The Maestro tasked them with creating a trend so powerful that it would consume Viralia entirely. The duo **racked** their brains for days, unsure of what to do.

rack [ræk]
v. 使受折磨；使痛苦不堪

In the end, they came up with the idea of the "Mystery Box Challenge". The premise was simple: people would buy a mystery box, filled with unknown items, and film themselves unboxing it. The **anticipation** and excitement of the unknown would drive Viralians wild, and Click and Bait were sure it would take the town by storm.

anticipation [ænˌtɪsɪˈpeɪʃn]
n. 预料；预期；期盼

They launched the trend on social media, and it exploded almost instantly. Everyone in Viralia was participating, buying and selling mystery boxes left and right. The town was consumed by the craze, and people were becoming **obsessed**, spending all their time and money on mystery boxes.

obsessed [əbˈsest]
adj. 对……着迷；受……困扰

As the trend **spiraled** out of control, Click and Bait realized the monster they had created. They felt an overwhelming sense of guilt for their actions and the chaos they had caused. It was then that they understood the true nature of their challenges and The Maestro's sinister **motives**.

spiral [ˈspaɪrəl]
v. 螺旋式上升或下降；急剧增长

motive [ˈməʊtɪv]
n. 动机；原因；目的

Chapter 6: The **Reckoning**

reckoning [ˈrekənɪŋ]
n. 计算；算总账

Click and Bait decided they had to put an end to The Media Maestros and The Maestro's **manipulative** games. They started by exposing the truth about the pineapple pizza debate and Mayor Goodwin's scandal. They confessed their actions, apologized, and shared their story, revealing The Maestro and his wicked game.

manipulative [məˈnɪpjələtɪv]
adj. 善于操纵的；会控制的；会摆布人的

The people of Viralia, though upset, eventually forgave Click and Bait, as they saw the sincerity in their **remorse**. Mayor Goodwin's reputation was restored, and the pineapple pizza debate returned to being a friendly disagreement. Together, Click, Bait, and the citizens of Viralia decided to take on The Maestro and his twisted game.

remorse [rɪˈmɔːs]
n. 懊悔；自责

Chapter 7: The Final Showdown

Click and Bait, armed with their newfound sense of responsibility, created a powerful video that exposed The Maestro and his manipulative tactics. They shared the video with their friends and followers, urging everyone in Viralia to stand up against the influence of The Media Maestros.

As the video went viral, The Maestro's power began to **wane**. His control over the media started to **crumble**, and people all over town were waking up to the dangers of blindly following trends and sensational stories. Viralians started to question what they saw on their screens and think critically about the media they consumed.

wane [weɪn]
v. (月亮)缺，亏；衰落，减弱
crumble [ˈkrʌmbl]
v. 崩裂；坍塌；(使)破碎

Furious and desperate, The Maestro made a final attempt to regain control by launching a massive disinformation campaign. But Click, Bait, and the people of Viralia were ready. They banded together, debunking the false stories and spreading the truth far and wide.

furious [ˈfjʊəriəs]
adj. 狂怒的；猛烈的

Outsmarted and **outmaneuvered**, The Maestro's influence **evaporated**. The once-mysterious figure disappeared, and The Media Maestros website vanished without a trace. Click and Bait had defeated The Maestro, saving Viralia from his twisted games.

outmaneuver [ˌaʊtməˈnuːvə(r)]
v. 比……高明
evaporate [ɪˈvæpəreɪt]
v. (使)蒸发；(逐渐)消失

Epilogue: Lessons Learned

In the aftermath of their adventures, Click and Bait realized the power they held as content creators and influencers. They vowed to use their abilities for good, promoting honesty, critical thinking, and responsibility in the digital world.

Their experiences taught the people of Viralia valuable lessons about the power and influence of media. They learned to question what they saw, to think for themselves, and to be aware of the forces that may attempt to manipulate them.

With the town now free from the grasp of The Maestro, Click and Bait continued to entertain and inform their fellow citizens, using their influence for good. Their adventures in The Media Maestros would be remembered as a **cautionary** tale, reminding future generations of the importance of responsible media consumption and the power of unity in the face of manipulation.

cautionary [ˈkɔːʃənəri] *adj.* 警告的;告诫的

As for Click and Bait, they grew into responsible young adults who learned from their mistakes. They continued to create content that not only entertained but also educated their audience on the importance of media literacy. They worked with local schools and community groups, sharing their story and the lessons they learned with others.

The once inseparable duo became role models for the younger generation, proving that with great power comes great responsibility. They never forgot the wild and twisted adventures they had experienced as players in The Media Maestros, and they were determined to prevent others from falling into the same trap.

With their newfound purpose and the support of their community, Click and Bait went on to shape the media landscape of Viralia for the better. Their influence reached far beyond their town, eventually inspiring teenagers around the world to be mindful of the media they consumed and to always think critically about the messages they encountered.

In the end, the spectacular adventures of Click and Bait served as a powerful reminder of the potential for change when people come together, united against manipulation and **deception**. And it all started with two teenagers, their love for the digital world, and a mysterious game that would change their lives forever.

deception [dɪˈsepʃn] *n.* 欺骗;蒙骗;骗术;骗局

Exercises

I. Read the following statements and decide whether they are true (T) or false (F) according to the text.

1.Click and Bait reluctantly accepted the challenge after some serious consideration. T☐ F☐

2.The pineapple-topped pizza sales enjoyed huge success. T☐ F☐

3.Mayor Goodwin stole money meant for a local animal shelter for personal use. T☐ F☐

4.Click and Bait refused to confess their crimes in the end. T☐ F☐

5.The people of Viralia learned a lesson about the power and influence of media. T☐ F☐

II. Translate the following sentences into English, using the words given below.

1.她在小区的旧货甩卖上偶然发现了一个精致的花瓶。(stumble upon)

____

2.他为了解决难题,不断费尽脑筋。(rack one's brains)

____

3.他对手机游戏沉迷不已,每天都花费大量时间,影响了学业和社交生活。(obsessed)

____

4.他决心付诸行动,结束这段不愉快的争执。(put an end to)

____

5.他分享的有趣视频在几小时内就开始迅速传播,观看人数迅速增加。(go viral)

____

III. Question for consideration.

The underlined sentence "Their experiences taught the people of Viralia valuable lessons about the power and influence of media." shows the moral of this story. Please show your understanding of it with your own stories.

Cultural Notes

Forms of Mass Media

Mass media includes the diverse arrays of media that reach a large audience via mass communication.

Broadcast media

Main articles: Radio broadcasting and television

The sequencing of content in a broadcast is called a schedule. With all technological endeavours a number of technical terms and slang have developed.

Radio and television programs are distributed over frequency bands which are highly regulated in the United States. Such regulation includes determination of the width of the bands, range, licensing, types of receivers and transmitters used, and acceptable content.

Cable television programs are often broadcast simultaneously with radio and television programs, but have a more limited audience. By coding signals and requiring a cable converter box at individual recipients' locations, cable also enables subscription-based channels and pay-per-view services.

A broadcasting organisation may broadcast several programs simultaneously, through several channels (frequencies), for example BBC One and Two. On the other hand, two or more organisations may share a channel and each use it during a fixed part of the day, such as the Cartoon Network/Adult Swim. Digital radio and digital television may also transmit multiplexed programming, with several channels compressed into one ensemble.

When broadcasting is done via the Internet the term webcasting is often used. In 2004, a new phenomenon occurred when a number of technologies combined to produce podcasting. Podcasting is an asynchronous broadcast/narrowcast medium. Adam Curry and his associates, the Podshow, are principal proponents of podcasting.

Film

Main article: Film

The term "film" encompasses motion pictures as individual projects, as well as the field in general. The name comes from the photographic film (also called film stock), historically the primary medium for recording and displaying motion pictures. Many other terms for film exist, such as motion pictures (or just pictures and "picture"), the silver screen, photoplays, the cinema, picture shows, flicks and, most commonly, movies.

Films are produced by recording people and objects with cameras, or by creating them using animation techniques or special effects. Films comprise a series of individual frames, but when these images are shown in rapid succession, an illusion of motion is created. Flickering between frames is not seen because of an effect known as persistence of vision, whereby the eye retains a visual image for a fraction of a second after the source has been removed. Also of relevance is what causes the perception of motion: a psychological effect identified as beta movement.

Film has emerged as an important art form. They entertain, educate, enlighten and inspire audiences. Any film can become a worldwide attraction, especially with the addition of dubbing or subtitles that translate the original language.

Video games

A video game is a computer-controlled game in which a video display, such as a monitor or television set, is the primary feedback device. The term "computer game" also includes games which display only text or which use other methods, such as sound or vibration, as their primary feedback device. There always must also be some sort of input device, usually in the form of button/joystick combinations (on arcade games), a keyboard and mouse/trackball combination (computer games), a controller (console games), or a combination of any of the above. Also, more esoteric devices have been used for input, e.g., the player's motion. Usually there are rules and goals, but in more open-ended games the player may be free to do whatever they like within the confines of the virtual universe.

In common usage, an "arcade game" refers to a game designed to be played in an establishment in which patrons pay to play on a per-use basis. A "computer game" or "PC game" refers to a game that is played on a personal computer. A "Console game" refers to one that is played on a device specifically designed for the use of such, while interfacing with a standard television set. A "video game" (or "videogame") has evolved into a catchall phrase that encompasses the aforementioned along with any game made for any other device, including, but not limited to, advanced calculators, mobile phones, PDAs, etc.

Audio recording and reproduction

Sound recording and reproduction is the electrical or mechanical re-creation or amplification of sound, often as music. This involves the use of audio equipment such as microphones, recording devices and loudspeakers. From early beginnings with the invention of the phonograph using purely mechanical techniques, the field has advanced with the invention of electrical recording, the mass production of the 78 record, the magnetic wire recorder followed by the tape recorder, the vinyl LP record. The invention of the compact cassette in the 1960s, followed by Sony's Walkman, gave a major boost to the mass distribution of music recordings, and the invention of digital recording and the compact disc in 1983 brought massive improvements in ruggedness and quality. The most recent developments have been in digital audio players.

An album is a collection of related audio recordings, released together to the public, usually commercially.

The term record album originated from the fact that 78 RPM phonograph disc records were kept together in a book resembling a photo album. The first collection of records to be called an "album" was Tchaikovsky's *Nutcracker Suite*, release in April 1909 as a four-disc set by Odeon Records. It retailed for 16 shillings—about £15 in modern currency.

A music video (also promo) is a short film or video that accompanies a complete piece of music, most commonly a song. Modern music videos were primarily made and used as a marketing device intended to promote the sale of music recordings. Although the origins of music videos go back much further, they came into their own in the 1980s, when Music Television's format was based on them. In the 1980s, the term "rock video" was often used to describe this form of entertainment, although the term has fallen into disuse.

Music videos can accommodate all styles of filmmaking, including animation, live-action films, documentaries, and non-narrative, abstract film.

Internet media

Also: Digital media

The Internet (also known simply as "the Net" or less precisely as "the Web") is a more interactive medium of mass media, and can be briefly described as "a network of networks". Specifically, it is the worldwide, publicly accessible network of interconnected computer networks that transmit data by packet switching using the standard Internet Protocol (IP). It consists of millions of smaller domestic, academic, business and governmental networks, which together carry various information and services, such as email, online chat, file transfer, and the interlinked web pages and other documents of the World Wide Web.

Contrary to some common usage, the Internet and the World Wide Web are not synonymous: the Internet is the system of interconnected computer networks, linked by copper wires, fibre-optic cables, wireless connections etc.; the Web is the contents, or the interconnected documents, linked by hyperlinks and URLs. The World Wide Web is accessible through the Internet, along with many other services including email, file sharing and others described below.

Toward the end of the 20th century, the advent of the World Wide Web marked the first era in which most individuals could have a means of exposure on a scale comparable to that of mass media. Anyone with a web site has the potential to address a global audience, although serving to high levels of web traffic is still relatively expensive. It is possible that the rise of peer-to-peer technologies may have begun the process of making the cost of bandwidth manageable. Although a vast amount of information, imagery, and commentary (i.e. "content") has been made available, it is often difficult to determine the authenticity and reliability of information contained in web pages (in many cases, self-published). The invention of the Internet has also allowed breaking news stories to reach around the globe within minutes. This rapid growth of instantaneous, decentralised communication is often deemed likely to change mass media and its relationship to society.

"Cross-media" means the idea of distributing the same message through different media channels. A similar idea is expressed in the news industry as "convergence". Many authors understand cross-media publishing to be the ability to publish in both print and on the web without manual conversion effort. An increasing number of wireless devices with mutually incompatible data and screen formats make it even more difficult to achieve the objective "create once, publish many".

The Internet is quickly becoming the center of mass media. Everything is becoming accessible via the internet. Rather than picking up a newspaper, or watching the 10 o'clock news, people can log onto the internet to get the news they want, when they want it. For example, many workers listen to the radio through the Internet while sitting at their desk.

Even the education system relies on the Internet. Teachers can contact the entire class by sending one email. They may have web pages on which students can get another copy of the class outline or assignments. Some classes have class blogs in which students are required to post weekly, with students graded on their contributions.

Blogs (web logs)

Blogging, too, has become a pervasive form of media. A blog is a website, usually maintained by an individual, with regular entries of commentary, descriptions of events, or interactive media such as images or video. Entries are commonly displayed in reverse chronological order, with most recent posts shown on top. Many blogs provide commentary or news on a particular subject; others function as more personal online diaries. A typical blog combines text, images and other graphics, and links to other blogs, web pages, and related media. The ability for readers to leave comments in an interactive format is an important part of many blogs. Most blogs are primarily textual, although some focus on art (artlog), photographs (photoblog), sketchblog, videos (vlog), music (MP3 blog) and audio (podcasting), are part of a wider network of social media. Microblogging is another type of blogging which consists of blogs with very short posts.

RSS feeds

RSS is a format for syndicating news and the content of news-like sites, including major news sites like Wired, news-oriented community sites like Slashdot, and personal blogs. It is a family of Web feed formats used to publish frequently updated content such as blog entries, news headlines, and podcasts. An RSS document (which is called a "feed" or "web feed" or "channel") contains either a summary of content from an associated web site or the full text. RSS makes it possible for people to keep up with web sites in an automated manner that can be piped into special programs or filtered displays.

Podcast

Main article: Podcast

A podcast is a series of digital-media files which are distributed over the Internet using syndication feeds for playback on portable media players and computers. The term podcast, like broadcast, can refer either to the series of content itself or to the method by which it is syndicated; the latter is also called podcasting. The host or author of a podcast is often called a podcaster.

Mobile

Main article: Mobile media

Mobile phones were introduced in Japan in 1979 but became a mass media only in 1998 when the first downloadable ringing tones were introduced in Finland. Soon most forms of media content were introduced on mobile phones, tablets and other portable devices, and today the total value of media consumed on mobile vastly exceeds that of internet content, and was worth over $31 billion in 2007 (source Informa). The mobile media content includes over $8 billion worth of mobile music (ringing tones, ringback tones, truetones, MP3 files, karaoke, music videos, music streaming services, etc.); over $5 billion worth of mobile gaming; and various news, entertainment and advertising services. In Japan mobile phone books are so popular that five of the ten best-selling printed books were originally released as mobile phone books.

Similar to the internet, mobile is also an interactive media, but has far wider reach, with

3.3 billion mobile phone users at the end of 2007 to 1.3 billion internet users (source ITU). Like email on the internet, the top application on mobile is also a personal messaging service, but SMS text messaging is used by over 2.4 billion people. Practically all internet services and applications exist or have similar cousins on mobile, from search to multiplayer games to virtual worlds to blogs. Mobile has several unique benefits which many mobile media pundits claim make mobile a more powerful media than either TV or the internet, starting with mobile being permanently carried and always connected. Mobile has the best audience accuracy and is the only mass media with a built-in payment channel available to every user without any credit cards or PayPal accounts or even an age limit. Mobile is often called the 7th Mass Medium and either the fourth screen (if counting cinema, TV and PC screens) or the third screen (counting only TV and PC).

Unit Five　Geography

Text 1　How the National Weather Service Affects Our Lives

The National Weather Service (NWS) is the **federal** agency responsible for monitoring weather conditions across the United States. **Headquartered** in Silver Spring, Maryland, alongside its parent agency the National Oceanic and **Atmospheric** Administration (NOAA), NWS issues as many as 1.5 million forecasts per year. Even if you get your weather from a local TV or radio station, the Internet, or your smartphone's weather app, chances are NWS data was used to create that forecast. This is because the NWS is the nation's official source for weather forecast information, much like NASA is the official source for all things outer space.

Thunderstorm warnings, tornado warnings, winter-storm warnings—each of these originate with the NWS, and meteorologists nationwide pass them on to the viewers and listeners in their communities. In fact, forecasters, no matter what organization they work for, often consult NWS forecast maps and weather warnings (which are free and accessible via the NWS website) when creating their own forecasts.

In providing the public with up-to-the-minute forecasts, the NWS operates around the clock. This means that the organization's nearly

federal [ˈfedərəl] *adj.* 联邦制的
headquartered [ˌhedˈkwɔːtəd] *adj.* 总部在某地
atmospheric [ˌætməsˈferɪk] *adj.* 大气的

5,000 employees (including **meteorologists**, forecasters, **hydrologists** and a handful of administrative and IT staff) largely do too. Whether it is midday or the middle of the night, NWS meteorologists are **poring** over weather data to help keep you, your family, and your community informed and safe.

NWS monitors not only **current** weather but developing conditions as well. In May 2013, as early as five days before the EF-5 tornado struck Moore, Oklahoma, the NWS Storm Prediction Center and its weather forecast office—both based in Norman, Oklahoma—determined that a severe weather outbreak would soon be likely to develop in the state. Two hours before the tornado touched down, a tornado watch was issued, and half an hour before the tornado struck Moore, a tornado warning had been issued for the city. Had NWS not forewarned the public, the 24 **fatalities** and hundreds of injuries sustained by Moore residents would have undoubtedly been higher, especially since the tornado struck Plaza Towers Elementary School around the time the school would have been dismissing.

Observing and forecasting weather conditions across the United States and its territories is a big job. To streamline this task, the NWS is split into weather forecast offices, of which there are 122 **sprinkled** across the eastern, southern, central and western regions of the United States as well as Alaska, Hawaii, and the U.S. **Affiliated** Pacific Islands. Because each office only focuses on the weather in its surrounding 20 to 50 counties, and because NWS forecasters live where you do and are familiar with your region's weather patterns, you get the most accurate forecasts possible.

NWS forecasts are not just good for staying a step ahead of storms and deciding what to wear to work or school. They also **cater to** your leisure-weather needs. NWS issues recreational forecasts—

meteorologist [ˌmiːtiəˈrɒlədʒɪst] *n.* 气象学家

hydrologist [haiˈdrɒlədʒist] *n.* 水文学家

pore [pɔː(r)] *v.* 仔细打量

current [ˈkʌrənt] *adj.* 当前的

fatality [fəˈtæləti] *n.* (事故、战争、暴力事件、疾病中的)死亡

sprinkle [ˈsprɪŋkl] *v.* 撒;洒;把……撒在……上

affiliated [əˈfɪlieɪtɪd] *adj.* 隶属的

cater to 为……服务

forecasts that inform the public of weather conditions at **recreational** points of interest, such as mountain summits, lakes and beaches. Since the weather at these locations can vary greatly from city weather, forecasters closely monitor weather observing stations and **webcams** in the **vicinity** of these tourist spots in real time. They also consider how approaching weather systems may interact with the geography of higher **elevations** or waterways to create unique weather conditions.

It is all a part of the NWS' s mission to preserve life and property—a mission that includes keeping you safe as you plan outdoor adventures. **Avid** hikers can monitor NWS "mountain point forecasts" for a summary of the winds, temperatures, and rain or snow they may encounter at the tops of significant mountain peaks. Likewise, water-enthusiasts might like to consult "marine point forecasts", which **notify** communities near lakes, rivers, and coasts of water-related **hazards**, including winds, **rip currents**, wave heights, and flow rates.

No matter the occasion or the weather, the NWS has us covered.

By National Geographic Society

recreational [ˌrekriˈeɪʃənl] *adj.* 娱乐的

webcam [ˈwebkæm] *n.* 网络摄像头

vicinity [vəˈsɪnəti] *n.* 邻近地区

elevation [ˌelɪˈveɪʃn] *n.* 海拔

avid[ˈævɪd] *adj.* 热衷的

notify [ˈnəʊtɪfaɪ] *v.* 通知

hazard [ˈhæzəd] *n.* 危险

rip current (海洋)离岸流

Exercises

I. Read the text and find answers to the following questions.

1.How many ways of getting your weather are mentioned in paragraph 1?

____

2.Where is the National Weather Service?

____

3.What do forecasters do when creating their own forecasts?

____

4.What can we know if we consult “marine point forecasts”?

______

II. Translate the following sentences into English, using the words given below.

1.她不仅是一位演员，还是一个好妈妈。(not only...but also)

______

2.他开始关注这个话题。(focus on)

______

3.医生定时监测他的血压。(monitor)

______

4.我对这座城市很熟悉。(be familiar with)

______

III. Question for consideration.

In what way do weather forecasts benefit our lives?

Text 2 On Geology's Relation to Other Sciences

Geology is closely related to almost all the physical sciences. It's just as history is to moral subjects. A historian should be **profoundly acquainted** with ethics, politics, **jurisprudence**, the military art, and religion. In essence, the historian should grasp all branches of knowledge, which give **insight** into human affairs, or into the moral and intellectual nature of man. Likewise, a geologist should be well **versed** in chemistry, natural philosophy, **mineralogy**, zoology, comparative **anatomy** and botany. In short, geologists should be familiar with every science relating to organic and inorganic nature.

With these accomplishments, the historian and geologist would draw correct conclusions from the records left behind by former events. They would know what combination of causes similar effects now were relatable to. And they would often be able to infer information concerning many events of former ages that were never recorded.

But such extensive understanding of different fields of study is out of reach of any individual. It is therefore necessary that men who have devoted their lives to different branches should unite their efforts. The historian receives assistance from experts on ancient times and politics. In the same way, the geologist should ask the aid of naturalists. He should particularly gain the help of those who have studied the

profoundly [prə'faʊndli] *adv.* 极大地
acquaint [ə'kweɪnt] *v.* 使熟悉
jurisprudence [ˌdʒʊərɪs'pruːdns] *n.* 法学
insight ['ɪnsaɪt] *n.* 洞察力
versed [vɜːst] *adj.* 精通的
mineralogy [ˌmɪnə'rælədʒɪ] *n.* 矿物学
anatomy [ə'nætəmɪ] *n.* 解剖学

fossil remains of lost species of animals and plants.

To be fair, we can only compare one class of historical monuments to the records studied in geology—those that **unintentionally** leave clues about the past. The **canoes**, for example, and stone **hatchets** found in our **peat bogs**, offer an insight into the arts and manners of the earliest people who lived there; the buried coin fixes the date of the **reign** of some Roman emperor; the ancient military camp shows where invading armies once occupied ground, and the former method of constructing military defenses; the Egyptian **mummies** throw light on the art of **embalming**, burials, or how tall humans in ancient Egypt were.

No other class of **artifacts** is more **authentic**. But it's just one of the resources on which the historian relies. In geology, however, it is the only evidence we can draw from. For this reason, we must not expect to obtain a full and connected account of any series of events beyond the reach of history.

Geological monuments are frequently imperfect recorders of the past. Yet, at least their clues cannot be **misrepresented** on purpose. Our **inferences** may be wrong, in the same manner as we often mistake the nature and significance of phenomena observed in nature. Yet, our risk of making an error is **confined** to the interpretation, and, if this be correct, our information is certain.

By Charles Lyell, adapted by Newsela staff

fossil [ˈfɒsl]
n. 化石

unintentionally [ˌʌnɪnˈtenʃənəli]
adv. 无意地

canoe [kəˈnuː]
n. 独木舟

hatchet [ˈhætʃɪt]
n. 短柄小斧

peat [piːt]
n. 泥炭

bog [bɒg]
n. 沼泽(地区)

reign [reɪn]
n. 君主统治时期

mummy [ˈmʌmɪ]
n. 木乃伊

embalm [ɪmˈbɑːm]
v. 对(尸体)进行防腐处理

artifact [ˈɑːtɪfækt]
n. 人工制品，手工艺品(尤指有历史或文化价值的)

authentic [ɔːˈθentɪk]
adj. 真正的

misrepresent [ˌmɪsˌreprɪˈzent]
v. 歪曲

inference [ˈɪnfərəns]
n. 推理

confine [kənˈfaɪn]
v. 限制

Exercises

I. Read the following statements and decide whether they are true (T) or false (F) according to the text.

1.Geology is not closely related to any other physical sciences. T☐ F☐

2.In short, geologists should be familiar with every science relating to organic and inorganic nature. T☐ F☐

3.Clues that geological monuments offer are often misrepresented on purpose. T☐ F☐

4.We can date the reign of an emperor via buried coins. T☐ F☐

5.we can expect to obtain a full and connected account of any series of events beyond the reach of history. T☐ F☐

II. Paraphrase the following sentences from the text.

1.And they would often be able to infer information concerning many events of former ages that were never recorded.

____

2.He should particularly gain the help of those who have studied the fossil remains of lost species of animals and plants.

____

3.Our inferences may be wrong, in the same manner as we often mistake the nature and significance of phenomena observed in nature.

____

4.The buried coin fixes the date of the reign of some Roman emperor.

____

III. Question for consideration.

Since the article mentioned that geologists should cooperate with other kinds of physical scientists to explore the real mystery on earth, why do we divide the subjects into languages, mathematics, science, biology, politics, history, geography and so on?

Text 3 Reading Maps and Globes

Reading a map or globe

Map styles and symbols change from place to place. Most published maps share details in common. Maps should have a date to show when they are published. That way, people know the map is still correct.

Maps usually have names of places or labels. They have a **scale**, which helps us to understand how a distance on the map compares with the real world. They usually have symbols, too, like stars or black lines, which stand for something else. A good map has a guide to symbols, called a **key** or **legend**, to explain what the symbols mean.

There should be an arrow pointing north, or a compass rose that shows the four main directions we travel: north, south, east, west.

Latitude and longitude

World maps show imaginary lines of **latitude** and **longitude** on Earth. The distances between these lines are called degrees.

Lines of longitude, or **meridians**, are drawn up and down, from the North Pole to the South Pole. They show distances east or west from the **prime** meridian. The prime meridian is located at 0 degrees longitude. This meridian runs through the city of Greenwich, England.

scale [skeɪl]
n. 刻度

key [kiː]
n. 图例，符号说明
legend [ˈledʒənd]
n. 图例，说明

latitude [ˈlætɪtjuːd]
n. 纬度
longitude [ˈlɒndʒɪtjuːd]
n. 经度
meridian [məˈrɪdɪən]
n. 子午线
prime [praɪm]
adj. 主要的

Lines of latitude are drawn left and right. The most important line of latitude is the **equator**, located perfectly in the middle of a map.

equator [ɪˈkweɪtə(r)] *n.* 赤道

There are 360 degrees in a circle. Longitude measures to 180 degrees east or west (180 + 180 = 360) until arriving at a point in the mid-Pacific Ocean.

Latitude runs to the North Pole (90 degrees north) and the South Pole (90 degrees south). That adds up to 360 degrees if we see a globe in cross section (90 + 90 on one side, 90 + 90 on the other).

A line of latitude meets a line of longitude on a map. For example, the Empire State Building in New York City is located at 40.7484 degrees N, 73.9857 degrees W. That means it is 40.7484 degrees north of the equator. It is 73.9857 degrees west of the prime meridian. This gives us an exact location.

Map symbols

On a typical map, black lines usually stand for roads. Circles or stars stand for cities. Dotted lines often represent railroads. Green and brown might shade real-world features, such as green for forests, brown for deserts. Different mapmakers may choose to use symbols differently. As a result, it is important to always check a map's key.

Advantages of globes

Globes are **clunky** and more expensive than maps. However, they give a closer representation of what the Earth really looks like. Globes also show how Earth is tilted. This is related to how long the days and seasons are. In a dark room, a person can shine a flashlight on one side of a globe. This demonstrates how sunlight reaches half the **tilted** Earth while leaving the rest in shadow, depending on the season.

clunky [ˈklʌŋki] *adj.* 笨重过时的

tilted [ˈtɪltɪd] *adj.* 倾斜的

By Encyclopaedia Britannica, adapted by Newsela staff

Exercises

I. Read the text and fill in the blanks with correct words.

1.A good map has a guide _______ symbols, called a key or legend, to e _______ what the symbols mean.

2.Longitude measures to 180 degrees east _______ west (180 + 180 = 360) until a _______ at a point in the mid-Pacific Ocean.

3. Green and brown might s _______ real-world features, such as green _______ forests, brown _______ deserts.

4. This d _______ how sunlight reaches half the t _______ Earth while leaving the rest in shadow, depending _______ the season.

II. Translate the following phrases into English.

代表____________________ 贯穿____________________

指向北____________________ 位于____________________

III. Question for consideration.

Do you know any other signs on the map? What do they stand for?

Text 4 Why the Equinox Ushers in the Arrival of Spring

Every six months, once in March and again in September, an **equinox** splits Earth's day almost in half, giving us about 12 hours of daylight and 12 of night.

On March 19, 2024, the **vernal** equinox will signal the coming of spring for the Northern **Hemisphere**. Then, in September, nature will once again bring us the autumnal equinox, the time of year that **ushers in** fall in the North. Those dates are **swapped** for the vernal and autumnal equinoxes in the Southern Hemisphere. (Here's why each season begins twice.)

Our planet normally orbits the sun on an axis that's **tilted** 23.5 degrees, meaning that the hemispheres trade off getting more warmth from the sun. Two times a year, Earth's orbit and its **axial** tilt combine so that the sun sits right above Earth's Equator, casting the dividing line between the light and dark parts of the planet—the so-called **terminator**, or twilight zone—through the North and South Poles.

The terminator doesn't perfectly divide the planet into dark and light; Earth's atmosphere bends sunlight by 37 miles (60 kilometers), which equals half a degree. That means one half of the planet is still a little more lit than the other, even on an equinox.

Earth isn't the only planet that experiences equinoxes: Every

equinox [ˈiːkwɪnɒks] *n.* 春分

vernal [ˈˈvɜːnl] *adj.* 春天的

hemisphere [ˈhemɪsfɪə(r)] *n.* 半球

usher in 开启

swap [swɒp] *v.* 交换

tilt [tɪlt] *v.* 倾斜

axial [ˈæksiəl] *adj.* 轴线的

terminator [ˈtɜrmɪneɪtə(r)] *n.* 明暗界限；卫星或行星圆盘照明和未照明部分的分界线

planet in our solar system has them. In 2009, the Cassini **probe** in orbit around Saturn captured an equinox on the ringed planet. As on Earth, equinoxes occur every half-year on Saturn, but that equals 15 years on Earth, making Cassini's photo session a unique event.

Ancient cultures have tracked the equinoxes in different ways over the **millennia**. From constructed monuments, like **pyramids**, to stone engravings that acted as calendars, to churches that incorporated the sun into their architecture, civilizations marked the passing of the sun and the seasons with great accuracy.

Some cultures continue to celebrate the equinox today, like the Lakota Tribe of the U.S. Midwest. The Lakota connect the earth with the sky by making tobacco from the red willow tree, which matches the Dried Willow **constellation**, where the sun rises on the spring equinox. They smoke this **sacred** tobacco in a ceremony marking the return of longer days.

By Lori Cuthbert, from National Geography Society

probe [prəʊb]
n. 探测仪；传感器

millennia [mɪˈleniə]
n. 一千年
pyramid [ˈpɪrəmɪd]
n. 金字塔

constellation [ˌkɒnstəˈleɪʃn]
n. 星座
sacred [ˈseɪkrɪd]
adj. 神圣的

Exercises

I. Read the text and find answers to the following questions.

1.How often does an equinox occur?

____

2.Why does the length of day and night change throughout the year?

____

3.What role does Earth's atmosphere play during equinoxes?

____

4.What is paragraph 6 mainly about?

____

II. Translate the following sentences into English, using the words given below.

1.春节的到来预示着新的一年的开始。(usher in)

____

2.他举手示意大家安静下来。(signal)

____

3.这场比赛的胜利将天平倾向了我们这一边。(tilt)

____

4.在质量和价格之间总是需要权衡取舍。(rade off)

____

III. Question for consideration.

How can we discover the arrival of equinox?

Text 5 Dating Fossils in Rocks Gives Us a Timeline of Human Evolution

Koobi Fora is a rock **formation** in Kenya. It is located on the shore of Lake Turkana. Koobi Fora is made up of **sedimentary** rock, a type of rock that forms when sediment, or sand and soil, builds up in **layers**. Since 1968, scientists have been studying Koobi Fora's rocks. They have found more than 10,000 fossils in the Koobi Fora rock formation, including the fossils of hominins, our human ancestors. These fossils have helped scientists study the history of human evolution.

formation [fɔːˈmeɪʃn]
n. 组成;形成;组成物
sediment [ˈsedɪmənt]
n. 沉淀物

layer [ˈleɪə(r)]
n. 层

The area around Turkana has changed over time. The region once had forests, grasslands and lakes, and an active volcano. Volcanoes shoot out ash and rock. Sometimes, the ash and rock fall straight back to earth. Other times, these materials are carried away by air or rivers. This volcanic matter can settle at the bottom of lakes or rivers. Over time, it is packed together into a special kind of rock called **tuff**.

tuff [tʌf]
n. 凝灰岩

Koobi Fora Blocks Rise

Tuff layers can contain an unstable **isotope** of **potassium**. When rocks are very old, scientists use a technique called **potassium-argon** dating on them. This method can reveal the approximate age of the rocks. Over time, the unstable potassium isotopes in the rocks

isotope [ˈaɪsətəʊp]
n. 同位素
potassium [pəˈtæsiəm]
n. 钾
argon [ˈɑːgɒn]
n. 氩

decay. They turn into a stable isotope of argon. Scientists can look at the relationship between the potassium isotope and argon isotope. This tells them when the tuff layer cooled off and solidified into rock.

decay [dɪˈkeɪ]
v. 衰退

Then, the scientists can estimate the age of the fossils in the rock. Picture a specific layer of rock. Any fossils above it are younger than that layer. Any fossils below it are older than that layer. This means that older fossils and rocks are found deeper in the Earth. This idea is called the law of **superposition** and it is an important law in geology, which is the study of rocks.

superposition [ˌsuːpəpəˈzɪʃn]
n. 叠加法

Extreme Heat Can Distort Dating

Dating fossils helps us understand the past, but it is not a perfect technique. For example, extreme heat can change the way that elements act in the rock. This throws off the results of **radiometric** dating.

radiometric [ˌreɪdiəʊˈmetrɪk]
adj. 辐射度测量的

Another problem that scientists face when dating fossils is that fossils are often stuck within rocks and are a similar color to their surrounding rock. As a result, they **blend** in with their surroundings. Sometimes, only a small part of a fossil is showing, which also makes the fossil hard to spot.

blend [blend]
v. (和某物)混合

Fossils can also be **fragile**. They may be broken into small pieces. Scientists have to use their skills and patience to put small pieces back together, like a **jigsaw** puzzle. Fossil dating takes skills and experience.

fragile [ˈfrædʒaɪl]
adj. 易碎的

jigsaw [ˈdʒɪgsɔː]
n. 拼图玩具

When scientists discover a fossil, they name it. Each fossil has its own special name. This helps scientists keep track of where and in what order fossils are found. One example of a fossil name is "KNM-ER 1813". In this example, the letters tell us the location where this fossil was found. "KNM" stands for Kenya National Museum. "ER" stands for East Rudolf, from the older name of Lake Turkana. The numbers also tell us information about the fossil. In this example, "1813" means that it was the 1,813th fossil found in the area.

From National Geographic Society

Exercises

I. Choose the best answer to each of the following questions based on the information from the text.

1.Tuff layers can contain an unstable isotope of (   ).

A.copper　　B.potassium

2. Over time, the unstable potassium isotope in the rock decays into a stable isotope of (   ).

A.argon　　B.sulfur

3.(   ) can change the way that elements act in the rock.

A.Extreme heat　　B.Nothing

4.Fossils are often (   ).

A.stuck within rocks　　B.discovered quickly

II. Fill in the blanks with the words or phrases given below. Change the form where necessary.

locate on	keep track of	stands for	solidify
make up of	fall straight back	blend in with	throw off
shoot out	carry away		

1.Koobi Fora ____________ sedimentary rock, a type of rock that forms when sediment, or sand and soil, builds up in layers.

2.The officer asked to ____________ the suspect's actions.

3. Those materials ___________ by professor Li. Please come back tomorrow to pick them up.

4.The rope loosened and he ___________ to the ground.

5.The buildings have been designed to ___________ their surroundings.

6.It is our collective duty in this age to ___________ such idiocy, and work honorably toward our intent.

7.As soon as the stopper was removed, water ___________ of the gun.

8."The book's by T.C.Smith." "What does 'T.C.' ___________ ?"

9.Chongqing ___________ the southwest of China.

10.The Energy Department plans to ___________ the deadly waste in a high-tech billion-dollar factory.

III. Question for consideration.

Fossils are extremely difficult to find and study, so why do we bother to study fossils?

Cultural Notes

9 Reasons to Study Geography

You may not have paid the closest attention in geography classes in school. And who can blame you? It's not always easy to recognize *why* you should study geography right off the bat. So: Why study geography? The truth is that geography is a highly relevant and important type of knowledge for anyone to have. Here are 9 reasons why you should study geography.

1. Look smart

Let's be honest: we all care about what other people think of us. That's why our first important reason for studying geography is that it makes you look smart. Knowing basic geography can help you avoid embarrassing moments, impress a date, maybe even land a job.

But geography doesn't just make you *look* smart. It actually does make you smarter, as our next reasons show.

2. Put the news in context

How are you supposed to understand the news if you don't know geography? Knowing geography helps put current events in context

3. Chart the course of history

Geography not only puts current events in perspective, it helps us understand history. Geography shapes the course of world history. Want to better understand history? Study geography.

4. Build navigation skills

The most basic skill in navigation is understanding the "lay of the land". Studying geography helps develop spatial thinking. Those skills could come in handy if you get lost driving around town or in the wilderness!

5. Travel smart

Without a basic sense of geography, it's impossible to get the most out of travel experiences. If you're heading to Spain, do you want to see misty mountains, rocky coastlines, or searing-hot cities? These questions will decide whether you head to Torla, Basque Country, or Sevilla.

It'll also help you decide your route: it makes much more sense to hit up Lisbon, then Barcelona, and then Paris if you want to end in Germany (rather than the other way around). Study up to make your next vacation easier.

6. Understand your home

Geography allows you to understand the place where you live. People settle in specific places because of the landscape. For example, cities are almost always built on a river or other reliable water supply. What is the history of the place you live? How has the geography affected the area? These are the questions to ask to gain a deep understanding of your home.

7. Get a grasp on globalization

Globalization has been one of the biggest forces in world history for decades. The saying "it's a small world" reflects this change: the world is as big as it always was, but it's just more interconnected than ever. Understanding the changes that have swept the world as a result of this interconnection is impossible without appreciating the geography on which it is taking place.

8. Make sense of different cultures

Human culture is fundamentally place-based: the land determines or influences the cuisine, clothing, architecture, even social relationships. Every aspect of a culture is affected by its geography.

Geography helps you understand and appreciate the incredible diversity of cultures around the world. Like with news, geography puts culture in context. To understand a people, you have to know something about their land.

9. Prepare for the future

Geographic skills guide important decisions every day. From architecture to politics to business, the physical landscape frames the debates happening today that will be in the history books tomorrow.

https://www.brainscape.com/academy/9-reasons-to-study-geography/

Section B

Classics

Anne of Green Gables

CHAPTER I

Mrs. Rachel Lynde is Surprised

Mrs. Rachel Lynde lived just where the Avonlea main road dipped down into a little **hollow**, **fringed** with alders and ladies' eardrops and **traversed** by a **brook** that had its source away back in the woods of the old Cuthbert place; it was reputed to be an intricate, headlong brook in its earlier course through those woods, with dark secrets of pool and **cascade**; but by the time it reached Lynde's Hollow it was a quiet, well-conducted little stream, for not even a brook could run past Mrs. Rachel Lynde's door without due regard for decency and **decorum**; it probably was conscious that Mrs. Rachel was sitting at her window, keeping a sharp eye on everything that passed, from brooks and children up, and that if she noticed anything odd or out of place she would never rest until she had **ferreted** out the whys and wherefores thereof.

There are plenty of people in Avonlea and out of it, who can attend closely to their neighbor's business **by dint of** neglecting their own; but Mrs. Rachel Lynde was one of those capable creatures who can manage their own concerns and those of other folks into the

hollow [ˈhɒləʊ]
n. 凹陷处;坑洼处
fringed [frɪndʒd]
adj. 加穗的
traverse [trəˈvɜːs]
v. 横越
brook [brʊk]
n. 溪
cascade [kæˈskeɪd]
n. 小瀑布
decorum [dɪˈkɔːrəm]
n. 礼貌得体
ferret [ˈferɪt]
v. 查获
by dint of
凭借

bargain. She was a notable housewife; her work was always done and well done; she "ran" the Sewing Circle, helped run the Sunday-school, and was the strongest **prop** of the Church Aid Society and Foreign Missions Auxiliary. Yet with all this Mrs. Rachel found abundant time to sit for hours at her kitchen window, knitting "cotton warp" **quilts**—she had knitted sixteen of them, as Avonlea housekeepers were wont to tell in awed voices—and keeping a sharp eye on the main road that crossed the hollow and wound up the steep red hill beyond. Since Avonlea occupied a little triangular **peninsula jutting** out into the Gulf of St. Lawrence with water on two sides of it, anybody who went out of it or into it had to pass over that hill road and so run the unseen **gauntlet** of Mrs. Rachel's all-seeing eye.

She was sitting there one afternoon in early June. The sun was coming in at the window warm and bright; the **orchard** on the slope below the house was in a bridal flush of pinky-white bloom, **hummed** over by **a myriad of** bees. Thomas Lynde—a **meek** little man whom Avonlea people called "Rachel Lynde's husband"—was sowing his late **turnip** seed on the hill field beyond the barn; and Matthew Cuthbert ought to have been sowing his on the big red brook field away over by Green Gables. Mrs. Rachel knew that he ought because she had heard him tell Peter Morrison the evening before in William J. Blair's store over at Carmody that he meant to sow his turnip seed the next afternoon. Peter had asked him, of course, for Matthew Cuthbert had never been known to volunteer information about anything in his whole life.

And yet here was Matthew Cuthbert, at half-past three on the afternoon of a busy day, **placidly** driving over the hollow and up the hill; moreover, he wore a white collar and his best suit of clothes, which was plain proof that he was going out of Avonlea; and he had

bargain [ˈbɑːgən]
n. 交易

prop [prɒp]
n. 支柱

quilt [kwɪlt]
n. 绗缝草被

peninsula [pəˈnɪnsjələ]
n. 半岛
jut [dʒʌt]
v. 伸出

gauntlet [ˈgɔːntlət]
n. 铁手套

orchard [ˈɔːtʃəd]
n. 果园

hum [hʌm]
v. 哼(曲子)
a myriad of [ˈmɪrɪəd]
无数
meek [miːk]
adj. 温顺的
turnip [ˈtɜːnɪp]
n. 芜菁;蔓菁

placidly [ˈplæsɪdli]
adv. 平静地

the **buggy** and the **sorrel** mare, which **betokened** that he was going a considerable distance. Now, where was Matthew Cuthbert going and why was he going there?

buggy [ˈbʌgi]
n. 轻便马车
sorrel [ˈsɒrəl]
adj. 栗色的
betoken [bɪˈtəʊkən]
v. 表示
deftly [ˈdeftli]
adv. 灵巧地

Had it been any other man in Avonlea, Mrs. Rachel, **deftly** putting this and that together, might have given a pretty good guess as to both questions. But Matthew so rarely went from home that it must be something pressing and unusual which was taking him; he was the shyest man alive and hated to have to go among strangers or to any place where he might have to talk. Matthew, dressed up with a white collar and driving in a buggy, was something that didn't happen often. Mrs. Rachel, ponder as she might, could make nothing of it and her afternoon's enjoyment was spoiled.

"I'll just step over to Green Gables after tea and find out from Marilla where he's gone and why," the worthy woman finally concluded. "He doesn't generally go to town this time of year and he never visits; if he'd run out of turnip seed he wouldn't dress up and take the buggy to go for more; he wasn't driving fast enough to be going for a doctor. Yet something must have happened since last night to start him off. I'm clean puzzled, that's what, and I won't know a minute's peace of mind or **conscience** until I know what has taken Matthew Cuthbert out of Avonlea today."

conscience [ˈkɒnʃəns]
n. 良心

Accordingly, after tea Mrs. Rachel set out; she had not far to go; the big, **rambling**, orchard-**embowered** house where the Cuthberts lived was a **scant** quarter of a mile up the road from Lynde's Hollow. To be sure, the long lane made it a good deal further. Matthew Cuthbert's father, as shy and silent as his son after him, had got as far away as he possibly could from his fellow men without actually **retreating** into the woods when he founded his **homestead**. Green Gables was built at the furthest edge of his cleared land and there it was to this

rambling [ˈræmblɪŋ]
adj. 规划凌乱的；向四处延伸的
embower [ɪmˈbaʊə]
v. 使(花木等)覆盖
scant [skænt]
adj. 不足的
retreat [rɪˈtriːt]
v. 撤退
homestead [ˈhəʊmsted]
n. 农庄

day, barely visible from the main road along which all the other Avonlea houses were so sociably situated. Mrs. Rachel Lynde did not call living in such a place living at all.

"It's just staying, that's what," she said as she stepped along the deep-rutted, grassy lane bordered with wild rose **bushes**. "It's no wonder Matthew and Marilla are both a little odd, living away back here by themselves. Trees aren't much company, though dear knows if they were there'd be enough of them. I'd rather look at people. To be sure, they seem contented enough; but then, I suppose, they're used to it. A body can get used to anything, even to being hanged, as the Irishman said."

bush [bʊʃ]
n. 灌木;丛林

With this Mrs. Rachel stepped out of the lane into the backyard of Green Gables. Very green and neat and **precise** was that yard, set about on one side with great **patriarchal willows** and the other with prim Lombardies. Not a stray stick nor stone was to be seen, for Mrs. Rachel would have seen it if there had been. Privately she was of the opinion that Marilla Cuthbert swept that yard over as often as she swept her house. One could have eaten a meal off the ground without **overbrimming** the **proverbial peck of dirt**.

precise [prɪˈsaɪs]
adj. 精确的
patriarchal [ˌpeɪtriˈɑːrkl]
adj. 族长的
willow [ˈwɪləʊ]
n. 柳树

overbrim [əʊvəˈbrɪm]
v. 溢出
proverbial peck of dirt
一小撮尘土

Mrs. Rachel rapped smartly at the kitchen door and stepped in when bidden to do so. The kitchen at Green Gables was a cheerful apartment—or would have been cheerful if it had not been so painfully clean as to give it something of the appearance of an unused **parlour**. Its windows looked east and west; through the west one, looking out on the back yard, came a flood of **mellow** June sunlight; but the east one, **whence** you got a glimpse of the bloom white cherry-trees in the left orchard and nodding, slender **birches** down in the hollow by the brook, was greened over by a tangle of **vines**. Here sat Marilla Cuthbert, when she sat at all, always slightly distrustful of sunshine, which

parlour [ˈpɑːlə(r)]
n. 客厅

mellow [ˈmeləʊ]
adj. 成熟的
whence [wens]
adv. 从哪里
birch [bɜːtʃ]
n. 桦树
vine [vaɪn]
n. 藤蔓

seemed to her too dancing and irresponsible a thing for a world which was meant to be taken seriously; and here she sat now, knitting, and the table behind her was laid for supper.

Mrs. Rachel, before she had fairly closed the door, had taken a mental note of everything that was on that table. There were three plates laid, so that Marilla must be expecting some one home with Matthew to tea; but the dishes were everyday dishes and there was only crab-apple **preserves** and one kind of cake, so that the expected company could not be any particular company. Yet what of Matthew's white collar and the sorrel mare? Mrs. Rachel was getting fairly dizzy with this unusual mystery about quiet, unmysterious Green Gables.

preserve [prɪˈzɜːv] *n.* 果酱

"Good evening, Rachel," Marilla said **briskly**. "This is a real fine evening, isn't it? Won't you sit down? How are all your folks?"

briskly [ˈbrɪskli] *adv.* 麻利地

Something that for lack of any other name might be called friendship existed and always had existed between Marilla Cuthbert and Mrs. Rachel, in spite of—or perhaps because of—their dissimilarity.

Marilla was a tall, thin woman, with angles and without curves; her dark hair showed some gray streaks and was always twisted up in a hard little knot behind with two wire **hairpins** stuck aggressively through it. She looked like a woman of narrow experience and rigid conscience, which she was; but there was a saving something about her mouth which, if it had been ever so slightly developed, might have been considered indicative of a sense of humor.

hairpin [ˈheəpɪn] *n.* 发夹

"We're all pretty well," said Mrs. Rachel. "I was kind of afraid you weren't, though, when I saw Matthew starting off today. I thought maybe he was going to the doctor's."

Marilla's lips **twitched** understandingly. She had expected Mrs. Rachel up; she had known that the sight of Matthew jaunting off so unaccountably would be too much for her neighbor's curiosity.

twitch [twɪtʃ] *v.* 抽搐

"Oh, no, I'm quite well although I had a bad headache yesterday," she said. "Matthew went to Bright River. We're getting a little boy from an orphan **asylum** in Nova Scotia and he's coming on the train tonight."

asylum [ə'saɪləm] *n.* (政治)庇护

If Marilla had said that Matthew had gone to Bright River to meet a kangaroo from Australia Mrs. Rachel could not have been more astonished. She was actually stricken dumb for five seconds. It was unsupposable that Marilla was making fun of her, but Mrs. Rachel was almost forced to suppose it.

"Are you in earnest, Marilla?" she demanded when voice returned to her.

"Yes, of course," said Marilla, as if getting boys from orphan asylums in Nova Scotia were part of the usual spring work on any well-regulated Avonlea farm instead of being an unheard of innovation.

Mrs. Rachel felt that she had received a severe mental jolt. She thought in exclamation points. A boy! Marilla and Matthew Cuthbert of all people adopting a boy! From an orphan asylum! Well, the world was certainly turning upside down! She would be surprised at nothing after this! Nothing!

"What on earth put such a notion into your head?" she demanded **disapprovingly**.

disapprovingly [ˌdɪsə'pruːvɪŋli] *adv.* 不赞成地

This had been done without her advice being asked, and must perforce be disapproved.

"Well, we've been thinking about it for some time— all winter in fact," returned Marilla. "Mrs. Alexander Spencer was up here one day before Christmas and she said she was going to get a little girl from the asylum over in Hopeton in the spring. Her cousin lives there and Mrs. Spencer has visited here and knows all about it. So Matthew and I have talked it over off and on ever since. We thought we'd get a boy.

Matthew is getting up in years, you know—he's sixty—and he isn't so **spry** as he once was. His heart troubles him a good deal. And you know how desperate hard it's got to be to get hired help. There's never anybody to be had but those stupid, half-grown little French boys; and as soon as you do get one broke into your ways and taught something he's up and off to the lobster **canneries** or the States. At first Matthew suggested getting a Home boy. But I said 'no' flat to that. 'They may be all right—I'm not saying they're not—but no London street Arabs for me,' I said. 'Give me a native born at least. There'll be a risk, no matter who we get. But I'll feel easier in my mind and sleep sounder at nights if we get a born Canadian.' So in the end we decided to ask Mrs. Spencer to pick us out one when she went over to get her little girl. We heard last week she was going, so we sent her word by Richard Spencer's folks at Carmody to bring us a smart, likely boy of about ten or eleven. We decided that would be the best age—old enough to be of some use in doing chores right off and young enough to be trained up proper. We mean to give him a good home and schooling. We had a telegram from Mrs. Alexander Spencer today—the mail-man brought it from the station—saying they were coming on the five-thirty train tonight. So Matthew went to Bright River to meet him. Mrs. Spencer will drop him off there. Of course she goes on to White Sands station herself."

spry [spraɪ] *adj.* 充满活力的

cannery ['kænəri] *n.* 罐头食品厂

Mrs. Rachel prided herself on always speaking her mind; she **proceeded** to speak it now, having adjusted her mental attitude to this amazing piece of news.

proceed [prə'siːd] *v.* 继续做(或从事、进行)

"Well, Marilla, I'll just tell you plain that I think you're doing a mighty foolish thing—a risky thing, that's what. You don't know what you're getting. You're bringing a strange child into your house and home and you don't know a single thing about him nor what his

disposition is like nor what sort of parents he had nor how he's likely to turn out. Why, it was only last week I read in the paper how a man and his wife up west of the Island took a boy out of an orphan asylum and he set fire to the house at night—set it on purpose, Marilla—and nearly **burnt them to a crisp** in their beds. And I know another case where an adopted boy used to suck the eggs—they couldn't break him of it. If you had asked my advice in the matter—which you didn't do, Marilla—I'd have said for mercy's sake not to think of such a thing, that's what."

This Job's comforting seemed neither to offend nor to alarm Marilla. She knitted steadily on.

"I don't deny there's something in what you say, Rachel. I've had some **qualms** myself. But Matthew was terrible set on it. I could see that, so I gave in. It's so seldom Matthew sets his mind on anything that when he does I always feel it's my duty to give in. And as for the risk, there's risks in pretty near everything a body does in this world. There's risks in people's having children of their own if it comes to that—they don't always turn out well. And then Nova Scotia is right close to the Island. It isn't as if we were getting him from England or the States. He can't be much different from ourselves."

"Well, I hope it will turn out all right," said Mrs. Rachel in a tone that plainly indicated her painful doubts. "Only don't say I didn't warn you if he burns Green Gables down or puts **strychnine** in the well—I heard of a case over in New Brunswick where an orphan asylum child did that and the whole family died in fearful agonies. Only, it was a girl in that instance."

"Well, we're not getting a girl," said Marilla, as if poisoning wells were a purely feminine accomplishment and not to be **dreaded** in the case of a boy. "I'd never dream of taking a girl to bring up. I

disposition [ˌdɪspəˈzɪʃn] *n.* 性情

burnt...to a crisp 完全烧毁；付之一炬

qualm [kwɑːm] *n.* 疑虑

strychnine [ˈstrɪkniːn] *n.* 马钱子碱

dread [ˈdred] *v.* 极为害怕

wonder at Mrs. Alexander Spencer for doing it. But there, she wouldn't shrink from adopting a whole orphan asylum if she took it into her head."

Mrs. Rachel would have liked to stay until Matthew came home with his imported orphan. But reflecting that it would be a good two hours at least before his arrival she concluded to go up the road to Robert Bell's and tell the news. It would certainly make a **sensation** second to none, and Mrs. Rachel dearly loved to make a sensation. So she took herself away, somewhat to Marilla's relief, for the latter felt her doubts and fears reviving under the influence of Mrs. Rachel's **pessimism**.

"Well, of all things that ever were or will be!" **ejaculated** Mrs. Rachel when she was safely out in the lane. "It does really seem as if I must be dreaming. Well, I'm sorry for that poor young one and no mistake. Matthew and Marilla don't know anything about children and they'll expect him to be wiser and steadier that his own grandfather, if so be he's ever had a grandfather, which is doubtful. It seems **uncanny** to think of a child at Green Gables somehow; there's never been one there, for Matthew and Marilla were grown up when the new house was built—if they ever were children, which is hard to believe when one looks at them. I wouldn't be in that orphan's shoes for anything. My, but I pity him, that's what."

So said Mrs. Rachel to the wild rose bushes out of the **fulness** of her heart; but if she could have seen the child who was waiting patiently at the Bright River station at that very moment her pity would have been still deeper and more profound.

sensation [sen'seɪʃn] *n.* 轰动

pessimism ['pesɪmɪzəm] *n.* 悲观主义

ejaculate [ɪ'dʒækjuleɪt] *v.* 突然说出

uncanny [ʌn'kæni] *adj.* 异常的；难以解释的

fulness ['fʊlnəs] *n.* 充实

CHAPTER II

Matthew Cuthbert is surprised

Matthew Cuthbert and the sorrel mare **jogged** comfortably over the eight miles to Bright River. It was a pretty road, running along between **snug farmsteads**, with now and again a bit of **balsamy fir** wood to drive through or a hollow where wild plums hung out their filmy bloom. The air was sweet with the breath of many apple orchards and the **meadows** sloped away in the distance to horizon **mists** of pearl and purple; while "the little birds sang as if it were the one day of summer in all the year".

Matthew enjoyed the drive after his own fashion, except during the moments when he met women and had to nod to them—for in Prince Edward island you are supposed to nod to all and sundry you meet on the road whether you know them or not.

Matthew dreaded all women except Marilla and Mrs. Rachel; he had an uncomfortable feeling that the mysterious creatures were secretly laughing at him. He may have been quite right in thinking so, for he was an odd-looking **personage**, with an **ungainly** figure and long iron-gray hair that touched his **stooping** shoulders, and a full, soft brown beard which he had worn ever since he was twenty. In fact, he had looked at twenty very much as he looked at sixty, lacking a little of the grayness.

When he reached Bright River there was no sign of any train; he thought he was too early, so he tied his horse in the yard of the small Bright River hotel and went over to the station house. The long platform was almost deserted; the only living creature in sight being a girl who was sitting on a pile of **shingles** at the extreme end. Matthew, barely noting that it was a girl, sidled past her as quickly as possible

jog [dʒɒg]
v. 慢跑

snug [snʌg]
adj. 温暖舒适的
farmstead ['fɑːmsted]
n. 农舍及附近建筑物
balsamy ['bɔːlsəmɪ]
adj. 香膏的
fir [fɜː(r)]
n. 冷杉
meadow ['medəʊ]
n. 草地
mist [mɪst]
n. 薄雾

personage ['pɜːsənɪdʒ]
n. 名人
ungainly [ʌn'geɪnli]
adj. 笨手笨脚的
stoop [stuːp]
v. 向前向下弯曲

shingles ['ʃɪŋglz]
n. 木瓦

without looking at her. Had he looked he could hardly have failed to notice the tense **rigidity** and expectation of her attitude and expression. She was sitting there waiting for something or somebody and, since sitting and waiting was the only thing to do just then, she sat and waited with all her might and main.

rigidity [rɪˈdʒɪdəti] *n.* 僵硬

Matthew **encountered** the stationmaster locking up the ticket office **preparatory to** going home for supper, and asked him if the five-thirty train would soon be along.

encounter [ɪnˈkaʊntə(r)] *v.* 遭遇

preparatory to sth. 作为某事的准备;在某事之前

"The five-thirty train has been in and gone half an hour ago," answered that brisk official. "But there was a passenger dropped off for you—a little girl. She's sitting out there on the shingles. I asked her to go into the ladies' waiting room, but she informed me gravely that she preferred to stay outside. 'There was more scope for imagination,' she said. She's a case, I should say."

"I'm not expecting a girl," said Matthew blankly. "It's a boy I've come for. He should be here. Mrs. Alexander Spencer was to bring him over from Nova Scotia for me."

The stationmaster whistled.

"Guess there's some mistake," he said. "Mrs. Spencer came off the train with that girl and gave her into my charge. Said you and your sister were adopting her from an orphan asylum and that you would be along for her presently. That's all I know about it—and I haven't got any more orphans concealed **hereabouts**."

hereabouts [ˌhɪərəˈbaʊts] *adv.* 在这附近

"I don't understand," said Matthew helplessly, wishing that Marilla was at hand to cope with the situation.

"Well, you'd better question the girl," said the station-master carelessly. "I dare say she'll be able to explain—she's got a tongue of her own, that's certain. Maybe they were out of boys of the brand you wanted."

He walked **jauntily** away, being hungry, and the unfortunate Matthew was left to do that which was harder for him than bearding a lion in its **den**—walk up to a girl—a strange girl—an orphan girl—and demand of her why she wasn't a boy. Matthew groaned in spirit as he turned about and **shuffled** gently down the platform towards her.

She had been watching him ever since he had passed her and she had her eyes on him now. Matthew was not looking at her and would not have seen what she was really like if he had been, but an ordinary observer would have seen this: A child of about eleven, **garbed** in a very short, very tight, very ugly dress of yellowish-gray **wincey**. She wore a faded brown sailor hat and beneath the hat, extending down her back, were two **braids** of very thick, **decidedly** red hair. Her face was small, white and thin, also much freckled; her mouth was large and so were her eyes, which looked green in some lights and moods and gray in others.

So far, the ordinary observer; an extraordinary observer might have seen that the chin was very pointed and pronounced; that the big eyes were full of spirit and **vivacity**; that the mouth was sweet-lipped and expressive; that the forehead was broad and full; in short, our **discerning** extraordinary observer might have concluded that no **commonplace** soul inhabited the body of this stray woman-child of whom shy Matthew Cuthbert was so **ludicrously** afraid.

Matthew, however, was spared the **ordeal** of speaking first, for as soon as she concluded that he was coming to her she stood up, **grasping** with one thin brown hand the handle of a shabby, old-fashioned carpet-bag; the other she held out to him.

"I suppose you are Mr. Matthew Cuthbert of Green Gables?" she said in a peculiarly clear, sweet voice. "I'm very glad to see you. I was beginning to be afraid you weren't coming for me and I was

jauntily [ˈdʒɔːntɪli]
adv. 轻快地

den [den]
n. 兽穴

shuffle [ˈʃʌfl]
v. 拖着脚走

garbed [ɡɑːbd]
adj. 以……方式穿着
wincey [ˈwɪnsi]
n. 一种织物

braid [breɪd]
n. 辫子
decidedly [dɪˈsaɪdɪdli]
adv. 明显地;无疑地

vivacity [vɪˈvæsəti]
n. 活力

discerning [dɪˈsɜːnɪŋ]
adj. 有识别力的
commonplace [ˈkɒmənpleɪs]
adj. 平凡的
ludicrously [ˈluːdɪkrəsli]
adv. 荒谬地
ordeal [ɔːˈdiːl]
n. 严酷的考验
grasp [ɡrɑːsp]
v. 抓紧;抓牢

imagining all the things that might have happened to prevent you. I had made up my mind that if you didn't come for me to-night I'd go down the track to that big wild cherry-tree at the bend, and climb up into it to stay all night. I wouldn't be a bit afraid, and it would be lovely to sleep in a wild cherry-tree all white with bloom in the moonshine, don't you think? You could imagine you were dwelling in **marble** halls, couldn't you? And I was quite sure you would come for me in the morning, if you didn't to-night."

marble [ˈmɑːbl]
n. 大理石

Matthew had taken the **scrawny** little hand awkwardly in his; then and there he decided what to do. He could not tell this child with the **glowing** eyes that there had been a mistake; he would take her home and let Marilla do that. She couldn't be left at Bright River anyhow, no matter what mistake had been made, so all questions and explanations might as well be **deferred** until he was safely back at Green Gables.

scrawny [ˈskrɔːni]
adj. 干瘦的

glowing [ˈgləʊɪŋ]
adj. 发光的

defer [dɪˈfɜː(r)]
v. 推迟

"I'm sorry I was late," he said shyly. "Come along. The horse is over in the yard. Give me your bag."

"Oh, I can carry it," the child responded cheerfully. "It isn't heavy. I've got all my worldly goods in it, but it isn't heavy. And if it isn't carried in just a certain way the handle pulls out—so I'd better keep it because I know the exact **knack** of it. It's an extremely old carpet-bag. Oh, I'm very glad you've come, even if it would have been nice to sleep in a wild cherry-tree. We've got to drive a long piece, haven't we? Mrs. Spencer said it was eight miles. I'm glad because I love driving. Oh, it seems so wonderful that I'm going to live with you and belong to you. I've never belonged to anybody—not really. But the asylum was the worst. I've only been in it four months, but that was enough. I don't suppose you ever were an orphan in an asylum, so you can't possibly understand what it is like. It's worse

knack [næk]
n. 技能

than anything you could imagine. Mrs. Spencer said it was **wicked** of me to talk like that, but I didn't mean to be wicked. It's so easy to be wicked without knowing it, isn't it? They were good, you know—the asylum people. But there is so little **scope** for the imagination in an asylum—only just in the other orphans. It was pretty interesting to imagine things about them—to imagine that perhaps the girl who sat next to you was really the daughter of a belted **earl**, who had been stolen away from her parents in her **infancy** by a cruel nurse who died before she could **confess**. I used to lie awake at nights and imagine things like that, because I didn't have time in the day. I guess that's why I'm so thin—I am dreadful thin, ain't I? There isn't a pick on my bones. I do love to imagine I'm nice and **plump**, with **dimples** in my elbows."

With this Matthew's companion stopped talking, partly because she was out of breath and partly because they had reached the buggy. Not another word did she say until they had left the village and were driving down a steep little hill, the road part of which had been cut so deeply into the soft soil, that the banks, fringed with blooming wild cherry-trees and slim white **birches**, were several feet above their heads.

The child put out her hand and broke off a branch of wild **plum** that brushed against the side of the buggy.

"Isn't that beautiful? What did that tree, leaning out from the bank, all white and **lacy**, make you think of?" she asked.

"Well now, I dunno," said Matthew.

"Why, a bride, of course—a bride all in white with a lovely misty **veil**. I've never seen one, but I can imagine what she would look like. I don't ever expect to be a **bride** myself. I'm so homely nobody will ever want to marry me—unless it might be a foreign **missionary**. I

wicked [ˈwɪkɪd] *adj.* 邪恶的

scope [skəʊp] *n.* 范围

earl [ɜːl] *n.* (英国)伯爵

infancy [ˈɪnfənsi] *n.* 婴儿期

confess [kənˈfes] *v.* 承认

plump [plʌmp] *adj.* 丰满的

dimple [ˈdɪmpl] *n.* 酒窝

birch [bɜːtʃ] *n.* 桦树

plum [plʌm] *n.* 李子

lacy [ˈleɪsi] *adj.* 蕾丝的

veil [veɪl] *n.* 面纱

bride [braɪd] *n.* 新娘

missionary [ˈmɪʃənri] *n.* 传教士

suppose a foreign missionary mightn't be very particular. But I do hope that some day I shall have a white dress. That is my highest ideal of **earthly bliss**. I just love pretty clothes. And I've never had a pretty dress in my life that I can remember—but of course it's all the more to look forward to, isn't it? And then I can imagine that I'm dressed **gorgeously**. This morning when I left the asylum I felt so ashamed because I had to wear this **horrid** old wincey dress. All the orphans had to wear them, you know. A merchant in Hopeton last winter donated three hundred yards of wincey to the asylum. Some people said it was because he couldn't sell it, but I'd rather believe that it was out of the kindness of his heart, wouldn't you? When we got on the train I felt as if everybody must be looking at me and pitying me. But I just went to work and imagined that I had on the most beautiful pale blue silk dress—because when you are imagining you might as well imagine something worth while—and a big hat all flowers and nodding **plumes**, and a gold watch, and kid gloves and boots. I felt cheered up right away and I enjoyed my trip to the Island with all my might. I wasn't a bit sick coming over in the boat. Neither was Mrs. Spencer although she generally is. She said she hadn't time to get sick, watching to see that I didn't fall **overboard**. She said she never saw the beat of me for **prowling** about. But if it kept her from being seasick it's a **mercy** I did prowl, isn't it? And I wanted to see everything that was to be seen on that boat, because I didn't know whether I'd ever have another opportunity. Oh, there are a lot more cherry-trees all in bloom! This Island is the bloomiest place. I just love it already, and I'm so glad I'm going to live here. I've always heard that Prince Edward Island was the prettiest place in the world, and I used to imagine I was living here, but I never really expected I would. It's delightful when your imaginations come true, isn't it? But those red

earthly [ˈɜːθli]
adj. 尘世的
bliss [blɪs]
n. 极乐

gorgeously [ˈɡɔːdʒəsli]
adv. 华丽地
horrid [ˈhɒrɪd]
adj. 非常讨厌的

plume [pluːm]
n. 羽毛

overboard [ˈəʊvəbɔːd]
adv. 从船上落水
prowl [praʊl]
v. 潜行
mercy [ˈmɜːsi]
n. 仁慈

roads are so funny. When we got into the train at Charlottetown and the red roads began to flash past I asked Mrs. Spencer what made them red and she said she didn't know and for pity's sake not to ask her any more questions. She said I must have asked her a thousand already. I suppose I had, too, but how you going to find out about things if you don't ask questions? And what does make the roads red?"

"Well now, I dunno," said Matthew.

"Well, that is one of the things to find out sometime. Isn't it splendid to think of all the things there are to find out about? It just makes me feel glad to be alive—it's such an interesting world. It wouldn't be half so interesting if we know all about everything, would it? There'd be no scope for imagination then, would there? But am I talking too much? People are always telling me I do. Would you rather I didn't talk? If you say so I'll stop. I can stop when I make up my mind to it, although it's difficult."

Matthew, much to his own surprise, was enjoying himself. Like most quiet folks he liked **talkative** people when they were willing to do the talking themselves and did not expect him to keep up his end of it. But he had never expected to enjoy the society of a little girl. Women were bad enough in all conscience, but little girls were worse. He **detested** the way they had of **sidling** past him **timidly**, with sidewise glances, as if they expected him to gobble them up at a mouthful if they ventured to say a word. That was the Avonlea type of well-bred little girl. But this **freckled** witch was very different, and although he found it rather difficult for his slower intelligence to keep up with her brisk mental processes he thought that he "kind of liked her **chatter**". So he said as shyly as usual:

"Oh, you can talk as much as you like. I don't mind."

"Oh, I'm so glad. I know you and I are going to get along to-

talkative [ˈtɔːkətɪv] *adj.* 健谈的

detest [dɪˈtest] *v.* 厌恶
sidle [ˈsaɪdl] *v.* 羞怯地走
timidly [ˈtɪmɪdli] *adv.* 胆怯地
freckled [ˈfrekld] *adj.* 有雀斑的

chatter [ˈtʃætə(r)] *v.* 喋喋不休

gether fine. It's such a relief to talk when one wants to and not be told that children should be seen and not heard. I've had that said to me a million times if I have once. And people laugh at me because I use big words. But if you have big ideas you have to use big words to express them, haven't you?"

"Well now, that seems reasonable," said Matthew.

"Mrs. Spencer said that my tongue must be hung in the middle. But it isn't—it's firmly **fastened** at one end. Mrs. Spencer said your place was named Green Gables. I asked her all about it. And she said there were trees all around it. I was gladder than ever. I just love trees. And there weren't any at all about the asylum, only a few poor weeny-teeny things out in front with little **whitewashed cagey** things about them. They just looked like **orphans** themselves, those trees did. It used to make me want to cry to look at them. I used to say to them, 'Oh, you poor little things! If you were out in a great big woods with other trees all around you and little mosses and Junebells growing over your roots and a brook not far away and birds singing in your **branches**, you could grow, couldn't you? But you can't where you are. I know just exactly how you feel, little trees.' I felt sorry to leave them behind this morning. You do get so attached to things like that, don't you? Is there a brook anywhere near Green Gables? I forgot to ask Mrs. Spencer that."

"Well now, yes, there's one right below the house."

"Fancy. It's always been one of my dreams to live near a brook. I never expected I would, though. Dreams don't often come true, do they? Wouldn't it be nice if they did? But just now I feel pretty nearly perfectly happy. I can't feel exactly perfectly happy because—well, what color would you call this?"

She **twitched** one of her long **glossy** braids over her thin shoul-

fasten [ˈfɑːsn]
v. 系牢

whitewash [ˈwaɪtwɒʃ]
v. 粉饰
cagey [ˈkeɪdʒi]
adj. 守口如瓶的；讳莫如深的
orphan [ˈɔːfn]
n. 孤儿

branch [brɑːntʃ]
n. 树枝

twitch [twɪtʃ]
v. 抽动
glossy [ˈglɒsi]
adj. 光滑的

der and held it up before Matthew's eyes. Matthew was not used to deciding on the **tints** of ladies' **tresses**, but in this case there couldn't be much doubt.

"It's red, ain't it?" he said.

The girl let the braid drop back with a **sigh** that seemed to come from her very toes and to **exhale** forth all the **sorrows** of the ages.

"Yes, it's red," she said **resignedly**. "Now you see why I can't be perfectly happy. Nobody could who has red hair. I don't mind the other things so much—the freckles and the green eyes and my **skinniness**. I can imagine them away. I can imagine that I have a beautiful rose-leaf **complexion** and lovely starry violet eyes. But I cannot imagine that red hair away. I do my best. I think to myself, 'Now my hair is a **glorious** black, black as the **raven**'s wing.' But all the time I know it is just plain red and it breaks my heart. It will be my lifelong sorrow. I read of a girl once in a novel who had a lifelong sorrow but it wasn't red hair. Her hair was pure gold **rippling** back from her **alabaster brow**. What is an alabaster brow? I never could find out. Can you tell me?"

"Well now, I'm afraid I can't," said Matthew, who was getting a little **dizzy**. He felt as he had once felt in his **rash** youth when another boy had **enticed** him on the merry-go-round at a picnic.

"Well, whatever it was it must have been something nice because she was **divinely** beautiful. Have you ever imagined what it must feel like to be divinely beautiful?"

"Well now, no, I haven't," confessed Matthew **ingenuously**.

"I have, often. Which would you rather be if you had the choice—divinely beautiful or **dazzlingly** clever or **angelically** good?"

"Well now, I—I don't know exactly."

"Neither do I. I can never decide. But it doesn't make much real

tint [tɪnt]
n. 色调
tresses ['tresɪz]
n. (女性的)长发

sigh [saɪ]
n. 叹息
exhale [eks'heɪl]
v. 呼气
sorrow ['sɒrəʊ]
n. 悲伤
resignedly [rɪ'zaɪnɪdli]
adv. 顺从地
skinniness ['skɪnɪnəs]
n. 瘦弱
complexion [kəm'plekʃn]
n. 面色
glorious ['glɔːriəs]
adj. 光荣的
raven ['reɪvn]
n. 渡鸦

ripple ['rɪpəl]
v. (使)起涟漪
alabaster brow ['æləbɑːstə(r)] [braʊ]
n. 雪白的额头

dizzy ['dɪzi]
adj. 头晕目眩的
rash [ræʃ]
adj. 鲁莽的
entice [ɪn'taɪs]
v. 引诱
divinely [dɪ'vaɪnli]
adv. 绝妙地
ingenuously [ɪn'dʒenjuəsli]
adv. 天真地
dazzlingly ['dæzlɪŋli]
adv. 眩目地
angelically [æn'dʒelɪkli]
adv. 天使般地

difference for it isn't likely I'll ever be either. It's certain I'll never be angelically good. Mrs. Spencer says—oh, Mr. Cuthbert! Oh, Mr. Cuthbert!! Oh, Mr. Cuthbert!!!"

That was not what Mrs. Spencer had said; neither had the child **tumbled** out of the buggy nor had Matthew done anything astonishing. They had simply rounded a **curve** in the road and found themselves in the "**Avenue**".

The "Avenue", so called by the Newbridge people, was a stretch of road four or five hundred yards long, completely **arched** over with huge, wide-spreading apple-trees, planted years ago by an **eccentric** old farmer. Overhead was one long **canopy** of snowy fragrant bloom. Below the boughs the air was full of a purple **twilight** and far ahead a **glimpse** of painted sunset sky shone like a great rose window at the end of a **cathedral aisle**.

Its beauty seemed to strike the child dumb. She leaned back in the buggy, her thin hands clasped before her, her face lifted **rapturously** to the white **splendour** above. Even when they had passed out and were driving down the long slope to Newbridge she never moved or spoke. Still with **rapt** face she gazed afar into the sunset west, with eyes that saw visions trooping splendidly across that glowing background. Through Newbridge, a **bustling** little village where dogs barked at them and small boys **hooted** and curious faces **peered** from the windows, they drove, still in silence. When three more miles had dropped away behind them the child had not spoken. She could keep silence, it was evident, as energetically as she could talk.

"I guess you're feeling pretty tired and hungry," Matthew **ventured** to say at last, accounting for her long **visitation** of dumbness with the only reason he could think of. "But we haven't very far to go now—only another mile."

tumble [ˈtʌmbl]
v. 跌倒
curve [kɜːv]
n. 曲线
avenue [ˈævənjuː]
n. 大街

arch [ɑːtʃ]
n. 拱门
eccentric [ɪkˈsentrɪk]
adj. 古怪的
canopy [ˈkænəpi]
n. 天篷
twilight [ˈtwaɪlaɪt]
n. 黄昏
glimpse [glɪmps]
n. 一瞥
cathedral [kəˈθiːdrəl]
n. 主教座堂
aisle [aɪl]
n. 过道
rapturously [ˈræptʃərəsli]
adv. 狂喜地
splendour [ˈsplendə(r)]
n. 壮丽
rapt [ræpt]
adj. 专心致志的
bustling [ˈbʌslɪŋ]
adj. 繁忙的
hoot [huːt]
v. 呼叫
peer [pɪə(r)]
v. 仔细看;端详

venture [ˈventʃə(r)]
v. 冒险
visitation [ˌvɪzɪˈteɪʃn]
n. 视察;巡视

She came out of her **reverie** with a deep sigh and looked at him with the dreamy **gaze** of a soul that had been wondering afar, star-led.

reverie [ˈrevəri] *n.* 幻想
gaze [geɪz] *n.* 凝视

"Oh, Mr. Cuthbert," she whispered, "that place we came through—that white place—what was it?"

"Well now, you must mean the Avenue," said Matthew after a few moments' profound reflection. "It is a kind of pretty place."

"Pretty? Oh, pretty doesn't seem the right word to use. Nor beautiful, either. They don't go far enough. Oh, it was wonderful—wonderful. It's the first thing I ever saw that couldn't be improved upon by imagination. It just satisfies me here"—she put one hand on her breast—"it made a **queer** funny ache and yet it was a pleasant ache. Did you ever have an ache like that, Mr. Cuthbert?"

queer [kwɪə(r)] *adj.* 奇怪的

"Well now, I just can't recollect that I ever had."

"I have it lots of time—whenever I see anything royally beautiful. But they shouldn't call that lovely place the Avenue. There is no meaning in a name like that. They should call it—let me see—the White Way of Delight. Isn't that a nice imaginative name? When I don't like the name of a place or a person I always imagine a new one and always think of them so. There was a girl at the asylum whose name was Hepzibah Jenkins, but I always imagined her as Rosalia DeVere. Other people may call that place the Avenue, but I shall always call it the White Way of Delight. Have we really only another mile to go before we get home? I'm glad and I'm sorry. I'm sorry because this drive has been so pleasant and I'm always sorry when pleasant things end. Something still pleasanter may come after, but you can never be sure. And it's so often the case that it isn't pleasanter. That has been my experience anyhow. But I'm glad to think of getting home. You see, I've never had a real home since I can remember. It gives me that pleasant ache again just to think of coming to a really truly home. Oh, isn't that pretty!"

They had driven over the crest of a hill. Below them was a pond, looking almost like a river so long and winding was it. A bridge spanned it midway and from there to its lower end, where an **amber-hued** belt of sand-hills shut it in from the dark blue gulf beyond, the water was a glory of many shifting hues—the most spiritual shadings of **crocus** and rose and **ethereal** green, with other elusive **tintings** for which no name has ever been found. Above the bridge the pond ran up into fringing groves of fir and **maple** and lay all darkly **translucent** in their **wavering** shadows. Here and there a wild plum leaned out from the bank like a white-**clad** girl tip-toeing to her own reflection. From the **marsh** at the head of the pond came the clear, **mournfully**-sweet **chorus** of the frogs. There was a little gray house peering around a white apple orchard on a slope beyond and, although it was not yet quite dark, a light was shining from one of its windows.

"That's Barry's pond," said Matthew.

"Oh, I don't like that name, either. I shall call it—let me see—the Lake of Shining Waters. Yes, that is the right name for it. I know because of the thrill. When I hit on a name that suits exactly it gives me a thrill. Do things ever give you a thrill?"

Matthew **ruminated**.

"Well now, yes. It always kind of gives me a thrill to see them ugly white **grubs** that **spade up** in the cucumber beds. I hate the look of them."

"Oh, I don't think that can be exactly the same kind of a thrill. Do you think it can? There doesn't seem to be much connection between grubs and lake of shining waters, does there? But why do other people call it Barry's pond?"

"I **reckon** because Mr. Barry lives up there in that house. Or-

amber-hued [ˈæmbə-hjuːd] *adj.* 琥珀色的
crocus [ˈkrəʊkəs] *n.* 番红花
ethereal [ɪˈθɪəriəl] *adj.* 优雅的
elusive [ɪˈluːsɪv] *adj.* 难以达到的
tint [tɪnt] *v.* 为……轻微染色
maple [ˈmeɪpl] *n.* 枫树
translucent [trænzˈluːsnt] *adj.* 半透明的
waver [ˈweɪvə(r)] *v.* 摇摆
-clad [klæd] *adj.* ……覆盖的
marsh [mɑːʃ] *n.* 沼泽地
mournfully [ˈmɔːnfəli] *adv.* 悲伤地
chorus [ˈkɔːrəs] *n.* 合唱曲

ruminate [ˈruːmɪneɪt] *v.* 沉思

grub [grʌb] *n.* 幼虫
spade up 挖掘

reckon [ˈrekən] *v.* 估计

chard Slope's the name of his place. If it wasn't for that big bush behind it you could see Green Gables from here. But we have to go over the bridge and round by the road, so it's near half a mile further."

"Has Mr. Barry any little girls? Well, not so very little either—about my size."

"He's got one about eleven. Her name is Diana."

"Oh!" with a long **indrawing** of breath. "What a perfectly lovely name!"

"Well now, I dunno. There's something dreadful heathenish about it, seems to me. I'd ruther Jane or Mary or some sensible name like that. But when Diana was born there was a schoolmaster boarding there and they gave him the naming of her and he called her Diana."

"I wish there had been a schoolmaster like that around when I was born, then. Oh, here we are at the bridge. I'm going to shut my eyes tight. I'm always afraid going over bridges. I can't help imagining that perhaps just as we get to the middle, they'll crumple up like a jack-knife and nip us. So I shut my eyes. But I always have to open them for all when I think we're getting near the middle. Because, you see, if the bridge did **crumple** up I'd want to see it crumple. What a jolly **rumble** it makes! I always like the rumble part of it. Isn't it splendid there are so many things to like in this world? There we're over. Now I'll look back. Good night, dear Lake of Shining Waters. I always say good night to the things I love, just as I would to people I think they like it. That water looks as if it was smiling at me."

When they had driven up the further hill and around a corner Matthew said:

"We're pretty near home now. That's Green Gables over—"

"Oh, don't tell me," she interrupted breathlessly, catching at his **partially** raised arm and shutting her eyes that she might not see his

indrawing [ˈɪndrɔːɪŋ]
n. 内收

crumple [ˈkrʌmpl]
v. (使)变皱
rumble [ˈrʌmbl]
n. 隆隆作响

partially [ˈpɑːʃəli]
adv. 部分地

gesture. "Let me guess. I'm sure I'll guess right."

She opened her eyes and looked about her. They were on the **crest** of a hill. The sun had set some time since, but the landscape was still clear in the mellow **afterlight**. To the west a dark church spire rose up against a **marigold** sky. Below was a little valley and beyond a long, gently-rising slope with snug farmsteads **scattered** along it. From one to another the child's eyes **darted**, eager and **wistful**. At last they **lingered** on one away to the left, far back from the road, dimly white with blossoming trees in the twilight of the surrounding woods. Over it, in the **stainless** southwest sky, a great crystal-white star was shining like a lamp of guidance and promise.

"That's it, isn't it?" she said, pointing.

Matthew slapped the reins on the sorrel's back delightedly.

"Well now, you've guessed it! But I reckon Mrs. Spencer described it so's you could tell."

"No, she didn't—really she didn't. All she said might just as well have been about most of those other places. I hadn't any real idea what it looked like. But just as soon as I saw it I felt it was home. Oh, it seems as if I must be in a dream. Do you know, my arm must be black and blue from the elbow up, for I've **pinched** myself so many times today. Every little while a horrible **sickening** feeling would come over me and I'd be so afraid it was all a dream. Then I'd pinch myself to see if it was real—until suddenly I remembered that even supposing it was only a dream I'd better go on dreaming as long as I could; so I stopped pinching. But it is real and we're nearly home."

With a sigh of **rapture** she relapsed into silence. Matthew stirred uneasily. He felt glad that it would be Marilla and not he who would have to tell this **waif** of the world that the home she longed for was not to be hers after all. They drove over Lynde's Hollow, where it was

crest [krest]
n. 山顶
afterlight [ˈɑːftəlaɪt]
n. 日落后的余晖
spire [ˈspaɪə(r)]
n. 尖塔
marigold [ˈmærɪɡəʊld]
n. 万寿菊
scatter [ˈskætə(r)]
v. 散开
dart [dɑːt]
v. (朝某人猛然)看,瞥
wistful [ˈwɪstfl]
adj. 伤感的
linger [ˈlɪŋɡə(r)]
v. 逗留
stainless [ˈsteɪnləs]
adj. 无瑕疵的
pinch [pɪntʃ]
v. 捏
sickening [ˈsɪkənɪŋ]
adj. 令人作呕的
rapture [ˈræptʃə(r)]
n. 狂喜
waif [weɪf]
n. 面黄肌瘦的小孩

already quite dark, but not so dark that Mrs. Rachel could not see them from her window **vantage**, and up the hill and into the long lane of Green Gables. By the time they arrived at the house Matthew was shrinking from the approaching revelation with an energy he did not understand. It was not of Marilla or himself he was thinking of the trouble this mistake was probably going to make for them, but of the child's disappointment. When he thought of that rapt light being **quenched** in her eyes he had an uncomfortable feeling that he was going to assist at murdering something—much the same feeling that came over him when he had to kill a lamb or calf or any other innocent little creature.

vantage [ˈvɑːntɪdʒ]
n. 优势

quench [kwentʃ]
v. 扑灭

The yard was quite dark as they turned into it and the **poplar** leaves were **rustling** silkily all round it.

poplar [ˈpɒplə(r)]
n. 杨树
rustle [ˈrʌsl]
v. 沙沙作响

"Listen to the trees talking in their sleep," she whispered, as he lifted her to the ground. "What nice dreams they must have!"

Then, holding tightly to the carpet-bag which contained "all her worldly goods", she followed him into the house.

CHAPTER III

Marilla Cuthbert is Surprised

Marilla came briskly forward as Matthew opened the door. But when her eyes fell of the odd little figure in the stiff, ugly dress, with the long braids of red hair and the eager, **luminous** eyes, she stopped short in amazement.

luminous [ˈluːmɪnəs]
adj. 发光的

"Matthew Cuthbert, who's that?" she ejaculated. "Where is the boy?"

"There wasn't any boy," said Matthew wretchedly. "There was only her."

He nodded at the child, remembering that he had never even

asked her name.

"No boy! But there must have been a boy," insisted Marilla. "We sent word to Mrs. Spencer to bring a boy."

"Well, she didn't. She brought her. I asked the station-master. And I had to bring her home. She couldn't be left there, no matter where the mistake had come in."

"Well, this is a pretty piece of business!" ejaculated Marilla.

During this dialogue the child had remained silent, her eyes **roving** from one to the other, all the animation fading out of her face. Suddenly she seemed to grasp the full meaning of what had been said. Dropping her precious carpet-bag she sprang forward a step and clasped her hands.

rove [ˈrəʊv]
v. 扫视

"You don't want me!" she cried. "You don't want me because I'm not a boy! I might have expected it. Nobody ever did want me. I might have known it was all too beautiful to last. I might have known nobody really did want me. Oh, what shall I do? I'm going to burst into tears!"

Burst into tears she did. Sitting down on a chair by the table, **flinging** her arms out upon it, and burying her face in them, she proceeded to cry stormily. Marilla and Matthew looked at each other **deprecatingly** across the stove. Neither of them knew what to say or do. Finally Marilla stepped lamely into the breach.

fling [flɪŋ]
v. 扔

deprecatingly [ˈdɛprɪkeɪtɪŋli]
adv. 责备地

"Well, well, there's no need to cry so about it."

"Yes, there is need!" The child raised her head quickly, revealing a tear-stained face and trembling lips. "You would cry, too, if you were an orphan and had come to a place you thought was going to be home and found that they didn't want you because you weren't a boy. Oh, this is the most tragical thing that ever happened to me!"

Something like a **reluctant** smile, rather rusty from long disuse,

reluctant [rɪˈlʌktənt]
adj. 不情愿的

mellowed Marilla's **grim** expression.

grim [grɪm] *adj.* 严肃的

"Well, don't cry any more. We're not going to turn you out-of-doors to-night. You'll have to stay here until we investigate this affair. What's your name?"

The child hesitated for a moment.

"Will you please call me Cordelia?" she said eagerly.

"Call you Cordelia? Is that your name?"

"No-o-o, it's not exactly my name, but I would love to be called Cordelia. It's such a perfectly elegant name."

"I don't know what on earth you mean. If Cordelia isn't your name, what is?"

"Anne Shirley," reluctantly **faltered** forth the owner of that name, "but, oh, please do call me Cordelia. It can't matter much to you what you call me if I'm only going to be here a little while, can it? And Anne is such an unromantic name."

falter [ˈfɔːltə(r)] *v.* 支支吾吾地说

"Unromantic fiddlesticks!" said the unsympathetic Marilla. "Anne is a real good plain sensible name. You've no need to be ashamed of it."

"Oh, I'm not ashamed of it," explained Anne, "only I like Cordelia better. I've always imagined that my name was Cordelia—at least, I always have of late years. When I was young I used to imagine it was Geraldine, but I like Cordelia better now. But if you call me Anne please call me Anne spelled with an E."

"What difference does it make how it's spelled?" asked Marilla with another rusty smile as she picked up the teapot.

"Oh, it makes such a difference. It looks so much nicer. When you hear a name pronounced can't you always see it in your mind, just as if it was printed out? I can; and A-n-n looks dreadful, but A-n-n-e looks so much more **distinguished**. If you'll only call me Anne

distinguished [dɪˈstɪŋgwɪʃt] *adj.* 卓越的

spelled with an E I shall try to **reconcile** myself to not being called Cordelia."

"Very well, then, Anne spelled with an E, can you tell us how this mistake came to be made? We sent word to Mrs. Spencer to bring us a boy. Were there no boys at the asylum?"

"Oh, yes, there was an abundance of them. But Mrs. Spencer said distinctly that you wanted a girl about eleven years old. And the **matron** said she thought I would do. You don't know how delighted I was. I couldn't sleep all last night for joy. Oh," she added **reproachfully**, turning to Matthew, "why didn't you tell me at the station that you didn't want me and leave me there? If I hadn't seen the White Way of Delight and the Lake of Shining Waters it wouldn't be so hard."

"What on earth does she mean?" demanded Marilla, staring at Matthew.

"She—she's just referring to some conversation we had on the road," said Matthew hastily. "I'm going out to put the mare in, Marilla. Have tea ready when I come back."

"Did Mrs. Spencer bring anybody over besides you?" continued Marilla when Matthew had gone out.

"She brought Lily Jones for herself. Lily is only five years old and she is very beautiful and had nut-brown hair. If I was very beautiful and had nut-brown hair would you keep me?"

"No. We want a boy to help Matthew on the farm. A girl would be of no use to us. Take off your hat. I'll lay it and your bag on the hall table."

Anne took off her hat **meekly**. Matthew came back presently and they sat down to supper. But Anne could not eat. In vain she **nibbled** at the bread and butter and pecked at the crab-apple preserve out of the

reconcile [ˈrekənsaɪl] *v.* 调和

matron [ˈmeɪtrən] *n.* 上年纪的已婚妇女

reproachfully [rɪˈprəʊtʃfəli] *adv.* 责备地

meekly [ˈmiːkli] *adv.* 温顺地

nibble [ˈnɪbl] *v.* 小口咬

little **scalloped** glass dish by her plate. She did not really make any **headway** at all.

scalloped [ˈskɒləpt] *adj.* 有扇形边缘的
headway [ˈhedweɪ] *n.* 取得(缓慢的或艰难的进展)

"You're not eating anything," said Marilla sharply, eying her as if it were a serious shortcoming. Anne sighed.

"I can't. I'm in the depths of despair. Can you eat when you are in the depths of despair?"

"I've never been in the depths of despair, so I can't say," responded Marilla.

"Weren't you? Well, did you ever try to imagine you were in the depths of despair?"

"No, I didn't."

"Then I don't think you can understand what it's like. It's very uncomfortable feeling indeed. When you try to eat a **lump** comes right up in your throat and you can't swallow anything, not even if it was a chocolate **caramel**. I had one chocolate caramel once two years ago and it was simply delicious. I've often dreamed since then that I had a lot of chocolate caramels, but I always wake up just when I'm going to eat them. I do hope you won't be offended because I can't eat. Everything is extremely nice, but still I cannot eat."

lump [lʌmp] *n.* 块,肿块
caramel [ˈkærəmel] *n.* 焦糖

"I guess she's tired," said Matthew, who hadn't spoken since his return from the barn. "Best put her to bed, Marilla."

Marilla had been wondering where Anne should be put to bed. She had prepared a couch in the kitchen **chamber** for the desired and expected boy. But, although it was neat and clean, it did not seem quite the thing to put a girl there somehow. But the spare room was out of the question for such a stray waif, so there remained only the east **gable** room. Marilla lighted a candle and told Anne to follow her, which Anne spiritlessly did, taking her hat and carpet-bag from the hall table as she passed. The hall was **fearsomely** clean; the little

chamber [ˈtʃeɪmbə(r)] *n.* 房间
gable [ˈgeɪbl] *n.* 山墙;三角墙
fearsomely [ˈfɪəsəmli] *adv.* 可怕地

gable chamber in which she presently found herself seemed still cleaner.

Marilla set the candle on a three-legged, three-cornered table and turned down the bedclothes.

"I suppose you have a **nightgown**?" she questioned.

Anne nodded.

"Yes, I have two. The matron of the asylum made them for me. They're fearfully **skimpy**. There is never enough to go around in an asylum, so things are always skimpy—at least in a poor asylum like ours. I hate skimpy night-dresses. But one can dream just as well in them as in lovely trailing ones, with **frills** around the neck, that's one **consolation**."

"Well, undress as quick as you can and go to bed. I'll come back in a few minutes for the candle. I daren't trust you to put it out yourself. You'd likely set the place on fire."

When Marilla had gone Anne looked around her wistfully. The whitewashed walls were so painfully bare and staring that she thought they must ache over their own **bareness**. The floor was bare, too, except for a round braided mat in the middle such as Anne had never seen before. In one corner was the bed, a high, old-fashioned one, with four dark, low-turned posts. In the other corner was the **aforesaid** three-corner table adorned with a fat, red velvet pin-**cushion** hard enough to turn the point of the most adventurous pin. Above it hung a little six-by-eight mirror. Midway between table and bed was the window, with an icy white muslin frill over it, and opposite it was the wash-stand. The whole apartment was of a rigidity not to be described in words, but which sent a shiver to the very marrow of Anne's bones. With a sob she hastily discarded her garments, put on the skimpy nightgown and sprang into bed where she **burrowed** face downward

nightgown [ˈnaɪtgaʊn]
n. 睡衣

skimpy [ˈskɪmpi]
adj. 小而暴露的

frill [frɪl]
n. 褶边

consolation [ˌkɒnsəˈleɪʃn]
n. 安慰

bareness [ˈbeənəs]
n. 赤露

aforesaid [əˈfɔːsed]
adj. 上述的

cushion [ˈkʊʃn]
n. 垫子

burrow [ˈbʌrəʊ]
v. (使……)钻到(……下面)

into the pillow and pulled the clothes over her head. When Marilla came up for the light various skimpy articles of **raiment** scattered most untidily over the floor and a certain **tempestuous** appearance of the bed were the only indications of any presence save her own.

She **deliberately** picked up Anne's clothes, placed them neatly on a prim yellow chair, and then, taking up the candle, went over to the bed.

"Good night," she said, a little awkwardly, but not unkindly.

Anne's white face and big eyes appeared over the bedclothes with a **startling** suddenness.

"How can you call it a good night when you know it must be the very worst night I've ever had?" she said reproachfully.

Then she **dived** down into **invisibility** again.

Marilla went slowly down to the kitchen and proceeded to wash the supper dishes. Matthew was smoking—a sure sign of **perturbation** of mind. He seldom smoked, for Marilla set her face against it as a **filthy** habit; but at certain times and seasons he felt driven to it and them Marilla winked at the practice, realizing that a mere man must have some vent for his emotions.

"Well, this is a pretty kettle of fish," she said **wrathfully**. "This is what comes of sending word instead of going ourselves. Richard Spencer's folks have twisted that message somehow. One of us will have to drive over and see Mrs. Spencer tomorrow, that's certain. This girl will have to be sent back to the asylum."

"Yes, I suppose so," said Matthew reluctantly. "You suppose so! Don't you know it?"

"Well now, she's a real nice little thing, Marilla. It's kind of a pity to send her back when she's so set on staying here."

"Matthew Cuthbert, you don't mean to say you think we ought to

raiment [ˈreɪmənt] *n.* 衣服
tempestuous [temˈpestʃuəs] *adj.* 风暴的
deliberately [dɪˈlɪbərətli] *adv.* 不慌不忙地
startling [ˈstɑːtlɪŋ] *adj.* 惊人的
dive [daɪv] *v.* 扑向，冲向
invisibility [ɪnˌvɪzəˈbɪləti] *n.* 隐形
perturbation [ˌpɜːtəˈbeɪʃn] *n.* 扰动
filthy [ˈfɪlθi] *adj.* 肮脏的
wrathfully [ˈrɒθfəli] *adv.* 愤怒地

keep her!"

Marilla's astonishment could not have been greater if Matthew had expressed a **predilection** for standing on his head.

"Well, now, no, I suppose not—not exactly," **stammered** Matthew, uncomfortably driven into a corner for his precise meaning. "I suppose—we could hardly be expected to keep her."

"I should say not. What good would she be to us?"

"We might be some good to her," said Matthew suddenly and unexpectedly.

"Matthew Cuthbert, I believe that child has **bewitched** you! I can see as plain as plain that you want to keep her."

"Well now, she's a real interesting little thing," persisted Matthew. "You should have heard her talk coming from the station."

"Oh, she can talk fast enough. I saw that at once. It's nothing in her favour, either. I don't like children who have so much to say. I don't want an orphan girl and if I did she isn't the style I'd pick out. There's something I don't understand about her. No, she's got to be **despatched** straight-way back to where she came from."

"I could hire a French boy to help me," said Matthew, "and she'd be company for you."

"I'm not suffering for company," said Marilla shortly. "And I'm not going to keep her."

"Well now, it's just as you say, of course, Marilla," said Matthew rising and putting his pipe away. "I'm going to bed."

To bed went Matthew. And to bed, when she had put her dishes away, went Marilla, **frowning** most **resolutely**. And up-stairs, in the east gable, a lonely, heart-hungry, friendless child cried herself to sleep.

predilection [ˌpriːdɪˈlekʃn] *n.* 偏爱

stammer [ˈstæmə(r)] *v.* 结结巴巴地说

bewitch [bɪˈwɪtʃ] *v.* 迷住;迷惑

despatch [dɪˈspætʃ] *v.* 派遣

frown [fraʊn] *v.* 皱眉

resolutely [ˈrezəluːtli] *adv.* 坚决地

CHAPTER IV

Morning at Green Gables

It was broad daylight when Anne awoke and sat up in bed, staring confusedly at the window through which a flood of cheery sunshine was pouring and outside of which something white and **feathery** waved across glimpses of blue sky.

feathery [ˈfeðəri]
adj. 羽毛般的

For a moment she could not remember where she was. First came a delightful thrill, as something very pleasant; then a horrible remembrance. This was Green Gables and they didn't want her because she wasn't a boy!

But it was morning and, yes, it was a cherry-tree in full bloom outside of her window. With a **bound** she was out of bed and across the floor. She pushed up the **sash**—it went up **stiffly** and **creakily**, as if it hadn't been opened for a long time, which was the case; and it stuck so tight that nothing was needed to hold it up.

bound [baʊnd]
n. 跳跃
sash [sæʃ]
n. 饰带
stiffly [ˈstɪfli]
adv. 僵硬地
creakily [kriːkili]
adv. 发出吱吱声地

Anne dropped on her knees and gazed out into the June morning, her eyes **glistening** with delight. Oh, wasn't it beautiful? Wasn't it a lovely place? Suppose she wasn't really going to stay here! She would imagine she was. There was scope for imagination here.

glisten [ˈglɪsn]
v. 闪光

A huge cherry-tree grew outside, so close that its **boughs** tapped against the house, and it was so thick-set with blossoms that hardly a leaf was to be seen. On both sides of the house was a big orchard, one of apple-trees and one of cherry-trees, also showered over with blossoms; and their grass was all sprinkled with **dandelions**. In the garden below were **lilac**-trees purple with flowers, and their dizzily sweet fragrance **drifted** up to the window on the morning wind.

bough [baʊ]
n. 大树枝

dandelion [ˈdændɪlaɪən]
n. 蒲公英
lilac [ˈlaɪlək]
n. 丁香紫
drift [drɪft]
v. 漂流

Below the garden a green field lush with **clover** sloped down to the hollow where the brook ran and where scores of white birches

clover [ˈkləʊvə(r)]
n. 三叶草

grew, upspringing airily out of an undergrowth suggestive of delightful possibilities in **ferns** and mosses and **woodsy** things generally. Beyond it was a hill, green and feathery with **spruce** and fir; there was a gap in it where the gray gable end of the little house she had seen from the other side of the Lake of Shining Waters was visible.

fern [fɜːn]
n. 蕨类植物
woodsy [ˈwʊdzi]
adj. 树林的
spruce [spruːs]
n. 云杉

Off to the left were the big barns and beyond them, away down over green, low-sloping fields, was a sparkling blue glimpse of sea.

Anne's beauty-loving eyes lingered on it all, taking everything greedily in. She had looked on so many unlovely places in her life, poor child; but this was as lovely as anything she had ever dreamed.

She **knelt** there, lost to everything but the loveliness around her, until she was startled by a hand on her shoulder. Marilla had come in unheard by the small dreamer.

kneel [niːl]
v. 跪下

"It's time you were dressed," she said **curtly**.

curtly [ˈkɜːtli]
adv. 简短地

Marilla really did not know how to talk to the child, and her uncomfortable ignorance made her crisp and curt when she did not mean to be.

Anne stood up and drew a long breath.

"Oh, isn't it wonderful?" she said, waving her hand comprehensively at the good world outside.

"It's a big tree," said Marilla, "and it blooms great, but the fruit don't amount to much never—small and **wormy**."

wormy [ˈwɜːmi]
adj. 有虫子的

"Oh, I don't mean just the tree; of course it's lovely—yes, it's radiantly lovely—it blooms as if it meant it—but I meant everything, the garden and the orchard and the brook and the woods, the whole big dear world. Don't you feel as if you just loved the world on a morning like this? And I can hear the brook laughing all the way up here. Have you ever noticed what cheerful things brooks are? They're always laughing. Even in winter-time I've heard them under the ice. I'm so glad there's a brook near Green Gables. Perhaps you think it doesn't make any difference to me when you're not going to keep me, but it does. I shall always like to remember that there is a brook at Green Gables even if I never see it again. If there wasn't a brook I'd be haunted by the uncomfortable feeling that there ought to be one. I'm not in the depths of despair this morning. I never can be in the morning. Isn't it a splendid thing that there are mornings? But I feel very sad. I've just been imagining that it was really me you wanted after all and that I was to stay here for ever and ever. It was a great comfort while it lasted. But the worst of imagining things is that the time comes when you have to stop and that hurts."

"You'd better get dressed and come down-stairs and never mind your imaginings," said Marilla as soon as she could get a word in edgewise. "Breakfast is waiting. Wash your face and comb your hair. Leave the window up and turn your bedclothes back over the foot of the bed. Be as smart as you can."

Anne could evidently be smart so some purpose for she was down-stairs in ten minutes' time, with her clothes neatly on, her hair brushed and braided, her face washed, and a comfortable consciousness **pervading** her soul that she had fulfilled all Marilla's requirements. As a matter of fact, however, she had forgotten to turn back the bedclothes.

pervade [pə'veɪd]
v. 弥漫

"I'm pretty hungry this morning," she announced as she slipped into the chair Marilla placed for her. "The world doesn't seem such a **howling wilderness** as it did last night. I'm so glad it's a sunshiny morning. But I like rainy mornings real well, too. All sorts of mornings are interesting, don't you think? You don't know what's going to happen through the day, and there's so much scope for imagination. But I'm glad it's not rainy today because it's easier to be cheerful and

howling ['haʊlɪŋ]
adj. 怒号的
wilderness ['wɪldənəs]
n. 荒野

bear up under **affliction** on a sunshiny day. I feel that I have a good deal to bear up under. It's all very well to read about sorrows and imagine yourself living through them heroically, but it's not so nice when you really come to have them, is it?"

affliction [ə'flɪkʃn]
n. 痛苦

"For pity's sake hold your tongue," said Marilla. "You talk entirely too much for a little girl."

Thereupon Anne held her tongue so **obediently** and thoroughly that her continued silence made Marilla rather nervous, as if in the presence of something not exactly natural. Matthew also held his tongue,—but this was natural,—so that the meal was a very silent one.

thereupon [ˌðeərə'pɒn]
adv. 于是
obediently [ə'biːdiəntli]
adv. 顺从地

As it progressed Anne became more and more abstracted, eating mechanically, with her big eyes fixed **unswervingly** and unseeingly on the sky outside the window. This made Marilla more nervous than ever; she had an uncomfortable feeling that while this odd child's body might be there at the table her spirit was far away in some remote airy cloudland, borne aloft on the wings of imagination. Who would want such a child about the place?

unswervingly
[ʌn'swɜːvɪŋli]
adv. 坚定不移地

Yet Matthew wished to keep her, of all **unaccountable** things! Marilla felt that he wanted it just as much this morning as he had the night before, and that he would go on wanting it. That was Matthew's way—take a whim into his head and cling to it with the most amazing silent persistency—a persistency ten times more **potent** and **effectual** in its very silence than if he had talked it out.

unaccountable
[ˌʌnə'kaʊntəbl]
adj. 无法解释的

potent ['pəʊtnt]
adj. 有力的
effectual [ɪ'fektʃuəl]
adj. 有效的

When the meal was ended Anne came out of her reverie and offered to wash the dishes.

"Can you wash dishes right?" asked Marilla distrustfully.

"Pretty well. I'm better at looking after children, though. I've had so much experience at that. It's such a pity you haven't any here for me to look after."

"I don't feel as if I wanted any more children to look after than I've got at present. You're problem enough in all conscience. What's to be done with you I don't know. Matthew is a most **ridiculous** man."

ridiculous [rɪ'dɪkjələs] *adj.* 荒谬的

"I think he's lovely," said Anne reproachfully. "He is so very sympathetic. He didn't mind how much I talked—he seemed to like it. I felt that he was a kindred spirit as soon as ever I saw him."

"You're both queer enough, if that's what you mean by kindred spirits," said Marilla with a sniff. "Yes, you may wash the dishes. Take plenty of hot water, and be sure you dry them well. I've got enough to attend to this morning for I'll have to drive over to White Sands in the afternoon and see Mrs. Spencer. You'll come with me and we'll settle what's to be done with you. After you've finished the dishes go up-stairs and make your bed."

Anne washed the dishes deftly enough, as Marilla who kept a sharp eye on the process, discerned. Later on she made her bed less successfully, for she had never learned the art of wrestling with a feather tick. But it was done somehow and smoothed down; and then Marilla, to get rid of her, told her she might go out-of-doors and amuse herself until dinner time.

Anne flew to the door, face alight, eyes glowing. On the very threshold she stopped short, wheeled about, came back and sat down by the table, light and glow as effectually blotted out as if some one had clapped an **extinguisher** on her.

extinguisher [ɪk'stɪŋgwɪʃə(r)] *n.* 灭火器

"What's the matter now?" demanded Marilla.

"I don't dare go out," said Anne, in the tone of a **martyr relinquishing** all earthly joys. "If I can't stay here there is no use in my loving Green Gables. And if I go out there and get **acquainted** with all those trees and flowers and the orchard and the brook I'll not be

martyr ['mɑːtə(r)] *n.* 殉道者

relinquish [rɪ'lɪŋkwɪʃ] *v.* 放弃

acquainted [ə'kweɪntɪd] *adj.* 熟悉的

able to help loving it. It's hard enough now, so I won't make it any harder. I want to go out so much—everything seems to be calling to me, 'Anne, Anne, come out to us. Anne, Anne, we want a playmate'—but it's better not. There is no use in loving things if you have to be torn from them, is there? And it's so hard to keep from loving things, isn't it? That was why I was so glad when I thought I was going to live here. I thought I'd have so many things to love and nothing to hinder me. But that brief dream is over. I am **resigned** to my fate now, so I don't think I'll go out for fear I'll get unresigned again. What is the name of that **geranium** on the window-sill, please?"

resigned [rɪ'zaɪnd] *adj.* 顺从的

geranium [dʒə'reɪniəm] *n.* 天竺葵

"That's the apple-scented geranium."

"Oh, I don't mean that sort of a name. I mean just a name you gave it yourself. Didn't you give it a name? May I give it one then? May I call it—let me see— Bonny would do—may I call it Bonny while I'm here? Oh, do let me!"

"Goodness, I don't care. But where on earth is the sense of naming a geranium?"

"Oh, I like things to have handles even if they are only geraniums. It makes them seem more like people. How do you know but that it hurts a geranium's feelings just to be called a geranium and nothing else? You wouldn't like to be called nothing but a woman all the time. Yes, I shall call it Bonny. I named that cherry-tree outside my bedroom window this morning. I called it Snow Queen because it was so white. Of course, it won't always be in blossom, but one can imagine that it is, can't one?"

"I never in all my life say or heard anything to equal her," muttered Marilla, beating a retreat down to the **cellar** after potatoes. "She is kind of interesting as Matthew says. I can feel already that I'm wondering what on earth she'll say next. She'll be casting a spell over me,

cellar ['selə(r)] *n.* 地窖

too. She's cast it over Matthew. That look he gave me when he went out said everything he said or hinted last night over again. I wish he was like other men and would talk things out. A body could answer back then and argue him into reason. But what's to be done with a man who just looks?"

Anne had **relapsed into** reverie, with her chin in her hands and her eyes on the sky, when Marilla returned from her cellar **pilgrimage**. There Marilla left her until the early dinner was on the table.

"I suppose I can have the mare and buggy this afternoon, Matthew?" said Marilla.

Matthew nodded and looked wistfully at Anne. Marilla **intercepted** the look and said **grimly**:

"I'm going to drive over to White Sands and settle this thing. I'll take Anne with me and Mrs. Spencer will probably make arrangements to send her back to Nova Scotia at once. I'll set your tea out for you and I'll be home in time to milk the cows."

Still Matthew said nothing and Marilla had a sense of having wasted words and breath. There is nothing more **aggravating** than a man who won't talk back—unless it is a woman who won't.

Matthew hitched the **sorrel** into the buggy in due time and Marilla and Anne set off. Matthew opened the yard gate for them and as they drove slowly through, he said, to nobody in particular as it seemed:

"Little Jerry Buote from the Creek was here this morning, and I told him I guessed I'd hire him for the summer."

Marilla made no reply, but she hit the unlucky sorrel such a **vicious** clip with the whip that the fat mare, unused to such treatment, **whizzed indignantly** down the lane at an alarming pace. Marilla looked back once as the buggy bounced along and saw that aggravating Matthew leaning over the gate, looking wistfully after them.

relapse into 重新陷入，故态复萌
pilgrimage [ˈpɪlɡrɪmɪdʒ] *n.* 朝圣之旅

intercept [ˌɪntəˈsept] *v.* 拦截
grimly [ˈɡrɪmli] *adv.* 严肃地

aggravating [ˈæɡrəveɪtɪŋ] *adj.* 恶化的
sorrel [ˈsɒrəl] *n.* 酸叶草

vicious [ˈvɪʃəs] *adj.* 残酷的
whizz [wɪz] *v.* 飞速行驶
indignantly [ɪnˈdɪɡnəntli] *adv.* 愤怒地

CHAPTER V

Anne's History

"Do you know," said Anne confidentially, "I've made up my mind to enjoy this drive. It's been my experience that you can nearly always enjoy things if you make up your mind firmly that you will. Of course, you must make it up firmly. I am not going to think about going back to the asylum while we're having our drive. I'm just going to think about the drive. Oh, look, there's one little early wild rose out! Isn't it lovely? Don't you think it must be glad to be a rose? Wouldn't it be nice if roses could talk? I'm sure they could tell us such lovely things. And isn't pink the most bewitching color in the world? I love it, but I can't wear it. Redheaded people can't wear pink, not even in imagination. Did you ever know of anybody whose hair was red when she was young, but got to be another color when she grew up?"

"No, I don't know as I ever did," said Marilla **mercilessly**, "and I shouldn't think it likely to happen in your case either."

mercilessly [ˈmɜːsɪləsli] *adv.* 无情地

Anne sighed.

"Well, that is another hope gone. 'My life is a perfect graveyard of buried hopes.' That's a sentence I read in a book once, and I say it over to comfort myself whenever I'm disappointed in anything."

"I don't see where the comforting comes in myself," said Marilla.

"Why, because it sounds so nice and romantic, just as if I were a heroine in a book, you know. I am so fond of romantic things, and a graveyard full of buried hopes is about as romantic a thing as one can imagine, isn't it? I'm rather glad I have one. Are we going across the Lake of Shining Waters today?"

"We're not going over Barry's pond, if that's what you mean by your Lake of Shining Waters. We're going by the shore road."

"Shore road sounds nice," said Anne dreamily. "Is it as nice as it sounds? Just when you said 'shore road' I saw it in a picture in my mind, as quick as that! And White Sands is a pretty name, too; but I don't like it as well as Avonlea. Avonlea is a lovely name. It just sounds like music. How far is it to White Sands?"

"It's five miles; and as you're evidently bent on talking you might as well talk to some purpose by telling me what you know about yourself."

"Oh, what I know about myself isn't really worth telling," said Anne eagerly. "If you'll only let me tell you what I imagine about myself you'll think it ever so much more interesting."

"No, I don't want any of your imaginings. Just you stick to bald facts. Begin at the beginning. Where were you born and how old are you?"

"I was eleven last March," said Anne, resigning herself to bald facts with a little sigh. "And I was born in Bolingbroke, Nova Scotia. My father's name was Walter Shirley, and he was a teacher in the Bolingbroke High School. My mother's name was Bertha Shirley. Aren't Walter and Bertha lovely names? I'm so glad my parents had nice names. It would be a real disgrace to have a father named—well, say Jedediah, wouldn't it?"

"I guess it doesn't matter what a person's name is as long as he behaves himself," said Marilla, feeling herself called upon to inculcate a good and useful moral.

"Well, I don't know." Anne looked thoughtful. "I read in a book once that a rose by any other name would smell as sweet, but I've never been able to believe it. I don't believe a rose would be as nice if it was called a thistle or a **skunk** cabbage. I suppose my father could

skunk [skʌŋk]
n. 北美臭鼬

have been a good man even if he had been called Jedediah; but I'm sure it would have been a cross. Well, my mother was a teacher in the high school, too, but when she married father she gave up teaching, of course. A husband was enough responsibility. Mrs. Thomas said that they were a pair of babies and as poor as church mice. They went to live in a weeny-teeny little yellow house in Bolingbroke. I've never seen that house, but I've imagined it thousands of times. I think it must have had honeysuckle over the parlor window and lilacs in the front yard and lilies of the valley just inside the gate. Yes, and muslin curtains in all the windows. Muslin curtains give a house such an air. I was born in that house. Mrs. Thomas said I was the homeliest baby she ever saw, I was so **scrawny** and tiny and nothing but eyes, but that mother thought I was perfectly beautiful. I should think a mother would be a better judge than a poor woman who came in to scrub, wouldn't you? I'm glad she was satisfied with me anyhow, I would feel so sad if I thought I was a disappointment to her—because she didn't live very long after that, you see. She died of fever when I was just three months old. I do wish she'd lived long enough for me to remember calling her mother. I think it would be so sweet to say 'mother', don't you? And father died four days afterwards from fever too. That left me an orphan and folks were at their wits' end, so Mrs. Thomas said, what to do with me. You see, nobody wanted me even then. It seems to be my fate. Father and mother had both come from places far away and it was well known they hadn't any relatives living. Finally Mrs. Thomas said she'd take me, though she was poor and had a drunken husband. She brought me up by hand. Do you know if there is anything in being brought up by hand that ought to make people who are brought up that way better than other people? Because whenever I was naughty Mrs. Thomas would ask me how I could be

scrawny [ˈskrɔːni] *adj.* 瘦弱的

such a bad girl when she had brought me up by hand—reproachful-like."

"Mr. and Mrs. Thomas moved away from Bolingbroke to Marysville, and I lived with them until I was eight years old. I helped look after the Thomas children—there were four of them younger than me—and I can tell you they took a lot of looking after. Then Mr. Thomas was killed falling under a train and his mother offered to take Mrs. Thomas and the children, but she didn't want me. Mrs. Thomas was at her wits' end, so she said, what to do with me. Then Mrs. Hammond from up the river came down and said she'd take me, seeing I was handy with children, and I went up the river to live with her in a little clearing among the **stumps**. It was a very lonesome place. I'm sure I could never have lived there if I hadn't had an imagination. Mr. Hammond worked a little **sawmill** up there, and Mrs. Hammond had eight children. She had twins three times. I like babies in moderation, but twins three times in succession is too much. I told Mrs. Hammond so firmly, when the last pair came. I used to get so dreadfully tired carrying them about."

stump [stʌmp] *n.* 树桩

sawmill [ˈsɔːmɪl] *n.* 锯木厂

"I lived up river with Mrs. Hammond over two years, and then Mr. Hammond died and Mrs. Hammond broke up housekeeping. She divided her children among her relatives and went to the States. I had to go to the asylum at Hopeton, because nobody would take me. They didn't want me at the asylum, either; they said they were overcrowded as it was. But they had to take me and I was there four months until Mrs. Spencer came."

Anne finished up with another sigh, of relief this time. Evidently she did not like talking about her experiences in a world that had not wanted her.

"Did you ever go to school?" demanded Marilla, turning the sorrel mare down the shore road.

"Not a great deal. I went a little the last year I stayed with Mrs. Thomas. When I went up river we were so far from a school that I couldn't walk it in winter and there was a vacation in summer, so I could only go in the spring and fall. But of course I went while I was at the asylum. I can read pretty well and I know ever so many pieces of poetry off by heart—'The Battle of Hohenlinden' and 'Edinburgh after Flodden', and 'Bingen of the Rhine', and most of the 'Lady of the Lake' and most of 'The Seasons' by James Thompson. Don't you just love poetry that gives you a **crinkly** feeling up and down your back? There is a piece in the Fifth Reader—'The Downfall of Poland'—that is just full of thrills. Of course, I wasn't in the Fifth Reader—I was only in the Fourth—but the big girls used to lend me theirs to read."

crinkly ['krɪŋkli] *adj.* 多皱纹的

"Were those women—Mrs. Thomas and Mrs. Hammond—good to you?" asked Marilla, looking at Anne out of the corner of her eye.

"O-o-o-h," faltered Anne. Her sensitive little face suddenly flushed scarlet and embarrassment sat on her **brow**. "Oh, they meant to be—I know they meant to be just as good and kind as possible. And when people mean to be good to you, you don't mind very much when they're not quite—always. They had a good deal to worry them, you know. It's very trying to have a drunken husband, you see; and it must be very trying to have twins three times in succession, don't you think? But I feel sure they meant to be good to me."

brow [braʊ] *n.* 额头

Marilla asked no more questions. Anne gave herself up to a silent rapture over the shore road and Marilla guided the sorrel abstractedly while she **pondered** deeply. Pity was suddenly stirring in her heart for the child. What a starved, unloved life she had had—a life of **drudgery** and poverty and neglect; for Marilla was shrewd enough to

ponder ['pɒndə(r)] *v.* 仔细考虑

drudgery ['drʌdʒəri] *n.* 苦工

read between the lines of Anne's history and divine the truth. No wonder she had been so delighted at the **prospect** of a real home. It was a pity she had to be sent back. What if she, Marilla, should indulge Matthew's unaccountable whim and let her stay? He was set on it; and the child seemed a nice, teachable little thing.

prospect ['prɒspekt] *n.* 前景

"She's got too much to say," thought Marilla, "but she might be trained out of that. And there's nothing rude or **slangy** in what she does say. She's ladylike. It's likely her people were nice folks."

slangy ['slæŋi] *adj.* 俚语的

The shore road was "woodsy and wild and lonesome". On the right hand, scrub firs, their spirits quite unbroken by long years of tussle with the gulf winds, grew thickly. On the left were the steep red sandstone cliffs, so near the track in places that a mare of less steadiness than the sorrel might have tried the nerves of the people behind her. Down at the base of the cliffs were heaps of surf-worn rocks or little sandy **coves inlaid** with **pebbles** as with ocean jewels; beyond lay the sea, **shimmering** and blue, and over it soared the gulls, their pinions flashing silvery in the sunlight.

cove [kəʊv] *n.* 小海湾
inlaid [ˌɪn'leɪd] *adj.* 镶嵌的
pebble ['pebl] *n.* 鹅卵石
shimmer ['ʃɪmə(r)] *v.* 微微发光

"Isn't the sea wonderful?" said Anne, rousing from a long, wide-eyed silence. "Once, when I lived in Marysville, Mr. Thomas hired an express **wagon** and took us all to spend the day at the shore ten miles away. I enjoyed every moment of that day, even if I had to look after the children all the time. I lived it over in happy dreams for years. But this shore is nicer than the Marysville shore. Aren't those gulls splendid? Would you like to be a gull? I think I would—that is, if I couldn't be a human girl. Don't you think it would be nice to wake up at sunrise and **swoop** down over the water and away out over that lovely blue all day; and then at night to fly back to one's nest? Oh, I can just imagine myself doing it. What big house is that just ahead, please?"

wagon ['wægən] *n.* 四轮马车
swoop [swuːp] *v.* 猛冲

"That's the White Sands Hotel. Mr. Kirke runs it, but the season hasn't begun yet. There are heaps of Americans come there for the summer. They think this shore is just about right."

"I was afraid it might be Mrs. Spencer's place," said Anne mournfully. "I don't want to get there. Somehow, it will seem like the end of everything."

CHAPTER VI

Marilla Makes Up Her Mind

Get there they did, however, in due season. Mrs. Spencer lived in a big yellow house at White Sands Cove, and she came to the door with surprise and welcome **mingled** on her **benevolent** face.

mingle [ˈmɪŋɡl]
v. 使混合
benevolent
[bəˈnevələnt]
adj. 仁慈的

"Dear, dear," she exclaimed, "you're the last folks I was looking for today, but I'm real glad to see you. You'll put your horse in? And how are you, Anne?"

"I'm as well as can be expected, thank you," said Anne smilelessly. A **blight** seemed to have descended on her.

blight [blaɪt]
n. (农作物等的)疫病

"I suppose we'll stay a little while to rest the mare," said Marilla, "but I promised Matthew I'd be home early. The fact is, Mrs. Spencer, there's been a queer mistake somewhere, and I've come over to see where it is. We send word, Matthew and I, for you to bring us a boy from the asylum. We told your brother Robert to tell you we wanted a boy ten or eleven years old."

"Marilla Cuthbert, you don't say so!" said Mrs. Spencer in distress. "Why, Robert sent word down by his daughter Nancy and she said you wanted a girl—didn't she Flora Jane?" appealing to her daughter who had come out to the steps.

"She certainly did, Miss Cuthbert," **corroborated** Flora Jane earnestly.

corroborate
[kəˈrɒbəreɪt]
v. 确证

"I'm dreadful sorry," said Mrs. Spencer. "It's too bad; but it certainly wasn't my fault, you see, Miss Cuthbert. I did the best I could and I thought I was following your instructions. Nancy is a terrible **flighty** thing. I've often had to scold her well for her **heedlessness**."

"It was our own fault," said Marilla resignedly. "We should have come to you ourselves and not left an important message to be passed along by word of mouth in that fashion. Anyhow, the mistake has been made and the only thing to do is to set it right. Can we send the child back to the asylum? I suppose they'll take her back, won't they?"

"I suppose so," said Mrs. Spencer thoughtfully, "but I don't think it will be necessary to send her back. Mrs. Peter Blewett was up here yesterday, and she was saying to me how much she wished she'd sent by me for a little girl to help her. Mrs. Peter has a large family, you know, and she finds it hard to get help. Anne will be the very girl for you. I call it positively **providential**."

Marilla did not look as if she thought Providence had much to do with the matter. Here was an unexpectedly good chance to get this unwelcome orphan off her hands, and she did not even feel grateful for it.

She knew Mrs. Peter Blewett only by sight as a small, shrewish-faced woman without an ounce of **superfluous** flesh on her bones. But she had heard of her. "A terrible worker and driver", Mrs. Peter was said to be; and discharged servant girls told fearsome tales of her temper and **stinginess**, and her family of pert, quarrelsome children. Marilla felt a **qualm** of conscience at the thought of handing Anne over to her tender mercies.

"Well, I'll go in and we'll talk the matter over," she said.

"And if there isn't Mrs. Peter coming up the lane this blessed minute!" exclaimed Mrs. Spencer, bustling her guests through the hall into the parlor, where a deadly chill struck on them as if the air had been strained so long through dark green, closely drawn blinds that it

flighty [ˈflaɪti] *adj.* 轻浮的
heedlessness [ˈhiːdləsnəs] *n.* 不注意

providential [ˌprɒvɪˈdenʃl] *adj.* 天缘巧合的

superfluous [suːˈpɜːfluəs] *adj.* 多余的

stinginess [ˈstɪndʒinəs] *n.* 小气
qualm [kwɔːm] *n.* 疑虑

had lost every particle of warmth it had ever possessed. "That is real lucky, for we can settle the matter right away. Take the armchair, Miss Cuthbert. Anne, you sit here on the **ottoman** and don't **wiggle**. Let me take your hats. Flora Jane, go out and put the kettle on. Good afternoon, Mrs. Blewett. We were just saying how fortunate it was you happened along. Let me introduce you two ladies. Mrs. Blewett, Miss Cuthbert. Please excuse me for just a moment. I forgot to tell Flora Jane to take the buns out of the oven."

ottoman [ˈɒtəmən]
n. 箱式凳
wiggle [ˈwɪɡl]
v. (使)扭动

Mrs. Spencer whisked away, after pulling up the blinds. Anne sitting **mutely** on the ottoman, with her hands clasped tightly in her lap, stared at Mrs. Blewett as one fascinated. Was she to be given into the keeping of this sharp-faced, sharp-eyed woman? She felt a lump coming up in her throat and her eyes smarted painfully. She was beginning to be afraid she couldn't keep the tears back when Mrs. Spencer returned, flushed and beaming, quite capable of taking any and every difficulty, physical, mental or spiritual, into consideration and settling it out of hand.

mutely [ˈmjuːtli]
adv. 默默地

"It seems there's been a mistake about this little girl, Mrs. Blewett," she said. "I was under the impression that Mr. and Miss Cuthbert wanted a little girl to adopt. I was certainly told so. But it seems it was a boy they wanted. So if you're still of the same mind you were yesterday, I think she'll be just the thing for you."

Mrs. Blewett darted her eyes over Anne from head to foot.

"How old are you and what's your name?" she demanded.

"Anne Shirley," faltered the shrinking child, not daring to make any **stipulations** regarding the spelling thereof, "and I'm eleven years old."

stipulation
[ˌstɪpjuˈleɪʃn]
n. 规定

"Humph! You don't look as if there was much to you. But you're wiry. I don't know but the wiry ones are the best after all.

Well, if I take you you'll have to be a good girl, you know—good and smart and respectful. I'll expect you to earn your keep, and no mistake about that. Yes, I suppose I might as well take her off your hands, Miss Cuthbert. The baby's awful **fractious**, and I'm clean worn out attending to him. If you like I can take her right home now."

fractious [ˈfrækʃəs] *adj.* 暴躁的

Marilla looked at Anne and softened at sight of the child's pale face with its look of mute misery—the misery of a helpless little creature who finds itself once more caught in the trap from which it had escaped. Marilla felt an uncomfortable **conviction** that, if she denied the appeal of that look, it would haunt her to her dying day. Moreover, she did not fancy Mrs. Blewett. To hand a sensitive, "high-strung" child over to such a woman! No, she could not take the responsibility of doing that!

conviction [kənˈvɪkʃn] *n.* 信念

"Well, I don't know," she said slowly. "I didn't say that Matthew and I had absolutely decided that we wouldn't keep her. In fact I may say that Matthew is disposed to keep her. I just came over to find out how the mistake had occurred. I think I'd better take her home again and talk it over with Matthew. I feel that I oughtn't to decide on anything without consulting him. If we make up our mind not to keep her we'll bring or send her over to you tomorrow night. If we don't you may know that she is going to stay with us. Will that suit you, Mrs. Blewett?"

"I suppose it'll have to," said Mrs. Blewett ungraciously.

During Marilla's speech a sunrise had been dawning on Anne's face. First the look of despair faded out; then came a faint flush of hope; here eyes grew deep and bright as morning stars. The child was quite **transfigured**; and, a moment later, when Mrs. Spencer and Mrs. Blewett went out in quest of a recipe the latter had come to borrow she sprang up and flew across the room to Marilla.

transfigure [trænsˈfɪgə(r)] *v.* 使改观

"Oh, Miss Cuthbert, did you really say that perhaps you would let me stay at Green Gables?" she said, in a breathless whisper, as if speaking aloud might shatter the glorious possibility. "Did you really say it? Or did I only imagine that you did?"

"I think you'd better learn to control that imagination of yours, Anne, if you can't distinguish between what is real and what isn't," said Marilla crossly. "Yes, you did hear me say just that and no more. It isn't decided yet and perhaps we will conclude to let Mrs. Blewett take you after all. She certainly needs you much more than I do."

"I'd rather go back to the asylum than go to live with her," said Anne passionately. "She looks exactly like a— like a **gimlet**."

gimlet ['gɪmlət] *n.* 螺丝锥

Marilla smothered a smile under the conviction that Anne must be reproved for such a speech.

"A little girl like you should be ashamed of talking so about a lady and a stranger," she said severely. "Go back and sit down quietly and hold your tongue and behave as a good girl should."

"I'll try to do and be anything you want me, if you'll only keep me," said Anne, returning meekly to her ottoman.

When they arrived back at Green Gables that evening Matthew met them in the lane. Marilla from afar had noted him prowling along it and guessed his motive. She was prepared for the relief she read in his face when he saw that she had at least brought back Anne back with her. But she said nothing, to him, relative to the affair, until they were both out in the yard behind the barn milking the cows. Then she briefly told him Anne's history and the result of the interview with Mrs. Spencer.

"I wouldn't give a dog I liked to that Blewett woman," said Matthew with unusual vim.

"I don't fancy her style myself," admitted Marilla, "but it's that or keeping her ourselves, Matthew. And since you seem to want her, I suppose I'm willing—or have to be. I've been thinking over the idea until I've got kind of used to it. It seems a sort of duty. I've never brought up a child, especially a girl, and I dare say I'll make a terrible mess of it. But I'll do my best. So far as I'm concerned, Matthew, she may stay."

Matthew's shy face was a glow of delight.

"Well now, I reckoned you'd come to see it in that light, Marilla," he said. "She's such an interesting little thing."

"It'd be more to the point if you could say she was a useful little thing," retorted Marilla, "but I'll make it my business to see she's trained to be that. And mind, Matthew, you're not to go interfering with my methods. Perhaps an old maid doesn't know much about bringing up a child, but I guess she knows more than an old bachelor. So you just leave me to manage her. When I fail it'll be time enough to put your oar in."

"There, there, Marilla, you can have your own way," said Matthew **reassuringly**. "Only be as good and kind to her as you can without spoiling her. I kind of think she's one of the sort you can do anything with if you only get her to love you."

Marilla sniffed, to express her contempt for Matthew's opinions concerning anything **feminine**, and walked off to the dairy with the pails.

"I won't tell her tonight that she can stay," she reflected, as she strained the milk into the creamers. "She'd be so excited that she wouldn't sleep a wink. Marilla Cuthbert, you're fairly in for it. Did you ever suppose you'd see the day when you'd be adopting an orphan girl? It's surprising enough; but not so surprising as that Matthew should be at the bottom of it, him that always seemed to have

reassuringly [ˌriːəˈʃʊərɪŋli] *adv.* 宽慰地

feminine [ˈfemənɪn] *adj.* 女性的

such a mortal dread of little girls. Anyhow, we've decided on the experiment and goodness only knows what will come of it."

CHAPTER VII

Anne Says Her Prayers

When Marilla took Anne up to bed that night she said stiffly:

"Now, Anne, I noticed last night that you threw your clothes all about the floor when you took them off. That is a very untidy habit, and I can't allow it at all. As soon as you take off any article of clothing fold it neatly and place it on the chair. I haven't any use at all for little girls who aren't neat."

"I was so **harrowed** up in my mind last night that I didn't think about my clothes at all," said Anne. "I'll fold them nicely tonight. They always made us do that at the asylum. Half the time, though, I'd forget, I'd be in such a hurry to get into bed nice and quiet and imagine things."

harrow [ˈhærəʊ] *v.* 折磨，使苦恼

"You'll have to remember a little better if you stay here," admonished Marilla. "There, that looks something like. Say your prayers now and get into bed."

"I never say any prayers," announced Anne.

Marilla looked horrified astonishment.

"Why, Anne, what do you mean? Were you never taught to say your prayers? God always wants little girls to say their prayers. Don't you know who God is, Anne?"

" 'God is a spirit, infinite, **eternal** and unchangeable, in his being, wisdom, power, holiness, justice, goodness, and truth,' " responded Anne **promptly** and **glibly**.

eternal [ɪˈtɜːnl] *adj.* 永恒的
promptly [ˈprɒmptli] *adv.* 迅速地
glibly [ˈglɪbli] *adv.* 未经思考地

Marilla looked rather relieved.

"So you do know something then, thank goodness! You're not

quite a heathen. Where did you learn that?"

"Oh, at the asylum Sunday-school. They made us learn the whole **catechism**. I liked it pretty well. There's something splendid about some of the words. 'Infinite, eternal and unchangeable.' Isn't that grand? It has such a roll to it—just like a big organ playing. You couldn't quite call it poetry, I suppose, but it sounds a lot like it, doesn't it?"

catechism [ˈkætəkɪzəm] n. 教理问答

"We're not talking about poetry, Anne—we are talking about saying your prayers. Don't you know it's a terrible wicked thing not to say your prayers every night? I'm afraid you are a very bad little girl."

"You'd find it easier to be bad than good if you had red hair," said Anne reproachfully. "People who haven't red hair don't know what trouble is. Mrs. Thomas told me that God made my hair red on purpose, and I've never cared about him since. And anyhow I'd always be too tired at night to bother saying prayers. People who have to look after twins can't be expected to say their prayers. Now, do you honestly think they can?"

Marilla decided that Anne's religious training must be begun at once. Plainly there was no time to be lost.

"You must say your prayers while you are under my roof, Anne."

"Why, of course, if you want me to," **assented** Anne cheerfully. "I'd do anything to **oblige** you. But you'll have to tell me what to say for this once. After I get into bed I'll imagine out a real nice prayer to say always. I believe that it will be quite interesting, now that I come to think of it."

assent [əˈsent] v. 同意
oblige [əˈblaɪdʒ] v. 强迫

"You must kneel down," said Marilla in embarrassment.

Anne knelt at Marilla's knee and looked up gravely.

"Why must people kneel down to pray? If I really wanted to pray I'll tell you what I'd do. I'd go out into a great big field all alone or into the deep, deep, woods, and I'd look up into the sky—up—up—up—into that lovely blue sky that looks as if there was no end to its blueness. And then I'd just feel a prayer. Well, I'm ready. What am I to say?"

Marilla felt more embarrassed than ever. She had intended to teach Anne the childish classic, "Now I lay me down to sleep." But she had, as I have told you, the glimmerings of a sense of humor—which is simply another name for a sense of fitness of things; and it suddenly occurred to her that simple little prayer, sacred to white-robed childhood **lisping** at motherly knees, was entirely unsuited to this freckled witch of a girl who knew and cared nothing about God's love, since she had never had it translated to her through the medium of human love.

lisp [lɪsp] v. 口齿不清

"You're old enough to pray for yourself, Anne," she said finally. "Just thank God for your blessings and ask him humbly for the things you want."

"Well, I'll do my best," promised Anne, burying her face in Marilla's lap. "Gracious heavenly Father—that's the way the ministers say it in church, so I suppose it's all right in private prayer, isn't it?" she interjected, lifting her head for a moment.

"Gracious heavenly Father, I thank Three for the White Way of Delight and the Lake of Shining Waters and Bonny and the Snow Queen. I'm really extremely grateful for them. And that's all the blessings I can think of just now to thank Thee for. As for the things I want, they're so numerous that it would take a great deal of time to name them all so I will only mention the two most important. Please let me stay at Green Gables; and please let me be good-looking when I grow up. I remain,

'Yours respectfully, Anne Shirley.'"

"There, did I do all right?" she asked eagerly, getting up. "I could have made it much more flowery if I'd had a little more time to think it over."

Poor Marilla was only preserved from complete collapse by remembering that it was not **irreverence**, but simply spiritual **ignorance** on the part of Anne that was responsible for this extraordinary **petition**. She tucked the child up in bed, mentally **vowing** that she should be taught a prayer the very next day, and was leaving the room with the light when Anne called her back.

irreverence [ɪ'revərəns] *n.* 不礼的行为
ignorance ['ɪgnərəns] *n.* 无知
petition [pə'tɪʃn] *n.* 请愿书
vow [vaʊ] *v.* 立誓
respectfully [rɪ'spektfəli] *adv.* 尊敬地

"I've just thought of it now. I should have said, 'Amen' in place of 'yours **respectfully**', shouldn't I? —the way the ministers do. I'd forgotten it, but I felt a prayer should be finished off in some way, so I put in the other. Do you suppose it will make any difference?"

"I—I don't suppose it will," said Marilla. "Go to sleep now like a good child. Good night."

"I can only say good night tonight with a clear **conscience**," said Anne, cuddling **luxuriously** down among her pillows.

conscience ['kɒnʃəns] *n.* 良知
luxuriously [lʌg'ʒʊəriəsli] *adv.* 舒适地

Marilla retreated to the kitchen, set the candle firmly on the table, and glared at Matthew.

"Matthew Cuthbert, it's about time somebody adopted that child and taught her something. She's next door to a perfect heathen. Will you believe that she never said a prayer in her life till tonight? I'll send her to the **manse** tomorrow and borrow the Peep of the Day series, that's what I'll do. And she shall go to Sunday-school just as soon as I can get some suitable clothes made for her. I foresee that I shall have my hands full. Well, well, we can't get through this world without our share of trouble. I've had a pretty easy life of it so far, but my time has come at last and I suppose I'll just have to make the best of it."

manse [mæns] *n.* 牧师住宅

CHAPTER VIII

Anne's Bringing-up Is Begun

For reasons best known to herself, Marilla did not tell Anne that she was to stay at Green Gables until the next afternoon. During the forenoon she kept the child busy with various tasks and watched over her with a keen eye while she did them. By noon she had concluded that Anne was smart and **obedient**, willing to work and quick to learn; her most serious shortcoming seemed to be a tendency to fall into daydreams in the middle of a task and forget all about it until such time as she was sharply recalled to earth by a **reprimand** or a **catastrophe**.

obedient [ə'biːdiənt] *adj.* 顺从的

reprimand ['reprɪmɑːnd] *n.* 谴责

catastrophe [kə'tæstrəfi] *n.* 灾难

When Anne had finished washing the dinner dishes she suddenly **confronted** Marilla with the air and expression of one **desperately** determined to learn the worst. Her thin little body trembled from head to foot; her face flushed and her eyes **dilated** until they were almost black; she clasped her hands tightly and said in an imploring voice:

confront [kən'frʌnt] *n.* 和……当面对证

desperately ['despərətli] *adv.* 迫切;非常

dilated [daɪ'leɪtɪd] *adj.* 扩大的

"Oh, please, Miss Cuthbert, won't you tell me if you are going to send me away or not? I've tried to be patient all the morning, but I really feel that I cannot bear not knowing any longer. It's a **dreadful** feeling. Please tell me."

dreadful ['dredfl] *adj.* 糟糕透顶的

"You haven't **scalded** the dishcloth in clean hot water as I told you to do," said Marilla immovably. "Just go and do it before you ask any more questions, Anne." Anne went and attended to the dishcloth. Then she returned to Marilla and fastened **imploring** eyes of the latter's face. "Well," said Marilla, unable to find any excuse for deferring her explanation longer, "I suppose I might as well tell you. Matthew and I have decided to keep you—that is, if you will try to be a good little girl and show yourself grateful. Why, child, whatever is the

scald [skɔːld] *v.* 烫伤

imploring [ɪm'plɔːrɪŋ] *adj.* 恳求的

matter?"

"I'm crying," said Anne in a tone of **bewilderment**. "I can't think why. I'm glad as glad can be. Oh, glad doesn't seem the right word at all. I was glad about the White Way and the cherry **blossoms**—but this! Oh, it's something more than glad. I'm so happy. I'll try to be so good. It will be uphill work, I expect, for Mrs. Thomas often told me I was desperately **wicked**. However, I'll do my very best. But can you tell me why I'm crying?"

"I suppose it's because you're all excited and worked up," said Marilla **disapprovingly**. "Sit down on that chair and try to calm yourself. I'm afraid you both cry and laugh far too easily. Yes, you can stay here and we will try to do right by you. You must go to school; but it's only a fortnight till vacation so it isn't worth, while for you to start before it opens again in September."

"What am I to call you?" asked Anne. "Shall I always say Miss Cuthbert? Can I call you Aunt Marilla?"

"No, you'll call me just plain Marilla. I'm not used to being called Miss Cuthbert and it would make me nervous."

"It sounds awfully disrespectful to just say Marilla," protested Anne.

"I guess there'll be nothing disrespectful in it if you're careful to speak respectfully. Everybody, young and old, in Avonlea calls me Marilla except the minister. He says Miss Cuthbert—when he thinks of it."

"I'd love to call you Aunt Marilla," said Anne **wistfully**. "I've never had an aunt or any relation at all— not even a grandmother. It would make me feel as if I really belonged to you. Can't I call you Aunt Marilla?"

"No. I'm not your aunt and I don't believe in calling people

bewilderment [bɪˈwɪldəmənt] *n.* 困惑

blossom [ˈblɒsəm] *n.* (树木的)花

wicked [ˈwɪkɪd] *adj.* 邪恶的

disapprovingly [ˌdɪsəˈpruːvɪŋli] *adv.* 不以为然地

wistfully [ˈwɪstfəli] *adv.* 伤感地

names that don't belong to them."

"But we could imagine you were my aunt."

"I couldn't," said Marilla grimly.

"Do you never imagine things different from what they really are?" asked Anne wide-eyed.

"No."

"Oh!" Anne drew a long breath. "Oh, Miss—Marilla, how much you miss!"

"I don't believe in imagining things different from what they really are," retorted Marilla. "When the Lord puts us in certain **circumstances**. He doesn't mean for us to imagine them away. And that reminds me. Go into the sitting room, Anne—be sure your feet are clean and don't let any flies in—and bring me out the **illustrated** card that's on the **mantelpiece**. The Lord's Prayer is on it and you'll devote your spare time this afternoon to learning it off by heart. There's to be no more of such praying as I heard last night."

"I suppose I was very awkward," said Anne **apologetically**, "but then, you see, I'd never had any practice. You couldn't really expect a person to pray very well the first time she tried, could you? I thought out a splendid prayer after I went to bed, just as I promised you I would. It was nearly as long as a minister's and so poetical. But would you believe it? I couldn't remember one word when I woke up this morning. And I'm afraid I'll never be able to think out another one as good. Somehow, things never are so good when they're thought out a second time. Have you ever noticed that?"

"Here is something for you to notice, Anne. When I tell you to do thing, I want you to obey me at once and not stand stock-still and discourse about it. Just you go and do as I **bid** you."

Anne **promptly** departed for the sitting-room across the hall; she

circumstance [ˈsɜːkəmstəns] *n.* 状况

illustrated [ˈɪləstreɪtɪd] *adj.* 有插图的

mantelpiece [ˈmæntlpiːs] *n.* 壁炉台

apologetically [əˌpɒləˈdʒetɪkli] *adv.* 道歉地

bid [bɪd] *v.* 吩咐

promptly [ˈprɒmptli] *adv.* 迅速地

failed to return; after waiting ten minutes Marilla laid down her knitting and marched after her with a grim expression. She found Anne standing motionless before a picture hanging on the wall between the two windows, with her eyes a star with dreams. The white and green light **strained** through apple trees and **clustering** vines outside fell over the rapt little figure with a half-unearthly radiance.

strain [streɪn]
v. 过滤
cluster ['klʌstə(r)]
v. 从生或聚集

"Anne, whatever are you thinking of?" demanded Marilla sharply.

Anne came back to earth with a start.

"That," she said, pointing to the picture—a rather vivid **chromo entitled**, "Christ Blessing Little Children"—"and I was just imagining I was one of them—that I was the little girl in the blue dress, standing off by herself in the corner as if she didn't belong to anybody, like me. She looks lonely and sad, don't you think? I guess she hadn't any father or mother of her own. But she wanted to be blessed, too, so she just crept shyly up on the outside of the crowd, hoping nobody would notice her—except him. I'm sure I know just how she felt. Her heart must have beat and her hands must have got cold, like mine did when I asked you if I could stay. She was afraid he mightn't notice her. But it's likely he did, don't you think? I've been trying to imagine it all out—her **edging** a little nearer all the time until she was quite close to him; and then he would look at her and put his hand on her hair and oh, such a thrill of joy as would run over her! But I wish the artist hadn't painted him so sorrowful looking. All His pictures are like that, if you've noticed. But I don't believe he could really have looked so sad or the children would have been afraid of him."

chromo ['krəʊməʊ]
n. 多彩石印版
entitled [ɪn'taɪtld]
adj. 标题为

edg ['edʒ]
v. 徐徐移动

"Anne," said Marilla, wondering why she had not broken into this speech long before, "you shouldn't talk that way. It's irreverent—positively irreverent."

Anne's eyes **marveled**.

marvel ['mɑːvl]
v. 惊讶

"Why, I felt just as reverent as could be. I'm sure I didn't mean to be irreverent."

"Well I don't suppose you did—but it doesn't sound right to talk so familiarly about such things. And another thing, Anne, when I send you after something you're to bring it at once and not fall into mooning and imagining before pictures. Remember that. Take that card and come right to the kitchen. Now, sit down in the corner and learn that prayer off by heart."

Anne set the card up against the **jugful** of apple blossoms she had brought in to decorate the dinner table—Marilla had eyed that decoration **askance**, but had said nothing—propped her chin on her hands, and fell to studying it **intently** for several silent minutes.

jugful [ˈdʒʌgfʊl] *adj.* 一壶的量

askance [əˈskæns] *adv.* 斜眼看

intently [ɪnˈtentli] *adv.* 专心地

"I like this," she announced at length. "It's beautiful. I've heard it before—I heard the **superintendent** of the asylum Sunday school say it over once. But I didn't like it then. He had such a cracked voice and he prayed it so **mournfully**. I really felt sure he thought praying was a disagreeable duty. This isn't poetry, but it makes me feel just the same way poetry does. 'Our Father who art in heaven hallowed be Thy name.' That is just like a line of music. Oh, I'm so glad you thought of making me learn this, Miss—Marilla."

superintendent [ˌsuːpərɪnˈtendənt] *n.* 主管

mournfully [ˈmɔːnfəli] *adv.* 悲痛地

"Well, learn it and hold your tongue," said Marilla shortly.

Anne tipped the vase of apple blossoms near enough to bestow a soft kiss on a pink-cupped but, and then studied diligently for some moments longer.

"Marilla," she demanded presently, "do you think that I shall ever have a bosom friend in Avonlea?"

"A—a what kind of friend?"

"A **bosom friend**—an intimate friend, you know—a really kindred spirit to whom I can confide my inmost soul. I've dreamed of

bosom [ˈbʊzəm] friend 亲密的朋友

meeting her all my life. I never really supposed I would, but so many of my loveliest dreams have come true all at once that perhaps this one will, too. Do you think it's possible?"

"Diana Barry lives over at Orchard Slope and she's about your age. She's a very nice little girl, and perhaps she will be a playmate for you when she comes home. She's visiting her aunt over at Carmody just now. You'll have to be careful how you behave yourself, though. Mrs. Barry is a very particular woman. She won't let Diana play with any little girl who isn't nice and good."

Anne looked at Marilla through the apple blossoms, her eyes **aglow** with interest.

aglow [ə'gləʊ]
adj. 光照融融

"What is Diana like? Her hair isn't red, is it? Oh, I hope not. It's bad enough to have red hair myself, but I positively couldn't endure it in a bosom friend."

"Diana is a very pretty little girl. She has black eyes and hair and rosy cheeks. And she is good and smart, which is better than being pretty."

Marilla was as fond of **morals** as the Duchess in Wonderland, and was firmly **convinced** that one should be **tacked on** to every **remark** made to a child who was being brought up.

But Anne waved the moral **inconsequently** aside and seized only on the delightful possibilities before it.

moral ['mɒrəl]
n. 品行
convinced [kən'vɪnst]
adj. 确信
tack on
附加，添加
remark [rɪ'mɑːk]
n. 评论
inconsequently
[ɪn'kɒnsɪkwəntli]
adv. 无所谓

"Oh, I'm so glad she's pretty. Next to being beautiful oneself—and that's impossible in my case—it would be best to have a beautiful bosom friend. When I lived with Mrs. Thomas she had a bookcase in her sitting room with glass doors. There weren't any books in it; Mrs. Thomas kept her best China and her preserves there—when she had any preserves to keep. One of the doors was broken. Mr. Thomas smashed it one night when he was slightly **intoxicated**. But the other

intoxicated
[ɪn'tɒksɪkeɪtɪd]
adj. 喝醉的

was whole and I used to pretend that my reflection in it was another little girl who lived in it. I called her Katie Maurice, and we were very intimate. I used to talk to her by the hour, especially on Sunday, and tell her everything. Katie was the comfort and **consolation** of my life. We used to pretend that the bookcase was **enchanted** and that if I only knew the spell I could open the door and step right into the room where Katie Maurice lived, instead of into Mrs. Thomas' shelves of preserves and China. And then Katie Maurice would have taken me by the hand and led me out into a wonderful place, all flowers and sunshine and fairies, and we would have lived there happy for ever after. When I went to live with Mrs. Hammond it just broke my heart to leave Katie Maurice. She felt it dreadfully, too, I know she did, for she was crying when she kissed me good-bye through the bookcase door. There was no bookcase at Mrs. Hammond's. But just up the river a little way from the house there was a long green little valley, and the loveliest echo lived there. It **echoed** back every word you said, even if you didn't talk a bit loud. So I imagined that it was a little girl called Violetta and we were great friends and I loved her almost as well as I loved Katie Maurice—not quite, but almost, you know. The night before I went to the asylum I said good-bye to Violetta, and oh, her good-bye came back to me in such sad, sad tones. I had become so attached to her that I hadn't the heart to imagine a bosom friend at the asylum, even if there had been any scope for imagination there."

"I think it's just as well there wasn't," said Marilla drily. "I don't approve of such goings-on. You seem to half believe your own imaginations. It will be well for you to have a real live friend to put such **nonsense** out of your head. But don't let Mrs. Barry hear you talking about your Katie Maurices and your Violettas or she'll think

consolation [ˌkɒnsəˈleɪʃn] *n.* 安慰

enchanted [ɪnˈtʃɑːntɪd] *adj.* 施过魔法的

echo [ˈekəʊ] *v.* （声音）回响，发出回声

nonsense [ˈnɒnsns] *n.* 荒谬的想法

you tell stories."

"Oh, I won't. I couldn't talk of them to everybody— their memories are too sacred for that. But I thought I'd like to have you know about them. Oh, look, here's a big bee just tumbled out of an apple blossom. Just think what a lovely place to live—in an apple blossom! Fancy going to sleep in it when the wind was rocking it. If I wasn't a human girl I think I'd like to be a bee and live among the flowers."

"Yesterday you wanted to be a sea gull," sniffed Marilla. "I think you are very **fickle** minded. I told you to learn that prayer and not talk. But it seems impossible for you to stop talking if you've got anybody that will listen to you. So go up to your room and learn it."

fickle [ˈfɪkl]
adj. 易变的

"Oh, I know it pretty nearly all now—all but just the last line."

"Well, never mind, do as I tell you. Go to your room and finish learning it well, and stay there until I call you down to help me get tea."

"Can I take the apple blossoms with me for company?" pleaded Anne.

"No; you don't want your room **cluttered** up with flowers. You should have left them on the tree in the first place."

clutter [ˈklʌtə(r)]
v. 凌乱地塞满

"I did feel a little that way, too," said Anne. "I kind of felt I shouldn't shorten their lovely lives by picking them—I wouldn't want to be picked if I were an apple blossom. But the **temptation** was **irresistible**. What do you do when you meet with an irresistible temptation?"

temptation [tempˈteɪʃn]
n. 诱惑
irresistible [ˌɪrɪˈzɪstəbl]
adj. 无法抗拒的

"Anne, did you hear me tell you to go to your room?"

Anne sighed, retreated to the east gable, and sat down in a chair by the window.

"There—I know this prayer. I learned that last sentence coming upstairs. Now I'm going to imagine things into this room so that they'll always stay imagined. The floor is covered with a white **velvet** carpet with pink roses all over it and there are pink silk curtains at the windows. The walls are hung with gold and silver **brocade tapestry**. The furniture is **mahogany**. I never saw any mahogany, but it does sound so luxurious. This is a couch all heaped with gorgeous silken cushions, pink and blue and **crimson** and gold, and I am reclining gracefully on it. I can see my reflection in that splendid big mirror hanging on the wall. I am tall and regal, clad in a gown of trailing white lace, with a pearl cross on my breast and pearls in my hair. My hair is of midnight darkness and my skin is a clear ivory pallor. My name is the Lady Cordelia Fitzgerald. No, it isn't—I can't make that seem real."

velvet [ˈvelvɪt] *n.* 天鹅绒
brocade [brəˈkeɪd] *n.* 锦缎
tapestry [ˈtæpəstri] *n.* 挂毯
mahogany [məˈhɒgəni] *n.* 桃花心木
crimson [ˈkrɪmzn] *adj.* 深红色的

She danced up to the little looking-glass and peered into it. Her pointed freckled face and solemn gray eyes peered back at her.

"You're only Anne of Green Gables," she said earnestly, "and I see you, just as you are looking now, whenever I try to imagine I'm the Lady Cordelia. But it's a million times nicer to be Anne of Green Gables than Anne of nowhere in particular, isn't it?"

She bent forward, kissed her reflection **affectionately**, and **betook herself** to the open window.

affectionately [əˈfekʃənətli] *adv.* 深情地
betake herself 前往,去(某处)

"Dear Snow Queen, good afternoon. And good afternoon dear birches down in the hollow. And good afternoon, dear gray house up on the hill. I wonder if Diana is to be my bosom friend. I hope she will, and I shall love her very much. But I must never quite forget Katie Maurice and Violetta. They would feel so hurt if I did and I'd hate to hurt anybody's feelings, even a little bookcase girl's or a little echo girl's. I must be careful to remember them and send them a kiss every day."

Anne blew a couple of airy kisses from her fingertips past the cherry blossoms and then, with her chin in her hands, **drifted** luxuriously out on a sea of daydreams.

drift ['drɪft]
v. 不知不觉陷入

CHAPTER IX

Mrs. Rachel Lynde Is Properly Horrified

Anne had been a fortnight at Green Gables before Mrs. Lynde arrived to inspect her. Mrs. Rachel, to do her justice, was not to blame for this. A severe and unseason-able attack of grippe had confined that good lady to her house ever since the occasion of her last visit to Green Gables. Mrs. Rachel was not often sick and had a well-defined **contempt** for people who were; but grippe, she **asserted**, was like no other illness on earth and could only be interpreted as one of the special visitations of Providence. As soon as her doctor allowed her to put her foot out-of-doors she hurried up to Green Gables, **bursting with** curiosity to see Matthew and Marilla' s orphan, concerning whom all sorts of stories and suppositions had gone abroad in Avonlea.

contempt [kən'tempt]
n. 轻视
asserted [ə'sɜːtɪd]
adj. 宣称的

be bursting with sth.
充满某物

Anne had made good use of every waking moment of that fortnight. Already she was **acquainted** with every tree and **shrub** about the place. She had discovered that a **lane** opened out below the apple orchard and ran up through a belt of woodland; and she had explored it to its furthest end in all its delicious **vagaries** of brook and bridge, fir **coppice** and wild cherry arch, corners thick with fern, and branching byways of maple and mountain ash.

acquainted [ə'kweɪntɪd]
adj. 认识的(但不了解)
shrub [ʃrʌb]
n. 灌木
lane [leɪn]
n. (乡间)小路
vagaries ['veɪgəriz]
n. 变幻莫测
coppice ['kɒpɪs]
n. 矮林

She had made friends with the spring down in the hollow—that wonderful deep, clear icy-cold spring; it was set about with smooth red sandstones and rimmed in by great palm-like clumps of water fern; and beyond it was a log bridge over the brook.

That bridge led Anne' s dancing feet up over a wooded hill beyond, where **perpetual** twilight reigned under the straight, thick-growing firs and spruces; the only flowers there were myriads of delicate "June bells", those shyest and sweetest of woodland blooms, and a few pale, aerial starflowers, like the spirits of last year's blossoms. **Gossamers** glimmered like threads of silver among the trees and the fir boughs and tassels seemed to utter friendly speech.

All these raptured voyages of exploration were made in the odd half hours which she was allowed for play, and Anne talked Matthew and Marilla halfdeaf over her discoveries. Not that Matthew complained, to be sure; he listened to it all with a wordless smile of enjoyment on his face; Marilla permitted the "chatter" until she found herself becoming too interested in it, whereupon she always promptly **quenched** Anne by a curt command to hold her tongue.

Anne was out in the **orchard** when Mrs. Rachel came, wandering at her own sweet will through the lush, **tremulous** grasses splashed with **ruddy** evening sunshine; so that good lady had an excellent chance to talk her illness fully over, describing every ache and pulse beat with such evident enjoyment that Marilla thought even grippe must bring its **compensations**. When details were exhausted Mrs. Rachel introduced the real reason of her call.

"I've been hearing some surprising things about you and Matthew."

"I don't suppose you are any more surprised than I am myself," said Marilla. "I'm getting over my surprise now."

"It was too bad there was such a mistake," said Mrs. Rachel sympathetically. "Couldn't you have sent her back?"

"I suppose we could, but we decided not to. Matthew took a fancy to her. And I must say I like her myself—although I admit she has her faults. The house seems a different place already. She's a real

perpetual [pə'petʃuəl]
adj. 长期的

gossamer ['gɒsəmə(r)]
n. 蛛丝

quench [kwentʃ]
v. 止住

orchard ['ɔːtʃəd]
n. 果园

tremulous ['tremjələs]
adj. 抖动的

ruddy ['rʌdi]
adj. 红的

compensation [ˌkɒmpen'seɪʃn]
n. 补偿

bright little thing."

Marilla said more than she had intended to say when she began, for she read disapproval in Mrs. Rachel's expression.

"It's a great responsibility you've taken on yourself," said that lady gloomily, "especially when you've never had any experience with children. You don't know much about her or her real **disposition**, I suppose, and there's no guessing how a child like that will turn out. But I don't want to discourage you I'm sure, Marilla."

disposition [ˌdɪspəˈzɪʃn]
n. 性情

"I'm not feeling discouraged," was Marilla's dry response. "When I make up my mind to do a thing it stays made up. I suppose you'd like to see Anne. I'll call her in."

Anne came running in presently, her face sparkling with the delight of her orchard **rovings**; but, **abashed** at finding the delight herself in the unexpected presence of a stranger, she halted confusedly inside the door. She certainly was an odd-looking little creature in the short tight wincey dress she had worn from the asylum, below which her thin legs seemed ungracefully long. Her **freckles** were more numerous and **obtrusive** than ever; the wind had **ruffled** her hatless hair into over-brilliant disorder; it had never looked redder than at that moment.

rove [rəʊv]
v. 漫游
abashed [əˈbæʃt]
adj. 羞愧

freckle [ˈfrekl]
n. (皮肤)雀斑
obtrusive [əbˈtruːsɪv]
adj. 突出的
ruffle [ˈrʌfəl]
v. 把(平整的表面)弄乱(弄皱)

"Well, they didn't pick you for your looks, that's sure and certain," was Mrs. Rachel Lynde's **emphatic** comment. Mrs. Rachel was one of those delightful and popular people who pride themselves on speaking their mind without fear or favor. "She's terrible skinny and homely, Marilla. Come here, child, and let me have a look at you. Lawful heart, did any one ever see such freckles? And hair as red as carrots! Come here, child, I say."

emphatic [ɪmˈfætɪk]
adj. 强调的

Anne "came there", but not exactly as Mrs. Rachel expected. With one bound she crossed the kitchen floor and stood before Mrs.

Rachel, her face **scarlet** with anger, her lips **quivering**, and her whole **slender** form trembling from head to foot.

"I hate you," she cried in a choked voice, stamping her foot on the floor. "I hate you—I hate you—I hate you—" a louder stamp with each **assertion** of hatred. "How dare you call me skinny and ugly? How dare you say I'm freckled and redheaded? You are a rude, impolite, unfeeling woman!"

"Anne!" exclaimed Marilla in consternation.

But Anne continued to face Mrs. Rachel undauntedly, head up, eyes blazing, hands clenched, passionate **indignation exhaling** from her like an atmosphere.

"How dare you say such things about me?" she repeated **vehemently**. "How would you like to have such things said about you? How would you like to be told that you are fat and **clumsy** and probably hadn't a spark of imagination in you? I don't care if I do hurt your feelings by saying so! I hope I hurt them. You have hurt mine worse than they were ever hurt before even by Mrs. Thomas' intoxicated husband. And I'll never forgive you for it, never, never!"

Stamp! Stamp!

"Did anybody ever see such a temper!" exclaimed the horrified Mrs. Rachel.

"Anne go to your room and stay there until I come up," said Marilla, recovering her powers of speech with difficulty.

Anne, bursting into tears, rushed to the hall door, slammed it until the tins on the **porch** wall outside **rattled** in sympathy, and fled through the hall and up the stairs like a **whirlwind**. A **subdued** slam above told that the door of the east gable had been shut with equal **vehemence**.

"Well, I don't envy you your job bringing that up, Marilla," said

scarlet [ˈskɑːlət]
adj. 猩红的
quiver [ˈkwɪvə]
v. 颤抖,发抖
slender [ˈslendə(r)]
adj. 苗条的

assertion [əˈsɜːʃn]
n. 断言

indignation [ˌɪndɪɡˈneɪʃn]
n. 愤怒
exhale [eksˈheɪl]
v. 呼气
vehemently [ˈviːəməntli]
adv. 激烈地
clumsy [ˈklʌmzi]
adj. 笨拙的

porch [pɔːtʃ]
n. 门廊
rattle [ˈrætl]
v. 发出咔嗒声
whirlwind [ˈwɜːlwɪnd]
n. 旋风
subdued [səbˈdjuːd]
adj. (声音)压低的
vehemence [ˈviːəməns]
n. 激烈

Mrs. Rachel with unspeakable **solemnity**.

Marilla opened her lips to say she knew not what of apology or **deprecation**. What she did say was a surprise to herself then and ever afterwards.

"You shouldn't have twitted her about her looks, Rachel."

"Marilla Cuthbert, you don't mean to say that you are upholding her in such a terrible display of temper as we've just seen?" demanded Mrs. Rachel indignantly.

"No," said Marilla slowly, "I'm not trying to excuse her. She's been very naughty and I'll have to give her a talking to about it. But we must **make allowances** for her. She's never been taught what is right. And you were too hard on her, Rachel."

Marilla could not help tacking on that last sentence, although she was again surprised at herself for doing it. Mrs. Rachel got up with an air of offended dignity.

"Well, I see that I'll have to be very careful what I say after this, Marilla, since the fine feelings of orphans, brought from goodness knows where, have to be considered before anything else. Oh, no, I'm not vexed—don't worry yourself. I'm too sorry for you to leave any room for anger in my mind. You'll have your own troubles with that child. But if you'll take my advice—which I suppose you won't do, although I've brought up ten children and buried two—you'll do that 'talking to' you mention with a fair-sized birch switch. I should think that would be the most effective language for that kind of a child. Her temper matches her hair I guess. Well, good evening, Marilla. I hope you'll come down to see me often as usual. But you can't expect me to visit here again in a hurry, if I'm liable to be flown at and **insulted** in such a fashion. It's something new in my experience."

Whereat Mrs. Rachel swept out and away—if a fat woman who

solemnity [səˈlemnəti]
n. 庄重；严肃

deprecation [ˌdeprəˈkeɪʃn]
n. 贬低

make allowances
谅解，宽恕

insult [ɪnˈsʌlt]
v. 侮辱

always **waddled** could be said to sweep away—and Marilla with a very **solemn** face betook herself to the east gable.

On the way upstairs she **pondered** uneasily as to what she ought to do. She felt no little dismay over the scene that had just been enacted. How unfortunate that Anne should have displayed such temper before Mrs. Rachel Lynde, of all people! Then Marilla suddenly became aware of an uncomfortable and **rebuking** consciousness that she felt more humiliation over this than sorrow over the discovery of such a serious defect in Anne's disposition. And how was she to punish her? The **amiable** suggestion of the birch switch—to the efficiency of which all of Mrs. Rachel's own children could have **borne** smarting **testimony**—did not appeal to Marilla. She did not believe she could whip a child. No, some other method of punishment must be found to bring Anne to a proper realization of the enormity of her offense.

Marilla found Anne face downward on her bed, crying bitterly, quite oblivious of muddy boots on a clean **counterpane**.

"Anne," she said not ungently.

No answer.

"Anne," with greater **severity**, "get off that bed this minute and listen to what I have to say to you."

Anne **squirmed** off the bed and sat rigidly on a chair beside it, her face swollen and **tear-stained** and her eyes fixed stubbornly on the floor.

"This is a nice way for you to behave. Anne! Aren't you ashamed of yourself?"

"She hadn't any right to call me ugly and redheaded," retorted Anne, **evasive** and **defiant**.

"You hadn't any right to fly into such a fury and talk the way you

waddle [ˈwɒdl]
v. 摇摇摆摆地走
solemn [ˈsɒləm]
adj. 表情严肃的
ponder [ˈpɒndə(r)]
v. 仔细考虑

rebuke [rɪˈbjuːk]
v. 斥责

amiable [ˈeɪmiəbl]
adj. 和蔼可亲的
borne testimony to...
见证,作证

counterpane [ˈkaʊntəpeɪn]
n. 床罩

severity [sɪˈverəti]
n. 严重

squirm [skwɜːm]
v. 扭动
tear-stained [ˈtɪə steɪnd]
adj. 布满泪痕的

evasive [ɪˈveɪsɪv]
adj. 推诿的;回避提问的
defiant [dɪˈfaɪənt]
adj. 违抗的

did to her, Anne. I was ashamed of you— thoroughly ashamed of you. I wanted you to behave nicely to Mrs. Lynde, and instead of that you have disgraced me. I'm sure I don't know why you should lose your temper like that just because Mrs. Lynde said you were redhaired and homely. You say it yourself often enough."

"Oh, but there's such a difference between saying a thing yourself and hearing other people say it," wailed Anne. "You may know a thing is so, but you can't help hoping other people don't quite think it is. I suppose you think I have an awful temper, but I couldn't help it. When she said those things something just rose right up in me and choked me. I had to fly out at her."

"Well, you made a fine exhibition of yourself I must say. Mrs. Lynde will have a nice story to tell about you everywhere—and she'll tell it, too. It was a dreadful thing for you to lose your temper like that, Anne."

"Just imagine how you would feel if somebody told you to your face that you were skinny and ugly," pleaded Anne tearfully.

An old remembrance suddenly rose up before Marilla. She had been a very small child when she had heard one aunt say of her to another, "What a pity she is such a dark, homely little thing." Marilla was every day of fifty before the **sting** had gone out of that memory.

"I don't say that I think Mrs. Lynde was exactly right in saying what she did to you, Anne," she admitted in a softer tone. "Rachel is too outspoken. But that is no excuse for such behavior on your part. She was a stranger and an elderly person and my visitor—all three very good reasons why you should have been respectful to her. You were rude and **saucy** and"—Marilla had a saving **inspiration** of punishment—"you must go to her and tell her you are very sorry for your bad temper and ask her to forgive you."

sting [stɪŋ]
n. 刺伤

saucy [ˈsɔːsi]
adj. 粗鲁的
inspiration
[ˌɪnspəˈreɪʃn]
n. 灵感

"I can never do that," said Anne **determinedly** and darkly. "You can punish me in any way you like, Marilla. You can shut me up in a dark, damp **dungeon** inhabited by snakes and **toads** and feed me only on bread and water and I shall not complain. But I cannot ask Mrs. Lynde to forgive me."

"We're not in the habit of shutting people up in dark damp dungeons," said Marilla drily, "especially as they're rather scarce in Avonlea. But apologize to Mrs. Lynde you must and shall and you'll stay here in your room until you can tell me you're willing to do it."

"I shall have to stay here forever then," said Anne mournfully, "because I can't tell Mrs. Lynde I'm sorry I said those things to her. How can I? I'm not sorry. I'm sorry I've **vexed** you; but I'm glad I told her just what I did. It was a great satisfaction. I can't say I'm sorry when I'm not, can I? I can't even imagine I'm sorry."

"Perhaps your imagination will be in better working order by the morning," said Marilla, rising to depart. "You'll have the night to think over your conduct in and come to a better frame of mind. You said you would try to be a very good girl if we kept you at Green Gables, but I must say it hasn't seemed very much like it this evening."

Leaving this Parthian shaft to **rankle** in Anne's stormy bosom, Marilla descended to the kitchen, grievously troubled in mind and vexed in soul. She was as angry with herself as with Anne, because, whenever she recalled Mrs. Rachel's **dumbfounded** countenance her lips twitched with amusement and she felt a most **reprehensible** desire to laugh.

determinedly [dɪˈtɜːmɪndli] *adv.* 决然地
dungeon [ˈdʌndʒən] *n.* 地牢
toad [təʊd] *n.* 蟾蜍
vex [veks] *v.* 使恼怒
rankle [ˈræŋkl] *v.* 使人耿耿于怀
dumbfounded [dʌmˈfaʊndɪd] *adj.* 目瞪口呆的
reprehensible [ˌreprɪˈhensəbl] *adj.* 应斥责的

CHAPTER X

Anne's Apology

Marilla said nothing to Matthew about the affair that evening; but when Anne proved still **refractory** the next morning an explanation had to be made to account for her absence from the breakfast table. Marilla told Matthew the whole story, taking pains to impress him with a due sense of the **enormity** of Anne's behavior.

"It's a good thing Rachel Lynde got a calling down; she's a **meddlesome** old gossip," was Matthew's **consolatory rejoinder**.

"Matthew Cuthbert, I'm **astonished** at you. You know that Anne's behavior was dreadful, and yet you take her part! I suppose you'll be saying next thing that she oughtn't to be punished at all!"

"Well now—no—not exactly," said Matthew uneasily. "I reckon she ought to be punished a little. But don't be too hard on her, Marilla. Recollect she hasn't ever had anyone to teach her right. You're— you're going to give her something to eat, aren't you?"

"When did you ever hear of me starving people into good behavior?" demanded Marilla **indignantly**. "She'll have her meals regular, and I'll carry them up to her myself. But she'll stay up there until she's willing to apologize to Mrs. Lynde, and that's final, Matthew."

Breakfast, dinner, and supper were very silent meals—for Anne still remained **obdurate**. After each meal Marilla carried a well-filled tray to the east gable and brought it down later on not noticeably **depleted**.

Matthew eyed its last descent with a troubled eye. Had Anne eaten anything at all?

When Marilla went out that evening to bring the cows from the back **pasture**, Matthew, who had been hanging about the barns and

refractory [rɪ'fræktəri] *adj.* 难治的

enormity [ɪ'nɔːməti] *n.* 严重性

meddlesome ['medlsəm] *adj.* 爱管闲事的

consolatory [kən'sɒlətəri] *adj.* 安慰的

rejoinder [rɪ'dʒɔɪndə(r)] *n.* 反驳

astonished [ə'stɒnɪʃt] *adj.* 十分震惊的

indignantly [ɪn'dɪgnəntli] *adv.* 愤怒地

obdurate ['ɒbdjərət] *adj.* 顽固的

deplete [dɪ'pliːt] *v.* 减少，损耗

pasture ['pɑːstʃə(r)] *n.* 牧场

watching, slipped into the house with the air of a **burglar** and crept upstairs. As a general thing Matthew **gravitated** between the kitchen and the little bedroom off the hall where he slept; once in a while he **ventured** uncomfortably into the **parlour** or sitting room when the minister came to tea. But he had never been upstairs in his own house since the spring he helped Marilla paper the spare bedroom, and that was four years ago.

burglar [ˈbɜːglə(r)]
n. 入室行窃者
gravitate [ˈgrævɪteɪt]
v. 被……吸引到
venture [ˈventʃə(r)]
v. 冒险
parlour [ˈpɑːlə(r)]
n. 会客厅

He **tiptoed** along the hall and stood for several minutes outside the door of the east gable before he **summoned** courage to tap on it with his fingers and then open the door to peep in.

tiptoe [ˈtɪptəʊ]
v. 踮着脚走
summon [ˈsʌmən]
v. 鼓起(勇气)

Anne was sitting on the yellow chair by the window gazing mournfully out into the garden. Very small and unhappy she looked, and Matthew's heart **smote** him. He softly closed the door and tiptoed over to her.

smite [smaɪt]
v. 重击

"Anne," he whispered, as if afraid of being overheard, "how are you making it, Anne?"

Anne smiled **wanly**.

wanly [ˈwɒnli]
adv. 苍白地

"Pretty well. I imagine a good deal, and that helps to pass the time. Of course, it's rather lonesome. But then, I may as well get used to that."

Anne smiled again, bravely facing the long years of solitary **imprisonment** before her.

imprisonment
[ɪmˈprɪznmənt]
n. 监禁

Matthew recollected that he must say what he had come to say without loss of time, lest Marilla return prematurely. "Well now, Anne, don't you think you'd better do it and have it over with?" he whispered. "It'll have to be done sooner or later, you know, for Marilla's a dreadful determined woman—dreadful determined, Anne. Do it right off, I say, and have it over."

"Do you mean apologize to Mrs. Lynde?"

"Yes—apologize—that's the very word," said Matthew eagerly. "Just smooth it over so to speak. That's what I was trying to get at."

"I suppose I could do it to oblige you," said Anne thoughtfully. "It would be true enough to say I am sorry, because I am sorry now. I wasn't a bit sorry last night. I was mad clear through, and I stayed mad all night. I know I did because I woke up three times and I was just **furious** every time. But this morning it was over. I wasn't in a temper anymore—and it left a dreadful sort of goneness, too. I felt so ashamed of myself. But I just couldn't think of going and telling Mrs. Lynde so. It would be so **humiliating**. I made up my mind I'd stay shut up here forever rather than do that. But still—I'd do anything for you—if you really want me to—"

furious [ˈfjʊəriəs] *adj.* 狂怒的

humiliating [hjuːˈmɪlieɪtɪŋ] *adj.* 丢脸的

"Well now, of course I do. It's terrible lonesome downstairs without you. Just go and smooth things over—that's a good girl."

"Very well," said Anne **resignedly**. "I'll tell Marilla as soon as she comes in I've **repented**."

resignedly [rɪˈzaɪnɪdli] *adv.* 顺从地

repent [rɪˈpent] *v.* 后悔

"That's right—that's right, Anne. But don't tell Marilla I said anything about it. She might think I was putting my oar in and I promised not to do that."

"Wild horses won't drag the secret from me," promised Anne solemnly. "How would wild horses drag a secret from a person anyhow?"

But Matthew was gone, scared at his own success. He fled **hastily** to the remotest corner of the horse pasture lest Marilla should suspect what he had been up to. Marilla herself, upon her return to the house, was agreeably surprised to hear a plaintive voice calling, "Marilla" over the **banisters**.

hastily [ˈheɪstɪli] *adv.* 匆忙地

banisters [ˈbænɪstə(r)] *n.* (楼梯)扶手

"Well?" she said, going into the hall.

"I'm sorry I lost my temper and said rude things, and I'm willing to go and tell Mrs. Lynde so."

"Very well." Marilla's **crispness** gave no sign of her relief. She had been wondering what under the **canopy** she should do if Anne did not give in. "I'll take you down after milking."

Accordingly, after milking, behold Marilla and Anne walking down the lane, the former erect and **triumphant**, the latter drooping and dejected. But halfway down Anne's **dejection** vanished as if by **enchantment**. She lifted her head and stepped lightly along, her eyes fixed on the sunset sky and an air of subdued **exhilaration** about her. Marilla beheld the change disapprovingly. This was no meek **penitent** such as it **behooved** her to take into the presence of the offended Mrs. Lynde.

"What are you thinking of, Anne?" she asked sharply.

"I'm imagining out what I must say to Mrs. Lynde," answered Anne dreamily.

This was satisfactory—or should have been so. But Marilla could not rid herself of the notion that something in her scheme of punishment was going **askew**. Anne had no business to look so rapt and radiant.

Rapt and radiant Anne continued until they were in the very presence of Mrs. Lynde, who was sitting knitting by her kitchen window. Then the **radiance** vanished. Mournful penitence appeared on every feature. Before a word was spoken Anne suddenly went down on her knees before the astonished Mrs. Rachel and held out her hands **beseechingly**.

"Oh, Mrs. Lynde, I am so extremely sorry," she said with a quiver in her voice. "I could never express all my sorrow, no, not if I used up a whole dictionary. You must just imagine it. I behaved terribly to you—and I've disgraced the dear friends, Matthew and Marilla, who have let me stay at Green Gables although I'm not a boy. I'm a

crispness [ˈkrɪspnəs]
n.（言行）干脆利落，利索

canopy [ˈkænəpi]
n. 罩盖

triumphant [traɪˈʌmfənt]
adj. 扬扬得意的

dejection [dɪˈdʒekʃn]
n. 沮丧

enchantment [ɪnˈtʃɑːntmənt]
n. 被施魔法

exhilaration [ɪɡˌzɪləˈreɪʃn]
n. 兴奋

penitent [ˈpenɪtənt]
n. 忏悔者

behoove [bɪˈhəʊv]
v. 对……来说有必要

askew [əˈskjuː]
adj. 歪斜的

radiance [ˈreɪdiəns]
n. 光辉

beseechingly [bɪˈsiːtʃɪŋli]
adv. 恳求地

dreadfully wicked and ungrateful girl, and I deserve to be punished and cast out by respectable people forever. It was very **wicked** of me to fly into a temper because you told me the truth. It was the truth; every word you said was true. My hair is red and I'm freckled and skinny and ugly. What I said to you was true, too, but I shouldn't have said it. Oh, Mrs. Lynde, please, please, forgive me. If you refuse it will be a lifelong sorrow on a poor little orphan girl would you, even if she had a dreadful temper? Oh, I am sure you wouldn't. Please say you forgive me, Mrs. Lynde."

wicked [ˈwɪkɪd]
adj. 邪恶的

Anne **clasped** her hands together, bowed her head, and waited for the word of judgment.

clasp [klɑːsp]
v. 握紧

There was no mistaking her sincerity—it breathed in every tone of her voice. Both Marilla and Mrs. Lynde recognized its unmistakable ring. But the former understood in dismay that Anne was actually enjoying her valley of humiliation—was reveling in the **thoroughness** of her **abasement**. Where was the wholesome punishment upon which she, Marilla, had **plumed herself**? Anne had turned it into a species of positive pleasure.

thoroughness [ˈθʌrənəs]
n. 完全
abasement [əˈbeɪsmənt]
n. 表现低微
plume herself on...
以……自豪

Good Mrs. Lynde, not being overburdened with **perception**, did not see this. She only perceived that Anne had made a very thorough apology and all **resentment** vanished from her kindly, if somewhat **officious**, heart.

perception [pəˈsepʃn]
n. 认知
resentment [rɪˈzentmənt]
n. 愤恨
officious [əˈfɪʃəs]
adj. 爱发号施令的

"There, there, get up, child," she said heartily. "Of course I forgive you. I guess I was a little too hard on you, anyway. But I'm such an outspoken person. You just mustn't mind me, that's what. It can't be denied your hair is terrible red; but I knew a girl once—went to school with her, in fact—whose hair was every **mite** as red as yours when she was young, but when she grew up it darkened to a real handsome **auburn**. I wouldn't be a mite surprised if yours did, too—not a mite."

mite [maɪt]
n. 一点点
auburn [ˈɔːbən]
n. 红褐色

"Oh, Mrs. Lynde!" Anne drew a long breath as she rose to her feet. "You have given me a hope. I shall always feel that you are a benefactor. Oh, I could endure anything if I only thought my hair would be a handsome auburn when I grew up. It would be so much easier to be good if one's hair was a handsome auburn, don't you think? And now may I go out into your garden and sit on that bench under the apple-trees while you and Marilla are talking? There is so much more scope for imagination out there."

"Laws, yes, run along, child. And you can pick a bouquet of them white June lilies over in the corner if you like."

As the door closed behind Anne Mrs. Lynde got **briskly** up to light a lamp.

"She's a real odd little thing. Take this chair, Marilla; it's easier than the one you've got; I just keep that for the hired boy to sit on. Yes, she certainly is an odd child, but there is something kind of taking about her after all. I don't feel so surprised at you and Matthew keeping her as I did—nor so sorry for you, either. She may turn out all right. Of course, she has a **queer** way of expressing herself—a little too—well, too kind of **forcible**, you know; but she'll likely get over that now that she's come to live among civilized folks. And then, her temper's pretty quick, I guess; but there's one comfort, a child that has a quick temper, just blaze up and cool down, ain't never likely to be sly or **deceitful**. Preserve me from a sly child, that's what. On the whole, Marilla, I kind of like her."

When Marilla went home Anne came out of the **fragrant** twilight of the orchard with a sheaf of white narcissi in her hands.

"I apologized pretty well, didn't I?" she said proudly as they went down the lane. "I thought since I had to do it I might as well do it thoroughly."

briskly [ˈbrɪskli] *adv.* 麻利地

queer [kwɪə(r)] *adj.* 奇怪的

forcible [ˈfɔːsəbl] *adj.* 强行的；暴力的

deceitful [dɪˈsiːtfl] *adj.* 欺骗的

fragrant [ˈfreɪgrənt] *adj.* 芳香的

"You did it thoroughly, all right enough," was Marilla's comment. Marilla was dismayed at finding herself inclined to laugh over the recollection. She had also an uneasy feeling that she ought to scold Anne for apologizing so well; but then, that was ridiculous! She **compromised** with her conscience by saying severely:

"I hope you won't have occasion to make many more such apologies. I hope you'll try to control your temper now, Anne."

"That wouldn't be so hard if people wouldn't **twit** me about my looks," said Anne with a sigh. "I don't get cross about other things; but I'm so tired of being twitted about my hair and it just makes me boil right over. Do you suppose my hair will really be a handsome auburn when I grow up?"

"You shouldn't think so much about your looks, Anne. I'm afraid you are a very vain little girl."

"How can I be **vain** when I know I'm homely?" protested Anne. "I love pretty things; and I hate to look in the glass and see something that isn't pretty. It makes me feel so sorrowful—just as I feel when I look at any ugly thing. I pity it because it isn't beautiful."

"Handsome is as handsome does," quoted Marilla.

"I've had that said to me before, but I have my doubts about it," remarked skeptical Anne, **sniffing** at her **narcissi**. "Oh, aren't these flowers sweet! It was lovely of Mrs. Lynde to give them to me. I have no hard feelings against Mrs. Lynde now. It gives you a lovely, comfortable feeling to apologize and be forgiven, doesn't it? Aren't the stars bright tonight? If you could live in a star, which one would you pick? I'd like that lovely clear big one away over there above that dark hill."

"Anne, do hold your tongue." said Marilla, thoroughly worn out trying to follow the **gyrations** of Anne's thoughts.

compromise [ˈkɒmprəmaɪz]
v. 妥协

twit [twɪt]
n. 讥笑

vain [veɪn]
adj. 虚荣的

sniff [snɪf]
v. 嗅，闻
narcissi [nɑːˈsɪsaɪ]
n. 水仙花

gyration [dʒaɪˈreɪʃn]
n. 旋转

Anne said no more until they turned into their own lane. A little **gypsy** wind came down it to meet them, laden with the spicy perfume of young dew-wet ferns. Far up in the shadows a cheerful light **gleamed** out through the trees from the kitchen at Green Gables. Anne suddenly came close to Marilla and slipped her hand into the older woman's hard palm.

gypsy [ˈdʒɪpsi] *n.* 吉卜赛人

gleam [gliːm] *v.* 发微光

"It's lovely to be going home and know it's home," she said. "I love Green Gables already, and I never loved any place before. No place ever seemed like home. Oh, Marilla, I'm so happy. I could pray right now and not find it a bit hard."

Something warm and pleasant welled up in Marilla's heart at touch of that thin little hand in her own—a **throb** of the **maternity** she had missed, perhaps. Its very unaccustomedness and sweetness disturbed her. She hastened to restore her sensations to their normal calm by **inculcating** a moral.

throb [θrɒb] *n.* (有规律地)抽动

maternity [məˈtɜːnəti] *n.* 母性

inculcate [ˈɪnkʌlkeɪt] *v.* 谆谆教诲

"If you'll be a good girl you'll always be happy, Anne. And you should never find it hard to say your prayers."

"Saying one's prayers isn't exactly the same thing as praying," said Anne **meditatively**. "But I'm going to imagine that I'm the wind that is blowing up there in those tree tops. When I get tired of the trees I'll imagine I'm gently waving down here in the ferns—and then I'll fly over to Mrs. Lynde's garden and set the flowers dancing—and then I'll go with one great swoop over the clover field—and then I'll blow over the Lake of Shining Waters and ripple it all up into little sparkling waves. Oh, there's so much scope for imagination in a wind! So I'll not talk any more just now, Marilla."

meditative [ˈmedɪtətɪv] *adj.* 深思的

"Thanks be to goodness for that," breathed Marilla in devout relief.

CHAPTER XI

Anne's Impressions of Sunday-School

"Well, how do you like them?" said Marilla.

Anne was standing in the gable room, looking solemnly at three new dresses spread out on the bed. One was of **snuffy** colored **ging-ham** which Marilla had been tempted to buy from a peddler the preceding summer because it looked so serviceable; one was of black-and-white checkered sateen which she had picked up at a **bargain** counter in the winter; and one was a stiff print of an ugly blue shade which she had purchased that week at a Carmody store.

She had made them up herself, and they were all made **alike**—plain skirts fulled tightly to plain waists, with sleeves as plain as waist and skirt and tight as sleeves could be.

"I'll imagine that I like them," said Anne **soberly**.

"I don't want you to imagine it," said Marilla, offended. "Oh, I can see you don't like the dresses! What is the matter with them? Aren't they neat and clean and new?"

"Yes."

"Then why don't you like them?"

"They're—they're not—pretty," said Anne **reluctantly**.

"Pretty!" Marilla sniffed. "I didn't trouble my head about getting pretty dresses for you. I don't believe in **pampering** vanity, Anne, I'll tell you that right off. Those dresses are good, sensible, serviceable dresses, without any **frills** or **furbelows** about them, and they're all you'll get this summer. The brown gingham and the blue print will do you for school when you begin to go. The **sateen** is for church and Sunday school. I'll expect you to keep them neat and clean and not to tear them. I should think you'd be grateful to get most any-

snuffy [ˈsnʌfi]
adj. 鼻烟一样的
gingham [ˈgɪŋəm]
n. 格子棉布

bargain [ˈbɑːgən]
n. 便宜货

alike [əˈlaɪk]
adj. 相似的

soberly [ˈsəʊbəli]
adv. 冷静地

reluctantly [rɪˈlʌktəntli]
adv. 不情愿地

pamper [ˈpæmpə(r)]
v. 纵容

frill [frɪl]
n. 装饰
furbelow [ˈfɜːbɪləʊ]
n. 俗丽的装饰
sateen [sæˈtiːn]
n. 棉缎

thing after those skimpy **wincey** things you've been wearing."

wincey ['wɪnsi] *n.* 棉绒

"Oh, I am grateful," protested Anne. "But I'd be ever so much gratefuller if—if you'd made just one of them with puffed sleeves. Puffed sleeves are so fashionable now. It would give me such a thrill, Marilla, just to wear a dress with puffed sleeves."

"Well, you'll have to do without your thrill. I hadn't any material to waste on puffed sleeves. I think they are ridiculous-looking things anyhow. I prefer the plain, sensible ones."

"But I'd rather look ridiculous when everybody else does than plain and sensible all by myself," persisted Anne mournfully.

"Trust you for that! Well, hang those dresses carefully up in your closet, and then sit down and learn the Sunday school lesson. I got a **quarterly** from Mr. Bell for you and you'll go to Sunday school tomorrow," said Marilla, disappearing downstairs in high dudgeon.

quarterly ['kwɔːtəli] *n.* 季刊

Anne clasped her hands and looked at the dresses.

"I did hope there would be a white one with puffed sleeves," she whispered **disconsolately**. "I prayed for one, but I didn't much expect it on that account. I didn't suppose God would have time to bother about a little orphan girl's dress. I knew I'd just have to depend on Marilla for it. Well, fortunately I can imagine that one of them is of snow-white **muslin** with lovely lace frills and three-puffed sleeves."

disconsolately [dɪs'kɒnsələtli] *adv.* 悲伤地

muslin ['mʌzlɪn] *n.* 平纹细布

The next morning warnings of a sick headache prevented Marilla from going to Sunday-school with Anne.

"You'll have to go down and call for Mrs. Lynde, Anne." she said. "She'll see that you get into the right class. Now, mind you behave yourself properly. Stay to preaching afterwards and ask Mrs. Lynde to show you our **pew**. Here's a cent for collection. Don't stare at people and don't **fidget**. I shall expect you to tell me the text when you come home."

pew [pjuː] *n.* 教堂长椅

fidget ['fɪdʒɪt] *v.* 坐立不安

Anne started off **irreproachable**, arrayed in the stiff black-and-white sateen, which, while decent as regards length and certainly not open to the charge of **skimpiness**, contrived to emphasize every corner and angle of her thin figure. Her hat was a little, flat, glossy, new sailor, the extreme plainness of which had likewise much disappointed Anne, who had permitted herself secret visions of ribbon and flowers. The latter, however, were supplied before Anne reached the main road, for being confronted halfway down the lane with a golden frenzy of wind-stirred buttercups and a glory of wild roses, Anne promptly and liberally garlanded her hat with a heavy wreath of them. Whatever other people might have thought of the result it satisfied Anne, and she tripped **gaily** down the road, holding her ruddy head with its decoration of pink and yellow very proudly.

irreproachable [ˌɪrɪˈprəʊtʃəbl] *adj.* 无可指责的

skimp [skɪmp] *adj.* （衣、裙等）太短（小）的，暴露的

gaily [ˈgeɪli] *adv.* 欢乐地

When she had reached Mrs. Lynde's house she found that lady gone. **Nothing daunted**, Anne proceeded onward to the church alone. In the porch she found a crowd of little girls, all more or less gaily **attired** in whites and blues and pinks, and all staring with curious eyes at this stranger in their midst, with her extraordinary head **adornment**. Avonlea little girls had already heard queer stories about Anne. Mrs. Lynde said she had an awful temper; Jerry Buote, the hired boy at Green Gables, said she talked all the time to herself or to the trees and flowers like a crazy girl. They looked at her and whispered to each other behind their quarterlies. Nobody made any friendly advances, then or later on when the opening exercises were over and Anne found herself in Miss Rogerson's class.

nothing daunted 毫不气馁

attired [əˈtaɪəd] *adj.* 穿着……衣服

adornment [əˈdɔːnmənt] *n.* 装饰

Miss Rogerson was a middle-aged lady who had taught a Sunday-school class for twenty years. Her method of teaching was to ask the printed questions from the quarterly and look **sternly** over its edge at the particular little girl she thought ought to answer the question. She

sternly [ˈstɜːnli] *adv.* 严厉地

looked very often at Anne, and Anne, thanks to Marilla's **drilling**, answered promptly; but it may be questioned if she understood very much about either question or answer.

She did not think she liked Miss Rogerson, and she felt very miserable; every other little girl in the class had puffed sleeves. Anne felt that life was really not worth living without puffed sleeves.

"Well, how did you like Sunday school?" Marilla wanted to know when Anne came home. Her **wreath** having faded, Anne had **discarded** it in the lane, so Marilla was spared the knowledge of that for a time.

"I didn't like it a bit. It was horrid."

"Anne Shirley!" said Marilla rebukingly.

Anne sat down on the rocker with a long sigh, kissed one of Bonny's leaves, and waved her hand to a blossoming **fuchsia**.

"They might have been **lonesome** while I was away," she explained. "And now about the Sunday school. I behaved well, just as you told me. Mrs. Lynde was gone, but I went right on myself. I went into the church, with a lot of other little girls, and I sat in the corner of a pew by the window while the opening exercises went on. Mr. Bell made an awfully long prayer. I would have been dreadfully tired before he got through if I hadn't been sitting by that window. But it looked right out on the Lake of Shining Waters, so I just gazed at that and imagined all sorts of splendid things."

"You shouldn't have done anything of the sort. You should have listened to Mr. Bell."

"But he wasn't talking to me," protested Anne. "He was talking to God and he didn't seem to be very much interested in it, either. I think he thought God was too far off though. There was long row of white birches hanging over the lake and the sunshine fell down

drilling [drɪlɪŋ]
n. 训练

wreath [riːðz]
n. 花环
discard [dɪˈskɑːd]
v. 丢弃

fuchsia [ˈfjuːʃə]
n. 倒挂金钟(园林植物)
lonesome [ˈləʊnsəm]
adj. 寂寞的

through them, 'way', way down, deep into the water. Oh, Marilla, it was like a beautiful dream! It gave me a thrill and I just said, 'Thank you for it, God', two or three times."

"Not out loud, I hope," said Marilla anxiously.

"Oh, no, just under my breath. Well, Mr. Bell did get through at last and they told me to go into the classroom with Miss Rogerson's class. There were nine other girls in it. They all had puffed sleeves. I tried to imagine mine were puffed, too, but I couldn't. Why couldn't I? It was as easy as could be to imagine they were puffed when I was alone in the east gable, but it was awfully hard there among the others who had really truly puffs."

"You shouldn't have been thinking about your sleeves in Sunday school. You should have been attending to the lesson. I hope you knew it."

"Oh, yes; and I answered a lot of questions. Miss Rogerson asked ever so many. I don't think it was fair for her to do all the asking. There were lots I wanted to ask her, but I didn't like to because I didn't think she was **a kindred spirit**. Then all the other little girls recited a paraphrase. She asked me if I knew any. I told her I didn't, but I could recite, 'The Dog at His Master's Grave' if she liked. That's in the Third Royal Reader. It isn't a really truly religious piece of poetry, but it's so sad and **melancholy** that it might as well be. She said it wouldn't do and she told me to learn the nineteenth **paraphrase** for next Sunday. I read it over in church afterwards and it's splendid. There are two lines in particular that just thrill me."

"'Quick as the **slaughtered squadrons** fell. In Midian's evil day.'"

"I don't know what 'squadrons' means nor 'Midian', either, but it sounds so tragical. I can hardly wait until next Sunday to recite it. I'll practice it all the week. After Sunday school I asked Miss Roger-

a kindred spirit
志趣相投的人

melancholy ['melənkəli]
adj. 令人悲伤的

paraphrase ['pærəfreɪz]
n. 释义

slaughter ['slɔːtə(r)]
v. 屠杀

squadron ['skwɒdrən]
n. 中队

son—because Mrs. Lynde was too far away—to show me your pew. I sat just as still as I could and the text was Revelations, third chapter, second and third **verses**. It was a very long text. If I was a minister I'd pick the short, **snappy** ones. The **sermon** was awfully long, too. I suppose the minister had to match it to the text. I didn't think he was a bit interesting. The trouble with him seems to be that he hasn't enough imagination. I didn't listen to him very much. I just let my thoughts run and I thought of the most surprising things."

verse [vɜːs]
n. （歌曲、诗歌、《圣经》等的）一节
snappy [ˈsnæpi]
adj. （标题、词语等）简洁有趣的
sermon [ˈsɜːmən]
n. 布道

Marilla felt helplessly that all this should be sternly reproved, but she was hampered by the undeniable fact that some of the things Anne had said, especially about the minister's sermons and Mr. Bell's prayers, were what she herself had really thought deep down in her heart for years, but had never given expression to. It almost seemed to her that those secret, **unuttered**, critical thoughts had suddenly taken visible and accusing shape and form in the person of this outspoken **morsel** of neglected humanity.

unuttered [ˌʌnˈʌtəd]
adj. 未说出口的
morsel [ˈmɔːsl]
n. 一点儿

CHAPTER XII

A Solemn Vow and Promise

It was not until the next Friday that Marilla heard the story of the flower-**wreathed** hat. She came home from Mrs. Lynde's and called Anne to account.

wreathe [riːð]
v. 覆盖

"Anne, Mrs. Rachel says you went to church last Sunday with your hat rigged out ridiculous with roses and buttercups. What on earth put you up to such a **caper**? A pretty-looking object you must have been!"

caper [ˈkeɪpə(r)]
n. 雀跃

"Oh. I know pink and yellow aren't becoming to me," began Anne.

"Becoming **fiddlesticks**! It was putting flowers on your hat at

fiddlesticks [ˈfɪdlstɪks]
n. 胡扯，废话（用于表示不同意或不满）

all, no matter what color they were, that was ridiculous. You are the most **aggravating** child!"

aggravating [ˈægrəveɪtɪŋ] *adj.* 令人恼怒的

"I don't see why it's any more ridiculous to wear flowers on your hat than on your dress," protested Anne. "Lots of little girls there had bouquets pinned on their dresses. What's the difference?"

Marilla was not to be drawn from the safe concrete into **dubious** paths of the abstract.

dubious [ˈdjuːbiəsli] *adv.* 靠不住的

"Don't answer me back like that, Anne. It was very silly of you to do such a thing. Never let me catch you at such a trick again. Mrs. Rachel says she thought she would sink through the floor when she come in all **rigged out** like that. She couldn't get near enough to tell you to take them off till it was too late. She says people talked about it something dreadful. Of course, they would think I had no better sense than to let you go decked out like that."

rig somebody out 给(某人)穿上特别(奇异)的衣服

"Oh, I'm so sorry," said Anne, tears welling into her eyes. "I never thought you'd mind. The roses and buttercups were so sweet and pretty I thought they'd look lovely on my hat. Lots of the little girls had artificial flowers on their hats. I'm afraid I'm going to be a dreadful trial to you. Maybe you'd better send me back to the asylum. That would be terrible; I don't think I could endure it; most likely I would go into consumption; I'm so thin as it is, you see. But that would be better than being a trial to you."

"Nonsense," said Marilla, vexed at herself for having made the child cry. "I don't want to send you back to the asylum, I'm sure. All I want is that you should behave like other little girls and not make yourself ridiculous. Don't cry any more. I've got some news for you. Diana Barry came home this afternoon. I'm going up to see if I can borrow a skirt pattern from Mrs. Barry, and if you like you can come with me and get acquainted with Diana."

Anne rose to her feet, with clasped hands, the tears still **glistening** on her cheeks; the dish towel she had been **hemming** slipped **unheeded** to the floor.

glisten [ˈglɪsn]
v. 闪亮
hem [hem]
v. 给……缝褶边
unheeded [ʌnˈhiːdɪd]
adj. 被忽视的

"Oh, Marilla, I'm frightened—now that it has come I'm actually frightened. What if she shouldn't like me! It would be the most tragical disappointment of my life."

"Now, don't get into a **fluster**. And I do wish you wouldn't use such long words. It sounds so funny in a little girl. I guess Diana'll like you well enough. It's her mother you've got to reckon with. If she doesn't like you it won't matter how much Diana does. If she has heard about your **outburst** to Mrs. Lynde and going to church with buttercups round your hat, I don't know what she'll think of you. You must be polite and well behaved, and don't make any of your startling speeches. For pity's sake, if the child isn't actually trembling!"

fluster [ˈflʌstə(r)]
n. 慌乱，紧张，困惑
outburst [ˈaʊtbɜːst]
n. 爆发

Anne was trembling. Her face was pale and tense. "Oh, Marilla, you'd be excited, too, if you were going to meet a little girl you hoped to be your bosom friend and whose mother mightn't like you," she said as she hastened to get her hat.

They went over to Orchard Slope by the short cut across the brook and up the **firry** hill grove. Mrs. Barry came to the kitchen door in answer to Marilla's knock. She was a tall black-eyed, black-haired woman, with a very **resolute** mouth. She had the reputation of being very strict with her children.

firry [ˈfɜːri]
adj. 杉树的
resolute [ˈrezəluːt]
adj. 坚决的

"How do you do, Marilla?" she said cordially. "Come in. And this is the little girl you have adopted, I suppose?"

"Yes, this is Anne Shirley," said Marilla.

"Spelled with an E," gasped Anne, who, tremulous and excited as she was, was determined there should be no misunderstanding on that important point.

Mrs. Barry, not hearing or not comprehending, merely shook hands and said kindly:

"How are you?"

"I am well in body although considerable **rumpled** up in spirit, thank you ma'am," said Anne gravely. Then aside to Marilla in an audible whisper, "There wasn't anything startling in that, was there, Marilla?"

rumple ['rʌmpl]
v. 弄皱;弄乱

Diana was sitting on the sofa, reading a book which she dropped when the callers entered. She was a very pretty little girl, with her mother's black eyes and hair, and rosy cheeks, and the merry expression which was her inheritance from her father.

"This is my little girl Diana," said Mrs. Barry. "Diana, you might take Anne out into the garden and show her your flowers. It will be better for you than **straining** your eyes over that book. She reads entirely too much—"this to Marilla as the little girls went out—"and I can't prevent her, for her father aids and abets her. She's always poring over a book. I'm glad she has the prospect of a playmate—perhaps it will take her more out-of-doors."

strain ['streɪn]
v. 损伤

Outside in the garden, which was full of mellow sunset light streaming through the dark old firs to the west of it, stood Anne and Diana, gazing **bashfully** at each other over a clump of gorgeous tiger lilies.

bashfully ['bæʃfəli]
adv. 羞怯地

The Barry Garden was a bowery wilderness of flowers which would have delighted Anne's heart at any time less **fraught** with destiny. It was encircled by huge old willows and tall firs, beneath which flourished flowers that loved the shade. Prim, right-angled paths neatly bordered with **clamshells**, intersected it like moist red **ribbons** and in the beds between old-fashioned flowers ran riot. There were rosy bleeding-hearts and great splendid crimson **peonies**; white, fragrant

fraught [frɔːt]
adj. 充满(不愉快事物)的

clamshell ['klæmʃel]
n. 蛤壳状挖泥器
ribbon ['rɪbən]
n. 丝带
peony ['piːəni]
n. 芍药

narcissi and thorny, sweet Scotch roses; pink and blue and white columbines and lilac-tinted Bouncing Bets; clumps of southernwood and ribbon grass and mint; purple Adam-and-Eve, **daffodils**, and masses of sweet clover white with its delicate, fragrant, feathery sprays; scarlet lightning that shot its **fiery** lances over prim white musk-flowers; a garden it was where sunshine lingered and bees hummed, and winds, beguiled into **loitering**, purred and rustled.

daffodil [ˈdæfədɪl] *n.* 黄水仙

fiery [ˈfaɪəri] *adj.* 火一般的

loiter [ˈlɔɪtə(r)] *v.* 流浪

"Oh, Diana," said Anne at last, clasping her hands and speaking almost in a whisper, "oh, do you think you can like me a little—enough to be my bosom friend?"

Diana laughed. Diana always laughed before she spoke.

"Why, I guess so," she said frankly. "I'm awfully glad you've come to live at Green Gables. It will be jolly to have somebody to play with. There isn't any other girl who lives near enough to play with, and I've no sisters big enough."

"Will you swear to be my friend forever and ever?" demanded Anne eagerly.

Diana looked shocked.

"Why it's dreadfully wicked to swear," she said **rebukingly**.

rebuke [rɪˈbjuːk] *v.* 斥责

"Oh no, not my kind of swearing. There are two kinds, you know."

"I never heard of but one kind," said Diana doubtfully.

"There really is another. Oh, it isn't wicked at all. It just means vowing and promising solemnly."

"Well, I don't mind doing that," agreed Diana, relieved. "How do you do it?"

"We must join hands—so," said Anne gravely. "It ought to be over running water. We'll just imagine this path is running water. I'll repeat the **oath** first. I solemnly swear to be faithful to my bosom

oath [əʊθ] *n.* 誓言

friend, Diana Barry, as long as the sun and moon shall endure. Now you say it and put my name in."

Diana repeated the "oath" with a laugh fore and **aft**. Then she said:

aft [ɑːft]
adv. 后部

"You're a queer girl, Anne. I heard before that you were queer. But I believe I'm going to like you really well."

When Marilla and Anne went home Diana went with them as for as the log bridge. The two little girls walked with their arms about each other. At the brook they parted with many promises to spend the next afternoon together.

"Well, did you find Diana a kindred spirit?" asked Marilla as they went up through the garden of Green Gables.

"Oh yes," sighed Anne, blissfully unconscious of any **sarcasm** on Marilla's part. "Oh Marilla, I'm the happiest girl on Prince Edward Island this very moment. I assure you I'll say my prayers with a right good-will tonight. Diana and I are going to build a playhouse in Mr. William Bell's birch grove tomorrow. Can I have those broken pieces of china that are out in the woodshed? Diana's birthday is in February and mine is in March. Don't you think that is a very strange coincidence?

sarcasm [ˈsɑːkæzəm]
n. 讽刺

Diana is going to lend me a book to read. She says it's perfectly splendid and **tremendously** exciting. She's going to show me a place back in the woods where rice lilies grow. Don't you think Diana has got very soulful eyes? I wish I had **soulful** eyes. Diana is going to teach me to sing a song called "Nelly in the Hazel Dell." She's going to give me a picture to put up in my room; it's a perfectly beautiful picture, she says—a lovely lady in a pale blue silk dress. A sewing-machine agent gave it to her. I wish I had something to give Diana. I'm an inch taller than Diana, but she is ever so much fatter; she says

tremendously [trəˈmendəsli]
adv. 极好地

soulful [ˈsəʊlfl]
adj. 深情的

she'd like to be thin because it's so much more graceful, but I'm afraid she only said it to **soothe** my feelings. We're going to the shore some day to gather shells. We have agreed to call the spring down by the log bridge the Dryad's Bubble. Isn't that a perfectly elegant name? I read a story once about a spring called that. A dryad is sort of a grown-up fairy, I think."

soothe [suːð] *v.* 安慰

"Well, all I hope is you won't talk Diana to death," said Marilla. "But remember this in all your planning, Anne. You're not going to play all the time nor most of it. You'll have your work to do and it'll have to be done first."

Anne's cup of happiness was full, and Matthew caused it to overflow. He had just got home from a trip to the store at Carmody, and he sheepishly produced a small parcel from his pocket and handed it to Anne, with a **deprecatory** look at Marilla.

deprecatory [deprəˈkeɪtərɪ] *adj.* 不赞成的

"I heard you say you liked chocolate sweeties, so I got you some," he said.

"Humph," sniffed Marilla. "It'll ruin her teeth and stomach. There, there, child, don't look so dismal. You can eat those, since Matthew has gone and got them. He'd better have brought you **peppermints**. They're wholesome. Don't sicken yourself eating all them at once now."

peppermint [ˈpepəmɪnt] *n.* 薄荷

"Oh, no, indeed, I won't," said Anne eagerly. "I'll just eat one tonight, Marilla. And I can give Diana half of them, can't I? The other half will taste twice as sweet to me if I give some to her. It's delightful to think I have something to give her."

"I will say it for the child," said Marilla when Anne had gone to her gable, "she isn't stingy. I'm glad, for of all faults I detest **stinginess** in a child. Dear me, it's only three weeks since she came, and it seems as if she'd been here always. I can't imagine the place without

stinginess [ˈstɪndʒinəs] *n.* 吝啬

her. Now, don't be looking I told-you-so, Matthew. That's bad enough in a woman, but it isn't to be endured in a man. I'm perfectly willing to own up that I'm glad I **consented** to keep the child and that I'm getting fond of her, but don't you **rub** it in, Matthew Cuthbert."

consent [kən'sent]
n. 允许
rub [rʌb]
v. 摩擦

CHAPTER XIII

The Delights of Anticipation

"It's time Anne was in to do her sewing," said Marilla, glancing at the clock and then out into the yellow August afternoon where everything drowsed in the heat. "She stayed playing with Diana more than half an hour more I gave her leave to; and now she's **perched** out there on the woodpile talking to Matthew, nineteen to the dozen, when she knows perfectly well she ought to be at her work. And of course, he's listening to her like a perfect **ninny**. I never saw such an **infatuated** man. The more she talks and the odder the things she says, the more he's delighted evidently. Anne Shirley, you come right in here this minute, do you hear me!"

perch [pɜːtʃt]
v. 栖息

ninny ['nɪni]
n. 傻瓜
infatuated [ɪn'fætʃueɪtɪd]
adj. 痴情的

A series of **staccato** taps on the west window brought Anne flying in from the yard, eyes shining, cheeks faintly flushed with pink, **unbraided** hair streaming behind her in a torrent of brightness.

staccato [stə'kɑːtəʊ]
adj. 断奏的

unbraid [ʌn'breɪd]
v. 解开

"Oh, Marilla," she exclaimed breathlessly, "there's going to be a Sunday-school picnic next week—in Mr. Harmon Andrews's field, right near the lake of Shining Waters. And Mrs. Superintendent Bell and Mrs. Rachel Lynde are going to make ice cream—think of it, Marilla—ice cream! And, oh, Marilla, can I go to it?"

"Just look at the clock, if you please, Anne. What time did I tell you to come in?"

"Two o'clock—but isn't it splendid about the picnic, Marilla? Please can I go? Oh, I've never been to a picnic—I've dreamed of picnics, but I've never—"

"Yes, I told you to come at two o'clock. And it's a quarter to three. I'd like to know why you didn't obey me, Anne."

"Why, I meant to, Marilla, as much as could be. But you have no idea how fascinating Idlewild is. And then, of course, I had to tell Matthew about the picnic. Matthew is such a **sympathetic** listener. Please can I go?"

sympathetic [ˌsɪmpəˈθetɪk] *adj.* 同情的

"You'll have to learn to resist the fascination of Idle whatever-you-call-it. When I tell you to come in at a certain time I mean that time and not half an hour later. And you needn't stop to **discourse** with sympathetic listeners on your way, either. As for the picnic, of course you can go. You're a Sunday-school scholar, and it's not likely I'd refuse to let you go when all the other little girls are going."

discourse [ˈdɪskɔːs] *v.* 论述

"But—but," faltered Anne, "Diana says that everybody must take a basket of things to eat. I can't cook, as you know, Marilla, and—and—I don't mind going to a picnic without puffed sleeves so much, but I'd feel terribly humiliated if I had to go without a basket. It's been preying on my mind ever since Diana told me."

"Well, it needn't prey any longer. I'll bake you a basket."

"Oh, you dear good Marilla. Oh, you are so kind to me. Oh, I'm so much obliged to you."

Getting through with her "ohs" Anne cast herself into Marilla's arms and **rapturously** kissed her sallow cheek. It was the first time in her whole life that childish lips had voluntarily touched Marilla's face. Again that sudden sensation of startling sweetness thrilled her. She was secretly vastly pleased at Anne's impulsive caress, which was probably the reason why she said **brusquely**:

rapturously [ˈræptʃərəsli] *adv.* 兴高采烈地

brusquely [ˈbruːskli] *adv.* 唐突地

"There, there, never mind your kissing nonsense. I'd sooner see you doing strictly as you're told. As for cooking, I mean to begin giving you lessons in that some of these days. But you' re so **feather-brained**, Anne, I' ve been waiting to see if you' d sober down a little and learn to be steady before I begin. You' ve got to keep your wits about you in cooking and not stop in the middle of things to let your thoughts rove all over creation. Now, get out your **patchwork** and have your square done before teatime."

feather-brained [ˈfeðəbreɪnd] *adj.* 轻浮的

patchwork [ˈpætʃwɜːk] *n.* 拼布工艺

"I do not like patchwork," said Anne dolefully, hunting out her workbasket and sitting down before a little heap of red and white diamonds with a sigh. "I think some kinds of sewing would be nice; but there' s no scope for imagination in patchwork. It' s just one little seam after another and you never seem to be getting anywhere. But of course, I' d rather be Anne of Green Gables sewing patchwork than Anne of any other place with nothing to do but play. I wish time went as quick sewing patches as it does when I' m playing with Diana, though. Oh, we do have such elegant times, Marilla. I have to furnish most of the imagination, but I' m well able to do that. Diana is simply perfect in every other way. You know that little piece of land across the brook that runs up between our farm and Mr. Barry' s. It belongs to Mr. William Bell, and right in the corner there is a little ring of white birch trees—the most romantic spot, Marilla. Diana and I have our playhouse there. We call it Idlewild. Isn' t that a poetical name? I assure you it took me some time to think it out. I stayed awake nearly a whole night before I invented it. Then, just as I was dropping off to sleep, it came like an inspiration. Diana was **enraptured** when she heard it. We have got our house fixed up elegantly. You must come and see it, Marilla—won' t you? We have great big stones, all covered with moss, for seats, and boards from tree to tree for shelves. And we have all our dishes on them. Of course, they' re all broken but it' s the easiest thing in the world to imagine that they are whole. There' s a

enraptured [ɪnˈræptʃəd] *adj.* 狂喜的

piece of a plate with a spray of red and yellow ivy on it that is especially beautiful. We keep it in the parlor and we have the fairy glass there, too. The fairy glass is as lovely as a dream. Diana found it out in the woods behind their chicken house. It's all full of rainbows—just little young rainbows that haven't grown big yet—and Diana's mother told her it was broken off a hanging lamp they once had. But it's nice to imagine the fairies lost it one night when they had a ball, so we call it the fairy glass. Matthew is going to make us a table. Oh, we have named that little round pool over in Mr. Barry's field Willowmere. I got that name out of the book Diana lent me. That was a thrilling book, Marilla. The heroine had five lovers. I'd be satisfied with one, wouldn't you? She was very handsome and she went through great **tribulations**. She could faint as easy as anything. I'd love to be able to faint, wouldn't you, Marilla? It's so romantic. But I'm really very healthy for all I'm so thin. I believe I'm getting fatter, though. Don't you think I am? I look at my elbows every morning when I get up to see if any **dimples** are coming. Diana is having a new dress made with elbow sleeves. She is going to wear it to the picnic. Oh, I do hope it will be fine next Wednesday. I don't feel that I could endure the disappointment if anything happened to prevent me from getting to the picnic. I suppose I'd live through it, but I'm certain it would be a lifelong sorrow. It wouldn't matter if I got to a hundred picnics in after years; they wouldn't make up for missing this one. They're going to have boats on the Lake of Shining Waters—and ice cream, as I told you. I have never tasted ice cream. Diana tried to explain what it was like, but I guess ice cream is one of those things that are beyond imagination."

"Anne, you have talked even on for ten minutes by the clock," said Marilla. "Now, just for curiosity's sake, see if you can hold your

tribulation [ˌtrɪbjuˈleɪʃn] *n.* 苦难

dimples [ˈdɪmpl] *n.* 酒窝；笑靥

tongue for the same length of time."

Anne held her tongue as desired. But for the rest of the week, she talked picnic and thought picnic and dreamed picnic. On Saturday it rained and she worked herself up into such a frantic state lest it should keep on raining until and over Wednesday that Marilla made her sew an extra patchwork square by way of steadying her nerves.

On Sunday Anne confided to Marilla on the way home from church that she grew actually cold all over with excitement when the minister announced the picnic from the pulpit.

"Such a thrill as went up and down my back, Marilla! I don't think I'd ever really believed until then that there was honestly going to be a picnic. I couldn't help fearing I'd only imagined it. But when a minister says a thing in the pulpit you just have to believe it."

"You set your heart too much on things, Anne," said Marilla, with a sigh. "I'm afraid there'll be a great many disappointments in store for you through life."

"Oh, Marilla, looking forward to things is half the pleasure of them," **exclaimed** Anne. "You mayn't get the things themselves; but nothing can prevent you from having the fun of looking forward to them. Mrs. Lynde says, 'Blessed are they who expect nothing for they shall not be disappointed.' But I think it would be worse to expect nothing than to be disappointed."

exclaime [ɪkˈskleɪm]
v. 惊叫

Marilla wore her **amethyst brooch** to church that day as usual. Marilla always wore her amethyst brooch to church. She would have thought it rather **sacrilegious** to leave it off—as bad as forgetting her Bible or her collection dime. That amethyst brooch was Marilla's most treasured possession. A seafaring uncle had given it to her mother who in turn had **bequeathed** it to Marilla. It was an old-fashioned oval, containing a braid of her mother's hair, surrounded by

amethyst [ˈæməθɪst]
n. 紫水晶
brooch [brəʊtʃ]
n. 胸针
sacrilegious
[ˌsækrəˈlɪdʒəs]
adj. 该受天谴地

bequeath [bɪˈkwiːð]
v. 把……遗赠给

a border of very fine amethysts. Marilla knew too little about precious stones to realize how fine the amethysts actually were; but she thought them very beautiful and was always pleasantly conscious of their violet **shimmer** at her throat, above her good brown **satin** dress, even although she could not see it.

Anne had been **smitten** with delighted admiration when she first saw that brooch.

"Oh, Marilla, it's a perfectly elegant brooch. I don't know how you can pay attention to the sermon or the prayers when you have it on. I couldn't, I know. I think amethysts are just sweet. They are what I used to think diamonds were like. Long ago, before I had ever seen a diamond, I read about them and I tried to imagine what they would be like. I thought they would be lovely glimmering purple stones. When I saw a real diamond in a lady's ring one day, I was so disappointed I cried. Of course, it was very lovely but it wasn't my idea of a diamond. Will you let me hold the brooch for one minute, Marilla? Do you think amethysts can be the souls of good violets?"

shimmer [ˈʃɪmə(r)] *v.* 闪烁
satin [ˈsætɪn] *n.* 缎子
smit [ˈsmaɪt] *v.* 重击

CHAPTER XIV

Anne's Confession

On the Monday evening before the picnic Marilla came down from her room with a troubled face.

"Anne," she said to that small **personage**, who was shelling peas by the **spotless** table and singing, "Nelly of the Hazel Dell" with a **vigor** and expression that did credit to Diana's teaching, "did you see anything of my amethyst brooch? I thought I stuck it in my **pincushion** when I came home from church yesterday evening, but I can't find it anywhere."

"I—I saw it this afternoon when you were away at the Aid Soci-

personage [ˈpɜːsənɪdʒ] *n.* 名人
spotless [ˈspɒtləs] *adj.* 非常洁净的
vigor [ˈvɪɡə(r)] *n.* 活力
pincushion [ˈpɪnkʊʃn] *n.* 针垫

ety," said Anne, a little slowly. "I was passing your door when I saw it on the cushion, so I went in to look at it."

"Did you touch it?" said Marilla sternly.

"Y-e-e-s," admitted Anne, "I took it up and I pinned it on my breast just to see how it would look."

"You had no business to do anything of the sort. It's very wrong in a little girl to **meddle**. You shouldn't have gone into my room in the first place and you shouldn't have touched a brooch that didn't belong to you in the second. Where did you put it?"

meddle ['medl]
v. 干涉

"Oh, I put it back on the bureau. I hadn't it on a minute. Truly, I didn't mean to meddle, Marilla. I didn't think about its being wrong to go in and try on the brooch; but I see now that it was and I'll never do it again. That's one good thing about me. I never do the same naughty thing twice."

"You didn't put it back," said Marilla. "That brooch isn't anywhere on the **bureau**. You've taken it out or something, Anne."

bureau ['bjʊərəʊ]
n. 书桌

"I did put it back," said Anne quickly—pertly, Marilla thought. "I don't just remember whether I stuck it on the pincushion or laid it in the china tray. But I'm perfectly certain I put it back."

"I'll go and have another look," said Marilla, determining to be just. "If you put that brooch back it's there still. If it isn't I'll know you didn't, that's all!"

Marilla went to her room and made a thorough search, not only over the bureau but also in every other place she thought the brooch might possibly be. It was not to be found and she returned to the kitchen.

"Anne, the brooch is gone. By your own admission you were the last person to handle it. Now, what have you done with it? Tell me the truth at once. Did you take it out and lose it?"

"No, I didn't," said Anne solemnly, meeting Marilla's angry gaze squarely. "I never took the brooch out of your room and that is the truth, if I was to be led to the block for it—although I'm not very certain what a block is. So there, Marilla."

Anne's "so there" was only intended to emphasize her **assertion**, but Marilla took it as a display of **defiance**.

assertion [ə'sɜːʃn] *n.* 断言
defiance [dɪ'faɪəns] *n.* 违抗
falsehood ['fɔːlshʊd] *n.* 虚假

"I believe you are telling me a **falsehood**, Anne," she said sharply. "I know you are. There now, don't say anything more unless you are prepared to tell the whole truth. Go to your room and stay there until you are ready to confess."

"Will I take the peas with me?" said Anne **meekly**.

meekly ['miːkli] *adv.* 温顺地

"No, I'll finish shelling them myself. Do as I bid you."

When Anne had gone Marilla went about her evening tasks in a very disturbed state of mind. She was worried about her valuable brooch. What if Anne had lost it? And how wicked of the child to deny having taken it, when anybody could see she must have! With such an innocent face, too!

"I don't know what I wouldn't sooner have had happen," thought Marilla, as she nervously shelled the peas. "Of course, I don't suppose she meant to steal it or anything like that. She's just taken it to play with or help along that imagination of hers. She must have taken it, that's clear, for there hasn't been a soul in that room since she was in it, by her own story, until I went up tonight. And the brooch is gone, there's nothing surer. I suppose she has lost it and is afraid to own up for fear she'll be punished. It's a dreadful thing to think she tells falsehoods. It's a far worse thing than her fit of temper. It's a fearful responsibility to have a child in your house you can't trust. **Slyness** and untruthfulness—that's what she has displayed. I declare I feel worse about that than about the brooch. If she'd only have told

slyness ['slaɪnəs] *n.* 狡猾

the truth about it, I wouldn't mind so much."

Marilla went to her room at **intervals** all through the evening and searched for the brooch, without finding it. A bedtime visits to the east gable produced no result.

interval [ˈɪntəvl]
n. 间隔

Anne persisted in denying that she knew anything about the brooch but Marilla was only the more firmly convinced that she did.

She told Matthew the story the next morning. Matthew was **confounded** and puzzled; he could not so quickly lose faith in Anne but he had to admit that **circumstances** were against her.

confounded [kənˈfaʊndɪd]
adj. 混乱的;不知所措的

circumstances [ˈsɜːkəmstəns]
n. 环境

"You're sure it hasn't fell down behind the bureau?" was the only suggestion he could offer.

"I've moved the bureau and I've taken out the drawers and I've looked in every crack and **cranny**" was Marilla's positive answer. "The brooch is gone and that child has taken it and lied about it. That's the plain, ugly truth, Matthew Cuthbert, and we might as well look it in the face."

cranny [ˈkræni]
n. 裂缝

"Well now, what are you going to do about it?" Matthew asked **forlornly**, feeling secretly thankful that Marilla and not he had to deal with the situation. He felt no desire to put his oar in this time.

forlornly [fəˈlɔːnli]
adv. 孤苦伶仃地

"She'll stay in her room until she confesses," said Marilla grimly, remembering the success of this method in the former case. "Then we'll see. Perhaps we'll be able to find the brooch if she'll only tell where she took it; but in any case, she'll have to be severely punished, Matthew."

"Well now, you'll have to punish her," said Matthew, reaching for his hat. "I've nothing to do with it, remember. You warned me off yourself."

Marilla felt deserted by everyone. She could not even go to Mrs. Lynde for advice. She went up to the east gable with a very serious face and left it with a face more serious still. Anne **steadfastly** refused to confess. She persisted in asserting that she had not taken the brooch. The child had evidently been crying and Marilla felt a **pang** of pity which she **sternly repressed**. By night she was, as she expressed it, "beat out."

"You'll stay in this room until you confess, Anne. You can make up your mind to that," she said firmly.

"But the picnic is tomorrow, Marilla," cried Anne. "You won't keep me from going to that, will you? You'll just let me out for the afternoon, won't you? Then I'll stay here as long as you like afterwards cheerfully. But I must go to the picnic."

"You'll not go to picnics nor anywhere else until you've confessed, Anne."

"Oh, Marilla," gasped Anne.

But Marilla had gone out and shut the door.

Wednesday morning dawned as bright and fair as if expressly made to order for the picnic. Birds sang around Green Gables; the Madonna lilies in the garden sent out whiffs of perfume that entered in on viewless winds at every door and window, and wandered through halls and rooms like spirits of **benediction**. The birches in the hollow waved joyful hands as if watching for Anne's usual morning greeting from the east gable. But Anne was not at her window. When Marilla took her breakfast up to her, she found the child sitting **primly** on her bed, pale and resolute, with tight-shut lips and gleaming eyes.

"Marilla, I'm ready to confess."

"Ah!" Marilla laid down her tray. Once again her method had succeeded; but her success was very bitter to her. "Let me hear what you have to say then, Anne."

"I took the amethyst brooch," said Anne, as if repeating a lesson

steadfastly [ˈstedfɑːstli]
adv. 坚定地

pang [pæŋ]
n. 一阵剧痛
sternly [ˈstɜːnli]
adv. 严厉地
repressed [rɪˈprest]
adj. 压抑的

benediction
[ˌbenɪˈdɪkʃn]
n. 祝福

primly [ˈprɪmli]
adv. 一本正经地

she had learned. "I took it just as you said. I didn't mean to take it when I went in. But it did look so beautiful, Marilla, when I pinned it on my breast that I was overcome by an irresistible temptation. I imagined how perfectly thrilling it would be to take it to Idlewild and play I was the Lady Cordelia Fitzgerald. It would be so much easier to imagine I was the Lady Cordelia if I had a real amethyst brooch on. Diana and I make necklaces of roseberries but what are roseberries compared to amethysts? So I took the brooch. I thought I could put it back before you came home. I went all the way around by the road to lengthen out the time. When I was going over the bridge across the Lake of Shining Waters I took the brooch off to have another look at it. Oh, how it did shine in the sunlight! And then, when I was leaning over the bridge, it just slipped through my fingers—so—and went down—down—down, all purply sparkling, and sank forevermore beneath the Lake of Shining Waters. And that's the best I can do at confessing, Marilla."

Marilla felt hot anger surge up into her heart again. This child had taken and lost her treasured amethyst brooch and now sat there calmly reciting the details thereof without the least apparent **compunction** or **repentance**.

"Anne, this is terrible," she said, trying to speak calmly. "You are the very wickedest girl I ever heard of."

"Yes, I suppose I am," agreed Anne **tranquilly**. "And I know I'll have to be punished. It'll be your duty to punish me, Marilla. Won't you please get it over right off because I'd like to go to the picnic with nothing on my mind."

"Picnic, indeed! You'll go to no picnic today, Anne Shirley. That shall be your punishment. And it isn't half severe enough either for what you've done!"

"Not go to the picnic!" Anne **sprang** to her feet and **clutched**

compunction [kəmˈpʌŋkʃn] *n.* 内疚

repentance [rɪˈpentəns] *n.* 后悔

tranquilly [ˈtræŋkwɪli] *adv.* 平静地

spring [sprɪŋ] *v.* 跳跃

clutch [klʌtʃ] *v.* 抓紧

Marilla's hand. "But you promised me I might! Oh, Marilla, I must go to the picnic. That was why I confessed. Punish me any way you like but that. Oh, Marilla, please, please, let me go to the picnic. Think of the ice cream! For anything you know I may never have a chance to taste ice cream again."

Marilla **disengaged** Anne's **clinging** hands stonily.

"You needn't plead, Anne. You are not going to the picnic and that's final. No, not a word."

Anne realized that Marilla was not to be moved. She clasped her hands together, gave a piercing **shriek**, and then **flung** herself face downward on the bed, crying and **writhing** in an utter abandonment of disappointment and despair.

"For the land's sake!" gasped Marilla, hastening from the room. "I believe the child is crazy. No child in her senses would behave as she does. If she isn't she's **utterly** bad. Oh dear, I'm afraid Rachel was right from the first. But I've **put my hand to the plow** and I won't look back."

That was a dismal morning. Marilla worked fiercely and scrubbed the porch floor and the dairy shelves when she could find nothing else to do. Neither the shelves nor the porch needed it—but Marilla did. Then she went out and raked the yard.

When dinner was ready she went to the stairs and called Anne. A tear-stained face appeared, looking tragically over the **banisters**.

"Come down to your dinner, Anne."

"I don't want any dinner, Marilla," said Anne, **sobbingly**. "I couldn't eat anything. My heart is broken. You'll feel **remorse** of conscience someday, I expect, for breaking it, Marilla, but I forgive you. Remember when the time comes that I forgive you. But please don't ask me to eat anything, especially boiled pork and greens.

disengage [ˌdɪsɪn'geɪdʒ]
v. 使松开;解开
cling ['klɪŋ]
v. 紧紧抓住(抱住)

shriek [ʃriːk]
v. 尖叫
fling [flɪŋ]
v. (用力地)掷,扔,抛
writhe ['raɪð]
v. 翻滚

utterly ['ʌtəli]
adv. 完全地
put your hand to the plow 开始工作

banister ['bænɪstə(r)]
n. (楼梯)扶手.

sobbingly ['sɒbɪŋli]
adv. 哭泣地
remorse [rɪ'mɔːs]
n. 懊悔

Boiled pork and greens are so unromantic when one is in **affliction**."

Exasperated, Marilla returned to the kitchen and poured out her tale of woe to Matthew, who, between his sense of justice and his unlawful sympathy with Anne, was a miserable man.

"Well now, she shouldn't have taken the brooch, Marilla, or told stories about it," he admitted, mournfuly surveying his plateful of unromantic pork and greens as if he, like Anne, thought it a food unsuited to crises of feeling, "but she's such a little thing—such an interesting little thing. Don't you think it's pretty rough not to let her go to the picnic when she's so set on it?"

"Matthew Cuthbert, I'm amazed at you. I think I've let her off entirely too easy. And she doesn't appear to realize how wicked she's been at all—that's what worries me most. If she'd really felt sorry it wouldn't be so bad. And you don't seem to realize it, neither; you're making excuses for her all the time to yourself—I can see that."

"Well now, she's such a little thing," **feebly reiterated** Matthew. "And there should be allowances made, Marilla. You know she's never had any bringing up."

"Well, she's having it now." **retorted** Marilla.

The retort silenced Matthew if it did not convince him. That dinner was a very **dismal** meal. The only cheerful thing about it was Jerry Buote, the hired boy, and Marilla resented his cheerfulness as a personal insult.

When her dishes were washed and her bread **sponge** set and her hens fed Marilla remembered that she had noticed a small rent in her best black lace shawl when she had taken it off on Monday afternoon on returning from the Ladies' Aid.

She would go and mend it. The shawl was in a box in her trunk. As Marilla lifted it out, the sunlight, falling through the vines that clus-

affliction [əˈflɪkʃn]
n. 苦恼
exasperated
[ɪgˈzæspəreɪtɪd]
adj. 恼怒的

feebly [ˈfiːbli]
adj. 无力地
reiterate [riːˈɪtəreɪt]
v. 反复地说，重申

retort [rɪˈtɔːt]
v. 反驳

dismal [ˈdɪzməl]
adj. 忧郁的

sponge [spʌndʒ]
n. 海绵块

tered thickly about the window, struck upon something caught in the shawl—something that glittered and sparkled in facets of violet light. Marilla snatched at it with a gasp. It was the amethyst brooch, hanging to a thread of the lace by its catch!

"Dear life and heart," said Marilla blankly, "what does this mean? Here's my brooch safe and sound that I thought was at the bottom of Barry's pond. Whatever did that girl mean by saying she took it and lost it? I declare I believe Green Gables is bewitched. I remember now that when I took off my shawl Monday afternoon I laid it on the bureau for a minute. I suppose the brooch got caught in it somehow. Well!"

Marilla betook herself to the east gable, brooch in hand. Anne had cried herself out and was sitting dejectedly by the window.

"Anne Shirley," said Marilla solemnly, "I've just found my brooch hanging to my black lace **shawl**. Now I want to know what that rigmarole you told me this morning meant."

shawl [ʃɔːl]
n. 披肩

"Why, you said you'd keep me here until I **confessed**," returned Anne wearily, "and so I decided to confess because I was bound to get to the picnic. I thought out a confession last night after I went to bed and made it as interesting as I could. And I said it over and over so that I wouldn't forget it. But you wouldn't let me go to the picnic after all, so all my trouble was wasted."

confess [kən'fes]
v. 供认

Marilla had to laugh in spite of herself. But her conscience pricked her.

"Anne, you do beat all! But I was wrong—I see that now. I shouldn't have doubted your word when I'd never known you to tell a story. Of course, it wasn't right for you to confess to a thing you hadn't done—it was very wrong to do so. But I drove you to it. So if you'll forgive me, Anne, I'll forgive you and we'll start square again.

And now get yourself ready for the picnic."

Anne flew up like a rocket.

"Oh, Marilla, isn't it too late?"

"No, it's only two o'clock. They won't be more than well gathered yet and it'll be an hour before they have tea. Wash your face and comb your hair and put on your gingham. I'll fill a basket for you. There's plenty of stuff baked in the house. And I'll get Jerry to **hitch** up the **sorrel** and drive you down to the picnic ground."

"Oh, Marilla," exclaimed Anne, flying to the **washstand**. "Five minutes ago, I was so miserable I was wishing I'd never been born and now I wouldn't change places with an angel!"

That night a **thoroughly** happy, completely tired-out Anne returned to Green Gables in a state of **beatification** impossible to describe.

"Oh, Marilla, I've had a perfectly scrumptious time. **Scrumptious** is a new word I learned today. I heard Mary Alice Bell use it. Isn't it very expressive? Everything was lovely. We had a **splendid** tea and then Mr. Harmon Andrews took us all for a row on the Lake of Shining Waters—six of us at a time. And Jane Andrews nearly fell overboard. She was leaning out to pick water lilies and if Mr. Andrews hadn't caught her by her **sash** just in the nick of time she'd fallen in and probably been **drowned**. I wish it had been me. It would have been such a romantic experience to have been nearly drowned. It would be such a **thrilling** tale to tell. And we had the ice cream. Words fail me to describe that ice cream. Marilla, I assure you it was **sublime**."

That evening Marilla told the whole story to Matthew over her stocking basket.

"I'm willing to own up that I made a mistake," she concluded

hitch [hɪtʃ] *v.* 搭便车
sorrel [ˈsɒrəl] *n.* 酸叶草
washstand [ˈwɒʃstænd] *n.* 脸盆架

thoroughly [ˈθʌrəlɪ] *adv.* 极度地
beatification [biˌætɪfɪˈkeɪʃn] *n.* 宣福礼
scrumptious [ˈskrʌmpʃəs] *adj.* 美味的
splendid [ˈsplendɪd] *adj.* 非常好的

sash [sæʃ] *n.* 腰带
drown [draʊn] *v.* 淹死

thrilling [ˈθrɪlɪŋ] *adj.* 惊险的

sublime [səˈblaɪm] *adj.* 绝美的

candidly, "but I've learned a lesson. I have to laugh when I think of Anne's '**confession**', although I suppose I shouldn't for it really was a **falsehood**. But it doesn't seem as bad as the other would have been, somehow, and anyhow I'm responsible for it. That child is hard to understand in some respects. But I believe she'll turn out all right yet. And there's one thing certain, no house will ever be dull that she's in."

candidly [ˈkændɪdlɪ] *adv.* 坦白地
confession [kənˈfeʃn] *n.* 认罪
falsehood [ˈfɔːlshʊd] *n.* 谎言

CHAPTER XV

A Tempest in the School Teapot

"What a splendid day!" said Anne, drawing a long breath. "Isn't it good just to be alive on a day like this? I pity the people who aren't born yet for missing it. They may have good days, of course, but they can never have this one. And it's splendider still to have such a lovely way to go to school by, isn't it?"

"It's a lot nicer than going round by the road; that is so dusty and hot," said Diana practically, **peeping** into her dinner basket and mentally **calculating** if the three juicy, toothsome, raspberry tarts **reposing** there were divided among ten girls how many bites each girl would have.

peep [piːp] *v.* 窥视
calculate [ˈkælkjuleɪt] *v.* 计算
repose [rɪˈpəʊz] *v.* 被搁置在

The little girls of Avonlea school always pooled their lunches, and to eat three raspberry tarts all alone or even to share them only with one's best chum would have forever and ever **branded** as "awful mean" the girl who did it. And yet, when the tarts were divided among ten girls you just got enough to tantalize you.

brand [brænd] *v.* 丑化(某人)

The way Anne and Diana went to school was a pretty one. Anne thought those walks to and from school with Diana couldn't be improved upon even by imagination. Going around by the main road would have been so unromantic; but to go by Lover's **Lane** and Wil-

lane [leɪn] *n.* 小路

lowmere and Violet Vale and the Birch Path was romantic, if ever anything was.

Lover's Lane opened out below the **orchard** at Green Gables and stretched far up into the woods to the end of the Cuthbert farm. It was the way by which the cows were taken to the back **pasture** and the wood hauled home in winter. Anne had named it Lover's Lane before she had been a month at Green Gables.

"Not that lovers ever really walk there," she explained to Marilla, "but Diana and I are reading a perfectly magnificent book and there's a Lover's Lane in it. So we want to have one, too. And it's a very pretty name, don't you think? So romantic! We can't imagine the lovers into it, you know. I like that lane because you can think out loud there without people calling you crazy."

Anne, starting out alone in the morning, went down Lover's Lane as far as the brook. Here Diana met her, and the two little girls went on up the lane under the leafy arch of maples—"maples are such sociable trees," said Anne; "they're always rustling and **whispering** to you"—until they came to a rustic bridge. Then they left the lane and walked through Mr. Barry's back field and past Willowmere. Beyond Willowmere came Violet Vale—a little green **dimple** in the shadow of Mr. Andrew Bell's big woods. "Of course there are no **violets** there now," Anne told Marilla, "but Diana says there are millions of them in spring. Oh, Marilla, can't you just imagine you see them? It actually takes away my breath. I named it Violet Vale. Diana says she never saw the beat of me for hitting on fancy names for places. It's nice to be clever at something, isn't it? But Diana named the Birch Path. She wanted to, so I let her; but I'm sure I could have found something more **poetical** than plain Birch Path. Anybody can think of a name like that. But the Birch Path is one of the prettiest places in the world, Marilla."

orchard [ˈɔːtʃəd]
n. 果园

pasture [ˈpɑːstʃə(r)]
n. 牧场

whisper [ˈwɪspə(r)]
v. 耳语

dimple [ˈdɪmpl]
n. 酒窝

violet [ˈvaɪələt]
n. 紫罗兰

poetical [pəʊˈɛtɪk]
adj. 诗的

It was. Other people besides Anne thought so when they **stumbled** on it. It was a little narrow, twisting path, winding down over a long hill straight through Mr. Bell's woods, where the light came down **sifted** through so many **emerald** screens that it was as flawless as the heart of a diamond. It was fringed in all its length with slim young birches, white stemmed and lissom boughed; ferns and starflowers and wild lilies-of-the-valley and scarlet tufts of pigeonberries grew thickly along it; and always there was a delightful spiciness in the air and music of bird calls and the murmur and laugh of wood winds in the trees overhead. Now and then you might see a rabbit skipping across the road if you were quiet—which, with Anne and Diana, happened about once in a blue moon. Down in the valley the path came out to the main road and then it was just up the **spruce** hill to the school.

stumble [ˈstʌmbl]
v. 跌跌撞撞地走

sift [sɪft]
v. 筛

emerald [ˈemərəld]
adj. 翠绿色的

spruce [spruːs]
n. 云杉

The Avonlea school was a whitewashed building, low in the **eaves** and wide in the windows, furnished inside with comfortable substantial old-fashioned desks that opened and shut, and were carved all over their lids with the **initials** and **hieroglyphics** of three generations of school children. The schoolhouse was set back from the road and behind it was a dusky fir wood and a brook where all the children put their bottles of milk in the morning to keep cool and sweet until dinner hour.

eaves [iːvz]
n. 屋檐

initial [ɪˈnɪʃl]
n. (名字的)首字母

hieroglyphics
[ˌhaɪərəˈglɪfɪks]
n. 象形文字(指书写符号系统)

Marilla had seen Anne start off to school on the first day of September with many secret misgivings. Anne was such an odd girl. How would she get on with the other children? And how on earth would she ever manage to hold her tongue during school hours?

Things went better than Marilla feared, however. Anne came home that evening in high spirits.

"I think I'm going to like school here," she announced. "I don't think much of the master, through. He's all the time curling his mustache and making eyes at Prissy Andrews. Prissy is grown up, you know. She's sixteen and she's studying for the entrance examination into Queen's Academy at Charlottetown next year. Tillie Boulter says the master is dead gone on her. She's got a beautiful complexion and curly brown hair and she does it up so **elegantly**. She sits in the long seat at the back and he sits there,too, most of the time—to explain her lessons, he says. But Ruby Gillis says she saw him writing something on her slate and when Prissy read it she **blushed** as red as a beet and **giggled**; and Ruby Gillis says she doesn't believe it had anything to do with the lesson."

"Anne Shirley, don't let me hear you talking about your teacher in that way again," said Marilla sharply. "You don't go to school to criticize the master. I guess he can teach you something, and it's your business to learn. And I want you to understand right off that you are not to come home telling tales about him. That is something I won't encourage. I hope you were a good girl."

"**Indeed** I was," said Anne comfortably. "It wasn't so hard as you might imagine, either. I sit with Diana. Our seat is right by the window and we can look down to the Lake of Shining Waters. There are a lot of nice girls in school and we had scrumptious fun playing at dinnertime. It's so nice to have a lot of little girls to play with. But of course I like Diana best and always will. I adore Diana. I'm dreadfully far behind the others. They're all in the fifth book and I'm only in the fourth. I feel that it's kind of a **disgrace**. But there's not one of them has such an imagination as I have and I soon found that out. We had reading and geography and Canadian history and dictation today. Mr. Phillips said my spelling was disgraceful and he held up my slate so that everybody could see it, all marked over. I felt so **mortified**,

elegantly [ˈelɪgəntli] *adv.* 优美地

blush [blʌʃ] *v.* 脸红
giggle [ˈgɪgl] *v.* 咯咯地笑

indeed [ɪnˈdiːd] *adv.* 确实

disgrace [dɪsˈgreɪs] *n.* 耻辱

mortified [ˈmɔːtɪfaɪ] *adj.* 窘迫的

Marilla; he might have been politer to a stranger, I think. Ruby Gillis gave me an apple and Sophia Sloane lent me a lovely pink card with 'May I see you home?' on it. I'm to give it back to her tomorrow. And Tillie Boulter let me wear her bead ring all the afternoon. Can I have some of those pearl **beads** off the old **pincushion** in the **garret** to make myself a ring? And oh, Marilla, Jane Andrews told me that Minnie MacPherson told her that she heard Prissy Andrews tell Sara Gillis that I had a very pretty nose. Marilla, that is the first **compliment** I have ever had in my life and you can't imagine what a strange feeling it gave me. Marilla, have I really a pretty nose? I know you'll tell me the truth."

bead [biːd] *n.* (有孔的)珠子
pincushion ['pɪnkʊʃn] *n.* 针垫
garret ['gærət] *n.* 阁楼
compliment ['kɒmplɪmənt] *n.* 赞扬

"Your nose is well enough," said Marilla shortly. Secretly she thought Anne's nose was a remarkable pretty one; but she had no intention of telling her so.

That was three weeks ago and all had gone smoothly so far. And now, this crisp September morning, Anne and Diana were tripping **blithely** down the Birch Path, two of the happiest little girls in Avonlea.

blithely ['blaɪðli] *adv.* 无忧无虑地

"I guess Gilbert Blythe will be in school today," said Diana. "He's been visiting his cousins over in New Brunswick all summer and he only came home Saturday night. He's aw'fly handsome, Anne. And he **teases** the girls something terrible. He just **torments** our lives out."

tease [tiːz] *v.* 取笑
torment ['tɔːment] *v.* 折磨

Diana's voice indicated that she rather liked having her life tormented out than not.

"Gilbert Blythe?" said Anne. "Isn't his name that's written up on the porch wall with Julia Bell's and a big 'Take Notice' over them?"

"Yes," said Diana, **tossing** her head, "but I'm sure he doesn't

toss [tɒs] *v.* 甩(头)

like Julia Bell so very much. I've heard him say he studied the **mul-tiplication** table by her freckles."

multiplication [ˌmʌltɪplɪˈkeɪʃn] *n.* 乘法

"Oh, don't speak about **freckles** to me," implored Anne. "It isn't delicate when I've got so many. But I do think that writing take-notices up on the wall about the boys and girls is the silliest ever. I should just like to see anybody dare to write my name up with a boy's. Not, of course," she hastened to add, "that anybody would."

freckle [ˈfrekl] *n.* 雀斑

Anne sighed. She didn't want her name written up. But it was a little **humiliating** to know that there was no danger of it.

humiliating [hjuːˈmɪlieɪtɪŋ] *adj.* 羞辱性的

"Nonsense," said Diana, whose black eyes and glossy tresses had played such havoc with the hearts of Avonlea schoolboys that her name figured on the porch walls in half a dozen take-notices. "It's only meant as a joke. And don't you be too sure your name won't ever be written up. Charlie Sloane is dead gone on you. He told his mother—his mother, mind you—that you were the smartest girl in school. That's better than being good looking."

"No, it isn't," said Anne, **feminine** to the core. "I'd rather be pretty than clever. And I hate Charlie Sloane, I can't bear a boy with **goggle** eyes. If anyone wrote my name up with his I'd never get over it, Diana Barry. But it is nice to keep head of your class."

feminine [ˈfemənɪn] *adj.* 女性的

goggle [ˈgɒgl] *adj.* 瞪住的

"You'll have Gilbert in your class after this," said Diana, "and he's used to being head of his class, I can tell you. He's only in the fourth book although he's nearly fourteen. Four years ago his father was sick and had to go out to Alberta for his health and Gilbert went with him. They were there three years and Gil didn't go to school hardly any until they came back. You won't find it so easy to keep head after this, Anne."

"I'm glad," said Anne quickly. "I couldn't really feel proud of keeping head of little boys and girls of just nine or ten. I got up yesterday spelling '**ebullition**'. Josie Pye was head and, mind you, she peeped in her book. Mr. Phillips didn't see her—he was looking at Prissy Andrews—but I did. I just swept her a look of freezing **scorn** and she got as red as a beet and spelled it wrong after all."

"Those Pye girls are cheats all round," said Diana **indignantly**, as they climbed the fence of the main road. "Gertie Pye actually went and put her milk bottle in my place in the brook yesterday. Did you ever? I don't speak to her now."

When Mr. Phillips was in the back of the room hearing Prissy Andrews's Latin, Diana whispered to Anne,

"That's Gilbert Blythe sitting right across the **aisle** from you, Anne. Just look at him and see if you don't think he's handsome."

Anne looked accordingly. She had a good chance to do so, for the said Gilbert Blythe was absorbed in **stealthily** pinning the long yellow braid of Ruby Gillis, who sat in front of him, to the back of her seat. He was a tall boy, with curly brown hair, **roguish** hazel eyes, and a mouth twisted into a teasing smile. Presently Ruby Gillis started up to take a sum to the master; she fell back into her seat with a little shriek, believing that her hair was pulled out by the roots. Everybody looked at her and Mr. Phillips glared so sternly that Ruby began to cry. Gilbert had whisked the pin out of sight and was studying his history with the soberest face in the world; but when the commotion **subsided** he looked at Anne and winked with inexpressible **drollery**.

"I think your Gilbert Blythe is handsome," **confided** Anne to Diana, "but I think he's very bold. It isn't good manners to wink at a strange girl."

But it was not until the afternoon that things really began to happen.

Mr. Phillips was back in the corner explaining a problem in algebra to Prissy Andrews and the rest of the scholars were doing pretty

ebullition [ˌebəˈlɪʃən] *n.* 沸腾

scorn [skɔːn] *n.* 蔑视

indignantly [ɪnˈdɪgnəntli] *adv.* 愤怒地

aisle [aɪl] *n.* 走道

stealthily [ˈstelθɪli] *adv.* 秘密地

roguish [ˈrəʊgɪʃ] *adj.* 淘气的

subside [səbˈsaɪd] *v.* 平息

drollery [ˈdrəʊləri] *n.* 诙谐

confide [kənˈfaɪd] *v.* 吐露

much as they pleased eating green apples, whispering, drawing pictures on their slates, and driving crickets **harnessed** to **strings**, up and down aisle. Gilbert Blythe was trying to make Anne Shirley look at him and failing utterly, because Anne was at that moment totally oblivious not only to the very existence of Gilbert Blythe, but of every other scholar in Avonlea school itself. With her chin **propped** on her hands and her eyes fixed on the blue glimpse of the Lake of Shining Waters that the west window afforded, she was far away in a gorgeous dreamland hearing and seeing nothing save her own wonderful visions.

harness [ˈhɑːnɪs]
v. 给(马等)上挽具
string [strɪŋ]
n. 线;细绳

prop [prɒp]
v. 支撑,倚靠

Gilbert Blythe wasn't used to putting himself out to make a girl look at him and meeting with failure. She should look at him, that red-haired Shirley girl with the little pointed chin and the big eyes that weren't like the eyes of any other girl in Avonlea school.

Gilbert reached across the aisle, picked up the end of Anne's long red braid, held it out at arm's length and said in a piercing whisper:

"Carrots! Carrots!"

Then Anne looked at him with a vengeance!

She did more than look. She sprang to her feet, her bright fancies fallen into cureless ruin. She flashed one indignant glance at Gilbert from eyes whose angry sparkle was swiftly quenched in equally angry tears.

"You mean, hateful boy!" she exclaimed passionately. "How dare you!"

And then—thwack! Anne had brought her slate down on Gilbert's head and cracked it—slate not head—clear across.

Avonlea school always enjoyed a scene. This was an especially enjoyable one. Everybody said "Oh" in horrified delight. Diana **gasped**. Ruby Gillis, who was **inclined** to be **hysterical**, began to

gasp [gɑːsp]
v. 喘气
incline [ɪnˈklaɪn]
v. (使)倾向于
hysterical [hɪˈsterɪkl]
adj. 歇斯底里的

cry. Tommy Sloane let his team of crickets escape him altogether while he stared open-mouthed at the tableau.

Mr. Phillips **stalked** down the aisle and laid his hand heavily on Anne's shoulder.

stalk [stɔːk]
v. 怒冲冲地走

"Anne Shirley, what does this mean?" he said angrily. Anne returned no answer. It was asking too much of flesh and blood to expect her to tell before the whole school that she had been called "carrots". Gilbert it was who spoke up stoutly.

"It was my fault Mr. Phillips. I teased her."

Mr. Phillips paid no **heed** to Gilbert.

heed [hiːd]
n. 注意

"I am sorry to see a pupil of mine displaying such a temper and such a **vindictive** spirit," he said in a solemn tone, as if the mere fact of being a pupil of his ought to root out all evil passions from the hearts of small imperfect mortals. "Anne, go and stand on the platform in front of the blackboard for the rest of the afternoon."

vindictive [vɪnˈdɪktɪv]
adj. 怀恨的

Anne would have infinitely preferred a whipping to this punishment under which her sensitive spirit quivered as from a whiplash. With a white, set face she obeyed. Mr. Phillips took a chalk crayon and wrote on the blackboard above her head.

"Ann Shirley has a very bad temper. Ann Shirley must learn to control her temper," and then read it out loud so that even the primer class, who couldn't read writing, should understand it.

Anne stood there the rest of the afternoon with that legend above her. She did not cry or hang her head. Anger was still too hot in her heart for that and it sustained her **amid** all her **agony** of humiliation. With resentful eyes and passion-red cheeks she confronted alike Diana's sympathetic gaze and Charlie Sloane's indignant nods and Josie Pye's malicious smiles. As for Gilbert Blythe, she would not even look at him. She would never look at him again! She would never

amid [əˈmɪd]
prep. 在……过程中
agony [ˈæɡəni]
n. 极度痛苦

speak to him!!

When school was dismissed Anne **marched** out with her red head held high. Gilbert Blythe tried to **intercept** her at the porch door.

"I'm awfully sorry I made fun of your hair, Anne," he whispered **contritely**. "Honest I am. Don't be mad for keeps, now."

Anne swept by **disdainfully**, without look or sign of hearing. "Oh how could you, Anne?" breathed Diana as they went down the road half reproachfully, half **admiringly**. Diana felt that she could never have resisted Gilbert's plea.

"I shall never forgive Gilbert Blythe," said Anne firmly. "And Mr. Phillips spelled my name without an e, too. The iron has entered into my soul, Diana."

Diana hadn't the least idea what Anne meant but she understood it was something terrible.

"You mustn't mind Gilbert making fun of your hair," she said soothingly. "Why, he makes fun of all the girls. He laughs at mine because it's so black. He's called me a crow a dozen times; and I never heard him apologize for anything before, either."

"There's a great deal of difference between being called a crow and being called carrots," said Anne with dignity. "Gilbert Blythe has hurt my feelings excruciatingly, Diana."

It is possible the matter might have blown over without more **excruciation** if nothing else had happened. But when things begin to happen they are apt to keep on.

Avonlea scholars often spent noon hour picking gum in Mr. Bell's spruce grove over the hill and across his big pasture field. From there they could keep an eye on Eben Wright's house, where the master boarded. When they saw Mr. Phillips emerging **therefrom** they ran for the schoolhouse; but the distance being about three times lon-

march [mɑːtʃ]
v. 快步走
intercept [ˌɪntə'sept]
v. 拦截

contritely [kən'traɪtli]
adv. 懊悔地
disdainfully [dɪs'deɪnfəli]
adv. 轻蔑地
admiringly [əd'maɪərɪŋli]
adv. 钦佩地

excruciation [ɪkskruːʃɪ'eɪʃən]
n. 苦恼

therefrom [ˌðeə'frɒm]
adv. 从那里

ger than Mr. Wright's lane they were very **apt** to arrive there, breathless and gasping, some three minutes too late.

apt [æpt]
adj. 易于……的

On the following day Mr. Phillips was seized with one of his **spasmodic** fits of reform and announced before going home to dinner, that he should expect to find all the scholars in their seats when he returned. Anyone who came in late would be punished.

spasmodic [spæzˈmɒdɪk]
adj. 间歇性的

All the boys and some of the girls went to Mr. Bell's spruce grove as usual, fully intending to stay only long enough to "pick a chew". But spruce groves are **seductive** and yellow nuts of gum beguiling; they picked and **loitered** and **strayed**; and as usual the first thing that recalled them to a sense of the flight of time was Jimmy Glover shouting from the top of a **patriarchal** old spruce "Master's coming".

seductive [sɪˈdʌktɪv]
adj. 有魅力的
loiter [ˈlɔɪtə(r)]
v. 闲荡
stray [streɪ]
v. 走神
patriarchal [ˌpeɪtriˈɑːkl]
adj. 男人统治的

The girls who were on the ground, started first and managed to reach the schoolhouse in time but without a second to spare. The boys, who had to wriggle hastily down from the trees, were later; and Anne, who had not been picking gum at all but was wandering happily in the far end of the grove, waist deep among the bracken, singing softly to herself, with a wreath of rice lilies on her hair as if she were some wild **divinity** of the shadowy places, was latest of all. Anne could run like a deer, however; run she did with the impish result that she overtook the boys at the door and was swept into the schoolhouse among them just as Mr. Phillips was in the act of hanging up his hat.

divinity [dɪˈvɪnəti]
n. 神性

Mr. Phillips's brief reforming energy was over; he didn't want the bother of punishing a dozen pupils; but it was necessary to do something to save his word, so he looked about for a **scapegoat** and found it in Anne, who had dropped into her seat, gasping for breath, with a forgotten lily wreath hanging askew over one ear and giving her a particularly **rakish** and **dishevelled** appearance.

scapegoat [ˈskeɪpgəʊt]
n. 替罪羊
rakish [ˈreɪkɪʃ]
adj. 放荡不羁的
dishevelled [dɪˈʃevld]
adj. 凌乱的

"Anne Shirley, since you seem to be so fond of the boys' company we shall indulge your taste for it this afternoon," he said sarcastically. "Take those flowers out of your hair and sit with Gilbert Blythe."

The other boys **snickered**. Diana, turning pale with pity, **plucked** the wreath from Anne's hair and squeezed her hand. Anne stared at the master as if turned to stone.

snicker [ˈsnɪkə(r)]
v. 偷笑
pluck [plʌk]
v. 摘

"Did you hear what I said, Anne?" queried Mr. Phillips sternly.

"Yes, sir," said Anne slowly "but I didn't suppose you really meant it."

"I assure you I did"—still with the sarcastic inflection which all the children, and Anne especially, hated. It **flicked** on the raw. "Obey me at once."

flick [flɪk]
v. 轻弹

For a moment Anne looked as if she meant to disobey. Then, realizing that there was no help for it, she rose **haughtily**, stepped across the aisle, sat down beside Gilbert Blythe, and buried her face in her arms on the desk. Ruby Gillis, who got a glimpse of it as it went down, told the others going home from school that she'd "acksually never seen anything like it—it was so white, with awful little red spots in it".

haughtily [ˈhɔːtɪli]
adv. 傲慢地

To Anne, this was as the end of all things. It was bad enough to be **singled** out for punishment from among a dozen equally guilty ones; it was worse still to be sent to sit with a boy, but that that boy should be Gilbert Blythe was heaping insult on injury to a degree utterly unbearable. Anne felt that she could not bear it and it would be of no use to try. Her whole being seethed with shame and anger and humiliation.

single [ˈsɪŋgl]
v. 单独挑选

At first the other scholars looked and whispered and giggled and **nudged**. But as Anne never lifted her head and as Gilbert worked **fractions** as if his whole soul was absorbed in them and them only,

nudge [nʌdʒ]
v. (用肘)轻推
fractions [ˈfrækʃn]
n. 分数

they soon returned to their own tasks and Anne was forgotten. When Mr. Phillips called the history class out Anne should have gone, but Anne did not move, and Mr. Phillips, who had been writing some verses "To Priscilla" before he called the class, was thinking about an **obstinate** rhyme still and never missed her. Once, when nobody was looking, Gilbert took from his desk a little pink candy heart with a gold motto on it, "You are sweet", and slipped it under the **curve** of Anne's arm. Whereupon Anne arose, took the pink heart **gingerly** between the tips of her fingers, dropped it on the floor, ground it to powder beneath her heel, and resumed her position without **deigning** to **bestow** a glance on Gilbert.

When school went out Anne marched to her desk, **ostentatiously** took out everything therein, books and writing tablet, pen and ink, testament and arithmetic, and piled them neatly on her cracked slate.

"What are you taking all those things home for, Anne?" Diana wanted to know, as soon as they were out on the road. She had not dared to ask the question before.

"I am not coming back to school any more," said Anne. Diana gasped and stared at Anne to see if she meant it.

"Will Marilla let you stay home?" she asked.

"She'll have to," said Anne. "I'll never go to school to that man again."

"Oh, Anne!" Diana looked as if she were ready to cry. "I do think you're mean. What shall I do? Mr. Phillips will make me sit with that horrid Gertie Pye—I know he will because she is sitting alone. Do come back, Anne."

"I'd do almost anything in the world for you, Diana," said Anne sadly. "I'd let myself be **torn** limb from limb if it would do you any

obstinate [ˈɒbstɪnət]
adj. 棘手的

curve [kɜːv]
n. 曲线
gingerly [ˈdʒɪndʒəli]
adv. 小心翼翼地
deign [deɪn]
v. 屈尊
bestow [bɪˈstəʊ]
v. 赠予
ostentatiously [ˌɒstenˈteɪʃəsli]
adv. 炫耀地

tear [tɔːn]
v. 撕碎

good. But I can't do this, so please don't ask it. You **harrow** up my very soul."

harrow [ˈhærəʊ] *v.* 使苦恼

"Just think of all the fun you will miss," mourned Diana. "We are going to build the loveliest new house down by the brook; and we'll be playing ball next week and you've never played ball, Anne. It's tremendously exciting. And we're going to learn a new song—Jane Andrews is practicing it up now; and Alice Andrews is going to bring a new Pansy book next week and we're all going to read it out loud, chapter about, down by the brook. And you know you are so fond of reading out loud, Anne."

Nothing moved Anne in the least. Her mind was made up. She would not go to school to Mr. Phillips again; she told Marilla so when she got home.

"Nonsense," said Marilla.

"It isn't nonsense at all," said Anne, gazing at Marilla with solemn, reproachful eyes. "Don't you understand, Marilla? I've been **insulted**."

insult [ˈɪnsʌlt] *v.* 侮辱

"Insulted fiddlesticks! You'll go to school tomorrow as usual."

"Oh, no." Anne shook her head gently. "I'm not going back, Marilla. I'll learn my lessons at home and I'll be as good as I can be and hold my tongue all the time if it's possible at all. But I will not go back to school, I assure you."

Marilla saw something remarkably like **unyielding stubbornness** looking out of Anne's small face. She understood that she would have trouble in overcoming it; but she resolved wisely to say nothing more just then. "I'll run down and see Rachel about it this evening," she thought. "There's no use reasoning with Anne now. She's too worked up and I've an idea she can be awful stubborn if she takes the **notion**. Far as I can make out from her story, Mr. Phillips has been

unyielding [ʌnˈjiːldɪŋ] *adj.* 不屈的

stubbornness [ˈstʌbənnəs] *n.* 固执

notion [ˈnəʊʃn] *n.* 想法

carrying matters with a rather high hand. But it would never do to say so to her. I'll just talk it over with Rachel. She's sent ten children to school and she ought to know something about it. She'll have heard the whole story, too, by this time."

Marilla found Mrs. Lynde **knitting** quilts as industriously and cheerfully as usual.

knitting [ˈnɪtɪŋ] *v.* 编织

"I suppose you know what I've come about," she said, a little **shamefacedly**.

shamefacedly [ˌʃeɪmˈfeɪstli] *adv.* 谦卑地

Mrs. Rachel nodded.

"About Anne's fuss in school, I **reckon**," she said. "Tillie Boulter was in on her way home from school and told me about it."

reckon [ˈrekən] *v.* 预料

"I don't know what to do with her," said Marilla. "She declares she won't go back to school. I never saw a child so worked up. I've been expecting trouble ever since she started to school. I knew things were going too smooth to last. She's so high strung. What would you advise, Rachel?"

"Well, since you've asked my advice, Marilla," said Mrs. Lynde amiably—Mrs. Lynde dearly loved to be asked for advice—"I'd just humor her a little at first, that's what I'd do. It's my belief that Mr. Phillips was in the wrong. Of course, it doesn't do to say so to the children, you know. And of course he did right to punish her yesterday for giving way to temper. But today it was different. The others who were late should have been punished as well as Anne, that's what. And I don't believe in making the girls sit with the boys for punishment. It isn't **modest**. Tillie Boulter was real **indignant**. She took Anne's part right through and said all the scholars did too. Anne seems real popular among them, somehow. I never thought she'd take with them so well."

modest [ˈmɒdɪst] *adj.* 不太大的

indignant [ɪnˈdɪgnənt] *adj.* 愤愤不平的

"Then you really think I'd better let her stay home," said Marilla in amazement.

"Yes. That is I wouldn't say school to her again until she said it herself. Depend upon it, Marilla, she'll cool off in a week or so and be ready enough to go back of her own accord, that's what, while, if you were to make her go back right off, dear knows what freak or **tantrum** she'd take next and make more trouble than ever. The less fuss made the better, in my opinion. She won't miss much by not going to school, as far as that goes. Mr. Phillips isn't any good at all as a teacher. The order he keeps is **scandalous**, that's what, and he **neglects** the young fry and puts all his time on those big scholars he's getting ready for Queen's. He'd never have got the school for another year if his uncle hadn't been a **trustee**—The trustee, for he just leads the other two around by the nose, that's what. I declare, I don't know what education in this Island is coming to."

tantrum [ˈtæntrəm] n. 发脾气

scandalous [ˈskændələs] adj. 不可原谅的

neglect [nɪˈglekt] v. 忽视

trustee [trʌˈstiː] n. 受托人

Mrs. Rachel shook her head, as much as to say if she were only at the head of the educational system of the Province things would be much better managed.

Marilla took Mrs. Rachel's advice and not another word was said to Anne about going back to school. She learned her lessons at home, did her chores, and played with Diana in the chilly purple autumn twilights; but when she met Gilbert Blythe on the road or encountered him in Sunday school she passed him by with an icy contempt that was no **whit thawed** by his evident desire to appease her. Even Diana's efforts as a peacemaker were of no **avail**. Anne had evidently made up her mind to hate Gilbert Blythe to the end of life.

whit [wɪt] n. 一点点

thaw [θɔː] v. 融化

avail [əˈveɪl] n. 效用

As much as she hated Gilbert, however, did she love Diana, with all the love of her passionate little heart, equally intense in its likes and dislikes. One evening Marilla, coming in from the orchard with a basket of apples, found Anne sitting along by the east window in the twilight, crying bitterly.

"Whatever's the matter now, Anne?" she asked.

"It's about Diana," sobbed Anne luxuriously. "I love Diana so, Marilla. I cannot ever live without her. But I know very well when we grow up that Diana will get married and go away and leave me. And oh, what shall I do? I hate her husband—I just hate him furiously. I've been imagining it all out—the wedding and everything—Diana dressed in snowy **garments**, with a veil, and looking as beautiful and regal as a queen; and me the **bridesmaid**, with a lovely dress too, and puffed sleeves, but with a breaking heart hid beneath my smiling face. And then bidding Diana goodbye-e-e—" Here Anne broke down entirely and wept with increasing bitterness.

garment [ˈɡɑːmənt] n. 衣服
bridesmaid [ˈbraɪdzmeɪd] n. 伴娘

Marilla turned quickly away to hide her **twitching** face; but it was no use; she collapsed on the nearest chair and burst into such a **hearty** and unusual peal of laughter that Matthew, crossing the yard outside, **halted** in amazement. When had he heard Marilla laugh like that before?

twitch [twɪtʃ] v. 抽搐
hearty [ˈhɑːti] adj. 热情友好的
halt [hɒlt] v. 停止

"Well, Anne Shirley," said Marilla as soon as she could speak, "if you must borrow trouble, for pity's sake borrow it handier home. I should think you had an imagination, sure enough."

CHAPTER XVI

Diana Is Invited to Tea with Tragic Results

October was a beautiful month at Green Gables, when the birches in the hollow turned as golden as sunshine and the maples behind the orchard were royal crimson and the wild cherry trees along the lane put on the loveliest shades of dark red and bronzy green, while the fields sunned themselves in **aftermaths**.

aftermath [ˈɑːftəmæθ] n. 后果

Anne reveled in the world of color about her.

"Oh, Marilla," she exclaimed one Saturday morning, coming dancing in with her arms full of gorgeous **boughs**, "I'm so glad I live in a world where there are Octobers. It would be terrible if we just skipped from September to November, wouldn't it? Look at these maple branches. Don't they give you a thrill—several thrills? I'm going to **decorate** my room with them."

bough [baʊ]
n. 树枝

decorate ['dekəreɪt]
v. 装饰

"Messy things," said Marilla, whose aesthetic sense was not noticeably developed. "You clutter up your room entirely too much with out-of-doors stuff, Anne. Bedrooms were made to sleep in."

"Oh, and dream in too, Marilla. And you know one can dream so much better in a room where there are pretty things. I'm going to put these boughs in the old blue jug and set them on my table."

"Mind you don't drop leaves all over the stairs then. I'm going on a meeting of the Aid Society at Carmody this afternoon, Anne, and I won't likely be home before dark. You'll have to get Matthew and Jerry their supper, so mind you don't forget to put the tea to draw until you sit down at the table as you did last time."

"It was dreadful of me to forget," said Anne **apologetically**, "but that was the afternoon I was trying to think of a name for Violet Vale and it crowded other things out. Matthew was so good. He never **scolded** a bit. He put the tea down himself and said we could wait awhile as well as not. And I told him a lovely fairy story while we were waiting, so he didn't find the time long at all. It was a beautiful fairy story, Marilla. I forgot the end of it, so I made up an end for it myself and Matthew said he couldn't tell where the join came in."

apologetically
[əˌpɒlə'dʒetɪkli]
adv. 道歉地

scold [skəʊld]
v. 责骂

"Matthew would think it all right, Anne, if you took a notion to get up and have dinner in the middle of the night. But you keep your **wits** about you this time. And—I don't really know if I'm doing right—it may make you more **addle-pated** than ever—but you can

wit [wɪt]
n. 机智

addle-pated
['ædlˌpeɪtɪd]
adj. 头脑不清的

ask Diana to come over and spend the afternoon with you and have tea here."

"Oh, Marilla!" Anne clasped her hands. "How perfectly lovely! You are able to imagine things after all or else you'd never have understood how I've longed for that very thing. It will seem so nice and grown-**uppish**. No fear of my forgetting to put the tea to draw when I have company. Oh, Marilla, can I use the rosebud spray tea set?"

uppish [ˈʌpɪʃ] *adj.* 傲慢的

"No, indeed! The **rosebud** tea set! Well, what next? You know I never use that except for the minister or the Aids. You'll put down the old brown tea set. But you can open the little yellow crock of cherry preserves.

rosebud [ˈrəʊzbʌd] *n.* 玫瑰花蕾

It's time it was being used anyhow—I believe it's beginning to work. And you can cut some fruit cake and have some of the cookies and snaps."

"I can just imagine myself sitting down at the head of the table and pouring out the tea," said Anne, shutting her eyes **ecstatically**. "And asking Diana if she takes sugar! I know she doesn't but of course I'll ask her just as if I didn't know. And then pressing her to take another piece of fruit cake and another helping of preserves. Oh, Marilla, it's a wonderful **sensation** just to think of it. Can I take her into the spare room to lay off her hat when she comes? And then into the parlor to sit?"

ecstatically [ɪkˈstætɪkli] *adv.* 心醉神迷地

sensation [senˈseɪʃn] *n.* 感觉

"No. The sitting room will do for you and your company. But there's a bottle half full of raspberry cordial that was left over from the church social the other night. It's on the second shelf of the sitting-room closet and you and Diana can have it if you like, and a **cooky** to eat with it along in the afternoon, for I daresay Matthew'll be late coming in to tea since he's **hauling** potatoes to the vessel."

cooky [ˈkʊki] *n.* 饼干

haul [hɔːl] *v.* (用力)拖，拉，拽

Anne flew down to the hollow, past the Dryad's Bubble and up the spruce path to Orchard Slope, to ask Diana to tea. As a result just after Marilla had driven off to Carmody, Diana came over, dressed in her second-best dress and looking exactly as it is proper to look when asked out to tea. At other times she was **wont** to run into the kitchen without knocking; but now she knocked **primly** at the front door. And when Anne, dressed in her second best, as primly opened it, both little girls shook hands as gravely as if they had never met before. This unnatural solemnity lasted until after Diana had been taken to the east gable to lay off her hat and then had sat for ten minutes in the sitting room, **toes** in position.

wont [wəʊnt] *adj.* 习惯于
primly [ˈprɪmli] *adv.* 拘谨地
toe [təʊ] *n.* 脚趾

"How is your mother?" inquired Anne politely, just as if she had not seen Mrs. Barry picking apples that morning in excellent health and spirits.

"She is very well, thank you. I suppose Mr. Cuthbert is hauling potatoes to the Lily Sands this afternoon, is he?" said Diana, who had ridden down to Mr. Harmon Andrews's that morning in Matthew's cart.

"Yes. Our potato crop is very good this year. I hope your father's crop is good too."

"It is fairly good, thank you. Have you picked many of your apples yet?"

"Oh, ever so many," said Anne forgetting to be **dignified** and jumping up quickly. "Let's go out to the orchard and get some of the Red Sweetings, Diana. Marilla says we can have all that are left on the tree. Marilla is a very generous woman. She said we could have fruit cake and cherry preserves for tea. But it isn't good manners to tell your company what you are going to give them to eat, so I won't tell you what she said we could have to drink. Only it begins with an R and a C and it's bright red color. I love bright red drinks, don't you?

dignified [ˈdɪgnɪfaɪd] *adj.* 高贵的

They taste twice as good as any other color."

The orchard, with its great sweeping boughs that bent to the ground with fruit, proved so delightful that the little girls spent most of the afternoon in it, sitting in a grassy corner where the frost had spared the green and the mellow autumn sunshine lingered warmly, eating apples and talking as hard as they could. Diana had much to tell Anne of what went on in school. She had to sit with Gertie Pye and she hated it; Gertie squeaked her pencil all the time and it just made her—Diana's—blood run cold; Ruby Gillis had charmed all her warts away, true's you live, with a magic pebble that old Mary Joe from the Creek gave her. You had to rub the **warts** with the pebble and then throw it away over your left shoulder at the time of the new moon and the warts would all go. Charlie Sloane's name was written up with Em White's on the porch wall and Em White was awful mad about it; Sam Boulter had "**sassed**" Mr. Phillips in class and Mr. Phillips **whipped** him and Sam's father came down to the school and dared Mr. Phillips to lay a hand on one of his children again; and Mattie Andrews had a new red hood and a blue **crossover** with tassels on it and the airs she put on about it were perfectly sickening; and Lizzie Wright didn't speak to Mamie Wilson because Mamie Wilson's grown-up sister had cut out Lizzie Wright's grown-up sister with her **beau**; and everybody missed Anne so and wished she's come to school again; and Gilbert Blythe—

But Anne didn't want to hear about Gilbert Blythe. She jumped up hurriedly and said suppose they go in and have some raspberry cordial.

Anne looked on the second shelf of the room **pantry** but there was no bottle of raspberry cordial there. Search revealed it away back on the top shelf. Anne put it on a tray and set it on the table with a tum-

wart [wɔːt]
n. 疣

sass [sæs]
v. 对……出言不逊

whip [wɪp]
v. 鞭打

crossover
[ˈkrɒsəʊvə(r)]
n. 转型，变化

beau [bəʊ]
n. 情郎

pantry [ˈpæntri]
n. 食品贮藏室

bler.

"Now, please help yourself, Diana," she said politely. "I don't believe I'll have any just now. I don't feel as if I wanted any after all those apples."

Diana poured herself out a **tumblerful**, looked at its bright-red hue admiringly, and then sipped it **daintily**.

"That's awfully nice raspberry cordial, Anne," she said. "I didn't know raspberry cordial was so nice."

"I'm real glad you like it. Take as much as you want. I'm going to run out and **stir** the fire up. There are so many responsibilities on a person's mind when they're keeping house, isn't there?"

When Anne came back from the kitchen Diana was drinking her second glassful of cordial; and, being entreated **thereto** by Anne, she offered no particular objection to the drinking of a third. The tumblerfuls were generous ones and the raspberry cordial was certainly very nice.

"The nicest I ever drank," said Diana. "It's ever so much nicer than Mrs. Lynde's, although she **brags** of hers so much. It doesn't taste a bit like hers."

"I should think Marilla's raspberry cordial would probaly be much nicer than Mrs. Lynde's," said Anne loyally. "Marilla is a famous cook. She is trying to teach me to cook but I assure you, Diana, it is **uphill** work. There's so little scope for imagination in **cookery**. You just have to go by rules. The last time I made a cake I forgot to put the flour in. I was thinking the loveliest story about you and me, Diana. I thought you were desperately ill with smallpox and everybody **deserted** you, but I went **boldly** to your bedside and nursed you back to life; and then I took the smallpox and died and I was buried under those poplar trees in the graveyard and you planted a rose-

trumblerful [ˈtʌmbləfʊl]
n. 一平底玻璃杯的量
daintily [ˈdeɪntɪli]
adv. 讲究地

stir [stɜː(r)]
v. 搅拌

thereto [ˌðeəˈtuː]
adv. 随之

brag [bræg]
v. 自夸

uphill [ˌʌpˈhɪl]
adj. 漫长而艰难的
cookery [ˈkʊkəri]
n. 烹饪

desert [dɪˈzɜːt]
v. 离弃
boldly [ˈbəʊldli]
adv. 大胆地

bush by my grave and watered it with your tears; and you never, never forgot the friend of your youth who sacrificed her life for you. Oh, it was such a pathetic tale, Diana. The tears just rained down over my cheeks while I mixed the cake. But I forgot the flour and the cake was a dismal failure. Flour is so essential to cakes, you know. Marilla was very cross and I don't wonder. I'm a great **trial** to her. She was terribly mortified about the pudding sauce last week. We had a plum **pudding** for dinner on Tuesday and there was half the pudding and a pitcherful of sauce left over. Marilla said there was enough for another dinner and told me to set it on the pantry shelf and cover it. I meant to cover it just as much as could be, Diana, but when I carried it in I was imagining I was a nun—of course I'm a Protestant but I imagined I was a Catholic—taking the veil to bury a broken heart in **cloistered seclusion**; and I forgot all about covering the pudding sauce. I thought of it next morning and ran to the pantry. Diana, fancy if you can my extreme horror at finding a mouse drowned in that pudding sauce! I lifted the mouse out with a spoon and threw it out in the yard and then I washed the spoon in three waters. Marilla was out milking and I fully intended to ask her when she came in if I'd give the sauce to the pigs; but when she did come in I was imagining that I was a frost fairy going through the woods turning the trees red and yellow, whichever they wanted to be, so I never thought about the pudding sauce again and Marilla sent me out to pick apples. Well, Mr. and Mrs. Chester Ross from Spencervale came here that morning. You know they are very **stylish** people, especially Mrs. Chester Ross. When Marilla called me in dinner was all ready and everybody was at the table. I tried to be as polite and **dignified** as I could be, for I wanted Mrs. Chester Ross to think I was a ladylike little girl even if I wasn't pretty. Everything went right until I saw Marilla coming with

trial [ˈtraɪəl]
n. 惹麻烦的人

pudding [ˈpʊdɪŋ]
n. 布丁

cloistered [ˈklɔɪstəd]
adj. 与世隔绝的

seclusion [sɪˈkluːʒn]
n. 隐居

stylish [ˈstaɪlɪʃ]
adj. 时髦的

dignified [ˈdɪɡnɪfaɪd]
adj. 有尊严的

the plum pudding in one hand and the pitcher of pudding sauce warmed up, in the other. Diana, that was a terrible moment. I remembered everything and I just stood up in my place and shrieked out 'Marilla, you mustn't use that pudding sauce. There was a mouse drowned in it. I forgot to tell you before'. Oh, Diana, I shall never forget that awful moment if I live to be a hundred. Mrs. Chester Ross just looked at me and I thought I would sink through the floor with **mortification**. She is such a perfect housekeeper and fancy what she must have thought of us. Marilla turned red as fire but she never said a word—then. She just carried that sauce and pudding out and brought in some strawberry preserves. She even offered me some, but I couldn't swallow a mouthful. It was like **heaping** coals of fire on my head. After Mrs. Chester Ross went away, Marilla gave me a dreadful scolding. Why, Diana, what is the matter?"

mortification [ˌmɔːtɪfɪˈkeɪʃn] *n.* 屈辱

heap [hiːp] *v.* 堆积

Diana had stood up very unsteadily; then she sat down again, putting her hands to her head.

"I'm—I'm awful sick," she said, a little thickly. "I—I— must go right home."

"Oh, you mustn't dream of going home without your tea," cried Anne in distress. "I'll get it right off—I'll go and put the tea down this very minute."

"I must go home," repeated Diana, stupidly but **determinedly**.

determinedly [dɪˈtɜːmɪndli] *adv.* 决然地

"Let me get you a lunch anyhow," implored Anne. "Let me give you a bit of fruit cake and some of the cherry preserves. Lie down on the sofa for a little while and you'll be better. Where do you feel bad?"

"I must go home," said Diana, and that was all she would say. In vain Anne **pleaded**.

plead [pliːd] *v.* 恳求

"I never heard of company going home without tea," she mourned. "Oh, Diana, do you suppose that it's possible you're really taking the smallpox? If you are I'll go and nurse you, you can depend on that. I'll never **forsake** you. But I do wish you'd stay till after tea. Where do you feel bad?"

forsake [fə'seɪk] *v.* 抛弃

"I'm awful **dizzy**," said Diana.

dizzy ['dɪzi] *adj.* 头晕目眩的

And indeed, she walked very dizzily. Anne, with tears of disappointment in her eyes, got Diana's hat and went with her as far as the Barry yard fence. Then she wept all the way back to Green Gables, where she sorrowfully put the remainder of the raspberry cordial back into the pantry and got tea ready for Matthew and Jerry, with all the zest gone out of the performance.

The next day was Sunday and as the rain poured down in **torrents** from dawn till dusk Anne did not stir abroad from Green Gables. Monday afternoon Marilla sent her down to Mrs. Lynde's on an **errand**. In a very short space of time Anne came flying back up the lane with tears rolling down her cheeks. Into the kitchen she dashed and flung herself face **downward** on the sofa in an agony.

torrent ['tɒrənt] *n.* 激流

errand ['erənd] *n.* 差事

downward ['daʊnwəd] *adv.* 向下地

"Whatever has gone wrong now, Anne?" queried Marilla in doubt and dismay. "I do hope you haven't gone and been saucy to Mrs. Lynde again."

No answer from Anne save more tears and **stormier** sobs!

stormy ['stɔːmi] *adj.* 暴风雨般的

"Anne Shirley, when I ask you a question I want to be answered. Sit right up this very minute and tell me what you are crying about."

Anne sat up, tragedy **personified**.

personify [pə'sɒnɪfaɪ] *v.* 是……的化身(典型)

"Mrs. Lynde was up to see Mrs. Barry today and Mrs. Barry was in an awful state," she wailed. "She says that I set Diana drunk Saturday and sent her home in a disgraceful condition. And she says I must be a thoroughly bad, wicked little girl and she's never, never going to let Diana play with me again. Oh, Marilla, I'm just overcome with **woe**."

woe [wəʊ] *n.* 痛苦

Marilla stared in blank amazement.

"Set Diana drunk!" she said when she found her voice. "Anne are you or Mrs. Barry crazy? What **on earth** did you give her?"

on earth
究竟

"Not a thing but raspberry cordial," sobbed Anne. "I never thought raspberry cordial would set people drunk, Marilla—not even if they drank three big tumblerfuls as Diana did. Oh, it sounds so—so—like Mrs. Thomas's husband! But I didn't mean to set her drunk."

"Drunk fiddlesticks!" said Marilla, marching to the sitting room pantry. There on the shelf was a bottle which she at once recognized as one containing some of her three-year-old homemade **currant** wine for which she was celebrated in Avonlea, although certain of the stricter sort, Mrs. Barry among them, disapproved strongly of it. And at the same time Marilla recollected that she had put the bottle of raspberry cordial down in the cellar instead of in the pantry as she had told Anne.

currant['kʌrənt]
n. 小葡萄干

She went back to the kitchen with the wine bottle in her hand. Her face was twitching in spite of herself.

"Anne, you certainly have a genius for getting into trouble. You went and gave Diana currant wine instead of raspberry cordial. Didn't you know the difference yourself?"

"I never tasted it," said Anne. "I thought it was the cordial. I meant to be so—so—**hospitable**. Diana got awfully sick and had to go home. Mrs. Barry told Mrs. Lynde she was simply dead drunk. She just laughed silly-like when her mother asked her what was the matter and went to sleep and slept for hours. Her mother smelled her breath and knew she was drunk. She had a fearful headache all day yesterday. Mrs. Barry is so indignant. She will never believe but what I did it on purpose."

hospitable
[hɒ'spɪtəbl]
adj. 好客的

"I should think she would better punish Diana for being so **greedy** as to drink three glassfuls of anything," said Marilla shortly.

greedy ['griːdi]
adj. 贪吃的

"Why, three of those big glasses would have made her sick even if it had only been cordial. Well, this story will be a nice handle for those folks who are so down on me for making currant wine, although I haven't made any for three years ever since I found out that the minister didn't approve. I just kept that bottle for sickness. There, there, child, don't cry. I can't see as you were to blame although I'm sorry it happened so."

"I must cry," said Anne. "My heart is broken. The stars in their courses fight against me, Marilla. Diana and I are parted forever. Oh, Marilla, I little dreamed of this when first we **swore** our **vows** of friendship."

swear [sweə(r)] v. 发誓
vow [vaʊ] n. 誓约

"Don't be foolish, Anne. Mrs. Barry will think better of it when she finds you're not to blame. I suppose she thinks you've done it for a silly joke or something of that sort. You'd best go up this evening and tell her how it was."

"My courage fails me at the thought of facing Diana's injured mother," sighed Anne. "I wish you'd go, Marilla. You're so much more dignified than I am. Likely she'd listen to you quicker than to me."

"Well, I will," said Marilla, reflecting that it would probably be the wiser course. "Don't cry any more, Anne. It will be all right."

Marilla had changed her mind about it being all right by the time she got back from Orchard Slope.

Anne was watching for her coming and flew to the porch door to meet her.

"Oh, Marilla, I know by your face that it's been no use," she said sorrowfully. "Mrs. Barry won't forgive me?"

"Mrs. Barry indeed!" **snapped** Marilla. "Of all the unreasonable women I ever saw she's the worst. I told her it was all a mistake and

snap [snæp] v. 厉声说

you weren't to blame, but she just simply didn't believe me. And she rubbed it well in about my currant wine and how I'd always said it couldn't have the least effect on anybody. I just told her plainly that currant wine wasn't meant to be drunk three tumblerfuls at a time and that if a child I had to do with was so greedy I'd **sober** her up with a right good spanking."

Marilla **whisked** into the kitchen, **grievously** disturbed, leaving a very much distracted little soul in the porch behind her. Presently Anne stepped out **bareheaded** into the chill autumn dusk; very determinedly and steadily she took her way down through the sere clover field over the log bridge and up through the spruce grove, lighted by a pale little moon hanging low over the western woods. Mrs. Barry, coming to the door in answer to a timid knock, found a white-lipped eager-eyed suppliant on the doorstep.

Her face **hardened**. Mrs. Barry was a woman of strong prejudices and dislikes, and her anger was of the cold, **sullen** sort which is always hardest to overcome. To do her justice, she really believed Anne had made Diana drunk out of sheer malice **pretense**, and she was honestly anxious to preserve her little daughter from the **contamination** of further intimacy with such a child.

"What do you want?" she said stiffly.

Anne clasped her hands.

"Oh, Mrs. Barry, please forgive me. I did not mean to—to—intoxicate Diana. How could I? Just imagine if you were a poor little orphan girl that kind people had adopted and you had just one bosom friend in all the world. Do you think you would intoxicate her on purpose? I thought it was only raspberry cordial. I was firmly convinced it was raspberry cordial. Oh, please don't say that you won't let Diana play with me any more. If you do you will cover my life with a dark

sober [ˈsəʊbə(r)]
v.(使)醒酒

whisk [wɪsk]
v. 飞奔
grievously [ˈgriːvəsli]
adv. 极其痛苦地
bareheaded [ˌbeəˈhedɪd]
adj. 头上不戴东西(的)

harden [ˈhɑːdn]
v. 硬化
sullen [ˈsʌlən]
adj. 愠怒的

pretense [prɪˈtens]
n. 假象
contamination [kənˌtæmɪˈneɪʃn]
n. 污染

cloud of woe."

This speech which would have softened good Mrs. Lynde's heart in a twinkling, had no effect on Mrs. Barry except to **irritate** her still more. She was suspicious of Anne's big words and dramatic gestures and imagined that the child was making fun of her. So she said, coldly and cruelly:

"I don't think you are a fit little girl for Diana to associate with. You'd better go home and behave yourself."

Anne's lips quivered.

"Won't you let me see Diana just once to say farewell?" she implored.

"Diana has gone over to Carmody with her father," said Mrs. Barry, going in and shutting the door.

Anne went back to Green Gables calm with **despair**.

"My last hope is gone," she told Marilla. "I went up and saw Mrs. Barry myself and she treated me very **insultingly**. Marilla, I do not think she is a well-bred woman. There is nothing more to do except to pray and I haven't much hope that'll do much good because, Marilla, I do not believe that God himself can do very much with such an **obstinate** person as Mrs. Barry."

"Anne, you shouldn't say such things" rebuked Marilla, **striving** to overcome that **unholy** tendency to laughter which she was **dismayed** to find growing upon her. And indeed, when she told the whole story to Matthew that night, she did laugh heartily over Anne's tribulations.

But when she slipped into the east **gable** before going to bed and found that Anne had cried herself to sleep an unaccustomed softness crept into her face.

"Poor little soul," she murmured, lifting a loose curl of hair from

irritate [ˈɪrɪteɪt]
v. 激怒

despair [dɪˈspeə(r)]
n. 绝望

insultingly [ɪnˈsʌltɪŋli]
adv. 无礼地

obstinate [ˈɒbstɪnət]
adj. 执拗的

strive [ˈstraɪv]
v. 努力

unholy [ʌnˈhəʊli]
adj. 不神圣的

dismay [dɪsˈmeɪ]
v. 使诧异

gable [ˈgeɪbl]
n. 三角墙

the child's tear-stained face. Then she bent down and kissed the flushed cheek on the pillow.

CHAPTER XVII

A New Interest in Life

The next afternoon Anne, bending over her patchwork at the kitchen window, happened to glance out and beheld Diana down by the Dryad's Bubble beckoning mysteriously. In a **trice** Anne was out of the house and flying down to the **hollow**, astonishment and hope struggling in her expressive eyes. But the hope faded when she saw Diana's dejected countenance.

trice [traɪs]
n. 瞬间
hollow ['hɒləʊ]
n. 坑洼处

"Your mother hasn't **relented**?" she gasped.

relent [rɪ'lent]
v. 变宽容,变温和

Diana shook her head mournfully.

"No; and oh, Anne, she says I'm never to play with you again. I've cried and cried and I told her it wasn't your fault, but it wasn't any use. I had ever such a time **coaxing** her to let me come down and say good-bye to you. She said I was only to stay ten minutes and she's timing me by the clock."

coax ['kəʊks]
v. 劝诱

"Ten minutes isn't very long to say an eternal **farewell** in," said Anne tearfully. "Oh, Diana, will you promise faithfully never to forget me, the friend of your youth, no matter what dearer friends may **caress** thee?"

farewell [ˌfeə'wel]
n. 告别

caress [kə'res]
v. 爱抚

"Indeed I will," sobbed Diana, "and I'll never have another bosom friend—I don't want to have. I couldn't love anybody as I love you."

"Oh, Diana," cried Anne, clasping her hands, "do you love me?"

"Why, of course I do. Didn't you know that?"

"No." Anne drew a long breath. "I thought you liked me of course but I never hoped you loved me. Why, Diana, I didn't think anybody could love me. Nobody ever has loved me since I can remember. Oh, this is wonderful! It's a ray of light which will forever shine on the darkness of a path severed from thee, Diana. Oh, just say it once again."

"I love you **devotedly**, Anne," said Diana **stanchly**, "and I always will, you may be sure of that."

devotedly [dɪˈvəʊtɪdli] *adv.* 一心一意地
stanchly [ˈstɔːntʃli] *adv.* 忠实地

"And I will always love thee, Diana," said Anne, solemnly extending her hand. "In the years to come thy memory will shine like a star over my lonely life, as that last story we read together says. Diana, wilt thou give me a lock of thy jet-black tresses in parting to treasure forevermore?"

"Have you got anything to cut it with?" queried Diana, wiping away the tears which Anne's affecting accents had caused to flow afresh, and returning to **practicalities**.

practicality [ˌpræktɪˈkæləti] *n.* 可行性

"Yes. I've got my patchwork scissors in my apron pocket fortunately," said Anne. She solemnly clipped one of Diana's curls. "Fare thee well, my beloved friend. **Henceforth** we must be as strangers though living side by side. But my heart will ever be faithful to thee."

henceforth [ˌhensˈfɔːθ] *adv.* 从此之后

Anne stood and watched Diana out of sight, **mournfully** waving her hand to the latter whenever she turned to look back. Then she returned to the house, not a little **consoled** for the time being by this romantic parting.

mournfully [ˈmɔːnfəli] *adv.* 悲哀地
console [kənˈsəʊl] *v.* 安慰

"It is all over," she informed Marilla. "I shall never have another friend. I'm really worse off than ever before, for I haven't Katie Maurice and Violetta now. And even if I had it wouldn't be the same. Somehow, little dream girls are not satisfying after a real friend. Diana and I had such an affecting farewell down by the spring. It will be sacred in my memory forever. I used the most pathetic language I could think of and said 'thou' and 'thee'. 'Thou' and 'thee' seem so much more romantic than 'you'. Diana gave me a lock of her hair and I'm going to sew it up in a little bag and wear it around my neck all my life. Please see that it is buried with me, for I don't believe I'll live very long. Perhaps when she sees me lying cold and dead before her Mrs. Barry may feel **remorse** for what she has done and will let Diana come to my funeral."

"I don't think there is much fear of your dying of **grief** as long as you can talk, Anne," said Marilla unsympathetically.

The following Monday Anne surprised Marilla by coming down from her room with her basket of books on her arm and lips primmed up into a line of determination.

"I'm going back to school," she announced. "That is all there is left in life for me, now that my friend has been ruthlessly torn from me. In school I can look at her and **muse** over days departed."

"You'd better muse over your lessons and sums," said Marilla, **concealing** her delight at this development of the situation. "If you're going back to school I hope we'll hear no more of breaking slates over people's heads and such carryings on. Behave yourself and do just what your teacher tells you."

"I'll try to be a model pupil," agreed Anne **dolefully**. "There won't be much fun in it, I expect. Mr. Phillips said Minnie Andrews was a model pupil and there isn't a spark of imagination or life in her. She is just dull and **poky** and never seems to have a good time. But I feel so depressed that perhaps it will come easy to me now. I'm going round by the road. I couldn't bear to go by the Birch Path all alone. I should weep bitter tears if I did."

Anne was welcomed back to school with open arms. Her imagination had been sorely missed in games, her voice in the singing and her dramatic ability in the perusal aloud of books at dinner hour. Ruby Gil-

remorse [rɪˈmɔːs]
n. 懊悔

grief [griːf]
n.(尤指因某人去世引起的)悲痛

muse [mjuːz]
v. 沉思

conceal [kənˈsiːl]
v. 隐藏

dolefully [ˈdəʊlfəli]
adv. 悲哀地

poky [ˈpəʊki]
adj. 狭窄的

lis **smuggled** three blue **plums** over to her during testament reading; Ella May MacPherson gave her an enormous yellow pansy cut from the covers of a floral catalogue—a species of desk decoration much prized in Avonlea school. Sophia Sloane offered to teach her a perfectly elegant new pattern of knit lace, so nice for trimming **aprons**. Katie Boulter gave her a perfume bottle to keep slate water in, and Julia Bell copied carefully on a piece of pale pink paper scalloped on the edges the following **effusion**:

When twilight drops her curtain down
And pins it with a star
Remember that you have a friend
Though she may wander far.

"It's so nice to be appreciated," sighed Anne **rapturously** to Marilla that night.

The girls were not the only scholars who "appreciated" her. When Anne went to her seat after dinner hour—she had been told by Mr. Phillips to sit with the model Minnie Andrews—she found on her desk a big **luscious** "strawberry apple". Anne caught it up all ready to take a bite when she remembered that the only place in Avonlea where strawberry apples grew was in the old Blythe orchard on the other side of the Lake of Shining Waters. Anne dropped the apple as if it were a red-hot coal and **ostentatiously** wiped her fingers on her handkerchief. The apple lay **untouched** on her desk until the next morning, when little Timothy Andrews, who swept the school and kindled the fire, **annexed** it as one of his **perquisites**. Charlie Sloane's slate pencil, gorgeously **bedizened** with striped red and yellow paper, costing two cents where ordinary pencils cost only one, which he sent up to her after dinner hour, met with a more favorable reception. Anne was **graciously** pleased to accept it and rewarded the donor with a

smuggle [ˈsmʌgl]
v. 偷偷携带，夹带

plum [plʌm]
n. 李子

apron [ˈeɪprən]
n. 围裙

effusion [ɪˈfjuːʒn]
n. (强烈感情的)迸发

rapturously [ˈræptʃərəsli]
adv. 兴高采烈地

luscious [ˈlʌʃəs]
adj. 甘美的

ostentatiously [ˌɒstenˈteɪʃəsli]
adv. 铺张地

untouched [ʌnˈtʌtʃt]
adj. 未食用(或饮用)；未动

annexe [ˈæneks]
v. 强占，并吞

perquisite [ˈpɜːkwɪzɪt]
n. 津贴，额外收入

bedizen [bɪˈdaɪz(ə)n]
v. (诗文)将……装扮得过分艳丽

graciously [ˈgreɪʃəsli]
adv. 有礼貌地

smile which exalted that **infatuated** youth straightway into the seventh heaven of delight and caused him to make such fearful errors in his dictation that Mr. Phillips kept him in after school to rewrite it.

infatuated [ɪn'fætʃueɪtɪd] *adj.* 入迷的

But as,

The Caesar's pageant shorn of Brutus' bust,

Did but of Rome's best son remind her more.

So the marked absence of any **tribute** or recognition from Diana Barry who was sitting with Gertie Pye **embittered** Anne's little triumph.

tribute ['trɪbjuːt] *n.* 致敬

embitter [ɪm'bɪtə(r)] *v.* 使痛苦

"Diana might just have smiled at me once, I think," she mourned to Marilla that night. But the next morning a note most fearfully and wonderfully **twisted** and folded, and a small parcel were passed across to Anne.

twist ['twɪst] *v.* 使扭曲

Dear Anne (ran the former),

Mother says I'm not to play with you or talk to you even in school. It isn't my fault and don't be cross at me, because I love you as much as ever. I miss you awfully to tell all my secrets to and I don't like Gertie Pye one bit. I made you one of the new bookmarkers out of red tissue paper. They are awfully fashionable now and only three girls in school know how to make them. When you look at it remember, your true friend Diana Barry.

Anne read the note, kissed the bookmark, and **dispatched** a prompt reply back to the other side of the school.

dispatch [dɪ'spætʃ] *v.* 迅速处理

My own darling Diana:

Of course I am not **cross** at you because you have to obey your mother. Our spirits can **commune**. I shall keep your lovely present forever. Minnie Andrews is a very nice little girl—although she has no imagination— but after having been Diana's busum friend I cannot be Minnie's. Please excuse mistakes because my spelling isn't very good

cross [krɒs] *adj.* 恼怒的

commune ['kɒmjuːn] *v.* 与……默默分享

yet, although much improved. Yours until death us do part Anne or Cordelia Shirley.

P.S. I shall sleep with your letter under my pillow tonight. A. OR C.S.

Marilla **pessimistically** expected more trouble since Anne had again begun to go to school. But none developed. Perhaps Anne caught something of the "model" spirit from Minnie Andrews; at least she got on very well with Mr. Phillips **thenceforth**. She flung herself into her studies heart and soul, determined not to be outdone in any class by Gilbert Blythe. The rivalry between them was soon apparent; it was entirely good natured on Gilbert's side; but it is much to be feared that the same thing cannot be said of Anne, who had certainly an **unpraiseworthy** tenacity for holding grudges. She was as intense in her **hatreds** as in her loves. She would not stoop to admit that she meant to rival Gilbert in schoolwork, because that would have been to acknowledge his existence which Anne **persistently** ignored; but the **rivalry** was there and honors fluctuated between them. Now Gilbert was head of the spelling class; now Anne, with a toss of her long red **braids**, spelled him down. One morning Gilbert had all his sums done correctly and had his name written on the blackboard on the roll of honor; the next morning Anne, having **wrestled** wildly with **decimals** the entire evening before, would be first. One awful day they were ties and their names were written up together. It was almost as bad as a take-notice and Anne's mortification was as evident as Gilbert's satisfaction. When the written examinations at the end of each month were held the suspense was terrible. The first month Gilbert came out three marks ahead. The second Anne beat him by five. But her triumph was marred by the fact that Gilbert congratulated her heartily before the whole school. It would have been ever so much sweeter to her if he had felt the sting of his defeat.

pessimistically [ˌpesɪˈmɪstɪkli] *adv.* 悲观地

thenceforth [ˌðensˈfɔːθ] *adv.* 从那时起

unpraiseworthy [ʌnˈpreɪzwɜːði] *adj.* 不值得称赞的

hatred [ˈheɪtrɪd] *n.* 仇恨

persistently [pəˈsɪstəntli] *adv.* 固执地

rivalry [ˈraɪvlri] *n.* 竞争

braid [breɪd] *n.* 辫子

wrestle [ˈresl] *v.* 努力解决

decimals [ˈdesɪml] *n.* 小数

Mr. Phillips might not be a very good teacher; but a pupil so **inflexibly** determined on learning as Anne was could hardly escape making progress under any kind of teacher. By the end of the term Anne and Gilbert were both promoted into the fifth class and allowed to begin studying the elements of "the branches"—by which Latin, geometry, French, and algebra were meant. In geometry Anne met her Waterloo.

inflexibly [ɪnˈfleksəbli] *adv.* 不屈地

"It's perfectly awful stuff, Marilla," she groaned. "I'm sure I'll never be able to make head or tail of it. There is no scope for imagination in it at all. Mr. Phillips says I'm the worst **dunce** he ever saw at it. And Gil—I mean some of the others are so smart at it. It is extremely mortifying, Marilla."

dunce [dʌns] *n.* 傻瓜

"Even Diana gets along better than I do. But I don't mind being beaten by Diana. Even although we meet as strangers now I still love her with an inextinguishable love. It makes me very sad at times to think about her. But really, Marilla, one can't stay sad very long in such an interesting world, can one?"

CHAPTER XVIII

Anne to the Rescue

All things great are **wound** up with all things little. At first **glance** it might not seem that the decision of a certain Canadian Premier to include Prince Edward Island in a political tour could have much or anything to do with the fortunes of little Anne Shirley at Green Gables. But it had.

wind [wɪnd] *v.* 缠绕

glance [glɑːns] *n.* 瞥一眼

It was a January the Premier came, to address his loyal supporters and such of his nonsupporters as chose to be present at the monster mass meeting held in Charlottetown. Most of the Avonlea people were on Premier's side of politics; **hence** on the night of the meeting

hence [hens] *adv.* 因此

nearly all the men and a goodly proportion of the women had gone to town thirty miles away. Mrs. Rachel Lynde had gone too. Mrs. Rachel Lynde was a red-hot politician and couldn't have believed that the political **rally** could be carried through without her, although she was on the opposite side of politics. So she went to town and took her husband—Thomas would be useful in looking after the horse—and Marilla Cuthbert with her. Marilla had a **sneaking** interest in politics herself, and as she thought it might be her only chance to see a real live Premier, she promptly took it, leaving Anne and Matthew to keep house until her return the following day.

rally [ˈræli] *n.* 集会

sneaking [ˈsniːkɪŋ] *adj.* 暗中的

Hence, while Marilla and Mrs. Rachel were enjoying themselves hugely at the mass meeting, Anne and Matthew had the cheerful kitchen at Green Gables all to themselves. A bright fire was glowing in the old-fashioned Waterloo stove and blue-white frost crystals were shining on the **windowpanes**. Matthew nodded over a farmers' advocate on the sofa and Anne at the table studied her lessons with **grim** determination, despite **sundry** wistful glances at the clock shelf, where lay a new book that Jane Andrews had lent her that day. Jane had assured her that it was **warranted** to produce any number of thrills, or words to that effect, and Anne's fingers **tingled** to reach out for it. But that would mean Gilbert Blythe's triumph on the morrow. Anne turned her back on the clock shelf and tried to imagine it wasn't there.

windowpane [ˈwɪndəʊpeɪn] *n.* 窗玻璃

grim [ɡrɪm] *adj.* 坚定的

sundry [ˈsʌndri] *adj.* 杂项的

warrant [ˈwɒrənt] *v.* 保证

tingle [ˈtɪŋɡl] *v.* 刺痛

"Matthew, did you ever study geometry when you went to school?"

"Well now, no, I didn't," said Matthew, coming out of his doze with a start.

"I wish you had," sighed Anne, "because then you'd be able to sympathize with me. You can't sympathize properly if you've never studied it. It is **casting** a cloud over my whole life. I'm such a **dunce** at it, Matthew."

"Well now, I dunno," said Matthew soothingly. "I guess you're all right at anything. Mr. Phillips told me last week in Blair's store at Carmody that you was the smartest scholar in school and was making rapid progress. 'Rapid progress' was his very words. There's them as runs down Teddy Phillips and says he ain't much of a teacher, but I guess he's all right."

Matthew would have thought anyone who praised Anne was "all right".

"I'm sure I'd get on better with geometry if only he wouldn't change the letters," complained Anne. "I learn the proposition off by heart and then he draws it on the blackboard and puts different letters from what are in the book and I get all mixed up. I don't think a teacher should take such a mean advantage, do you? We're studying **agriculture** now and I've found out at last what makes the roads red. It's a great comfort. I wonder how Marilla and Mrs. Lynde are enjoying themselves. Mrs. Lynde says Canada is going to the dogs the way things are being run at Ottawa and that it's an awful warning to the **electors**. She says if women were allowed to vote we would soon see a blessed change. What way do you vote, Matthew?"

"**Conservative**," said Matthew promptly. To vote Conservative was part of Matthew's religion.

"Then I'm Conservative too," said Anne decidedly. "I'm glad because Gil—because some of the boys in school are **Grits**. I guess Mr. Phillips is a Grit too because Prissy Andrews's father is one, and Ruby Gillis says that when a man is courting he always has to agree with the girl's mother in religion and her father in politics. Is that true, Matthew?"

"Well now, I dunno," said Matthew.

cast [ˈkɑːst]
v. 投射

dunce [dʌns]
n. 愚笨的人

agriculture
[ˈæɡrɪkʌltʃə(r)]
n. 农学

elector [ɪˈlektə(r)]
n. 选举人

Conservative
[kənˈsɜːvətɪv]
n. 保守党党员，保守党支持者

Grits [ɡrɪts]
n. 自由党成员

"Did you ever go courting, Matthew?"

"Well now, no, I dunno's I ever did," said Matthew, who had certainly never thought of such a thing in his whole existence.

Anne reflected with her chin in her hands.

"It must be rather interesting, don't you think, Matthew? Ruby Gillis says when she grows up she's going to have ever so many beaus on the string and have them all crazy about her; but I think that would be too exciting. I'd rather have just one in his right mind. But Ruby Gillis knows a great deal about such matters because she has so many big sisters, and Mrs. Lynde says the Gillis girls have gone off like hot cakes. Mr. Phillips goes up to see Prissy Andrews nearly every evening. He says it is to help her with her lessons but Miranda Sloane is studying for Queen's too, and I should think she needed help a lot more than Prissy because she's ever so much stupider, but he never goes to help her in the evenings at all. There are a great many things in this world that I can't understand very well, Matthew."

"Well now, I dunno as I comprehend them all myself," acknowledged Matthew.

"Well, I suppose I must finish up my lessons. I won't allow myself to open that new book Jane lent me until I'm through. But it's a terrible **temptation**, Matthew. Even when I turn my back on it I can see it there just as plain. Jane said she cried herself sick over it. I love a book that makes me cry. But I think I'll carry that book into the sitting room and lock it in the jam closet and give you the key. And you must not give it to me, Matthew, until my lessons are done, not even if I implore you on my bended knees. It's all very well to say resist temptation, but it's ever so much easier to resist it if you can't get the key. And then shall I run down the cellar and get some russets, Matthew? Wouldn't you like some russets?"

temptation [temp'teɪʃn] *n.* 诱惑

"Well now, I dunno but what I would," said Matthew, who never ate **russets** but knew Anne's weakness for them.

Just as Anne emerged triumphantly from the cellar with her plateful of russets came the sound of flying footsteps on the icy board walk outside and the next moment the kitchen door was flung open and in rushed Diana Barry, white faced and breathless, with a shawl wrapped **hastily** around her head. Anne promptly let go of her candle and plate in her surprise, and plate, candle, and apples crashed together down the cellar ladder and were found at the bottom **embedded** in melted **grease**, the next day, by Marilla, who gathered them up and thanked mercy the house hadn't been set on fire.

"Whatever is the matter, Diana?" cried Anne. "Has your mother relented at last?"

"Oh, Anne, do come quick," implored Diana nervously. "Minnie May is awful sick—she's got **croup**. Young Mary Joe says—and Father and Mother are away to town and there's nobody to go for the doctor. Minnie May is awful bad and Young Mary Joe doesn't know what to do—and oh, Anne, I'm so scared!"

Matthew, without a word, reached out for cap and coat, slipped past Diana and away into the darkness of the yard.

"He's gone to harness the **sorrel mare** to go to Carmody for the doctor," said Anne, who was hurrying on hood and jacket. "I know it as well as if he'd said so. Matthew and I are such kindred spirits I can read his thoughts without words at all."

"I don't believe he'll find the doctor at Carmody," sobbed Diana. "I know that Dr. Blair went to town and I guess Dr. Spencer would go too. Young Mary Joe never saw anybody with croup and Mrs. Lynde is away. Oh, Anne!"

"Don't cry, Di," said Anne cheerily. "I know exactly what to do

russet [ˈrʌsɪt]
n. 赤褐色马铃薯

hastily [ˈheɪstɪli]
adv. 匆忙地

embed [ɪmˈbed]
v. 使融入

grease [griːs]
n. 油脂

croup [kruːp]
n. 哮吼

sorrel mare
栗色母马

for croup. You forget that Mrs. Hammond had twins three times. When you look after three pairs of twins you naturally get a lot of experience. They all had croup regularly. Just wait till I get the ipecac bottle—you mayn't have any at your house. Come on now."

The two little girls **hastened** out hand in hand and hurried through Lover's Lane and across the **crusted** field beyond, for the snow was too deep to go by the shorter wood way. Anne, although sincerely sorry for Minnie May, was far from being insensible to the romance of the situation and to the sweetness of once more sharing that romance with a kindred spirit.

hasten [ˈheɪsn] *v.* 急忙，赶快
crusted [ˈkrʌstɪd] *adj.* 有外壳

The night was clear and **frosty**, all **ebony** of shadow and silver of snowy slope; big stars were shining over the silent fields; here and there the dark pointed firs stood up with snow powdering their branches and the wind whistling through them. Anne thought it was truly delightful to go skimming through all this mystery and loveliness with your bosom friend who had been so long **estranged**.

frosty [ˈfrɒsti] *adj.* 严寒的
ebony [ˈebəni] *n.* 乌黑色
estranged [ɪˈstreɪndʒd] *adj.* 疏远的

Minnie May, aged three, was really very sick. She lay on the kitchen sofa **feverish** and restless, while her hoarse breathing could be heard all over the house. Young Mary Joe, a **buxom**, broad-faced French girl from the creek, whom Mrs. Barry had engaged to stay with the children during her absence, was helpless and **bewildered**, quite incapable of thinking what to do, or doing it if she thought of it.

feverish [ˈfiːvərɪʃ] *adj.* 发烧的
buxom [ˈbʌksəm] *adj.* 丰满的
bewildered [bɪˈwɪldəd] *adj.* 困惑的

Anne went to work with skill and promptness.

"Minnie May has croup all right; she's pretty bad, but I've seen them worse. First we must have lots of hot water. I declare, Diana, there isn't more than a **cupful** in the kettle! There, I've filled it up, and, Mary Joe, you may put some wood in the stove. I don't want to hurt your feelings but it seems to me you might have thought of this before if you'd any imagination. Now, I'll undress Minnie May and

cupful [ˈkʌpfʊl] *n.* 满杯

put her to bed and you try to find some soft flannel cloths, Diana. I'm going to give her a dose of **ipecac** first of all."

Minnie May did not take kindly to the ipecac but Anne had not brought up three pairs of twins for nothing. Down that ipecac went, not only once, but many times during the long, anxious night when the two little girls worked patiently over the suffering Minnie May, and Young Mary Joe, honestly anxious to do all she could, kept up a roaring fire and heated more water than would have been needed for a hospital of **croupy** babies.

It was three o'clock when Matthew came with a doctor, for he had been obliged to go all the way to Spencervale for one. But the pressing need for assistance was past. Minnie May was much better and was sleeping soundly.

"I was awfully near giving up in despair," explained Anne. "She got worse and worse until she was sicker than ever the Hammond twins were, even the last pair. I actually thought she was going to **choke** to death. I gave her every drop of ipecac in that bottle and when the last dose went down I said to myself—not to Diana or Young Mary Joe, because I didn't want to worry them any more than they were worried, but I had to say it to myself just to relieve my feelings—'This is the last **lingering** hope and I fear, tis a vain one.' But in about three minutes she coughed up the **phlegm** and began to get better right away. You must just imagine my relief, doctor, because I can't express it in words. You know there are some things that cannot be expressed in words."

"Yes, I know," nodded the doctor. He looked at Anne as if he were thinking some things about her that couldn't be expressed in words. Later on, however, he expressed them to Mr. and Mrs. Barry.

"That little redheaded girl they have over at Cuthbert's is as

ipecac [ˈɪpeˌkæk]
n. 吐根制剂

croupy [kruːpi]
adj. 哮吼性的

choke [tʃəʊk]
v. 窒息

lingering [ˈlɪŋgərɪŋ]
adj. 拖延的

phlegm [flem]
n. 痰

smart as they make 'em. I tell you she saved that baby's life, for it would have been too late by the time I got there. She seems to have a skill and presence of mind perfectly wonderful in a child of her age. I never saw anything like the eyes of her when she was explaining the case to me."

Anne had gone home in the wonderful, white-frosted winter morning, heavy eyed from loss of sleep, but still talking unweariedly to Matthew as they crossed the long white field and walked under the **glittering** fairy arch of the Lover's Lane maples.

glittering ['glɪtərɪŋ] *adj.* 华丽的

"Oh, Matthew, isn't it a wonderful morning? The world looks like something God had just imagined for his own pleasure, doesn't it? Those trees look as if I could blow them away with a breath—pouf! I'm so glad I live in a world where there are white frosts, aren't you? And I'm so glad Mrs. Hammond had three pairs of twins after all. If she hadn't I mightn't have known what to do for Minnie May. I'm real sorry I was ever cross with Mrs. Hammond for having twins. But, oh, Matthew, I'm so sleepy. I can't go to school. I just know I couldn't keep my eyes open and I'd be so stupid. But I hate to stay home, for Gil—some of the others will get head of the class, and it's so hard to get up again—although of course the harder it is the more satisfaction you have when you do get up, haven't you?"

"Well now, I guess you'll manage all right," said Matthew, looking at Anne's white little face and the dark shadows under her eyes. "You just go right to bed and have a good sleep. I'll do all the chores."

Anne accordingly went to bed and slept so long and soundly that it was well on in the white and rosy winter afternoon when she awoke and **descended** to the kitchen where Marilla, who had arrived home in the meantime, was sitting **knitting**.

descend [dɪ'send] *v.* 下来
knit ['nɪt] *v.* 编织

"Oh, did you see the Premier?" exclaimed Anne at once. "What did he look like Marilla?"

"Well, he never got to be Premier on account of his looks," said Marilla. "Such a nose as that man had! But he can speak. I was proud of being a Conservative. Rachel Lynde, of course, being a Liberal, had no use for him. Your dinner is in the oven, Anne, and you can get yourself some blue plum preserve out of the pantry. I guess you're hungry. Matthew has been telling me about last night. I must say it was fortunate you knew what to do. I wouldn't have had any idea myself, for I never saw a case of croup. There now, never mind talking till you've had your dinner. I can tell by the look of you that you're just full up with speeches, but they'll keep."

Marilla had something to tell Anne, but she did not tell it just then for she knew if she did Anne's consequent excitement would lift her clear out of the region of such material matters as **appetite** or dinner. Not until Anne had finished her saucer of blue plums did Marilla say:

appetite ['æpɪtaɪt]
n. 食欲

"Mrs. Barry was here this afternoon, Anne. She wanted to see you, but I wouldn't wake you up. She says you saved Minnie May's life, and she is very sorry she acted as she did in that affair of the currant wine. She says she knows now you didn't mean to set Diana drunk, and she hopes you'll forgive her and be good friends with Diana again. You're to go over this evening if you like for Diana can't **stir** outside the door on account of a bad cold she caught last night. Now, Anne Shirley, for pity's sake don't fly up into the air."

stir [stɜː(r)]
v. 行动

The warning seemed not unnecessary, so uplifted and **aerial** was Anne's expression and attitude as she sprang to her feet, her face irradiated with the flame of her spirit.

aerial ['eəriəl]
adj. 空气中的

"Oh, Marilla, can I go right now—without washing my dishes? I'll wash them when I come back, but I cannot tie myself down to anything so unromantic as dishwashing at this thrilling moment."

"Yes, yes, run along," said Marilla **indulgently**. "Anne Shirley—are you crazy? Come back this instant and put something on you. I might as well call to the wind. She's gone without a cap or **wrap**. Look at her tearing through the orchard with her hair streaming. It'll be a mercy if she doesn't catch her death of cold."

indulgently [ɪn'dʌldʒəntli] *adv.* 放纵地

wrap [ræp] *n.* 披肩

Anne came dancing home in the purple winter twilight across the snowy places. Afar in the southwest was the great shimmering, pearl-like sparkle of an evening star in a sky that was pale golden and **ethereal** rose over gleaming white spaces and dark glens of spruce. The tinkles of sleigh bells among the snowy hills came like **elfin** chimes through the frosty air, but their music was not sweeter than the song in Anne's heart and on her lips.

ethereal [ɪ'θɪəriəl] *adj.* 优雅的

elfin ['elfɪn] *adj.* 小巧玲珑的

"You see before you a perfectly happy person, Marilla," she announced. "I'm perfectly happy—yes, in spite of my red hair. Just at present I have a soul above red hair. Mrs. Barry kissed me and cried and said she was so sorry and she could never repay me. I felt fearfully embarrassed, Marilla, but I just said as politely as I could, 'I have no hard feelings for you, Mrs. Barry. I assure you once for all that I did not mean to **intoxicate** Diana and henceforth I shall cover the past with the mantle of oblivion.' That was a pretty **dignified** way of speaking wasn't it, Marilla?

intoxicate [ɪn'tɒksɪkeɪt] *v.* 使喝醉

dignified ['dɪgnɪfaɪd] *adj.* 庄严的

"I felt that I was heaping coals of fire on Mrs. Barry's head. And Diana and I had a lovely afternoon. Diana showed me a new fancy **crochet** stitch her aunt over at Carmody taught her. Not a soul in Avonlea knows it but us, and we **pledged** a solemn vow never to reveal it to anyone else. Diana gave me a beautiful card with a wreath of roses on it and a verse of poetry:

crochet ['krəʊʃeɪ] *n.* 钩针编织

pledge [pledʒ] *v.* 发誓

"If you love me as I love you,

Nothing but death can part us two.

"And that is true, Marilla. We're going to ask Mr. Phillips to let us sit together in school again, and Gertie Pye can go with Minnie Andrews. We had an elegant tea. Mrs. Barry had the very best china set out, Marilla, just as if I was real company. I can't tell you what a thrill it gave me. Nobody ever used their very best china on my account before. And we had fruit cake and pound cake and doughnuts and two kinds of preserves, Marilla. And Mrs. Barry asked me if I took tea and said, 'Pa, why don't you pass the biscuits to Anne?' It must be lovely to be grown up, Marilla, when just being treated as if you were is so nice."

"I don't know about that," said Marilla, with a brief sigh.

"Well, anyway, when I am grown up," said Anne decidedly, "I'm always going to talk to little girls as if they were too, and I'll never laugh when they use big words. I know from sorrowful experience how that hurts one's feelings. After tea Diana and I made **taffy**. The taffy wasn't very good, I suppose because neither Diana nor I had ever made any before. Diana left me to stir it while she buttered the plates and I forgot and let it burn; and then when we set it out on the platform to cool the cat walked over one plate and that had to be thrown away. But the making of it was **splendid** fun. Then when I came home Mrs. Barry asked me to come over as often as I could and Diana stood at the window and threw kisses to me all the way down to Lover's Lane. I assure you, Marilla, that I feel like praying tonight and I'm going to think out a special brand-new prayer in honor of the occasion."

taffy [ˈtæfi]
n. 太妃糖

splendid [ˈsplendɪd]
adj. 非常好的

CHAPTER XIX

A Concert, a Catastrophe and a Confession

"Marilla, can I go over to see Diana just for a minute?" asked Anne, running breathlessly down from the east gable one February evening.

"I don't see what you want to be **traipsing** about after dark for," said Marilla shortly. "You and Diana walked home from school together and then stood down there in the snow for half an hour more, your tongues going the whole blessed time, clickety-clack. So I don't think you're very badly off to see her again."

traipse [treɪps]
v. 疲惫地走;闲荡

"But she wants to see me," pleaded Anne. "She has something very important to tell me."

"How do you know she has?"

"Because she just **signaled** to me from her window. We have arranged a way to signal with our candles and cardboard. We set the candle on the window sill and make flashes by passing the cardboard back and forth. So many flashes mean a certain thing. It was my idea, Marilla."

signal [ˈsɪgnəl]
v. 发信号

"I'll **warrant** you it was," said Marilla emphatically. "And the next thing you'll be setting fire to the curtains with your signaling nonsense."

warrant [ˈwɒrənt]
v. 保证

"Oh, we're very careful, Marilla. And it's so interesting. Two flashes mean, 'Are you there?' Three mean 'yes' and four 'no'. Five mean, 'Come over as soon as possible, because I have something important to reveal.' Diana has just signaled five flashes, and I'm really suffering to know what it is."

"Well, you needn't suffer any longer," said Marilla **sarcastically**. "You can go, but you're to be back here in just ten minutes, re-

sarcastically [sɑːˈkæstɪkli]
adv. 讽刺地

member that."

Anne did remember it and was back in the stipulated time, although probably no mortal will ever know just what it cost her to **confine** the discussion of Diana's important communication within the limits of ten minutes. But at least she had made good use of them.

confine [kən'faɪn] *v.* 限制

"Oh, Marilla, what do you think? You know tomorrow is Diana's birthday. Well, her mother told her she could ask me to go home with her from school and stay all night with her. And her cousins are coming over from Newbridge in a big pung **sleigh** to go to the Debating Club concert at the hall tomorrow night. And they are going to take Diana and me to the concert—if you'll let me go, that is. You will, won't you, Marilla? Oh, I feel so excited."

sleigh [sleɪ] *n.* 雪橇

"You can calm down then, because you're not going. You're better at home in your own bed, and as for that club concert, it's all nonsense, and little girls should not be allowed to go out to such places at all."

"I'm sure the Debating Club is a most respectable affair," pleaded Anne.

"I'm not saying it isn't. But you're not going to begin **gadding** about to concerts and staying out all hours of the night. Pretty doings for children. I'm surprised at Mrs. Barry's letting Diana go."

gad [gæd] *v.* 游荡

"But it's such a very special occasion," mourned Anne, on the **verge** of tears. "Diana has only one birthday in a year. It isn't as if birthdays were common things, Marilla. Prissy Andrews is going to recite 'Curfew Must Not Ring Tonight'. That is such a good moral piece, Marilla, I'm sure it would do me lots of good to hear it. And the choir are going to sing four lovely **pathetic** songs that are pretty near as good as **hymns**. And oh, Marilla, the minister is going to take part; yes, indeed, he is; he's going to give an address. That will be just

verge [vɜːdʒ] *n.* 接近于

pathetic [pə'θetɪk] *adj.* 感伤的

hymn [hɪm] *n.* 赞美诗

about the same thing as a **sermon**. Please, mayn't I go, Marilla?"

"You heard what I said, Anne, didn't you? Take off your boots now and go to bed. It's past eight."

"There's just one more thing, Marilla," said Anne, with the air of producing the last shot in her locker. "Mrs. Barry told Diana that we might sleep in the spare-room bed. Think of the honor of your little Anne being put in the spare-room bed."

"It's an honor you'll have to get along without. Go to bed, Anne, and don't let me hear another word out of you."

When Anne, with tears rolling over her cheeks, had gone sorrowfully upstairs, Matthew, who had been apparently sound asleep on the lounge during the whole dialogue, opened his eyes and said decidedly:

"Well now, Marilla, I think you ought to let Anne go."

"I don't then," retorted Marilla. "Who's bringing this child up, Matthew, you or me?"

"Well now, you," admitted Matthew. "Don't interfere then."

"Well now, I ain't interfering. It ain't interfering to have your own opinion. And my opinion is that you ought to let Anne go."

"You'd think I ought to let Anne go to the moon if she took the notion, I've no doubt" was Marilla's **amiable rejoinder**. "I might have let her spend the night with Diana, if that was all. But I don't approve of this concert plan. She'd go there and catch cold like as not, and have her head filled up with nonsense and excitement. It would **unsettle** her for a week. I understand that child's **disposition** and what's good for it better than you, Matthew."

"I think you ought to let Anne go," repeated Matthew firmly. Argument was not his strong point, but holding fast to his opinion certainly was. Marilla gave a gasp of helplessness and took **refuge** in silence. The next morning, when Anne was washing the breakfast dishes

sermon [ˈsɜːmən]
n. 布道

amiable [ˈeɪmiəbl]
adj. 和蔼可亲的
rejoinder
[rɪˈdʒɔɪndə(r)]
n. 回答

unsettle [ʌnˈsetl]
v. 使心神不宁
disposition [ˌdɪspəˈzɪʃn]
n. 性情

refuge [ˈrefjuːdʒ]
n. 庇护

in the pantry, Matthew paused on his way out to the barn to say to Marilla again:

"I think you ought to let Anne go, Marilla."

For a moment Marilla looked things not lawful to be uttered. Then she **yielded** to the inevitable and said **tartly**:

"Very well, she can go, since nothing else'll please you."

Anne flew out of the pantry, dripping dishcloth in hand.

"Oh, Marilla, Marilla, say those blessed words again."

"I guess once is enough to say them. This is Matthew's doings and I wash my hands of it. If you catch **pneumonia** sleeping in a strange bed or coming out of that hot hall in the middle of the night, don't blame me, blame Matthew. Anne Shirley, you're dripping **greasy** water all over the floor. I never saw such a careless child."

"Oh, I know I'm a great **trial** to you, Marilla," said Anne **repentantly**. "I make so many mistakes. But then just think of all the mistakes I don't make, although I might. I'll get some sand and **scrub** up the spots before I go to school. Oh, Marilla, my heart was just set on going to that concert. I never was to a concert in my life, and when the other girls talk about them in school I feel so out of it. You didn't know just how I felt about it, but you see Matthew did. Matthew understands me, and it's so nice to be understood, Marilla."

Anne was too excited to do herself justice as to lessons that morning in school. Gilbert Blythe spelled her down in class and left her clear out of sight in mental **arithmetic**. Anne's consequent **humiliation** was less than it might have been, however, in view of the concert and the spare-room bed. She and Diana talked so constantly about it all day that with a stricter teacher than Mr. Phillips dire disgrace must **inevitably** have been their portion.

Anne felt that she could not have borne it if she had not been go-

yield [jiːld]
v. 让步
tartly [ˈtɑːtli]
adv. 刻薄地

pneumonia
[njuːˈməʊniə]
n. 肺炎

greasy [ˈgriːsi]
adj. 沾油脂的
trial [ˈtraɪəl]
n. 惹麻烦的人
repentantly
[rɪˈpentəntly]
adv. 后悔地
scrub [skrʌb]
v. 擦洗

arithmetic [əˈrɪθmətɪk]
n. 计算
humiliation
[hjuːˌmɪliˈeɪʃn]
n. 蒙羞

inevitably [ɪnˈevɪtəbli]
adv. 不可避免地

ing to the concert, for nothing else was discussed that day in school. The Avonlea Debating Club, which met **fortnightly** all winter, had had several smaller free entertainments; but this was to be a big affair, admission ten cents, in aid of the library. The Avonlea young people had been practicing for weeks, and all the scholars were especially interested in it by reason of older brothers and sisters who were going to take part. Everybody in school over nine years of age expected to go, except Carrie Sloane, whose father shared Marilla's opinions about small girls going out to night concerts. Carrie Sloane cried into her grammar all the afternoon and felt that life was not worth living.

For Anne the real excitement began with the **dismissal** of school and increased therefrom in **crescendo** until it reached to a crash of positive **ecstasy** in the concert itself. They had a "perfectly elegant tea"; and then came the delicious occupation of dressing in Diana's little room upstairs. Diana did Anne's front hair in the new pompadour style and Anne tied Diana's bows with the especial **knack** she possessed; and they experimented with at least half a dozen different ways of arranging their back hair. At last they were ready, cheeks scarlet and eyes glowing with excitement.

True, Anne could not help a little pang when she contrasted her plain black tam and shapeless, tight-sleeved, homemade gray-cloth coat with Diana's **jaunty** fur cap and smart little jacket. But she remembered in time that she had an imagination and could use it.

Then Diana's cousins, the Murrays from Newbridge, came; they all crowded into the big pung **sleigh**, among straw and furry robes. Anne **reveled** in the drive to the hall, slipping along over the satin-smooth roads with the snow **crisping** under the runners. There was a magnificent sunset, and the snowy hills and deep-blue water of the St. Lawrence Gulf seemed to rim in the splendour like a huge bowl of

fortnightly [ˈfɔːtnaɪtli] *adv.* 每两周地

dismissal [dɪsˈmɪsl] *n.* 解散

crescendo [krəˈʃendəʊ] *n.* 声音渐增

ecstasy [ˈekstəsi] *n.* 狂喜

knack [næk] *n.* 本领

jaunty [ˈdʒɔːnti] *adj.* 得意扬扬

sleigh [sleɪ] *n.* 雪橇

revel [ˈrevl] *v.* 狂欢

crisp [krɪsp] *v.* 踩上去咯吱作响

pearl and **sapphire** brimmed with wine and fire. Tinkles of sleigh bells and distant laughter, that seemed like the mirth of wood elves, came from every quarter.

sapphire ['sæfaɪə(r)]
n. 蓝宝石

"Oh, Diana," breathed Anne, squeezing Diana's mittened hand under the fur robe, "isn't it all like a beautiful dream? Do I really look the same as usual? I feel so different that it seems to me it must show in my looks."

"You look awfully nice," said Diana, who having just received a compliment from one of her cousins, felt that she ought to pass it on. "You've got the loveliest color."

The program that night was a series of "thrills" for at least one listener in the audience, and, as Anne assured Diana, every succeeding thrill was thrillier than the last. When Prissy Andrews, attired in a new pink-silk waist with a string of pearls about her smooth white throat and real **carnations** in her hair—rumor whispered that the master had sent all the way to town for them for her—"climbed the slimy ladder, dark without one ray of light," Anne shivered in luxurious sympathy; when the choir sang "Far Above the Gentle Daisies" Anne **gazed** at the ceiling as if it were **frescoed** with angels; when Sam Sloane proceeded to explain and illustrate "How Sockery Set a Hen" Anne laughed until people sitting near her laughed too, more out of sympathy with her than with amusement at a selection that was rather threadbare even in Avonlea; and when Mr. Phillips gave Mark Antony's **oration** over the dead body of Caesar in the most heartstirring tones—looking at Prissy Andrews at the end of every sentence—Anne felt that she could rise and mutiny on the spot if but one Roman citizen led the way.

carnation [kɑː'neɪʃn]
n. 康乃馨

gaze [geɪz]
v. 凝视

frescoed ['freskəʊd]
adj. 画有壁画的

oration [ɔː'reɪʃn]
n. 致辞

Only one number on the program failed to interest her. When Gilbert Blythe recited "Bingen on the Rhine" Anne picked up Rhoda

Murray's library book and read it until he had finished, when she sat **rigidly** stiff and motionless while Diana clapped her hands until they **tingled**.

rigidly [ˈrɪdʒɪdli] *adj.* 身体僵直地
tingle [ˈtɪŋgl] *v.* 感到刺痛

It was eleven when they got home, sated with **dissipation**, but with the exceeding sweet pleasure of talking it all over still to come. Everybody seemed asleep and the house was dark and silent. Anne and Diana tiptoed into the parlor, a long narrow room out of which the spare room opened. It was pleasantly warm and dimly lighted by the **embers** of a fire in the grate.

dissipation [ˌdɪsɪˈpeɪʃn] *n.* 放荡
ember [ˈembə(r)] *n.* 余火未尽的木块

"Let's undress here," said Diana. "It's so nice and warm."

"Hasn't it been a delightful time?" sighed Anne **rapturously**. "It must be splendid to get up and recite there. Do you suppose we will ever be asked to do it, Diana?"

rapturously [ˈræptʃərəsli] *adv.* 狂喜地

"Yes, of course, someday. They're always wanting the big scholars to recite. Gilbert Blythe does often and he's only two years older than us. Oh, Anne, how could you pretend not to listen to him? When he came to the line,

"There's another, not a sister, he looked right down at you."

"Diana," said Anne with **dignity**, "you are my bosom friend, but I cannot allow even you to speak to me of that person. Are you ready for bed? Let's run a race and see who'll get to the bed first."

dignity [ˈdɪgnəti] *n.* 尊严

The suggestion appealed to Diana. The two little white-clad figures flew down the long room, through the spare-room door, and bounded on the bed at the same moment. And then—something—moved beneath them, there was a **gasp** and a cry—and somebody said in **muffled** accents:

gasp [gɑːsp] *n.* 喘息
muffled [ˈmʌfld] *adj.* 模糊不清的

"Merciful goodness!"

Anne and Diana were never able to tell just how they got off that bed and out of the room. They only knew that after one **frantic** rush

frantic [ˈfræntɪk] *adj.* 疯狂的

they found themselves tiptoeing **shiveringly** upstairs.

shiver ['ʃɪvə(r)]
v. 颤抖

"Oh, who was it—what was it?" whispered Anne, her teeth chattering with cold and fright.

"It was Aunt Josephine," said Diana, gasping with laughter. "Oh, Anne, it was Aunt Josephine, however she came to be there. Oh, and I know she will be furious. It's dreadful—it's really dreadful—but did you ever know anything so funny, Anne?"

"Who is your Aunt Josephine?"

"She's father's aunt and she lives in Charlottetown. She's **awfully** old—seventy anyhow—and I don't believe she was ever a little girl. We were expecting her out for a visit, but not so soon. She's awfully prim and proper and she'll scold dreadfully about this, I know. Well, we'll have to sleep with Minnie May—and you can't think how she kicks."

awfully ['ɔːfli]
adv. 非常

Miss Josephine Barry did not appear at the early breakfast the next morning. Mrs. Barry smiled kindly at the two little girls.

"Did you have a good time last night? I tried to stay awake until you came home, for I wanted to tell you Aunt Josephine had come and that you would have to go upstairs after all, but I was so tired I fell asleep. I hope you didn't disturb your aunt, Diana."

Diana preserved a **discreet** silence, but she and Anne exchanged **furtive** smiles of guilty amusement across the table. Anne hurried home after breakfast and so remained in blissful ignorance of the disturbance which presently resulted in the Barry household until the late afternoon, when she went down to Mrs. Lynde's on an **errand** for Marilla.

discreet [dɪ'skriːt]
adj. 谨慎的
furtive ['fɜːtɪv]
adj. 偷偷摸摸的

errand ['erənd]
n. 差事

"So you and Diana nearly frightened poor old Miss Barry to death last night?" said Mrs. Lynde severely, but with a twinkle in her eye. "Mrs. Barry was here a few minutes ago on her way to Carmody.

She's feeling real worried over it. Old Miss Barry was in a terrible temper when she got up this morning—and Josephine Barry's temper is no joke, I can tell you that. She wouldn't speak to Diana at all."

"It wasn't Diana's fault," said Anne **contritely**. "It was mine. I suggested racing to see who would get into bed first."

contritely [kən'traɪtli] *adv.* 后悔地

"I knew it!" said Mrs. Lynde, with the **exultation** of a correct guesser. "I knew that idea came out of your head. Well, it's made a nice lot of trouble, that's what. Old Miss Barry came out to stay for a month, but she declares she won't stay another day and is going right back to town tomorrow, Sunday and all as it is. She'd have gone today if they could have taken her. She had promised to pay for a quarter's music lessons for Diana, but now she is determined to do nothing at all for such a tomboy. Oh, I guess they had a lively time of it there this morning. The Barrys must feel cut up. Old Miss Barry is rich and they'd like to keep on the good side of her. Of course, Mrs. Barry didn't say just that to me, but I'm a pretty good judge of human nature, that's what."

exultation [ˌegzʌl'teɪʃn] *n.* 得意

"I'm such an unlucky girl," mourned Anne. "I'm always getting into **scrapes** myself and getting my best friends—people I'd shed my heart's blood for—into them too. Can you tell me why it is so, Mrs. Lynde?"

scrape [skreɪp] *n.* 困境

"It's because you're too **heedless** and **impulsive**, child, that's what. You never stop to think—whatever comes into your head to say or do you say or do it without a moment's reflection."

heedless ['hiːdləs] *adj.* 不加注意的

impulsive [ɪm'pʌlsɪv] *adj.* 易冲动的

"Oh, but that's the best of it," protested Anne. "Something just flashes into your mind, so exciting, and you must out with it. If you stop to think it over you spoil it all. Haven't you never felt that yourself, Mrs. Lynde?"

No, Mrs. Lynde had not. She shook her head **sagely**.

sagely ['seɪdʒli] *adv.* 明智地

"You must learn to think a little, Anne, that's what. The proverb you need to go by is 'Look before you leap'—especially into spare-room beds."

Mrs. Lynde laughed comfortably over her mild joke, but Anne remained **pensive**. She saw nothing to laugh at in the situation, which to her eyes appeared very serious. When she left Mrs. Lynde's she took her way across the crusted fields to Orchard Slope. Diana met her at the kitchen door.

pensive [ˈpensɪv] *adj.* 忧伤的

"Your Aunt Josephine was very cross about it, wasn't she?" whispered Anne.

"Yes," answered Diana, **stifling** a giggle with an **apprehensive** glance over her shoulder at the closed sitting-room door. "She was fairly dancing with rage, Anne. Oh, how she scolded. She said I was the worst-behaved girl she ever saw and that my parents ought to be ashamed of the way they had brought me up. She says she won't stay and I'm sure I don't care. But Father and Mother do."

stifle [ˈstaɪfl] *v.* 强忍住,压抑
apprehensive [ˌæprɪˈhensɪv] *adj.* 担心的

"Why didn't you tell them it was my fault?" demanded Anne.

"It's likely I'd do such a thing, isn't it?" said Diana with just scorn. "I'm no **telltale**, Anne Shirley, and anyhow I was just as much to blame as you."

telltale [ˈteltеɪl] *n.* 告密者

"Well, I'm going in to tell her myself," said Anne resolutely.

Diana stared.

"Anne Shirley, you'd never! why—she'll eat you alive!"

"Don't frighten me any more than I am frightened," **implored** Anne. "I'd rather walk up to a cannon's mouth. But I've got to do it, Diana. It was my fault and I've got to confess. I've had practice in confessing, fortunately."

implore [ɪmˈplɔː(r)] *v.* 恳求

"Well, she's in the room," said Diana. "You can go in if you want to. I wouldn't dare. And I don't believe you'll do a bit of good."

With this encouragement Anne **bearded the lion in its den**—that is to say, walked resolutely up to the sitting-room door and knocked faintly. A sharp "Come in" followed.

beard the lion in its den 太岁头上动土

Miss Josephine Barry, thin, prim, and **rigid**, was knitting fiercely by the fire, her wrath quite **unappeased** and her eyes **snapping** through her gold-rimmed glasses. She wheeled around in her chair, expecting to see Diana, and beheld a white-faced girl whose great eyes were **brimmed** up with a mixture of desperate courage and shrinking terror.

rigid [ˈrɪdʒɪd] *adj.* 严格的
appease [əˈpiːz] *v.* 安抚
snap [ˈsnæp] *v.* (唰地)移到某位置
brim [brɪm] *v.* 溢出

"Who are you?" demanded Miss Josephine Barry, without ceremony.

"I'm Anne of Green Gables," said the small visitor **tremulously**, clasping her hands with her characteristic gesture, "and I've come to confess, if you please."

tremulously [ˈtremjələsli] *adv.* 发抖地

"Confess what?"

"That it was all my fault about jumping into bed on you last night. I suggested it. Diana would never have thought of such a thing, I am sure. Diana is a very ladylike girl, Miss Barry. So you must see how **unjust** it is to blame her."

unjust [ˌʌnˈdʒʌst] *adj.* 不公平的

"Oh, I must, hey? I rather think Diana did her share of the jumping at least. Such carryings on in a **respectable** house!"

respectable [rɪˈspektəbl] *adj.* 相当好的

"But we were only in fun," persisted Anne. "I think you ought to forgive us, Miss Barry, now that we've apologized. And anyhow, please forgive Diana and let her have her music lessons. Diana's heart is set on her music lessons, Miss Barry, and I know too well what it is to set your heart on a thing and not get it. If you must be cross with anyone, be cross with me. I've been so used in my early days to having people cross at me that I can **endure** it much better than Diana can."

endure [ɪnˈdjʊə(r)] *v.* 忍耐

Much of the snap had gone out of the old lady's eyes by this time and was replaced by a twinkle of amused interest. But she still said severely:

"I don't think it is any excuse for you that you were only in fun. Little girls never **indulged** in that kind of fun when I was young. You don't know what it is to be awakened out of a sound sleep, after a long and **arduous** journey, by two great girls coming **bounce** down on you."

"I don't know, but I can imagine," said Anne eagerly. "I'm sure it must have been very disturbing. But then, there is our side of it too. Have you any imagination, Miss Barry? If you have, just put yourself in our place. We didn't know there was anybody in that bed and you nearly scared us to death. It was simply awful the way we felt. And then we couldn't sleep in the spare room after being promised. I suppose you are used to sleeping in spare rooms. But just imagine what you would feel like if you were a little orphan girl who had never had such an honor."

All the snap had gone by this time. Miss Barry actually laughed—a sound which caused Diana, waiting in speechless anxiety in the kitchen outside, to give a great gasp of relief.

"I'm afraid my imagination is a little **rusty**—it's so long since I used it," she said. "I dare say your claim to sympathy is just as strong as mine. It all depends on the way we look at it. Sit down here and tell me about yourself."

"I am very sorry I can't," said Anne firmly. "I would like to, because you seem like an interesting lady, and you might even be a kindred spirit although you don't look very much like it. But it is my duty to go home to Miss Marilla Cuthbert. Miss Marilla Cuthbert is a very kind lady who has taken me to bring up properly. She is doing her best, but it is very discouraging work. You must not blame her because

indulge [ɪn'dʌldʒ]
v. 沉溺

arduous ['ɑːdʒuəs]
adj. 艰苦的

bounce [baʊns]
v. 弹跳

rusty ['rʌsti]
adj. 荒废的，生疏的

I jumped on the bed. But before I go I do wish you would tell me if you will forgive Diana and stay just as long as you meant to in Avonlea."

"I think perhaps I will if you will come over and talk to me occasionally," said Miss Barry.

That evening Miss Barry gave Diana a silver **bangle** bracelet and told the senior members of the household that she had unpacked her valise.

bangle [ˈbæŋgl] *n.* 手镯

"I've made up my mind to stay simply for the sake of getting better acquainted with that Anne-girl," she said frankly. "She amuses me, and at my time of life an amusing person is a **rarity**."

rarity [ˈreərəti] *n.* 珍品

Marilla's only comment when she heard the story was, "I told you so". This was for Matthew's benefit.

Miss Barry stayed her month out and over. She was a more agreeable guest than usual, for Anne kept her in good humor. They became firm friends.

When Miss Barry went away she said:

"Remember, you Anne-girl, when you come to town you're to visit me and I'll put you in my very sparest spare-room bed to sleep."

"Miss Barry was a kindred spirit, after all," Anne confided to Marilla. "You wouldn't think so to look at her, but she is. You don't find it right out at first, as in Matthew's case, but after a while you come to see it. Kindred spirits are not so scarce as I used to think. It's splendid to find out there are so many of them in the world."

CHAPTER XX

A Good Imagination Gone Wrong

Spring had come once more to Green Gables—the beautiful **capricious**, **reluctant** Canadian spring, lingering along through April

capricious [kəˈprɪʃəs] *adj.* 变幻莫测的

reluctant [rɪˈlʌktənt] *adj.* 不情愿的

and May in a **succession** of sweet, fresh, chilly days, with pink sunsets and miracles of **resurrection** and growth. The maples in Lover's Lane were red budded and little curly ferns pushed up around the Dryad's Bubble. Away up in the **barrens**, behind Mr. Silas Sloane's place, the Mayflowers blossomed out, pink and white stars of sweetness under their brown leaves. All the school girls and boys had one golden afternoon gathering them, coming home in the clear, echoing twilight with arms and baskets full of flowery spoil.

succession [sək'seʃn]
n. 连续的人(或事情)
resurrection [ˌrezə'rekʃn]
n. 复活
barren ['bærən]
n. 贫瘠地

"I'm so sorry for people who live in lands where there are no Mayflowers," said Anne. "Diana says perhaps they have something better, but there couldn't be anything better than Mayflowers, could there, Marilla? And Diana says if they don't know what they are like they don't miss them. But I think that is the saddest thing of all. I think it would be tragic, Marilla, not to know what Mayflowers are like and not to miss them. Do you know what I think Mayflowers are, Marilla? I think they must be the souls of the flowers that died last summer and this is their heaven. But we had a splendid time today, Marilla. We had our lunch down in a big mossy hollow by an old well—such a romantic spot. Charlie Sloane dared Arty Gillis to jump over it, and Arty did because he wouldn't take a dare. Nobody would in school. It is very fashionable to dare. Mr. Phillips gave all the Mayflowers he found to Prissy Andrews and I heard him to say 'sweets to the sweet'. He got that out of a book, I know; but it shows he has some imagination. I was offered some Mayflowers too, but I rejected them with scorn. I can't tell you the person's name because I have vowed never to let it cross my lips. We made wreaths of the Mayflowers and put them on our hats; and when the time came to go home we marched in procession down the road, two by two, with our **bouquets** and wreaths, singing 'My Home on the Hill'. Oh, it was so thrilling,

bouquet [bu'keɪ]
n. 花束

Marilla. All Mr. Silas Sloane's folks rushed out to see us and everybody we met on the road stopped and stared after us. We made a real sensation."

"Not much wonder! Such silly doings!" was Marilla's response.

After the Mayflowers came the violets, and Violet Vale was empurpled with them. Anne walked through it on her way to school with **reverent** steps and **worshiping** eyes, as if she trod on holy ground.

reverent ['revərənt] *adj.* 虔诚的
worship ['wɜːʃɪp] *v.* 崇拜

"Somehow," she told Diana, "when I'm going through here I don't really care whether Gil—whether anybody gets ahead of me in class or not. But when I'm up in school it's all different and I care as much as ever. There's such a lot of different Annes in me. I sometimes think that is why I'm such a troublesome person. If I was just the one Anne it would be ever so much more comfortable, but then it wouldn't be half so interesting."

One June evening, when the orchards were pink blossomed again, when the frogs were singing silverly sweet in the marshes about the head of the Lake of Shining Waters, and the air was full of the **savor** of clover fields and **balsamic** fir woods, Anne was sitting by her gable window. She had been studying her lessons, but it had grown too dark to see the book, so she had fallen into wide-eyed **reverie**, looking out past the boughs of the Snow Queen, once more bestarred with its tufts of blossom.

savor ['seɪvə(r)] *n.* 气味
balsamic [bɔːlsæmɪk] *adj.* 香脂的
reverie ['revəri] *n.* 幻想

In all essential respects the little gable chamber was unchanged. The walls were as white, the pincushion as hard, the chairs as stiffly and yellowly upright as ever. Yet the whole character of the room was altered. It was full of a new vital, pulsing personality that seemed to pervade it and to be quite independent of schoolgirl books and dresses and ribbons, and even of the cracked blue jug full of apple blossoms on the table. It was as if all the dreams, sleeping and waking, of its vivid occupant had taken a visible although unmaterial form and had **tapestried** the bare room with splendid filmy tissues of rainbow and moonshine. Presently Marilla came briskly in with some of Anne's freshly ironed school **aprons**. She hung them over a chair and sat down with a short sigh. She had had one of her headaches that afternoon, and although the pain had gone she felt weak and "**tuckered** out", as she expressed it. Anne looked at her with eyes **limpid** with sympathy.

"I do truly wish I could have had the headache in your place, Marilla. I would have endured it joyfully for your sake."

"I guess you did your part in attending to the work and letting me rest," said Marilla. "You seem to have got on fairly well and made fewer mistakes than usual. Of course, it wasn't exactly necessary to starch Matthew's handkerchiefs! And most people when they put a pie in the oven to warm up for dinner take it out and eat it when it gets hot instead of leaving it to be burned to a crisp. But that doesn't seem to be your way evidently."

Headaches always left Marilla somewhat sarcastic.

"Oh, I'm so sorry," said Anne **penitently**. "I never thought about that pie from the moment I put it in the oven till now, although I felt instinctively that there was something missing on the dinner table. I was firmly resolved, when you left me in charge this morning, not to imagine anything, but keep my thoughts on facts. I did pretty well until I put the pie in, and then an irresistible **temptation** came to me to imagine I was an **enchanted** princess shut up in a lonely tower with a handsome knight riding to my rescue on a coal-black steed. So that is how I came to forget the pie. I didn't know I starched the handkerchiefs. All the time I was ironing I was trying to think of a name for a new island Diana and I have discovered up the brook. It's the most

tapestry [ˈtæpəstri] *v.* 用挂毯装饰

apron [ˈeɪprən] *n.* 围裙

tucker [ˈtʌkə(r)] *v.* 使疲倦

limpid [ˈlɪmpɪd] *adj.* 清澈的

penitent [ˈpenɪtənt] *adj.* 悔过的

temptation [tempˈteɪʃn] *n.* 诱惑

enchanted [ɪnˈtʃɑːntɪd] *adj.* 着了魔的

ravishing spot, Marilla. There are two maple trees on it and the brook flows right around it. At last, it struck me that it would be splendid to call it Victoria Island because we found it on the Queen's birthday. Both Diana and I are very loyal. But I'm sorry about that pie and the handkerchiefs. I wanted to be extra good today because it's an anniversary. Do you remember what happened this day last year, Marilla?"

"No, I can't think of anything special."

"Oh, Marilla, it was the day I came to Green Gables. I shall never forget it. It was the turning point in my life. Of course it wouldn't seem so important to you. I've been here for a year and I've been so happy. Of course, I've had my troubles, but one can live down troubles. Are you sorry you kept me, Marilla?"

"No, I can't say I'm sorry," said Marilla, who sometimes wondered how she could have lived before Anne came to Green Gables, "no, not exactly sorry. If you've finished your lessons, Anne, I want you to run over and ask Mrs. Barry if she'll lend me Diana's apron pattern."

"Oh—it's—it's too dark," cried Anne.

"Too dark? Why, it's only twilight. And goodness knows you've gone over often enough after dark."

"I'll go over early in the morning," said Anne eagerly. "I'll get up at sunrise and go over, Marilla."

"What has got into your head now, Anne Shirley? I want that pattern to cut out your new apron this evening. Go at once and be smart too."

"I'll have to go around by the road, then," said Anne, taking up her hat reluctantly.

"Go by the road and waste half an hour! I'd like to catch you!"

"I can't go through the Haunted Wood, Marilla," cried Anne desperately.

Marilla stared.

"The Haunted Wood! Are you crazy? What under the canopy is the **Haunted** Wood?"

"The spruce wood over the brook," said Anne in a whisper.

"**Fiddlesticks**! There is no such thing as a haunted wood anywhere. Who has been telling you such stuff?"

"Nobody," confessed Anne. "Diana and I just imagined the wood was haunted. All the places around here are so—so—commonplace. We just got this up for our own amusement. We began it in April. A haunted wood is so very romantic, Marilla. We chose the spruce grove because it's so **gloomy**. Oh, we have imagined the most **harrowing** things. There's a white lady walks along the brook just about this time of the night and wrings her hands and utters wailing cries. She appears when there is to be a death in the family. And the ghost of a little murdered child haunts the corner up by Idlewild; it creeps up behind you and lays its cold fingers on your hand—so. Oh, Marilla, it gives me a **shudder** to think of it. And there's a headless man **stalks** up and down the path and **skeletons glower** at you between the boughs. Oh, Marilla, I wouldn't go through the Haunted Wood after dark now for anything. I'd be sure that white things would reach out from behind the trees and grab me."

"Did ever anyone hear the like!" ejaculated Marilla, who had listened in dumb amazement. "Anne Shirley, do you mean to tell me you believe all that wicked nonsense of your own imagination?"

"Not believe exactly," faltered Anne. "At least, I don't believe it in daylight. But after dark, Marilla, it's different. That is when ghosts walk."

"There are no such things as ghosts, Anne."

haunted [ˈhɔːntɪd]
adj. 闹鬼的

fiddlesticks [ˈfɪdlstɪks]
n. 胡说

gloomy [ˈgluːmi]
adj. 黑暗的
harrowing [ˈhærəʊɪŋ]
adj. 令人伤心的

shudder [ˈʃʌdə(r)]
n. 发抖
stalk [stɔːk]
v. 跟踪
skeleton [ˈskelɪtn]
n. 骨瘦如柴的人
glower [ˈglaʊə(r)]
v. 怒视

"Oh, but there are, Marilla," cried Anne eagerly. "I know people who have seen them. And they are respectable people. Charlie Sloane says that his grandmother saw his grandfather driving home the cows one night after he'd been buried for a year. You know Charlie Sloane's grandmother wouldn't tell a story for anything. She's a very religious woman. And Mrs. Thomas's father was pursued home one night by a lamb of fire with its head cut off hanging by a strip of skin. He said he knew it was the spirit of his brother and that it was a warning he would die within nine days. He didn't, but he died two years after, so you see it was really true. And Ruby Gillis says—"

"Anne Shirley," interrupted Marilla firmly, "I never want to hear you talking in this fashion again. I've had my doubts about that imagination of yours right along, and if this is going to be the outcome of it, I won't **countenance** any such doings. You'll go right over to Barry's, and you'll go through that spruce grove, just for a lesson and a warning to you. And never let me hear a word out of your head about haunted woods again."

countenance [ˈkaʊntənəns] v. 支持

Anne might **plead** and cry as she liked—and did, for her terror was very real. Her imagination had run away with her and she held the spruce grove in **mortal dread** after nightfall. But Marilla was **inexorable**. She marched the shrinking ghostseer down to the spring and ordered her to proceed straightaway over the bridge and into the dusky **retreats** of wailing ladies and headless specters beyond.

plead [pliːd] v. 恳求

mortal dread 极度地恐惧

inexorable [ɪnˈeksərəbl] adj. 不可阻挡的

retreat [rɪˈtriːt] n. 隐居处

"Oh, Marilla, how can you be so cruel?" sobbed Anne. "What would you feel like if a white thing did snatch me up and carry me off?"

"I'll risk it," said Marilla unfeelingly. "You know I always mean what I say. I'll cure you of imagining ghosts into places. March, now."

Anne marched. That is, she **stumbled** over the bridge and went

stumble [ˈstʌmbl] v. 绊脚

shuddering up the horrible dim path beyond. Anne never forgot that walk. Bitterly did she repent the license she had given to her imagination. The goblins of her fancy **lurked** in every shadow about her, reaching out their cold, **fleshless** hands to grasp the terrified small girl who had called them into being. A white strip of birch bark blowing up from the hollow over the brown floor of the grove made her heart stand still. The long-drawn wail of two old boughs rubbing against each other brought out the **perspiration** in beads on her forehead. The swoop of bats in the darkness over her was as the wings of **unearthly** creatures. When she reached Mr. William Bell' s field she fled across it as if pursued by an army of white things, and arrived at the Barry kitchen door so out of breath that she could hardly gasp out her request for the apron pattern. Diana was away so that she had no excuse to linger. The dreadful return journey had to be faced. Anne went back over it with shut eyes, preferring to take the risk of dashing her brains out among the boughs to that of seeing a white thing. When she finally stumbled over the log bridge she drew one long shivering breath of relief.

"Well, so nothing caught you?" said Marilla unsympathetically.

"Oh, Mar—Marilla," chattered Anne, "I' ll b-b-be contt-tented with c-c-commonplace places after this."

CHAPTER XXI

A New Departure in Flavorings

"Dear me, there is nothing but meetings and partings in this world, as Mrs. Lynde says," remarked Anne **plaintively**, putting her **slate** and books down on the kitchen table on the last day of June and wiping her red eyes with a very damp handkerchief. "Wasn' t it fortunate, Marilla, that I took an extra handkerchief to school today? I had a

lurk [lɜːk]
v. 潜伏
fleshless [fleʃles]
adj. 瘦的

perspiration
[ˌpɜːspəˈreɪʃn]
n. 汗水

unearthly
[ʌnˈɜːθli]
adj. 怪异的

plaintively
[ˈpleɪntɪvli]
adv. 悲哀地
slate [sleɪt]
n. 石板

presentiment that it would be needed."

"I never thought you were so fond of Mr. Phillips that you'd require two handkerchiefs to dry your tears just because he was going away," said Marilla.

"I don't think I was crying because I was really so very fond of him," reflected Anne. "I just cried because all the others did. It was Ruby Gillis started it. Ruby Gillis has always declared she hated Mr. Phillips, but just as soon as he got up to make his farewell speech she burst into tears. Then all the girls began to cry, one after the other. I tried to hold out, Marilla. I tried to remember the time Mr. Phillips made me sit with Gil—with a, boy; and the time he spelled my name without an e on the blackboard; and how he said I was the worst dunce he ever saw at geometry and laughed at my spelling; and all the times he had been so horrid and sarcastic; but somehow, I couldn't, Marilla, and I just had to cry too. Jane Andrews has been talking for a month about how glad she'd be when Mr. Phillips went away and she declared she'd never shed a tear. Well, she was worse than any of us and had to borrow a handkerchief from her brother—of course the boys didn't cry—because she hadn't brought one of her own, not expecting to need it. Oh, Marilla, it was **heart-rending**. Mr. Phillips made such a beautiful farewell speech beginning, 'The time has come for us to part.' It was very affecting. And he had tears in his eyes too, Marilla. Oh, I felt dreadfully sorry and **remorseful** for all the times I'd talked in school and drawn pictures of him on my slate and made fun of him and Prissy. I can tell you I wished I'd been a model pupil like Minnie Andrews. She hadn't anything on her conscience. The girls cried all the way home from school. Carrie Sloane kept saying every few minutes, 'The time has come for us to part,' and that would start us off again whenever we were in any danger of cheering up. I do feel dread-

presentiment [prɪˈzentɪmənt] *n.* 预感

heart-rending [ˈhɑːtˌrendɪŋ] *adj.* 令人悲痛的

remorseful [rɪˈmɔːsfl] *adj.* 悔恨的

fully sad, Marilla. But one can't feel quite in the depths of despair with two months' vacation before them, can they, Marilla? And besides, we met the new minister and his wife coming from the station. For all I was feeling so bad about Mr. Phillips going away I couldn't help taking a little interest in a new minister, could I? His wife is very pretty. Not exactly regally lovely, of course—it wouldn't do, I suppose, for a minister to have a **regally** lovely wife, because it might set a bad example. Mrs. Lynde says the minister's wife over at Newbridge sets a very bad example because she dresses so fashionably. Our new minister's wife was dressed in blue muslin with lovely puffed **sleeves** and a hat trimmed with roses. Jane Andrews said she thought puffed sleeves were too worldly for a minister's wife, but I didn't make any such **uncharitable** remark, Marilla, because I know what it is to long for puffed sleeves. Besides, she's only been a minister's wife for a little while, so one should make allowances, shouldn't they? They are going to board with Mrs. Lynde until the manse is ready."

regally [ˈriːɡəli]
adv. 像帝王地

sleeve [sliːv]
n. 袖套

uncharitable [ʌnˈtʃærɪtəbl]
adj. 刻薄的

If Marilla, in going down to Mrs. Lynde's that evening, was **actuated** by any motive save her avowed one of returning the quilting frames she had borrowed the preceding winter, it was an amiable weakness shared by most of the Avonlea people. Many a thing Mrs. Lynde had lent, sometimes never expecting to see it again, came home that night in charge of the borrowers **thereof**. A new minister, and moreover a minister with a wife, was a lawful object of curiosity in a quiet little country settlement where sensations were few and far between.

actuate [ˈæktʃueɪt]
v. 驱使

thereof [ˌðeərˈɒv]
adv. 在其中

Old Mr. Bentley, the minister whom Anne had found lacking in imagination, had been pastor of Avonlea for eighteen years. He was a **widower** when he came, and a widower he remained, despite the fact

widower [ˈwɪdəʊə(r)]
n. 鳏夫

that gossip regularly married him to this, that, or the other one, every year of his **sojourn**. In the preceding February he had resigned his charge and departed amid the regrets of his people, most of whom had the affection born of long **intercourse** for their good old minister in spite of his shortcomings as an orator. Since then the Avonlea church had enjoyed a variety of religious **dissipation** in listening to the many and various candidates and "supplies" who came Sunday after Sunday to preach on trial. These stood or fell by the judgment of the fathers and mothers in Israel; but a certain small, red-haired girl who sat **meekly** in the corner of the old Cuthbert pew also had her opinions about them and discussed the same in full with Matthew, Marilla always declining from principle to criticize ministers in any shape or form.

"I don't think Mr. Smith would have done, Matthew" was Anne's final summing up. "Mrs. Lynde says his delivery was so poor, but I think his worst fault was just like Mr. Bentley's—he had no imagination. And Mr. Terry had too much; he let it run away with him just as I did mine in the matter of the Haunted Wood. Besides, Mrs. Lynde says his theology wasn't sound. Mr. Gresham was a very good man and a very religious man, but he told too many funny stories and made the people laugh in church; he was **undignified**, and you must have some dignity about a minister, mustn't you, Matthew? I thought Mr. Marshall was decidedly attractive; but Mrs. Lynde says he isn't married, or even engaged, because she made special inquiries about him, and she says it would never do to have a young unmarried minister in Avonlea, because he might marry in the **congregation** and that would make trouble. Mrs. Lynde is a very farseeing woman, isn't she, Matthew? I'm very glad they've called Mr. Allan. I liked him because his sermon was interesting and he prayed as if he meant it and not just

sojourn [ˈsɒdʒən]
n. 逗留

intercourse [ˈɪntəkɔːs]
n. 交流

dissipation [ˌdɪsɪˈpeɪʃn]
n. 挥霍;浪费

meekly [ˈmiːkli]
adv. 温顺地

undignified [ʌnˈdɪɡnɪfaɪd]
adj. 不庄重的

congregation [ˌkɒŋɡrɪˈɡeɪʃn]
n. (教堂的)会众

as if he did it because he was in the habit of it. Mrs. Lynde says he isn't perfect, but she says she supposes we couldn't expect a perfect minister for seven hundred and fifty dollars a year, and anyhow his theology is sound because she questioned him thoroughly on all the points of doctrine. And she knows his wife's people and they are most respectable and the women are all good housekeepers. Mrs. Lynde says that sound doctrine in the man and good housekeeping in the woman make an ideal combination for a minister's family."

The new minister and his wife were a young, pleasant-faced couple, still on their honeymoon, and full of all good and beautiful enthusiasms for their chosen lifework. Avonlea opened its heart to them from the start. Old and young liked the frank, cheerful young man with his high ideals, and the bright, gentle little lady who assumed the mistress-ship of the manse. With Mrs. Allan Anne fell **promptly** and wholeheartedly in love. She had discovered another kindred spirit.

promptly [ˈprɒmptli] *adv.* 迅速地

"Mrs. Allan is perfectly lovely," she announced one Sunday afternoon. "She's taken our class and she's a splendid teacher. She said right away she didn't think it was fair for the teacher to ask all the questions, and you know, Marilla, that is exactly what I've always thought. She said we could ask her any question we liked and I asked ever so many. I'm good at asking questions, Marilla."

"I believe you" was Marilla's emphatic comment. "Nobody else asked any except Ruby Gillis, and she asked if there was to be a Sunday-school picnic this summer. I didn't think that was a very proper question to ask because it hadn't any connection with the lesson—the lesson was about Daniel in the lions' den— but Mrs. Allan just smiled and said she thought there would be. Mrs. Allan has a lovely smile; she has such exquisite dimples in her cheeks. I wish I had dimples in my cheeks, Marilla. I'm not half so skinny as I was when I came here, but I have no dimples yet. If I had perhaps I could influence people for good. Mrs. Allan said we ought always to try to influence other people for good. She talked so nice about everything. I never knew before that religion was such a cheerful thing. I always thought it was kind of **melancholy**, but Mrs. Allan's isn't, and I'd like to be a Christian if I could be one like her. I wouldn't want to be one like Mr. Superintendent Bell."

melancholy ['melənkəli] *adj.* 哀伤的

"It's very naughty of you to speak so about Mr. Bell," said Marilla severely. "Mr. Bell is a real good man."

"Oh, of course he's good," agreed Anne, "but he doesn't seem to get any comfort out of it. If I could be good, I'd dance and sing all day because I was glad of it. I suppose Mrs. Allan is too old to dance and sing and of course it wouldn't be dignified in a minister's wife. But I can just feel she's glad she's a Christian and that she'd be one even if she could get to heaven without it."

"I suppose we must have Mr. and Mrs. Allan up to tea someday soon," said Marilla reflectively. "They've been most everywhere but here. Let me see. Next Wednesday would be a good time to have them. But don't say a word to Matthew about it, for if he knew they were coming he'd find some excuse to be away that day. He'd got so used to Mr. Bentley he didn't mind him, but he's going to find it hard to get acquainted with a new minister, and a new minister's wife will frighten him to death."

"I'll be as secret as the dead," assured Anne. "But oh, Marilla, will you let me make a cake for the occasion? I'd love to do something for Mrs. Allan, and you know I can make a pretty good cake by this time."

"You can make a layer cake," promised Marilla.

Monday and Tuesday great preparations went on at Green

Gables. Having the minister and his wife to tea was a serious and important **undertaking**, and Marilla was determined not to be eclipsed by any of the Avonlea housekeepers. Anne was wild with excitement and delight. She talked it all over with Diana Tuesday night in the twilight, as they sat on the big red stones by the Dryad' s Bubble and made rainbows in the water with little **twigs** dipped in fir balsam.

undertaking [ˌʌndəˈteɪkɪŋ] *n.* 任务

twig [twɪg] *n.* 细枝

"Everything is ready, Diana, except my cake which I' m to make in the morning, and the baking-powder biscuits which Marilla will make just before teatime. I assure you, Diana, that Marilla and I have had a busy two days of it. It' s such a responsibility having a minister' s family to tea. I never went through such an experience before. You should just see our **pantry**. It' s a sight to behold. We' re going to have **jellied** chicken and cold tongue. We' re to have two kinds of jelly, red and yellow, and whipped cream and lemon pie, and cherry pie, and three kinds of cookies, and fruit cake, and Marilla' s famous yellow plum preserves that she keeps especially for ministers, and pound cake and layer cake, and biscuits as **aforesaid**; and new bread and old both, in case the minister is **dyspeptic** and can' t eat new. Mrs. Lynde says ministers are dyspeptic, but I don' t think Mr. Allan has been a minister long enough for it to have had a bad effect on him. I just grow cold when I think of my layer cake. Oh, Diana, what if it shouldn' t be good! I dreamed last night that I was chased all around by a fearful goblin with a big layer cake for a head."

pantry [ˈpæntri] *n.* 食品贮藏室

jellied [ˈdʒelid] *adj.* 做成胶冻状的

aforesaid [əˈfɔːsɛd] *adj.* 上述的

dyspeptic [dɪsˈpeptɪk] *adj.* 消化不良的

"It' ll be good, all right," assured Diana, who was a very comfortable sort of friend. "I' m sure that piece of the one you made that we had for lunch in Idlewild two weeks ago was perfectly elegant."

"Yes; but cakes have such a terrible habit of turning out bad just when you especially want them to be good," sighed Anne, setting a particularly well-balsamed twig afloat. "However, I suppose I shall just have to trust to Providence and be careful to put in the flour. Oh, look, Diana, what a lovely rainbow! Do you suppose the dryad will come out after we go away and take it for a scarf?"

"You know there is no such thing as a dryad," said Diana. Diana's mother had found out about the Haunted Wood and had been decidedly angry over it. As a result, Diana had **abstained** from any further imitative flights of imagination and did not think it **prudent** to cultivate a spirit of belief even in harmless **dryads**.

abstain [əbˈsteɪn]
v. 放弃
prudent [ˈpruːdnt]
adj. 谨慎的
dryad [ˈdraɪæd]
adj. 林中女仙

"But it's so easy to imagine there is," said Anne. "Every night before I go to bed, I look out of my window and wonder if the dryad is really sitting here, combing her locks with the spring for a mirror. Sometimes I look for her footprints in the dew in the morning. Oh, Diana, don't give up your faith in the dryad!"

Wednesday morning came. Anne got up at sunrise because she was too excited to sleep. She had caught a severe cold in the head by reason of her **dabbling** in the spring on the preceding evening; but nothing short of absolute **pneumonia** could have quenched her interest in **culinary** matters that morning. After breakfast she proceeded to make her cake. When she finally shut the oven door upon it she drew a long breath.

dabble [ˈdæbl]
v. 玩水
pneumonia [njuːˈməʊniə]
n. 肺炎
culinary [ˈkʌlɪnəri]
adj. 烹饪的

"I'm sure I haven't forgotten anything this time, Marilla. But do you think it will rise? Just suppose perhaps the baking powder isn't good? I used it out of the new can. And Mrs. Lynde says you can never be sure of getting good baking powder nowadays when everything is so **adulterated**. Mrs. Lynde says the Government ought to take the matter up, but she says we'll never see the day when a Tory Government will do it. Marilla, what if that cake doesn't rise?"

adulterate [əˈdʌltəreɪt]
v. 掺假

"We'll have plenty without it" was Marilla's **unimpassioned** way of looking at the subject.

unimpassioned [ʌnɪmˈpæʃnd]
adj. 没有激情的

The cake did rise, however, and came out of the oven as light and feathery as golden foam. Anne, flushed with delight, clapped it together with layers of ruby jelly and, in imagination, saw Mrs. Allan eating it and possibly asking for another piece!

"You'll be using the best tea set, of course, Marilla," she said. "Can I fix the table with ferns and wild roses?"

"I think that's all nonsense," sniffed Marilla. "In my opinion it's the eatables that matter and not **flummery** decorations."

flummery [ˈflʌməri]
n. 废话

"Mrs. Barry had her table decorated," said Anne, who was not entirely **guiltless** of the wisdom of the serpent, "and the minister paid her an elegant **compliment**. He said it was a feast for the eye as well as the palate."

guiltless [ˈgɪltləs]
adj. 无罪的
compliment [ˈkɒmplɪmənt]
n. 赞美

"Well, do as you like," said Marilla, who was quite determined not to be **surpassed** by Mrs. Barry or anybody else. "Only mind you leave enough room for the dishes and the food."

surpass [səˈpɑːs]
v. 超过

Anne laid herself out to decorate in a manner and after a fashion that should leave Mrs. Barry's nowhere. Having abundance of roses and ferns and a very artistic taste of her own, she made that tea table such a thing of beauty that when the minister and his wife sat down to it they **exclaimed** in chorus over it loveliness.

exclaim [ɪkˈskleɪm]
v. 呼喊

"It's Anne's doings," said Marilla, grimly just; and Anne felt that Mrs. Allan's approving smile was almost too much happiness for this world.

Matthew was there, having been **inveigled** into the party only goodness and Anne knew how. He had been in such a state of shyness and nervousness that Marilla had given him up in despair, but Anne took him in hand so successfully that he now sat at the table in his best clothes and white collar and talked to the minister not uninterestingly. He never said a word to Mrs. Allan, but that perhaps was not to be ex-

inveigle [ɪnˈveɪgl]
v. 诱骗

pected.

All went merry as a marriage bell until Anne's layer cake was passed. Mrs. Allan, having already been helped to a **bewildering** variety, declined it. But Marilla, seeing the disappointment on Anne's face, said smilingly:

"Oh, you must take a piece of this, Mrs. Allan. Anne made it on purpose for you."

"In that case I must **sample** it," laughed Mrs. Allan, helping herself to a **plump** triangle, as did also the minister and Marilla.

Mrs. Allan took a **mouthful** of hers and a most peculiar expression crossed her face; not a word did she say, however, but steadily ate away at it. Marilla saw the expression and **hastened** to taste the cake.

"Anne Shirley!" she exclaimed, "what on earth did you put into that cake?"

"Nothing but what the recipe said, Marilla," cried Anne with a look of **anguish**. "Oh, isn't it all right?"

"All right! It's simply horrible. Mr. Allan, don't try to eat it. Anne, taste it yourself. What flavoring did you use?"

"Vanilla," said Anne, her face **scarlet** with **mortification** after tasting the cake. "Only vanilla. Oh, Marilla, it must have been the baking powder. I had my suspicions of that bak—"

"Baking powder fiddlesticks! Go and bring me the bottle of vanilla you used."

Anne fled to the pantry and returned with a small bottle partially filled with a brown liquid and labeled yellowly, "Best Vanilla."

Marilla took it, **uncorked** it, smelled it.

"Mercy on us, Anne, you've flavored that cake with anodyne **liniment**. I broke the liniment bottle last week and poured what was left into an old empty vanilla bottle. I suppose it's partly my fault—I

bewildering [bɪˈwɪldərɪŋ] *adj.* 让人困惑的

sample [ˈsɑːmpl] *v.* 品尝

plump [plʌmp] *adj.* 丰满的

mouthful [ˈmaʊθfʊl] *n.* 一口(的量)

hasten [ˈheɪsn] *v.* 加速

anguish [ˈæŋgwɪʃ] *n.* 极度痛苦

scarlet [ˈskɑːlət] *adj.* 鲜红的

mortification [ˌmɔːtɪfɪˈkeɪʃn] *n.* 窘迫

uncork [ˌʌnˈkɔːk] *v.* 打开……的瓶塞

liniment [ˈlɪnəmənt] *n.* 镇痛擦剂油

should have warned you—but for pity's sake why couldn't you have smelled it?"

Anne **dissolved** into tears under this double **disgrace**.

"I couldn't—I had such a cold!" And with this she fairly fled to the gable chamber, where she cast herself on the bed and wept as one who refuses to be comforted.

Presently a light step sounded on the stairs and somebody entered the room.

"Oh, Marilla," sobbed Anne, without looking up, "I'm disgraced forever. I shall never be able to live this down. It will get out—things always do get out in Avonlea. Diana will ask me how my cake turned out and I shall have to tell her the truth. I shall always be pointed at as the girl who **flavoured** a cake with anodyne liniment. Gil—the boys in school will never get over laughing at it. Oh, Marilla, if you have a spark of Christian pity don't tell me that I must go down and wash the dishes after this. I'll wash them when the minister and his wife are gone, but I cannot ever look Mrs. Allan in the face again. Perhaps she'll think I tried to poison her. Mrs. Lynde says she knows an orphan girl who tried to poison her **benefactor**. But the liniment isn't poisonous. It's meant to be taken internally—although not in cakes. Won't you tell Mrs. Allan so, Marilla?"

"Suppose you jump up and tell her so yourself," said a merry voice.

Anne flew up, to find Mrs. Allan standing by her bed, surveying her with laughing eyes.

"My dear little girl, you mustn't cry like this," she said, **genuinely** disturbed by Anne's **tragic** face. "Why, it's all just a funny mistake that anybody might make."

"Oh, no, it takes me to make such a mistake," said Anne

dissolve [dɪ'zɒlv]
v. 禁不住
disgrace [dɪs'greɪs]
n. 丢脸

flavour ['fleɪvə(r)]
v. 调味

benefactor
['benɪfæktə(r)]
n. 捐助者

genuinely ['dʒenjuɪnli]
adv. 真正地
tragic ['trædʒɪk]
adj. 悲痛的

forlornly. "And I wanted to have that cake so nice for you, Mrs. Allan."

"Yes, I know, dear. And I assure you I appreciate your kindness and thoughtfulness just as much as if it had turned out all right. Now, you mustn't cry any more, but come down with me and show me your flower garden. Miss Cuthbert tells me you have a little plot all your own. I want to see it, for I'm very much interested in flowers."

Anne permitted herself to be led down and comforted, reflecting that it was really providential that Mrs. Allan was a kindred spirit. Nothing more was said about the liniment cake, and when the guests went away Anne found that she had enjoyed the evening more than could have been expected, considering that terrible incident. Nevertheless, she sighed deeply.

"Marilla, isn't it nice to think that tomorrow is a new day with no mistakes in it yet?"

"I'll **warrant** you'll make plenty in it," said Marilla. "I never saw your beat for making mistakes, Anne."

"Yes, and well I know it," admitted Anne **mournfully**. "But have you ever noticed one encouraging thing about me, Marilla? I never make the same mistake twice."

"I don't know as that's much benefit when you're always making new ones."

"Oh, don't you see, Marilla? There must be a limit to the mistakes one person can make, and when I get to the end of them, then I'll be through with them. That's a very comforting thought."

"Well, you'd better go and give that cake to the pigs," said Marilla. "It isn't fit for any human to eat, not even Jerry Boute."

forlornly [fə'lɔːnli]
adv. 凄凉地

warrant ['wɒrənt]
v. 保证

mournfully ['mɔːnfəli]
adv. 悲痛地

CHAPTER XXII

Anne Is Invited Out to Tea

"And what are your eyes popping out of your head about. Now?" asked Marilla, when Anne had just come in from a run to the post office. "Have you discovered another kindred spirit?" Excitement hung around Anne like a **garment**, shone in her eyes, **kindled** in every feature. She had come dancing up the lane, like a wind-blown **sprite**, through the **mellow** sunshine and lazy shadows of the August evening.

garment ['gɑːmənt]
n. (一件)衣服
kindle ['kɪndl]
v. 点燃
sprite [spraɪt]
n. 小精灵
mellow ['meləʊ]
n. 柔和的

"No, Marilla, but oh, what do you think? I am invited to tea at the manse tomorrow afternoon! Mrs. Allan left the letter for me at the post office. Just look at it, Marilla. 'Miss Anne Shirley, Green Gables.' That is the first time I was ever called 'Miss'. Such a thrill as it gave me! I shall cherish it forever among my choicest treasures."

"Mrs. Allan told me she meant to have all the members of her Sunday-school class to tea in turn," said Marilla, regarding the wonderful event very coolly. "You needn't get in such a fever over it. Do learn to take things calmly, child."

For Anne to take things calmly would have been to change her nature. All "spirit and fire and dew," as she was, the pleasures and pains of life came to her with **trebled** intensity. Marilla felt this and was **vaguely** troubled over it, realizing that the ups and downs of existence would probably bear hardly on this **impulsive** soul and not sufficiently understanding that the equally great capacity for delight might more than **compensate**. Therefore, Marilla conceived it to be her duty to drill Anne into a tranquil uniformity of **disposition** as impossible and alien to her as to a dancing sunbeam in one of the brook shallows. She did not make much headway, as she sorrowfully admitted to herself. The downfall of some dear hope or plan plunged Anne

treble ['trebl]
v. 成为三倍
vaguely ['veɪgli]
adv. 含糊地
impulsive [ɪm'pʌlsɪv]
adj. 易冲动的
compensate
['kɒmpenseɪt]
v. 弥补
disposition
[ˌdɪspə'zɪʃn]
n. 性格

into "deeps of affliction." The fulfillment thereof **exalted** her to dizzy realms of delight. Marilla had almost begun to despair of ever fashioning this waif of the world into her model little girl of **demure** manners and prim **deportment**. Neither would she have believed that she really liked Anne much better as she was.

exalt [ɪɡ'zɔːlt] v. 赞扬

demure [dɪ'mjʊə(r)] adj. 娴静的

deportment [dɪ'pɔːtmənt] n. 仪态

Anne went to bed that night speechless with misery because Matthew had said the wind was round northeast and he feared it would be a rainy day tomorrow. The rustle of the poplar leaves about the house worried her, it sounded so like **pattering** raindrops, and the full, faraway roar of the gulf, to which she listened delightedly at other times, loving its strange, **sonorous**, haunting rhythm, now seemed like a prophecy of storm and disaster to a small maiden who particularly wanted a fine day. Anne thought that the morning would never come.

patter ['pætə(r)] v. 发出轻快的拍打声

sonorous ['sɒnərəs] adj. 浑厚的

But all things have an end, even nights before the day on which you are invited to take tea at the manse. The morning, in spite of Matthew's predictions, was fine and Anne's spirits soared to their highest. "Oh, Marilla, there is something in me today that makes me just love everybody I see," she exclaimed as she washed the breakfast dishes. "You don't know how good I feel! Wouldn't it be nice if it could last? I believe I could be a model child if I were just invited out to tea every day. But oh, Marilla, it's a solemn occasion too. I feel so anxious. What if I shouldn't behave properly? You know I never had tea at a manse before, and I'm not sure that I know all the rules of **etiquette**, although I've been studying the rules given in the Etiquette Department of the Family Herald ever since I came here. I'm so afraid I'll do something silly or forget to do something I should do. Would it be good manners to take a second helping of anything if you wanted to very much?"

etiquette ['etɪkət] n. 礼节

"The trouble with you, Anne, is that you're thinking too much about yourself. You should just think of Mrs. Allan and what would be nicest and most agreeable to her," said Marilla, hitting for once in her life on a very sound and **pithy** piece of advice. Anne instantly realized this.

pithy [ˈpɪθi]
adj. 简练的

"You are right, Marilla. I'll try not to think about myself at all."

Anne evidently got through her visit without any serious breach of "etiquette", for she came home through the twilight, under a great, high-sprung sky gloried over with trails of **saffron** and rosy cloud, in a beatified state of mind and told Marilla all about it happily, sitting on the big red-sandstone slab at the kitchen door with her tired curly head in Marilla's gingham lap.

saffron [ˈsæfrən]
adj. 藏红色的

A cool wind was blowing down over the long harvest fields from the rims of firry western hills and whistling through the poplars. One clear star hung over the orchard and the fireflies were **flitting** over in Lover's Lane, in and out among the ferns and rustling boughs. Anne watched them as she talked and somehow felt that wind and stars and fireflies were all **tangled** up together into something **unutterably** sweet and enchanting.

flit [flɪt]
v. 轻快掠过

tangle [ˈtæŋgl]
v. 使缠绕
unutterably [ʌnˈʌtərəbli]
adv. 非言语所能表地

"Oh, Marilla, I've had a most fascinating time. I feel that I have not lived in vain and I shall always feel like that even if I should never be invited to tea at a manse again. When I got there Mrs. Allan met me at the door. She was dressed in the sweetest dress of pale-pink **organdy**, with dozens of frills and elbow sleeves, and she looked just like a seraph. I really think I'd like to be a minister's wife when I grow up, Marilla. A minister mightn't mind my red hair because he wouldn't be thinking of such **worldly** things. But then of course one would have to be naturally good and I'll never be that, so I suppose there's no use in thinking about it. Some people are naturally good, you know, and others are not. I'm one of the others. Mrs. Lynde says I'm full of original sin. No matter how hard I try to be good I can

organdy [ˈɔːgəndi]
n. 蝉翼纱

worldly [ˈwɜːldli]
adj. 世俗的

never make such a success of it as those who are naturally good. It's a good deal like geometry, I expect. But don't you think the trying so hard ought to count for something? Mrs. Allan is one of the naturally good people. I love her passionately. You know there are some people, like Matthew and Mrs. Allan that you can love right off without any trouble. And there are others, like Mrs. Lynde, that you have to try very hard to love. You know you ought to love them because they know so much and are such active workers in the church, but you have to keep reminding yourself of it all the time or else you forget. There was another little girl at the manse to tea, from the White Sands Sunday school. Her name was Lauretta Bradley, and she was a very nice little girl. Not exactly a kindred spirit, you know, but still very nice. We had an elegant tea, and I think I kept all the rules of etiquette pretty well. After tea Mrs. Allan played and sang and she got Lauretta and me to sing too. Mrs. Allan says I have a good voice and she says I must sing in the Sunday-school choir after this. You can't think how I was thrilled at the mere thought. I've longed so to sing in the Sunday-school choir, as Diana does, but I feared it was an honor I could never **aspire** to. Lauretta had to go home early because there is a big concert in the White Sands Hotel tonight and her sister is to recite at it. Lauretta says that the Americans at the hotel give a concert every fortnight in aid of the Charlottetown hospital, and they ask lots of the White Sands people to recite. Lauretta said she expected to be asked herself someday. I just gazed at her in awe. After she had gone Mrs. Allan and I had a heart-to-heart talk. I told her everything—about Mrs. Thomas and the twins and Katie Maurice and Violetta and coming to Green Gables and my troubles over geometry. And would you believe it, Marilla? Mrs. Allan told me she was a dunce at geometry too. You don't know how that encouraged me. Mrs. Lynde came to the manse

aspire [ə'spaɪə(r)] *v.* 渴望

just before I left, and what do you think, Marilla? The trustees have hired a new teacher and it's a lady. Her name is Miss Muriel Stacy. Isn't that a romantic name? Mrs. Lynde says they've never had a female teacher in Avonlea before and she thinks it is a dangerous innovation. But I think it will be splendid to have a lady teacher, and I really don't see how I'm going to live through the two weeks before school begins. I'm so impatient to see her."

CHAPTER XXIII

Anne Comes to Grief in an Affair of Honor

Anne had to live through more than two weeks, as it happened. Almost a month having **elapsed** since the liniment cake episode, it was high time for her to get into fresh trouble of some sort, little mistakes, such as **absentmindedly** emptying a pan of skim milk into a basket of yarn balls in the pantry instead of into the pigs' bucket, and walking clean over the edge of the log bridge into the brook while wrapped in imaginative reverie, not really being worth counting.

elapse [ɪˌlæps]
v. (时间)流逝

absentmindedly
[ˌæbsənt'maɪndɪdli]
adv. 心不在焉地

A week after the tea at the manse Diana Barry gave a party.

"Small and select," Anne assured Marilla. "Just the girls in our class."

They had a very good time and nothing untoward happened until after tea, when they found themselves in the Barry garden, a little tired of all their games and ripe for any **enticing** form of mischief which might present itself. This presently took the form of "daring".

enticing [ɪn'taɪsɪŋ]
adj. 迷人的

Daring was the fashionable amusement among the Avonlea small fry just then. It had begun among the boys, but soon spread to the girls, and all the silly things that were done in Avonlea that summer because the doers thereof were "dared" to do them would fill a book by themselves.

First of all, Carrie Sloane dared Ruby Gillis to climb to a certain point in the huge old willow tree before the front door; which Ruby Gillis, **albeit** in mortal dread of the fat green caterpillars with which said tree was infested and with the fear of her mother before her eyes if she should tear her new muslin dress, **nimbly** did, to the **discomfiture** of the aforesaid Carrie Sloane. Then Josie Pye dared Jane Andrews to hop on her left leg around the garden without stopping once or putting her right foot to the ground; which Jane Andrews gamely tried to do, but gave out at the third corner and had to confess herself defeated.

albeit [ˌɔːlˈbiːɪt] *conj.* 尽管

nimbly [ˈnɪmbli] *adv.* 敏捷地

discomfiture [dɪsˈkʌmfɪtʃə(r)] *n.* 尴尬

Josie's triumph being rather more pronounced than good taste permitted, Anne Shirley dared her to walk along the top of the board fence which bounded the garden to the east. Now, to "walk" board fences requires more skill and steadiness of head and heel than one might suppose who has never tried it. But Josie Pye, if **deficient** in some qualities that make for popularity, had at least a natural and inborn gift, duly cultivated, for walking board fences. Josie walked the Barry fence with an **airy** unconcern which seemed to imply that a little thing like that wasn't worth a "dare". Reluctant admiration greeted her **exploit**, for most of the other girls could appreciate it, having suffered many things themselves in their efforts to walk fences. Josie descended from her perch, flushed with victory, and darted a defiant glance at Anne.

deficient [dɪˈfɪʃnt] *adj.* 有缺陷的

airy [ˈeəri] *adj.* 无所谓的

exploit [ɪkˈsplɔɪt] *n.* 英勇的行为

Anne **tossed** her red braids.

toss [tɒs] *v.* 甩

"I don't think it's such a very wonderful thing to walk a little, low, board fence," she said. "I knew a girl in Marysville who could walk the ridgepole of a roof."

"I don't believe it," said Josie flatly. "I don't believe anybody could walk a ridgepole. you couldn't, anyhow."

"Couldn't I?" cried Anne rashly.

"Then I dare you to do it," said Josie defiantly. "I dare you to climb up there and walk the ridgepole of Mr. Barry's kitchen roof."

Anne turned pale, but there was clearly only one thing to be done. She walked toward the house, where a ladder was leaning against the kitchen roof. All the fifth-class girls said, "Oh!" partly in excitement, partly in **dismay**.

dismay [dɪs'meɪ] *n.* 沮丧

"Don't you do it, Anne," **entreated** Diana. "You'll fall off and be killed. Never mind Josie Pye. It isn't fair to dare anybody to do anything so dangerous."

entreat [ɪn'triːt] *v.* 恳求

"I must do it. My honor is at stake," said Anne solemnly. "I shall walk that ridgepole, Diana, or perish in the attempt. If I am killed you are to have my pearl bead ring."

Anne climbed the ladder amid breathless silence, gained the ridgepole, balanced herself **uprightly** on that **precarious** footing, and started to walk along it, dizzily conscious that she was uncomfortably high up in the world and that walking ridgepoles was not a thing in which your imagination helped you out much. Nevertheless, she managed to take several steps before the catastrophe came. Then she swayed, lost her balance, stumbled, staggered, and fell, sliding down over the sun-baked roof and crashing off it through the tangle of Virginia creeper beneath—all before the dismayed circle below could give a simultaneous, terrified shriek.

uprightly ['ʌpraɪt] *adv.* 正直地

precarious [prɪ'keəriəs] *adj.* 不稳固的

If Anne had tumbled off the roof on the side up which she had **ascended** Diana would probably have fallen heir to the pearl bead ring then and there. Fortunately, she fell on the other side, where the roof extended down over the porch so nearly to the ground that a fall therefrom was a much less serious thing. Nevertheless, when Diana and the other girls had rushed **frantically** around the house—except

ascend [ə'send] *v.* 登上

frantically ['fræntɪkli] *adv.* 疯狂地

Ruby Gillis, who remained as if rooted to the ground and went into **hysterics**—they found Anne lying all white and limp among the wreck and ruin of the Virginia creeper.

hysterics [hɪˈsterɪks] *n.* 歇斯底里

"Anne, are you killed?" shrieked Diana, throwing herself on her knees beside her friend. "Oh, Anne, dear Anne, speak just one word to me and tell me if you're killed."

To the **immense** relief of all the girls, and especially of Josie Pye, who, in spite of lack of imagination, had been seized with horrible visions of a future branded as the girl who was the cause of Anne Shirley's early and tragic death, Anne sat dizzily up and answered uncertainly:

immense [ɪˈmens] *adj.* 巨大的

"No, Diana, I am not killed, but I think I am **rendered** unconscious."

render [ˈrendə(r)] *v.* 使处于(某种状态)

"Where?" sobbed Carrie Sloane. "Oh, where, Anne?" Before Anne could answer Mrs. Barry appeared on the scene. At sight of her Anne tried to scramble to her feet, but sank back again with a sharp little cry of pain.

"What's the matter? Where have you hurt yourself?" demanded Mrs. Barry.

"My ankle," gasped Anne. "Oh, Diana, please find your father and ask him to take me home. I know I can never walk there. And I'm sure I couldn't hop so far on one foot when Jane couldn't even hop around the garden."

Marilla was out in the orchard picking a panful of summer apples when she saw Mr. Barry coming over the log bridge and up the slope, with Mrs. Barry beside him and a whole procession of little girls trailing after him. In his arms he carried Anne, whose head lay limply against his shoulder.

At that moment Marilla had a **revelation**. In the sudden stab of

revelation [ˌrevəˈleɪʃn] *n.* 揭露,茅塞顿开

fear that pierced her very heart she realized what Anne had come to mean to her. She would have admitted that she liked Anne—nay, that she was very fond of Anne. But now she knew as she hurried wildly down the slope that Anne was dearer to her than anything else on earth.

"Mr. Barry, what has happened to her?" she gasped, more white and shaken than the self-contained, sensible Marilla had been for many years.

Anne herself answered, lifting her head.

"Don't be very frightened, Marilla. I was walking the ridgepole and I fell off. I expect I have **sprained** my ankle. But, Marilla, I might have broken my neck. Let us look on the bright side of things."

sprain [spreɪn] *v.* 扭伤(关节)

"I might have known you'd go and do something of the sort when I let you go to that party," said Marilla, sharp and **shrewish** in her very relief. "Bring her in here, Mr. Barry, and lay her on the sofa. Mercy me, the child has gone and fainted!"

shrewish [ˈʃruːɪʃ] *adj.* 爱争吵且脾气坏的

It was quite true. Overcome by the pain of her injury, Anne had one more of her wishes granted to her. She had fainted dead away.

Matthew, hastily **summoned** from the harvest field, was straightway **dispatched** for the doctor, who in due time came, to discover that the injury was more serious than they had supposed. Anne's ankle was broken.

summon [ˈsʌmən] *v.* 召集
dispatch [dɪˈspætʃ] *v.* 派遣

That night, when Marilla went up to the east gable, where a white-faced girl was lying, a **plaintive** voice greeted her from the bed.

plaintive [ˈpleɪntɪv] *adj.* 忧伤的

"Aren't you very sorry for me, Marilla?"

"It was your own fault," said Marilla, **twitching** down the blind and lighting a lamp.

twitch [twɪtʃ] *v.* 抽搐

"And that is just why you should be sorry for me," said Anne, "because the thought that it is all my own fault is what makes it so hard. If I could blame it on anybody I would feel so much better. But what would you have done, Marilla, if you had been dared to walk a ridgepole?"

"I'd have stayed on good firm ground and let them dare away. Such **absurdity**!" said Marilla.

absurdity [əbˈsɜːdəti] *n.* 荒谬

Anne sighed.

"But you have such strength of mind, Marilla. I haven't. I just felt that I couldn't bear Josie Pye's scorn. She would have **crowed** over me all my life. And I think I have been punished so much that you needn't be very cross with me, Marilla. It's not a bit nice to faint, after all. And the doctor hurt me dreadfully when he was setting my ankle. I won't be able to go around for six or seven weeks and I'll miss the new lady teacher. She won't be new any more by the time I'm able to go to school. And Gil—everybody will get ahead of me in class. Oh, I am an afflicted mortal. But I'll try to bear it all bravely if only you won't be cross with me, Marilla."

crow [krəʊ] *v.* (尤指在其他人不成功时)扬扬自得地夸口

"There, there, I'm not cross," said Marilla. "You're an unlucky child, there's no doubt about that; but as you say, you'll have the suffering of it. Here now, try and eat some supper."

"Isn't it fortunate I've got such an imagination?" said Anne. "It will help me through splendidly, I expect. What do people who haven't any imagination do when they break their bones, do you suppose, Marilla?"

Anne had good reason to bless her imagination many a time and oft during the **tedious** seven weeks that followed. But she was not solely dependent on it. She had many visitors and not a day passed without one or more of the schoolgirls dropping in to bring her flowers and books and tell her all the happenings in the **juvenile** world of Avonlea.

tedious [ˈtiːdiəs] *adj.* 乏味的

juvenile [ˈdʒuːvənaɪl] *adj.* 少年的

"Everybody has been so good and kind, Marilla," sighed Anne

happily, on the day when she could first limp across the floor. "It isn't very pleasant to be laid up; but there is a bright side to it, Marilla. You find out how many friends you have. Why, even Superintendent Bell came to see me, and he's really a very fine man. Not a kindred spirit, of course; but still I like him and I'm awfully sorry I ever criticized his prayers. I believe now he really does mean them, only he has got into the habit of saying them as if he didn't. He could get over that if he'd take a little trouble. I gave him a good broad hint. I told him how hard I tried to make my own little private prayers interesting. He told me all about the time he broke his ankle when he was a boy. It does seem so strange to think of Superintendent Bell ever being a boy. Even my imagination has its limits, for I can't imagine that. When I try to imagine him as a boy I see him with gray whiskers and spectacles, just as he looks in Sunday school, only small. Now, it's so easy to imagine Mrs. Allan as a little girl. Mrs. Allan has been to see me fourteen times. Isn't that something to be proud of, Marilla? When a minister's wife has so many claims on her time! She is such a cheerful person to have visit you, too. She never tells you it's your own fault and she hopes you'll be a better girl on account of it. Mrs. Lynde always told me that when she came to see me; and she said it in a kind of way that made me feel she might hope I'd be a better girl but didn't really believe I would. Even Josie Pye came to see me. I received her as politely as I could, because I think she was sorry she dared me to walk a ridgepole. If I had been killed she would had to carry a dark burden of remorse all her life. Diana has been a faithful friend. She's been over every day to cheer my lonely pillow. But oh, I shall be so glad when I can go to school for I've heard such exciting things about the new teacher. The girls all think she is perfectly sweet. Diana says she has the loveliest fair curly hair and such fascinating eyes. She dresses beautifully, and her sleeve **puffs** are bigger than anybody else's in Avonlea. Every other Friday afternoon she has recitations and everybody has to say a piece or take part in a dialogue. Oh, it's just glorious to think of it. Josie Pye says she hates it but that is just because Josie has so little imagination. Diana and Ruby Gillis and Jane Andrews are preparing a dialogue, called 'A Morning Visit', for next Friday. And the Friday afternoons they don't have recitations Miss Stacy takes them all to the woods for a 'field' day and they study ferns and flowers and birds. And they have physical culture exercises every morning and evening. Mrs. Lynde says she never heard of such goings on and it all comes of having a lady teacher. But I think it must be splendid and I believe I shall find that Miss Stacy is a kindred spirit."

puff [pʌf]
n. 织物打褶且凸起的部分

"There's one thing plain to be seen, Anne," said Marilla, "and that is that your fall off the Barry roof hasn't injured your tongue at all."

CHAPTER XXIV

Miss Stacy and Her Pupils Get Up a Concert

It was October again when Anne was ready to go back to school—a glorious October, all red and gold, with mellow mornings when the valleys were filled with **delicate** mists as if the spirit of autumn had poured them in for the sun to drain—**amethyst**, pearl, silver, rose, and smoke-blue. The dews were so heavy that the fields **glistened** like cloth of silver and there were such heaps of rustling leaves in the hollows of many-stemmed woods to run **crisply** through. The Birch Path was a **canopy** of yellow and the ferns were sear and brown all along it. There was a tang in the very air that inspired the hearts of small maidens tripping, unlike snails, swiftly and willingly to school; and it was jolly to be back again at the little brown desk beside Diana, with Ruby Gillis nodding across the aisle and Carrie Sloane

delicate ['delɪkət]
adj. 柔和的
amethyst ['æməθɪst]
n. 紫水晶

glisten ['glɪsn]
v. 闪光
crisply ['krɪspli]
adv. 凉爽地
canopy ['kænəpi]
n. 天蓬

sending up notes and Julia Bell passing a "chew" of gum down from the back seat. Anne drew a long breath of happiness as she sharpened her pencil and arranged her picture cards in her desk. Life was certainly very interesting.

In the new teacher she found another true and helpful friend. Miss Stacy was a bright, sympathetic young woman with the happy gift of winning and holding the affections of her pupils and bringing out the best that was in them mentally and morally. Anne expanded like a flower under this **wholesome** influence and carried home to the admiring Matthew and the critical Marilla glowing accounts of schoolwork and aims.

wholesome [ˈhəʊlsəm] *adj.* 有益健康的

"I love Miss Stacy with my whole heart, Marilla. She is so ladylike and she has such a sweet voice. When she pronounces my name I feel instinctively that she's spelling it with an E. We had recitations this afternoon. I just wish you could have been there to hear me recite 'Mary, Queen of Scots.' I just put my whole soul into it. Ruby Gillis told me coming home that the way I said the line, 'Now for my father's arm,' she said, 'my woman's heart farewell,' just made her blood run cold."

"Well now, you might recite it for me some of these days, out in the barn," suggested Matthew.

"Of course I will," said Anne **meditatively**, "but I won't be able to do it so well, I know. It won't be so exciting as it is when you have a whole schoolful before you hanging breathlessly on your words. I know I won't be able to make your blood run cold."

meditative [ˈmedɪtətɪv] *adj.* 沉思的

"Mrs. Lynde says it made her blood run cold to see the boys climbing to the very tops of those big trees on Bell's hill after crows' nests last Friday," said Marilla. "I wonder at Miss Stacy for encouraging it."

"But we wanted a crow's nest for nature study," explained Anne. "That was on our field afternoon. Field afternoons are splendid, Marilla. And Miss Stacy explains everything so beautifully. We have to write compositions on our field afternoons and I write the best ones."

"It's very vain of you to say so then. You'd better let your teacher say it."

"But she did say it, Marilla. And indeed, I'm not vain about it. How can I be, when I'm such a dunce at geometry? Although I'm really beginning to see through it a little, too. Miss Stacy makes it so clear. Still, I'll never be good at it and I assure you it is a **humbling** reflection. But I love writing compositions. Mostly Miss Stacy lets us choose our own subjects; but next week we are to write a composition on some **remarkable** person. It's hard to choose among so many remarkable people who have lived. Mustn't it be splendid to be remarkable and have compositions written about you after you're dead? Oh, I would dearly love to be remarkable. I think when I grow up I'll be a trained nurse and go with the Red Crosses to the field of battle as a messenger of mercy. That is, if I don't go out as a foreign **missionary**. That would be very romantic, but one would have to be very good to be a missionary, and that would be a stumbling block. We have physical culture exercises every day, too. They make you graceful and promote **digestion**."

"Promote fiddlesticks!" said Marilla, who honestly thought it was all nonsense.

But all the field afternoons and recitation Fridays and physical culture **contortions** paled before a project which Miss Stacy brought forward in November. This was that the scholars of Avonlea school should get up a concert and hold it in the hall on Christmas Night, for

humbling [ˈhʌmblɪŋ] *adj.* 令人谦卑的

remarkable [rɪˈmɑːkəbl] *adj.* 不寻常的

missionary [ˈmɪʃənri] *n.* 传教士

digestion [daɪˈdʒestʃən] *n.* 消化

contortion [kənˈtɔːʃn] *n.* 扭曲

the **laudable** purpose of helping to pay for a schoolhouse flag. The pupils one and all taking **graciously** to this plan, the preparations for a program were begun at once. And of all the excited performers-elect none was so excited as Anne Shirley, who threw herself into the undertaking heart and soul, hampered as she was by Marilla's disapproval. Marilla thought it all rank foolishness.

"It's just filling your heads up with nonsense and taking time that ought to be put on your lessons," she grumbled. "I don't approve of children's getting up concerts and racing about to practices. It makes them vain and forward and fond of **gadding**."

"But think of the worthy object," **pleaded** Anne. "A flag will cultivate a spirit of **patriotism**, Marilla."

"Fudge! There's precious little patriotism in the thoughts of any of you. All you want is a good time."

"Well, when you can combine patriotism and fun, isn't it all right? Of course, it's real nice to be getting up a concert. We're going to have six choruses and Diana is to sing a solo. I'm in two dialogues—'The Society for the Suppression of Gossip' and 'The Fairy Queen'. The boys are going to have a dialogue too. And I'm to have two recitations, Marilla. I just tremble when I think of it, but it's a nice thrilly kind of tremble. And we're to have a tableau at the last—'Faith, Hope and Charity'. Diana and Ruby and I are to be in it, all draped in white with flowing hair. I'm to be hope, with my hands clasped—so—and my eyes uplifted. I'm going to practice my recitations in the garret. Don't be alarmed if you hear me **groaning**. I have to groan **heart-rendingly** in one of them, and it's really hard to get up a good artistic groan, Marilla. Josie Pye is sulky because she didn't get the part she wanted in the dialogue. She wanted to be the fairy queen. That would have been ridiculous, for who ever heard of a fairy queen as fat as

laudable [ˈlɔːdəbl] *adj.* 值得赞美的
graciously [ˈgreɪʃəsli] *adv.* 亲切地

gad [gæd] *v.* 闲逛
plead [pliːd] *v.* 恳求
patriotism [ˈpætriətɪzəm] *n.* 爱国主义

groan [grəʊn] *v.* 呻吟
heartrending [ˈhaːt rɛndɪŋ] *adv.* 令人悲痛的

Josie? Fairy queens must be **slender**. Jane Andrews is to be the queen and I am to be one of her maids of honor. Josie says she thinks a red-haired fairy is just as ridiculous as a fat one, but I do not let myself mind what Josie says. I'm to have a wreath of white roses on my hair and Ruby Gillis is going to lend me her slippers because I haven't any of my own. It's necessary for fairies to have slippers, you know. You couldn't imagine a fairy wearing boots, could you? Especially with **copper** toes? We are going to decorate the hall with creeping spruce and fir mottoes with pink tissue-paper roses in them. And we are all to march in two by two after the audience is seated, while Emma White plays a march on the organ. Oh, Marilla, I know you are not so enthusiastic about it as I am, but don't you hope your little Anne will distinguish herself?"

"All I hope is that you'll behave yourself. I'll be heartily glad when all this fuss is over and you'll be able to settle down. You are simply good for nothing just now with your head **stuffed** full of dialogues and groans and tableaus. As for your tongue, it's a marvel it's not clean worn out."

Anne sighed and **betook** herself to the back yard, over which a young new moon was shining through the leafless poplar boughs from an apple-green western sky, and where Matthew was splitting wood. Anne perched herself on a block and talked the concert over with him, sure of an appreciative and sympathetic listener in this instance at least.

"Well now, I reckon it's going to be a pretty good concert. And I expect you'll do your part fine," he said, smiling down into her eager, **vivacious** little face. Anne smiled back at him. Those two were the best of friends and Matthew thanked his stars many a time and oft that he had nothing to do with bringing her up. That was Marilla's **exclusive** duty; if it had been his he would have been worried over

slender [ˈslendə(r)] *adj.* 苗条的

copper [ˈkɒpə(r)] *adj.* 铜的

stuffed [stʌft] *adj.* 塞满了的

betake [bɪˈteɪk] *v.* 去往

vivacious [vɪˈveɪʃəs] *adj.* 活泼的

exclusive [ɪkˈskluːsɪv] *adj.* 专有的

frequent conflicts between inclination and said duty. As it was, he was free to, "spoil Anne"—Marilla's phrasing—as much as he liked. But it was not such a bad arrangement after all; a little "appreciation" sometimes does quite as much good as all the **conscientious** "bringing up" in the world.

conscientious [ˌkɒnʃiˈenʃəs] *adj.* 勤勉认真的

CHAPTER XXV

Matthew Insists on Puffed Sleeves

Matthew was having a bad ten minutes of it. He had come into the kitchen, in the twilight of a cold, gray December evening, and had sat down in the woodbox corner to take off his heavy boots, unconscious of the fact that Anne and a bevy of her schoolmates were having a practice of "The Fairy Queen" in the sitting room. Presently they came trooping through the hall and out into the kitchen, laughing and chattering **gaily**. They did not see Matthew, who shrank **bashfully** back into the shadows beyond the woodbox with a boot in one hand and a bootjack in the other, and he watched them shyly for the aforesaid ten minutes as they put on caps and jackets and talked about the dialogue and the concert. Anne stood among them, bright eyed and **animated** as they; but Matthew suddenly became conscious that there was something about her different from her mates. And what worried Matthew was that the difference impressed him as being something that should not exist. Anne had a brighter face, and bigger, **starrier** eyes, and more delicate features than the other; even shy, unobservant Matthew had learned to take note of these things; but the difference that disturbed him did not consist in any of these respects. Then in what did it consist?

gaily [ˈɡeɪli] *adv.* 快乐地

bashfully [ˈbæʃfəli] *adv.* 羞怯地

animated [ˈænɪmeɪtɪd] *adj.* 生气勃勃的

starry [ˈstɑːri] *adj.* 布满星星的

Matthew was haunted by this question long after the girls had gone, arm in arm, down the long, hard-frozen lane and Anne had betaken herself to her books. He could not refer it to Marilla, who, he felt, would be quite sure to sniff **scornfully** and remark that the only difference she saw between Anne and the other girls was that they sometimes kept their tongues quiet while Anne never did. This, Matthew felt, would be no great help.

scornfully [ˈskɔːnfəli]
adv. 轻蔑地

He had **recourse** to his pipe that evening to help him study it out, much to Marilla's disgust. After two hours of smoking and hard reflection Matthew arrived at a solution of his problem. Anne was not dressed like the other girls!

recourse [rɪˈkɔːs]
n. 求助

The more Matthew thought about the matter the more he was convinced that Anne never had been dressed like the other girls—never since she had come to Green Gables. Marilla kept her clothed in plain, dark dresses, all made after the same unvarying pattern. If Matthew knew there was such a thing as fashion in dress it was as much as he did; but he was quite sure that Anne's sleeves did not look at all like the sleeves the other girls wore. He recalled the cluster of little girls he had seen around her that evening—all gay in waists of red and blue and pink and white—and he wondered why Marilla always kept her so plainly and **soberly gowned**.

soberly [ˈsəʊbəli]
adv. 素净地
gowned [gaʊnd]
adj. 穿长袍的

Of course, it must be all right. Marilla knew best and Marilla was bringing her up. Probably some wise, **inscrutable** motive was to be served thereby. But surely it would do no harm to let the child have one pretty dress—something like Diana Barry always wore. Matthew decided that he would give her one; that surely could not be objected to as an **unwarranted** putting in of his oar. Christmas was only a fortnight off. A nice new dress would be the very thing for a present. Matthew, with a sigh of satisfaction, put away his pipe and went to bed, while Marilla opened all the doors and **aired** the house.

inscrutable
[ɪnˈskruːtəbl]
adj. 无法理解

unwarranted
[ʌnˈwɒrəntɪd]
adj. 不合理的

air [eə(r)]
v. 使通风

The very next evening Matthew betook himself to Carmody to

buy the dress, determined to get the worst over and have done with it. It would be, he felt assured, no **trifling ordeal**. There were some things Matthew could buy and prove himself no mean bargainer; but he knew he would be at the mercy of shopkeepers when it came to buying a girl's dress.

trifling [ˈtraɪflɪŋ] *adj.* 微不足道的
ordeal [ɔːˈdiːl] *n.* 折磨

After much **cogitation** Matthew **resolved** to go to Samuel Lawson's store instead of William Blair's. To be sure, the Cuthberts always had gone to William Blair's; it was almost as much a matter of conscience with them as to attend the Presbyterian church and vote Conservative. But William Blair's two daughters frequently waited on customers there and Matthew held them in absolute dread. He could **contrive** to deal with them when he knew exactly what he wanted and could point it out; but in such a matter as this, requiring explanation and **consultation**, Matthew felt that he must be sure of a man behind the counter. So he would go to Lawson's, where Samuel or his son would wait on him.

cogitation [ˌkɒdʒɪˈteɪʃn] *n.* 仔细思考
resolve [rɪˈzɒlv] *v.* 决定,决意
contrive [kənˈtraɪv] *v.* 设法
consultation [ˌkɒnslˈteɪʃn] *n.* 咨询

Alas! Matthew did not know that Samuel, in the recent expansion of his business, had set up a lady clerk also; she was a niece of his wife's and a very dashing young person indeed, with a huge, drooping **pompadour**, big, rolling brown eyes, and a most extensive and **bewildering** smile. She was dressed with exceeding smartness and wore several bangle **bracelets** that glittered and **rattled** and tinkled with every movement of her hands. Matthew was covered with confusion at finding her there at all; and those bangles completely wrecked his wits **at one fell swoop**.

pompadour [ˈpɒmpədɔː] *n.* 往后梳头发
bewildering [bɪˈwɪldərɪŋ] *adj.* 让人困惑的
bracelet [ˈbreɪslət] *n.* 手镯
rattle [ˈrætl] *v.* 发出咔嗒咔嗒的声音
at one fell swoop 一下子;一举

"What can I do for you this evening, Mr. Cuthbert?" Miss Lucilla Harris inquired, **briskly** and **ingratiatingly**, tapping the counter with both hands.

briskly [ˈbrɪskli] *adv.* 轻快地
ingratiatingly [ɪnˈgreɪʃieɪtɪŋli] *adv.* 讨好地

"Have you any—any—any—well now, say any garden rakes?"

stammered Matthew.

Miss Harris looked somewhat surprised, as well she might, to hear a man inquiring for garden rakes in the middle of December.

"I believe we have one or two left over," she said, "but they're upstairs in the **lumber** room. I'll go and see." During her absence Matthew collected his **scattered** senses for another effort.

When Miss Harris returned with the rake and cheerfully inquired: "Anything else tonight, Mr. Cuthbert?" Matthew took his courage in both hands and replied: "Well now, since you suggest it, I might as well—take—that is—look at—buy some—some hayseed."

Miss Harris had heard Matthew Cuthbert called odd. She now concluded that he was entirely crazy.

"We only keep **hayseed** in the spring," she explained **loftily**. "We've none on hand just now."

"Oh, certainly—certainly—just as you say," stammered unhappy Matthew, seizing the rake and making for the door. At the **threshold** he recollected that he had not paid for it and he turned miserably back. While Miss Harris was counting out his change he **rallied** his powers for a final desperate attempt.

"Well now—if it isn't too much trouble—I might as well—that is—I'd like to look at—at—some sugar."

"White or brown?" queried Miss Harris patiently.

"Oh—well now—brown," said Matthew **feebly**.

"There's a barrel of it over there," said Miss Harris, shaking her bangles at it. "It's the only kind we have."

"I'll—I'll take twenty pounds of it," said Matthew, with beads of **perspiration** standing on his forehead.

Matthew had driven halfway home before he was his own man again. It had been a **gruesome** experience, but it served him right, he

stammer [ˈstæmə(r)] *v.* 结结巴巴地说

lumber [ˈlʌmbə(r)] *n.* 木材

scattered [ˈskætəd] *adj.* 分散的

hayseed [ˈheɪsiːd] *n.* 干草种子

loftily [ˈlɒftɪli] *adv.* 傲慢地

threshold [ˈθreʃhəʊld] *n.* 门槛

rally [ˈræli] *v.* 召集

feebly [ˈfiːbli] *adv.* 衰弱地

perspiration [ˌpɜːspəˈreɪʃn] *n.* 汗

gruesome [ˈgruːsəm] *adj.* 可怕的

thought, for committing the **heresy** of going to a strange store. When he reached home he hid the rake in the tool house, but the sugar he carried in to Marilla.

heresy [ˈherəsi]
n. 异教

"Brown sugar!" exclaimed Marilla. "Whatever possessed you to get so much? You know I never use it except for the hired man's **porridge** or black fruit cake. Jerry's gone and I've made my cake long ago. It's not good sugar, either—it's coarse and dark—William Blair doesn't usually keep sugar like that."

porridge [ˈpɒrɪdʒ]
n. 粥

"I—I thought it might come in handy sometime," said Matthew, making good his escape.

When Matthew came to think the matter over he decided that a woman was required to cope with the situation. Marilla was out of the question. Matthew felt sure she would throw cold water on his project at once. Remained only Mrs. Lynde; for of no other woman in Avonlea would Matthew have dared to ask advice. To Mrs. Lynde he went accordingly, and that good lady promptly took the matter out of the **harassed** man's hands.

harassed [ˈhærəst]
adj. 疲倦的

"Pick out a dress for you to give Anne? To be sure I will. I'm going to Carmody tomorrow and I'll attend to it. Have you something particular in mind? No? Well, I'll just go by my own judgment then. I believe a nice rich brown would just suit Anne, and William Blair has some new gloria in that's real pretty. Perhaps you'd like me to make it up for her, too, seeing that if Marilla was to make it Anne would probably get wind of it before the time and spoil the surprise? Well, I'll do it. No, it isn't a mite of trouble. I like sewing. I'll make it to fit my niece, Jenny Gillis, for she and Anne are as like as two peas as far as figure goes."

"Well now, I'm much obliged," said Matthew, "and— and—I **dunno**—but I'd like—I think they make the sleeves different nowa-

dunno [dəˈnəʊ]
v. 我不知道

days to what they used to be. If it wouldn't be asking too much I—I'd like them made in the new way."

"Puffs? Of course. You needn't worry a speck more about it, Matthew. I'll make it up in the very latest fashion," said Mrs. Lynde. To herself she added when Matthew had gone:

"It'll be a real satisfaction to see that poor child wearing something **decent** for once. The way Marilla dresses her is positively ridiculous, that's what, and I've ached to tell her so plainly a dozen times. I've held my tongue though, for I can see Marilla doesn't want advice and she thinks she knows more about bringing children up than I do for all she's an old maid. But that's always the way. Folks that has brought up children know that there's no hard and fast method in the world that'll suit every child. But them as never have think it's all as plain and easy as Rule of Three— just set your three terms down so fashion, and the sum'll work out correct. But flesh and blood don't come under the head of **arithmetic** and that's where Marilla Cuthbert makes her mistake. I suppose she's trying to cultivate a spirit of **humility** in Anne by dressing her as she does; but it's more likely to cultivate envy and discontent. I'm sure the child must feel the difference between her clothes and the other girls'. But to think of Matthew taking notice of it! That man is waking up after being asleep for over sixty years."

Marilla knew all the following fortnight that Matthew had something on his mind, but what it was she could not guess, until Christmas Eve, when Mrs. Lynde brought up the new dress. Marilla behaved pretty well on the whole, although it is very likely she distrusted Mrs. Lynde's **diplomatic** explanation that she had made the dress because Matthew was afraid Anne would find out about it too soon if Marilla made it.

decent [ˈdiːsnt] *adj.* 像样的

arithmetic [əˈrɪθmətɪk] *n.* 算数

humility [hjuːˈmɪləti] *n.* 谦逊

diplomatic [ˌdɪpləˈmætɪk] *adj.* 外交的

"So this is what Matthew has been looking so mysterious over and **grinning** about to himself for two weeks, is it?" she said a little stiffly but tolerantly. "I knew he was up to some foolishness. Well, I must say I don't think Anne needed any more dresses. I made her three good, warm, serviceable ones this fall, and anything more is sheer **extravagance**. There's enough material in those sleeves alone to make a waist, I declare there is. You'll just **pamper** Anne's **vanity**, Matthew, and she's as vain as a peacock now. Well, I hope she'll be satisfied at last, for I know she's been **hankering** after those silly sleeves ever since they came in, although she never said a word after the first. The puffs have been getting bigger and more ridiculous right along; they're as big as balloons now. Next year anybody who wears them will have to go through a door sideways."

grin [grɪn] *v.* 露牙齿笑

extravagance [ɪk'strævəgəns] *n.* 奢侈

pamper ['pæmpə(r)] *v.* 娇惯

vanity ['vænəti] *n.* 虚荣心

hanker ['hæŋkə] *v.* 渴望

Christmas morning broke on a beautiful white world. It had been a very mild December and people had looked forward to a green Christmas; but just enough snow fell softly in the night to **transfigure** Avonlea. Anne peeped out from her frosted gable window with delighted eyes. The firs in the Haunted Wood were all feathery and wonderful; the birches and wild cherry trees were outlined in pearl; the plowed fields were stretches of snowy dimples; and there was a crisp tang in the air that was glorious. Anne ran downstairs singing until her voice **re-echoed** through Green Gables.

transfigure [træns'fɪgə(r)] *v.* 美化

re-echo [ˌriː'ɛkəʊ] *v.* 回响

"Merry Christmas, Marilla! Merry Christmas, Matthew! Isn't it a lovely Christmas? I'm so glad it's white. Any other kind of Christmas doesn't seem real, does it? I don't like green Christmases. They're not green—they're just nasty faded browns and grays. What makes people call them green? Why—why—Matthew, is that for me? Oh, Matthew!"

Matthew had **sheepishly** unfolded the dress from its paper

sheepishly ['ʃiːpɪʃli] *adv.* 窘迫地

swathings and held it out with a **deprecatory** glance at Marilla, who feigned to be **contemptuously** filling the teapot, but nevertheless watched the scene out of the corner of her eye with a rather interested air.

Anne took the dress and looked at it in **reverent** silence. Oh, how pretty it was—a lovely soft brown gloria with all the gloss of silk; a skirt with **dainty** frills and shirrings; a waist elaborately pintucked in the most fashionable way, with a little ruffle of filmy lace at the neck. But the sleeves—they were the crowning glory! Long elbow cuffs, and above them two beautiful puffs divided by rows of shirring and bows of brown-silk ribbon.

"That's a Christmas present for you, Anne," said Matthew shyly. "Why—why—Anne, don't you like it? Well now—well now."

For Anne's eyes had suddenly filled with tears.

"Like it! Oh, Matthew!" Anne laid the dress over a chair and clasped her hands. "Matthew, it's perfectly **exquisite**. Oh, I can never thank you enough. Look at those sleeves! Oh, it seems to me this must be a happy dream."

"Well, well, let us have breakfast," interrupted Marilla. "I must say, Anne, I don't think you needed the dress; but since Matthew has got it for you, see that you take good care of it. There's a hair **ribbon** Mrs. Lynde left for you. It's brown, to match the dress. Come now, sit in."

"I don't see how I'm going to eat breakfast," said Anne **rapturously**. "Breakfast seems so **commonplace** at such an exciting moment. I'd rather feast my eyes on that dress. I'm so glad that puffed sleeves are still fashionable. It did seem to me that I'd never get over it if they went out before I had a dress with them. I'd never have felt quite satisfied, you see. It was lovely of Mrs. Lynde to give me the ribbon too. I feel that I ought to be a very good girl indeed. It's at times

swathe [sweɪð]
v. 包
deprecatory [ˈdɛprɪkeɪtəri]
adj. 反对的
contemptuously [kənˈtemptʃuəsli]
adv. 轻蔑地
reverent [ˈrevərənt]
adj. 充满敬意的
dainty [ˈdeɪnti]
adj. 精致的

exquisite [ɪkˈskwɪzɪt]
adj. 精美的

ribbon [ˈrɪbən]
n. 丝带

rapturously [ˈræptʃərəsli]
adv. 狂喜地
commonplace [ˈkɒmənpleɪs]
adj. 常见的

like this I'm sorry I'm not a model little girl; and I always resolve that I will be in future. But somehow it's hard to carry out your resolutions when irresistible **temptations** come. Still, I really will make an extra effort after this."

temptation [temp'teɪʃn] *n.* 诱惑

When the commonplace breakfast was over Diana appeared, crossing the white log bridge in the hollow, a gay little figure in her **crimson ulster**. Anne flew down the slope to meet her.

crimson ['krɪmzn] *adj.* 深红色的
ulster ['ʌlstə] *n.* 一种大衣

"Merry Christmas, Diana! And oh, it's a wonderful Christmas. I've something splendid to show you. Matthew has given me the loveliest dress, with such sleeves. I couldn't even imagine any nicer."

"I've got something more for you," said Diana breathlessly. "Here—this box. Aunt Josephine sent us out a big box with ever so many things in it—and this is for you. I'd have brought it over last night, but it didn't come until after dark, and I never feel very comfortable coming through the Haunted Wood in the dark now."

Anne opened the box and **peeped** in. First a card with "For the Anne-girl and Merry Christmas," written on it; and then, a pair of the daintiest little kid slippers, with **beaded** toes and satin bows and glistening buckles.

peep [piːp] *v.* 窥视

beaded ['biːdɪd] *adj.* 珠状的

"Oh," said Anne, "Diana, this is too much. I must be dreaming."

"I call it providential," said Diana. "You won't have to borrow Ruby's slippers now, and that's a blessing, for they're two sizes too big for you, and it would be awful to hear a fairy shuffling. Josie Pye would be delighted. Mind you, Rob Wright went home with Gertie Pye from the practice night before last. Did you ever hear anything equal to that?"

All the Avonlea scholars were in a fever of excitement that day, for the hall had to be decorated and a last grand **rehearsal** held.

rehearsal [rɪ'hɜːsl] *n.* 排练

The concert came off in the evening and was a pronounced success. The little hall was crowded; all the performers did excellently well, but Anne was the bright particular star of the occasion, as even envy, in the shape of Josie Pye, dared not deny.

"Oh, hasn't it been a brilliant evening?" sighed Anne, when it was all over and she and Diana were walking home together under a dark, starry sky.

"Everything went off very well," said Diana practically. "I guess we must have made as much as ten dollars. Mind you, Mr. Allan is going to send an account of it to the Charlottetown papers."

"Oh, Diana, will we really see our names in print? It makes me thrill to think of it. Your solo was perfectly elegant, Diana. I felt prouder than you did when it was **encored**. I just said to myself, 'It is my dear bosom friend who is so honored.'"

encore [ˈɒŋkɔː(r)] *v.* 再次演唱

"Well, your recitations just brought down the house, Anne. That sad one was simply splendid."

"Oh, I was so nervous, Diana. When Mr. Allan called out my name I really cannot tell how I ever got up on that platform. I felt as if a million eyes were looking at me and through me, and for one dreadful moment I was sure I couldn't begin at all. Then I thought of my lovely **puffed** sleeves and took courage. I knew that I must live up to those sleeves, Diana. So I started in, and my voice seemed to be coming from ever so far away. I just felt like a parrot. It's providential that I practiced those recitations so often up in the garret, or I'd never have been able to get through. Did I groan all right?"

puffed [pʌft] *adj.* 疏松的

"Yes, indeed, you **groaned** lovely," assured Diana.

groan [grəʊn] *v.* 抱怨

"I saw old Mrs. Sloane wiping away tears when I sat down. It was splendid to think I had touched somebody's heart. It's so romantic to take part in a concert, isn't it? Oh, it's been a very memorable occasion indeed."

"Wasn't the boys' dialogue fine?" said Diana. "Gilbert Blythe was just splendid. Anne, I do think it's awful mean the way you treat Gil. Wait till I tell you. When you ran off the platform after the fairy dialogue one of your roses fell out of your hair. I saw Gil pick it up and put it in his breast pocket. There now. You're so romantic that I'm sure you ought to be pleased at that."

"It's nothing to me what that person does," said Anne loftily. "I simply never waste a thought on him, Diana."

That night Marilla and Matthew, who had been out to a concert for the first time in twenty years, sat for a while by the kitchen fire after Anne had gone to bed.

"Well now, I guess our Anne did as well as any of them," said Matthew proudly.

"Yes, she did," admitted Marilla. "She's a bright child, Matthew. And she looked real nice too. I've been kind of opposed to this concert **scheme**, but I suppose there's no real harm in it after all. Anyhow, I was proud of Anne tonight, although I'm not going to tell her so."

scheme [skiːm] *n.* 计划

"Well now, I was proud of her and I did tell her so 'fore she went upstairs," said Matthew. "We must see what we can do for her some of these days, Marilla. I guess she'll need something more than Avonlea school by and by."

"There's time enough to think of that," said Marilla. "She's only thirteen in March. Though tonight it struck me she was growing quite a big girl. Mrs. Lynde made that dress a mite too long, and it makes Anne look so tall. She's quick to learn and I guess the best thing we can do for her will be to send her to Queen's after a spell. But nothing need be said about that for a year or two yet."

"Well now, it'll do no harm to be thinking it over off and on," said Matthew. "Things like that are all the better for lots of thinking over."

CHAPTER XXVI

The Story Club Is Formed

Junior Avonlea found it hard to settle down to humdrum existence again. To Anne in particular things seemed fearfully flat, stale, and **unprofitable** after the **goblet** of excitement she had been sipping for weeks. Could she go back to the former quiet pleasures of those **faraway** days before the concert? At first, as she told Diana, she did not really think she could.

unprofitable [ʌn'prɒfɪtəbl] *adj.* 无利润的
goblet ['gɒblət] *n.* 高脚杯
faraway ['fɑːrəweɪ] *adj.* 遥远的

"I' m positively certain, Diana, that life can never be quite the same again as it was in those olden days," she said mournfully, as if referring to a period of at least fifty years back. "Perhaps after a while I' ll get used to it, but I' m afraid concerts spoil people for everyday life. I suppose that is why Marilla disapproves of them. Marilla is such a **sensible** woman. It must be a great deal better to be sensible; but still, I don' t believe I' d really want to be a sensible person, because they are so unromantic. Mrs. Lynde says there is no danger of my ever being one, but you can never tell. I feel just now that I may grow up to be sensible yet. But perhaps that is only because I' m tired. I simply couldn' t sleep last night for ever so long. I just lay awake and imagined the concert over and over again. That' s one splendid thing about such affairs—it' s so lovely to look back to them."

sensible ['sensəbl] *adj.* 明智的

Eventually, however, Avonlea school slipped back into its old groove and took up its old interests. To be sure, the concert left traces. Ruby Gillis and Emma White, who had quarreled over a point of **precedence** in their platform seats, no longer sat at the same desk, and a promising friendship of three years was broken up. Josie Pye and Julia Bell did not "speak" for three months, because Josie Pye had told Bessie Wright that Julia Bell' s bow when she got up to recite

precedence ['presɪdəns] *n.* 领先

made her think of a chicken jerking its head, and Bessie told Julia. None of the Sloanes would have any dealings with the Bells, because the Bells had declared that the Sloanes had too much to do in the program, and the Sloanes had retorted that the Bells were not capable of doing the little they had to do properly. Finally, Charlie Sloane fought Moody Spurgeon MacPherson, because Moody Spurgeon had said that Anne Shirley put on airs about her recitations, and Moody Spurgeon was "licked"; consequently Moody Spurgeon's sister, Ella May, would not "speak" to Anne Shirley all the rest of the winter. With the exception of these trifling frictions, work in Miss Stacy's little kingdom went on with regularity and smoothness.

The winter weeks slipped by. It was an unusually mild winter, with so little snow that Anne and Diana could go to school nearly every day by way of the Birch Path. On Anne's birthday they were tripping lightly down it, keeping eyes and ears alert amid all their chatter, for Miss Stacy had told them that they must soon write a composition on "A Winter's Walk in the Woods," and it behooved them to be observant.

"Just think, Diana, I'm thirteen years old today," remarked Anne in an awed voice. "I can scarcely realize that I'm in my teens. When I woke this morning it seemed to me that everything must be different. You've been thirteen for a month, so I suppose it doesn't seem such a novelty to you as it does to me. It makes life seem so much more interesting. In two more years, I'll be really grown up. It's a great comfort to think that I'll be able to use big words then without being laughed at."

"Ruby Gillis says she means to have a beau as soon as she's fifteen," said Diana.

"Ruby Gillis thinks of nothing but beaus," said Anne **disdainfully**. "She's actually delighted when anyone writes her name up in a

disdainfully [dɪsˈdeɪnfəli] *adj.* 轻蔑地

take-notice for all she pretends to be so mad. But I'm afraid that is an uncharitable speech. Mrs. Allan says we should never make **unchari-table** speeches; but they do slip out so often before you think, don't they? I simply can't talk about Josie Pye without making an uncharitable speech, so I never mention her at all. You may have noticed that. I'm trying to be as much like Mrs. Allan as I possibly can, for I think she's perfect. Mr. Allan thinks so too. Mrs. Lynde says he just worships the ground she treads on and she doesn't really think it right for a minister to set his affections so much on a mortal being. But then, Diana, even ministers are human and have their **besetting** sins just like everybody else. I had such an interesting talk with Mrs. Allan about besetting sins last Sunday afternoon. There are just a few things it's proper to talk about on Sundays and that is one of them. My besetting sin is imagining too much and forgetting my duties. I'm striving very hard to overcome it and now that I'm really thirteen perhaps I'll get on better."

uncharitable [ʌn'tʃærɪtəbl] *adj.* 苛刻的

beset [bɪ'set] *v.* 困扰

"In four more years, we'll be able to put our hair up," said Diana. "Alice Bell is only sixteen and she is wearing hers up, but I think that's ridiculous. I shall wait until I'm seventeen."

"If I had Alice Bell's crooked nose," said Anne decidedly, "I wouldn't—but there! I won't say what I was going to because it was extremely uncharitable. Besides, I was comparing it with my own nose and that's **vanity**. I'm afraid I think too much about my nose ever since I heard that compliment about it long ago. It really is a great comfort to me. Oh, Diana, look, there's a rabbit. That's something to remember for our woods composition. I really think the woods are just as lovely in winter as in summer. They're so white and still, as if they were asleep and dreaming pretty dreams."

vanity ['vænəti] *n.* 自负

"I won't mind writing that composition when its time comes," sighed Diana. "I can manage to write about the woods, but the one we're to hand in Monday is terrible. The idea of Miss Stacy telling us to write a story out of our own heads!"

"Why, it's as easy as wink," said Anne.

"It's easy for you because you have an imagination," retorted Diana, "but what would you do if you had been born without one? I suppose you have your composition all done?"

Anne nodded, trying hard not to look virtuously **complacent** and failing miserably.

complacent [kəm'pleɪsnt] *adj.* 自满的

"I wrote it last Monday evening. It's called 'The Jealous Rival; or In Death Not Divided'. I read it to Marilla and she said it was stuff and nonsense. Then I read it to Matthew and he said it was fine. That is the kind of critic I like. It's a sad, sweet story. I just cried like a child while I was writing it. It's about two beautiful **maidens** called Cordelia Montmorency and Geraldine Seymour who lived in the same village and were **devotedly** attached to each other. Cordelia was a regal brunette with a coronet of midnight hair and duskly flashing eyes. Geraldine was a queenly blonde with hair like spun gold and velvety purple eyes."

maiden ['meɪdn] *n.* 少女

devotedly [dɪ'vəʊtɪdli] *adv.* 忠实地

"I never saw anybody with purple eyes," said Diana **dubiously**.

dubiously ['djuːbiəsli] *adv.* 怀疑地

"Neither did I. I just imagined them. I wanted something out of the common. Geraldine had an alabaster brow too. I've found out what an alabaster brow is. That is one of the advantages of being thirteen. You know so much more than you did when you were only twelve."

"Well, what became of Cordelia and Geraldine?" asked Diana, who was beginning to feel rather interested in their fate.

"They grew in beauty side by side until they were sixteen. Then Bertram DeVere came to their native village and fell in love with the fair Geraldine. He saved her life when her horse ran away with her in a carriage, and she fainted in his arms and he carried her home three miles; because, you understand, the carriage was all smashed up. I found it rather hard to imagine the proposal because I had no experience to go by. I asked Ruby Gillis if she knew anything about how men proposed because I thought she'd likely be an authority on the subject, having so many sisters married. Ruby told me she was hid in the hall pantry when Malcolm Andres proposed to her sister Susan. She said Malcolm told Susan that his dad had given him the farm in his own name and then said, 'What do you say, darling pet, if we **get hitched** this fall?' And Susan said, 'Yes—no—I don't know—let me see'—and there they were, engaged as quick as that. But I didn't think that sort of a proposal was a very romantic one, so in the end I had to imagine it out as well as I could. I made it very flowery and poetical and Bertram went on his knees, although Ruby Gillis says it isn't done nowadays. Geraldine accepted him in a speech a page long. I can tell you I took a lot of trouble with that speech. I rewrote it five times and I look upon it as my masterpiece. Bertram gave her a diamond ring and a ruby necklace and told her they would go to Europe for a wedding tour, for he was **immensely** wealthy. But then, alas, shadows began to darken over their path. Cordelia was secretly in love with Bertram herself and when Geraldine told her about the engagement, she was simply furious, especially when she saw the necklace and the diamond ring. All her affection for Geraldine turned to bitter hate and she vowed that she should never marry Bertram. But she pretended to be Geraldine's friend the same as ever. One evening they were standing on the bridge over a rushing **turbulent** stream and Cordelia, thinking they were alone, pushed Geraldine over the brink with a wild, mocking, 'Ha, ha, ha'. But Bertram saw it all and he at

get hitched
结婚

immensely [ɪ'mensli]
adv. 极其地

turbulent ['tɜːbjələnt]
adj. 动乱的

once plunged into the current, exclaiming, 'I will save thee, my **peerless** Geraldine.' But alas, he had forgotten he couldn't swim, and they were both drowned, clasped in each other's arms. Their bodies were washed ashore soon afterwards. They were buried in the one grave and their funeral was most **imposing**, Diana. It's so much more romantic to end a story up with a funeral than a wedding. As for Cordelia, she went insane with **remorse** and was shut up in a lunatic asylum. I thought that was a poetical **retribution** for her crime."

"How perfectly lovely!" sighed Diana, who belonged to Matthew's school of critics. "I don't see how you can make up such thrilling things out of your own head, Anne. I wish my imagination was as good as yours."

"It would be if you'd only **cultivate** it," said Anne cheeringly. "I've just thought of a plan, Diana. Let you and me have a story club all our own and write stories for practice. I'll help you along until you can do them by yourself. You ought to cultivate your imagination, you know. Miss Stacy says so. Only we must take the right way. I told her about the Haunted Wood, but she said we went the wrong way about it in that."

This was how the story club came into existence. It was limited to Diana and Anne at first, but soon it was extended to include Jane Andrews and Ruby Gillis and one or two others who felt that their imaginations needed cultivating. No boys were allowed in it—although Ruby Gillis opined that their admission would make it more exciting—and each member had to produce one story a week.

"It's extremely interesting," Anne told Marilla. "Each girl has to read her story out loud and then we talk it over. We are going to keep them all sacredly and have them to read to our **descendants**. We each write under a nom-de-plume. Mine is Rosamond Montmorency.

peerless [ˈpɪələs]
adj. 杰出的

imposing [ɪmˈpəʊzɪŋ]
adj. 壮观的

remorse [rɪˈmɔːs]
n. 懊悔，悔恨

retribution [ˌretrɪˈbjuːʃn]
n. 报应

cultivate [ˈkʌltɪveɪt]
v. 培育

descendant [dɪˈsendənt]
n. 后代

All the girls do pretty well. Ruby Gillis is rather **sentimental**. She puts too much lovemaking into her stories and you know too much is worse than too little. Jane never puts any because she says it makes her feel so silly when she had to read it out loud. Jane's stories are extremely sensible. Then Diana puts too many murders into hers. She says most of the time she doesn't know what to do with the people so she kills them off to get rid of them. I mostly always have to tell them what to write about, but that isn't hard for I've millions of ideas."

sentimental [ˌsentɪˈmentl] *adj.* 多愁善感的

"I think this story-writing business is the foolishest yet," **scoffed** Marilla. "You'll get a pack of **nonsense** into your heads and waste time that should be put on your lessons. Reading stories is bad enough but writing them is worse."

scoff [skɒf] *v.* 嘲笑
nonsense [ˈnɒnsns] *n.* 无意义的事

"But we're so careful to put a moral into them all, Marilla," explained Anne. "I insist upon that. All the good people are rewarded and all the bad ones are suitably punished. I'm sure that must have a wholesome effect. The moral is the great thing. Mr. Allan says so. I read one of my stories to him and Mrs. Allan and they both agreed that the moral was excellent. Only they laughed in the wrong places. I like it better when people cry. Jane and Ruby almost always cry when I come to the pathetic parts. Diana wrote her Aunt Josephine about our club and her Aunt Josephine wrote back that we were to send her some of our stories. So we copied out four of our very best and sent them. Miss Josephine Barry wrote back that she had never read anything so **amusing** in her life. That kind of puzzled us because the stories were all very pathetic and almost everybody died. But I'm glad Miss Barry liked them. It shows our club is doing some good in the world. Mrs. Allan says that ought to be our object in everything. I do really try to make it my object but I forget so often when I'm having fun. I hope I shall be a little like Mrs. Allan when I grow up. Do you think there is

amusing [əˈmjuːzɪŋ] *adj.* 有趣的

any **prospect** of it, Marilla?"

"I shouldn't say there was a great deal" was Marilla's encouraging answer. "I'm sure Mrs. Allan was never such a silly, forgetful little girl as you are."

"No; but she wasn't always so good as she is now either," said Anne seriously. "She told me so herself—that is, she said she was a dreadful **mischief** when she was a girl and was always getting into scrapes. I felt so encouraged when I heard that. Is it very **wicked** of me, Marilla, to feel encouraged when I hear that other people have been bad and mischievous? Mrs. Lynde says it is. Mrs. Lynde says she always feels shocked when she hears of anyone ever having been naughty, no matter how small they were. Mrs. Lynde says she once heard a minister **confess** that when he was a boy, he stole a strawberry tart out of his aunt's pantry and she never had any respect for that minister again. Now, I wouldn't have felt that way. I'd have thought that it was real noble of him to confess it, and I'd have thought what an encouraging thing it would be for small boys nowadays who do naughty things and are sorry for them to know that perhaps they may grow up to be ministers in spite of it. That's how I'd feel, Marilla."

"The way I feel at present, Anne," said Marilla, "is that it's high time you had those dishes washed. You've taken half an hour longer than you should with all your chattering. Learn to work first and talk afterwards."

CHAPTER XXVII

Vanity and **Vexation** of Spirit

Marilla, walking home one late April evening from an Aid meeting, realized that the winter was over and gone with the thrill of de-

prospect [ˈprɒspekt] *n.* 希望

mischief [ˈmɪstʃɪf] *n.* 淘气鬼
wicked [ˈwɪkɪd] *adj.* 邪恶的

confess [kənˈfes] *v.* 坦白

vanity [ˈvænəti] *n.* 自负
vexation [vekˈseɪʃn] *n.* 烦恼

light that spring never fails to bring to the oldest and saddest as well as to the youngest and merriest. Marilla was not given to subjective analysis of her thoughts and feelings. She probably imagined that she was thinking about the Aids and their **missionary** box and the new carpet for the **vestry** room, but under these reflections was a harmonious consciousness of red fields smoking into pale-purply mists in the declining sun, of long, sharp-pointed fir shadows falling over the meadow beyond the brook, of still, crimson-budded maples around a mirrorlike wood pool, of a wakening in the world and a stir of hidden pulses under the gray sod. The spring was abroad in the land and Marilla's sober, middle-aged step was lighter and swifter because of its deep, primal gladness.

missionary [ˈmɪʃənri] *adj.* 传教(士)的
vestry [ˈvestri] *n.* (教堂的)祭衣圣器储藏室

Her eyes dwelt **affectionately** on Green Gables, peering through its network of trees and reflecting the sunlight back from its windows in several little **coruscations** of glory. Marilla, as she picked her steps along the damp lane, thought that it was really a satisfaction to know that she was going home to a briskly snapping wood fire and a table nicely spread for tea, instead of to the cold comfort of old Aid meeting evenings before Anne had come to Green Gables.

affectionately [əˈfekʃənətli] *adv.* 关爱地
coruscation [kɒrəˈskeɪʃən] *n.* 闪光

Consequently, when Marilla entered her kitchen and found the fire black out, with no sign of Anne anywhere, she felt justly disappointed and **irritated**. She had told Anne to be sure and have tea ready at five o'clock, but now she must hurry to take off her second-best dress and prepare the meal herself against Matthew's return from **plowing**.

irritated [ˈɪrɪteɪtɪd] *adj.* 恼怒的
plough [plaʊ] *v.* 耕

"I'll settle Miss Anne when she comes home," said Marilla grimly, as she **shaved** up kindlings with a carving knife and with more **vim** than was strictly necessary. Matthew had come in and was waiting patiently for his tea in his corner. "She's gadding off some-

shave [ʃeɪv] *v.* 削去，刮掉
vim [vɪm] *n.* 活力

where with Diana, writing stories or practicing dialogues or some such **tomfoolery**, and never thinking once about the time or her duties. She's just got to be pulled up short and sudden on this sort of thing. I don't care if Mrs. Allan does say she's the brightest and sweetest child she ever knew. She may be bright and sweet enough, but her head is full of nonsense and there's never any knowing what shape it'll break out in next. Just as soon as she grows out of one **freak**, she takes up with another. But there! Here I am saying the very thing I was so **riled** with Rachel Lynde for saying at the Aid today. I was really glad when Mrs. Allan spoke up for Anne, for if she hadn't. I know I'd have said something too sharp to Rachel before everybody. Anne's got plenty of faults, goodness knows, and far be it from me to deny it. But I'm bringing her up and not Rachel Lynde, who'd pick faults in the Angel Gabriel himself if he lived in Avonlea. Just the same, Anne has no business to leave the house like this when I told her she was to stay home this afternoon and look after things. I must say, with all her faults, I never found her **disobedient** or untrustworthy before and I'm really sorry to find her so now."

"Well now, I dunno," said Matthew, who, being patient and wise and, above all, hungry, had **deemed** it best to let Marilla talk her **wrath** out **unhindered**, having learned by experience that she got through with whatever work was on hand much quicker if not delayed by **untimely** argument. "Perhaps you're judging her too hasty, Marilla. Don't call her untrustworthy until you're sure she has disobeyed you. Mebbe it can all be explained—Anne's a great hand at explaining."

"She's not here when I told her to stay," **retorted** Marilla. "I reckon she'll find it hard to explain that to my satisfaction. Of course, I knew you'd take her part, Matthew. But I'm bringing her up, not you."

tomfoolery [tɒm'fuːləri]
n. 愚蠢的行为

freak [friːk]
n. 怪人

rile [raɪl]
v. 激怒

disobedient [ˌdɪsə'biːdiənt]
adj. 不服从的

deem [diːm]
v. 认为

wrath [rɒθ]
n. 盛怒

unhindered [ʌn'hɪndəd]
adj. 不受阻碍的

untimely [ʌn'taɪmli]
adj. 不合时宜的

retort [rɪ'tɔːt]
v. 反驳

It was dark when supper was ready, and still no sign of Anne, coming hurriedly over the log bridge or up Lover's Lane, breathless and **repentant** with a sense of neglected duties. Marilla washed and put away the dishes grimly. Then, wanting a candle to light her way down the **cellar**, she went up to the east gable for the one that generally stood on Anne's table. Lighting it, she turned around to see Anne herself lying on the bed, face downward among the pillows.

repentant [rɪ'pentənt] *adj.* 后悔的

cellar ['selə(r)] *n.* 地下室

"Mercy on us," said astonished Marilla, "have you been asleep, Anne?"

"No," was the muffled reply.

"Are you sick then?" demanded Marilla anxiously, going over to the bed.

Anne **cowered** deeper into her pillows as if **desirous** of hiding herself forever from mortal eyes.

cower ['kaʊə(r)] *v.* 畏缩

desirous [dɪ'zaɪərəs] *adj.* 渴望

"No. But please, Marilla, go away and don't look at me. I'm in the depths of despair and I don't care who gets head in class or writes the best composition or sings in the Sunday-school choir any more. Little things like that are of no importance now because I don't suppose I'll ever be able to go anywhere again. My career is closed. Please, Marilla, go away and don't look at me."

"Did anyone ever hear the like?" the **mystified** Marilla wanted to know. "Anne Shirley, whatever is the matter with you? What have you done? Get right up this minute and tell me. This minute, I say. There now, what is it?"

mystify ['mɪstɪfaɪ] *v.* 迷惑

Anne had slid to the floor in despairing obedience.

"Look at my hair, Marilla," she whispered.

Accordingly, Marilla lifted her candle and looked **scrutinizingly** at Anne's hair, flowing in heavy masses down her back. It certainly had a very strange appearance.

scrutinize ['skruːtənaɪz] *v.* 仔细查看

"Anne Shirley, what have you done to your hair? Why, it's green!"

Green it might be called, if it were any earthly color—a **queer**, dull, **bronzy** green, with streaks here and there of the original red to heighten the **ghastly** effect. Never in all her life had Marilla seen anything so **grotesque** as Anne's hair at that moment.

"Yes, it's green," **moaned** Anne. "I thought nothing could be as bad as red hair. But now I know it's ten times worse to have green hair. Oh, Marilla, you little know how **utterly wretched** I am."

"I little know how you got into this fix, but I mean to find out," said Marilla. "Come right down to the kitchen—it's too cold up here—and tell me just what you've done. I've been expecting something queer for some time. You haven't got into any scrape for over two months, and I was sure another one was due. Now, then, what did you do to your hair?"

"I **dyed** it."

"Dyed it! Dyed your hair! Anne Shirley, didn't you know it was a wicked thing to do?"

"Yes, I knew it was a little wicked," admitted Anne. "But I thought it was worthwhile to be a little wicked to get rid of red hair. I counted the cost, Marilla. Besides, I meant to be extra good in other ways to make up for it."

"Well," said Marilla **sarcastically**, "if I'd decided it was worthwhile to dye my hair, I'd have dyed it a **decent** color at least. I wouldn't have dyed it green."

"But I didn't mean to dye it green, Marilla," **protested** Anne dejectedly. "If I was wicked, I meant to be wicked to some purpose. He said it would turn my hair a beautiful raven black—he positively assured me that it would. How could I doubt his word, Marilla? I know

queer [kwɪə(r)]
adj. 奇怪的
bronze [brɒnz]
adj. 青铜色的
ghastly [ˈɡɑːstli]
adj. 可怕的
grotesque [ɡrəʊˈtesk]
adj. 怪诞的
moan [məʊn]
v. 抱怨
utterly [ˈʌtəli]
adv. 完全地
wretched [ˈretʃɪd]
adj. 悲惨的

dye [daɪ]
v. 染色

sarcastically [sɑːˈkæstɪkli]
adv. 挖苦地
decent [ˈdiːsnt]
adj. 得体的
protest [prəˈtest]
v. 抗议

what it feels like to have your word doubted. And Mrs. Allan says we should never **suspect** anyone of not telling us the truth unless we have proof that they're not. I have proof now—green hair is proof enough for anybody. But I hadn't then and I believed every word he said implicitly."

suspect [sə'spekt] *v.* 怀疑

"Who said? Who are you talking about?"

"The **peddler** that was here this afternoon. I bought the dye from him."

peddler ['pedlə(r)] *n.* 流动小贩

"Anne Shirley, how often have I told you never to let one of those Italians in the house! I don't believe in encouraging them to come around at all."

"Oh, I didn't let him in the house. I remembered what you told me, and I went out, carefully shut the door, and looked at his things on the step. Besides, he wasn't an Italian—he was a German Jew. He had a big box full of very interesting things and he told me he was working hard to make enough money to bring his wife and children out from Germany. He spoke so feelingly about them that it touched my heart. I wanted to buy something from him to help him in such a worthy object. Then all at once I saw the bottle of hair dye. The peddler said it was **warranted** to dye any hair a beautiful raven black and wouldn't wash off. In a trice I saw myself with beautiful raven-black hair and the **temptation** was **irresistible**. But the price of the bottle was seventy-five cents and I had only fifty cents left out of my chicken money. I think the peddler had a very kind heart, for he said that, seeing it was me, he'd sell it for fifty cents and that was just giving it away. So I bought it, and as soon as he had gone I came up here and applied it with an old hairbrush as the directions said. I used up the whole bottle, and oh, Marilla, when I saw the dreadful color it turned my hair I repented of being wicked, I can tell you. And I've been

warrant ['wɒrənt] *v.* 担保

temptation [temp'teɪʃn] *n.* 诱惑

irresistible [ˌɪrɪ'zɪstəbl] *adj.* 无法抑制的

repenting ever since."

"Well, I hope you'll repent to good purpose," said Marilla severely, "and that you've got your eyes opened to where your vanity has led you, Anne. Goodness knows what's to be done. I suppose the first thing is to give your hair a good washing and see if that will do any good."

Accordingly, Anne washed her hair, scrubbing it **vigorously** with soap and water, but for all the difference it made she might as well have been scouring its original red. The peddler had certainly spoken the truth when he declared that the dye wouldn't wash off, however his **veracity** might be **impeached** in other respects.

"Oh, Marilla, what shall I do?" questioned Anne in tears. "I can never live this down. People have pretty well forgotten my other mistakes—the liniment cake and setting Diana drunk and flying into a temper with Mrs. Lynde. But they'll never forget this. They will think I am not respectable. Oh, Marilla, 'what a **tangled** web we weave when first we practice to **deceive**.' That is poetry, but it is true. And oh, how Josie Pye will laugh! Marilla, I cannot face Josie Pye. I am the unhappiest girl in Prince Edward Island."

Anne's unhappiness continued for a week. During that time, she went nowhere and shampooed her hair every day. Diana alone of outsiders knew the fatal secret, but she promised solemnly never to tell, and it may be stated here and now that she kept her word. At the end of the week Marilla said decidedly:

"It's no use, Anne. That is fast dye if ever there was any. Your hair must be cut off; there is no other way. You can't go out with it looking like that."

Anne's lips **quivered**, but she realized the bitter truth of Marilla's remarks. With a **dismal** sigh she went for the scissors.

repent [rɪ'pent]
v. 悔恨

vigorously ['vɪgərəsli]
adv. 精力旺盛地

veracity [və'ræsəti]
n. 真实
impeach [ɪm'piːtʃ]
v. 控告

tangled ['tæŋgld]
adj. 纠缠的
deceive [dɪ'siːv]
v. 欺骗

quiver ['kwɪvə(r)]
v. 颤抖
dismal ['dɪzməl]
adj. 忧郁的

"Please cut it off at once, Marilla, and have it over. Oh, I feel that my heart is broken. This is such an unromantic **affliction**. The girls in books lose their hair in fevers or sell it to get money for some good deed, and I'm sure I wouldn't mind losing my hair in some such fashion half so much. But there is nothing comforting in having your hair cut off because you've dyed it a dreadful color, is there? I'm going to weep all the time you're cutting it off, if it won't **interfere**. It seems such a tragic thing."

affliction [ə'flɪkʃn]
n. 苦难

interfere [ˌɪntə'fɪə(r)]
v. 干扰

Anne wept then, but later on, when she went upstairs and looked in the glass, she was calm with despair. Marilla had done her work thoroughly and it had been necessary to **shingle** the hair as closely as possible. The result was not becoming, to state the case as mildly as may be. Anne **promptly** turned her glass to the wall.

shingle ['ʃɪŋgl]
v. 剪成平顶发式

promptly ['prɒmptli]
adj. 迅速地

"I'll never, never look at myself again until my hair grows," she exclaimed passionately.

Then she suddenly righted the glass.

"Yes, I will, too. I'd do **penance** for being wicked that way. I'll look at myself every time I come to my room and see how ugly I am. And I won't try to imagine it away, either. I never thought I was vain about my hair, of all things, but now I know I was, in spite of its being red, because it was so long and thick and **curly**. I expect something will happen to my nose next."

penance ['penəns]
n. 忏悔

curly ['kɜːli]
adj. 卷曲的

Anne's clipped head made a sensation in school on the following Monday, but to her **relief** nobody guessed the real reason for it, not even Josie Pye, who, however, did not fail to **inform** Anne that she looked like a perfect **scarecrow**.

"I didn't say anything when Josie said that to me," Anne **confided** that evening to Marilla, who was lying on the sofa after one of her headaches, "because I thought it was part of my punishment and I

relief [rɪ'liːf]
n. 轻松

inform [ɪn'fɔːm]
v. 通知

scarecrow ['skeəkrəʊ]
n. 稻草人

confide [kən'faɪd]
v. 吐露

ought to bear it patiently. It's hard to be told you look like a scarecrow and I wanted to say something back. But I didn't. I just swept her one **scornful** look and then I forgave her. It makes you feel very **virtuous** when you forgive people, doesn't it? I mean to devote all my energies to being good after this and I shall never try to be beautiful again. Of course, it's better to be good. I know it is, but it's sometimes so hard to believe a thing even when you know it. I do really want to be good, Marilla, like you and Mrs. Allan and Miss Stacy, and grow up to be a credit to you. Diana says when my hair begins to grow to tie a black velvet **ribbon** around my head with a bow at one side. She says she thinks it will be very becoming. I will call it a snood—that sounds so romantic. But am I talking too much, Marilla? Does it hurt your head?"

scornful [ˈskɔːnfl] *adj.* 轻蔑的
virtuous [ˈvɜːtʃuəs] *adj.* 道德高尚的
ribbon [ˈrɪbən] *n.* 丝带

"My head is better now. It was terrible bad this afternoon, though. These headaches of mine are getting worse and worse. I'll have to see a doctor about them. As for your chatter, I don't know that I mind it—I've got so used to it."

Which was Marilla's way of saying that she liked to hear it.

CHAPTER XXVIII

An Unfortunate Lily Maid

"OF course you must be Elaine, Anne," said Diana. "I could never have the courage to float down there."

"Nor I," said Ruby Gillis, with a shiver. "I don't mind **floating** down when there's two or three of us in the flat and we can sit up. It's fun then. But to lie down and pretend I was dead—I just couldn't. I'd die really of **fright**."

"Of course, it would be romantic," **conceded** Jane Andrews, "but I know I couldn't keep **still**. I'd be popping up every minute or so to see where I was and if I wasn't **drifting** too far out. And you

float [ˈfləʊt] *v.* 浮动
fright [fraɪt] *n.* 惊吓
concede [kənˈsiːd] *v.* 承认
still [stɪl] *adj.* 静止的
drift [drɪft] *v.* 飘移

know, Anne, that would **spoil** the effect."

"But it's so ridiculous to have a **red-headed** Elaine," mourned Anne. "I'm not afraid to float down and I'd love to be Elaine. But it's ridiculous just the same. Ruby ought to be Elaine because she is so **fair** and has such lovely long golden hair—Elaine had 'all her bright hair streaming down', you know. And Elaine was the lily maid. Now, a red-haired person cannot be a lily maid."

"Your **complexion** is just as fair as Ruby's," said Diana **earnestly**, "and your hair is ever so much darker than it used to be before you cut it."

"Oh, do you really think so?" exclaimed Anne, flushing **sensitively** with delight. "I've sometimes thought it was myself—but I never **dared** to ask anyone for fear she would tell me it wasn't. Do you think it could be called auburn now, Diana?"

"Yes, and I think it is real pretty," said Diana, looking admiringly at the short, silky curls that clustered over Anne's head and were held in place by a very **jaunty** black velvet ribbon and bow.

They were standing on the bank of the pond, below Orchard Slope, where a little headland fringed with birches ran out from the bank; at its tip was a small wooden platform built out into the water for the convenience of fishermen and duck hunters. Ruby and Jane were spending the midsummer afternoon with Diana, and Anne had come over to play with them.

Anne and Diana had spent most of their playtime that summer on and about the pond. Idlewild was a thing of the past, Mr. Bell having **ruthlessly** cut down the little circle of trees in his back pasture in the spring. Anne had sat among the **stumps** and wept, not without an eye to the romance of it; but she was speedily **consoled**, for, after all, as she and Diana said, big girls of thirteen, going on fourteen, were too

spoil [spɔɪl]
v. 破坏
red-headed [ˌred'hedɪd]
adj. 红发的

fair [feə(r)]
adj. 白皙的

complexion [kəm'plekʃn]
n. 肤色
earnestly ['ɜːnɪstli]
adv. 真挚地
sensitively ['sensətɪvli]
adj. 敏感地

dare [deə(r)]
v. 敢于

jaunty ['dʒɔːnti]
adj. 快活的

ruthlessly ['ruːθləsli]
adv. 无情地
stump [stʌmp]
n. 树桩
console [kən'səʊl]
v. 安慰

old for such childish amusements as playhouses, and there were more fascinating sports to be found about the pond. It was splendid to fish for **trout** over the bridge and the two girls learned to row themselves about in the little flat-bottomed **dory** Mr. Barry kept for duck shooting.

trout [traʊt]
n. 鳟鱼
dory [ˈdɔːri]
n. 平底小渔船

It was Anne's idea that they dramatize Elaine. They had studied Tennyson's poem in school the preceding winter, the Superintendent of Education having **prescribed** it in the English course for the Prince Edward Island schools. They had analyzed and **parsed** it and torn it to pieces in general until it was a wonder there was any meaning at all left in it for them, but at least the fair lily maid and Lancelot and Guinevere and King Arthur had become very real people to them, and Anne was **devoured** by secret regret that she had not been born in Camelot. Those days, she said, were so much more romantic than the present.

prescribe [prɪˈskraɪb]
v. 规定
parse [pɑːz]
v. 分析
devour [dɪˈvaʊə(r)]
v. 吞没

Anne's plan was **hailed** with enthusiasm. The girls had discovered that if the flat were pushed off from the landing place it would drift down with the current under the bridge and finally **strand** itself on another headland lower down which ran out at a **curve** in the pond. They had often gone down like this and nothing could be more convenient for playing Elaine.

hail [heɪl]
v. 赞扬,称颂
strand [strænd]
v. 使滞留
curve [kɜːv]
n. 曲线

"Well, I'll be Elaine," said Anne, yielding **reluctantly**, for, although she would have been delighted to play the principal character, yet her artistic sense demanded fitness for it and this, she felt, her limitations made impossible. "Ruby, you must be King Arthur and Jane will be Guinevere and Diana must be Lancelot. But first you must be the brothers and the father. We can't have the old **dumb servitor** because there isn't room for two in the flat when one is lying down. We must pall the barge all its length in blackest samite. That old black shawl of your mother's will be just the thing, Diana."

reluctantly [rɪˈlʌktəntli]
adv. 不情愿地
dumb [dʌm]
adj. 哑的
servitor [ˈsɜːvɪtə(r)]
n. 男仆

The black shawl having been **procured**, Anne spread it over the flat and then lay down on the bottom, with closed eyes and hands folded over her breast.

procure [prə'kjʊə(r)] *v.* 获得

"Oh, she does look really dead," whispered Ruby Gillis nervously, watching the still, white little face under the flickering shadows of the birches. "It makes me feel frightened, girls. Do you suppose it's really right to act like this? Mrs. Lynde says that all play-acting is **abominably** wicked."

abominably [ə'bɒmɪnəbli] *adv.* 令人厌恶地

"Ruby, you shouldn't talk about Mrs. Lynde," said Anne severely. "It **spoils** the effect because this is hundreds of years before Mrs. Lynde was born. Jane, you arrange this. It's silly for Elaine to be talking when she's dead."

spoil [spɔɪl] *v.* 破坏

Jane rose to the occasion. Cloth of gold for **coverlet** there was none, but an old piano scarf of yellow Japanese crepe was an excellent **substitute**. A white lily was not **obtainable** just then, but the effect of a tall blue iris placed in one of Anne's folded hands was all that could be desired.

coverlet ['kʌvələt] *n.* 床罩

substitute ['sʌbstɪtjuːt] *n.* 替代物

obtainable [əb'teɪnəbl] *adj.* 可得到的

"Now, she's all ready," said Jane. "We must kiss her quiet brows and, Diana, you say, 'Sister, farewell forever', and Ruby, you say, 'Farewell, sweet sister', both of you as sorrowfully as you possibly can. Anne, for goodness sake, smile a little. You know Elaine 'lay as though she smiled'. That's better. Now push the flat off."

The flat was accordingly pushed off, scraping roughly over an old embedded **stake** in the process. Diana and Jane and Ruby only waited long enough to see it caught in the current and headed for the bridge before **scampering** up through the woods, across the road, and down to the lower headland where, as Lancelot and Guinevere and the King, they were to be in readiness to receive the lily maid.

stake [steɪk] *n.* 篱笆桩

scamper ['skæmpə(r)] *v.* 蹦蹦跳跳

For a few minutes Anne, drifting slowly down, enjoyed the romance of her situation to the full. Then something happened not at all romantic. The flat began to **leak**. In a very few moments it was necessary for Elaine to scramble to her feet, pick up her cloth of gold coverlet and pall of blackest samite and gaze blankly at a big crack in the bottom of her barge through which the water was literally pouring. That sharp stake at the landing had torn off the strip of batting nailed on the flat. Anne did not know this, but it did not take her long to realize that she was in a dangerous **plight**. At this rate the flat would fill and sink long before it could drift to the lower headland. Where were the oars? Left behind at the landing!

leak [liːk] *v.* 渗漏

plight [plaɪt] *n.* 困境

Anne gave one gasping little scream which nobody ever heard; she was white to the lips, but she did not lose her self-possession. There was one chance—just one.

"I was horribly frightened," she told Mrs. Allan the next day, "and it seemed like years while the flat was drifting down to the bridge and the water rising in it every moment. I prayed, Mrs. Allan, most earnestly, but I didn't shut my eyes to pray, for I knew the only way God could save me was to let the flat float close enough to one of the bridge piles for me to climb up on it. You know the piles are just old tree trunks and there are lots of knots and old branch stubs on them. It was proper to pray, but I had to do my part by watching out and right well I knew it. I just said, 'Dear God, please take the flat close to a pile and I'll do the rest,' over and over again.

Under such circumstances you don't think much about making a flowery prayer. But mine was answered, for the flat bumped right into a pile for a minute and I flung the scarf and the shawl over my shoulder and scrambled up on a big providential stub. And there I was, Mrs. Allan, clinging to that slippery old pile with no way of getting up or down. It was a very unromantic position, but I didn't think about that at the time. You don't think much about romance when you have just escaped from a watery grave. I said a grateful prayer at once and then I gave all my attention to holding on tight, for I knew I should probably have to depend on human aid to get back to dry land."

The flat drifted under the bridge and then promptly sank in midstream. Ruby, Jane, and Diana, already awaiting it on the lower headland, saw it disappear before their very eyes and had not a doubt but that Anne had gone down with it. For a moment they stood still, white as sheets, frozen with horror at the tragedy; then, shrieking at the tops of their voices, they started on a frantic run up through the woods, never pausing as they crossed the main road to glance the way of the bridge. Anne, clinging desperately to her precarious **foothold**, saw their flying **forms** and heard their shrieks. Help would soon come, but meanwhile her position was a very uncomfortable one.

foothold [ˈfʊthəʊld]
n. 立足点
form [fɔːm]
n. 形式

The minutes passed by, each seeming an hour to the unfortunate lily maid. Why didn't somebody come? Where had the girls gone? Suppose they had fainted, one and all! Suppose nobody ever came! Suppose she grew so tired and **cramped** that she could hold on no longer! Anne looked at the wicked green depths below her, **wavering** with long, oily shadows, and shivered. Her imagination began to suggest all manner of gruesome possibilities to her.

cramped [kræmpt]
adj. 拥挤的
waver [ˈweɪvə(r)]
v. 摇曳

Then, just as she thought she really could not **endure** the ache in her arms and wrists another moment, Gilbert Blythe came rowing under the bridge in Harmon Andrews's dory!

endure [ɪnˈdjʊə(r)]
v. 忍受

Gilbert glanced up and, much to his amazement, beheld a little white scornful face looking down upon him with big, frightened but also scornful gray eyes.

"Anne Shirley! How on earth did you get there?" he exclaimed.

Without waiting for an answer, he pulled close to the pile and extended his hand. There was no help for it; Anne, clinging to Gilbert Blythe's hand, scrambled down into the dory, where she sat, **drabbled** and furious, in the stern with her arms full of dripping shawl and wet crepe. It was certainly extremely difficult to be dignified under the circumstances!

"What has happened, Anne?" asked Gilbert, taking up his oars. "We were playing Elaine" explained Anne frigidly, without even looking at her rescuer, "and I had to drift down to Camelot in the barge—I mean the flat. The flat began to leak and I climbed out on the pile. The girls went for help. Will you be kind enough to row me to the landing?"

Gilbert **obligingly** rowed to the landing and Anne, disdaining assistance, sprang nimbly on shore.

"I'm very much obliged to you," she said haughtily as she turned away. But Gilbert had also sprung from the boat and now laid a detaining hand on her arm.

"Anne," he said hurriedly, "look here. Can't we be good friends? I'm awfully sorry I made fun of your hair that time. I didn't mean to **vex** you and I only meant it for a joke. Besides, it's so long ago. I think your hair is awfully pretty now—honest I do. Let's be friends."

For a moment Anne hesitated. She had an odd, newly awakened consciousness under all her outraged dignity that the half-shy, half-eager expression in Gilbert's hazel eyes was something that was very good to see. Her heart gave a quick, queer little beat. But the bitterness of her old **grievance** promptly **stiffened** up her wavering determination. That scene of two years before flashed back into her **recollection** as vividly as if it had taken place yesterday. Gilbert had called her "carrots" and had brought about her disgrace before the whole school. Her **resentment**, which to other and older people might be as

drabbled [ˈdræbəld]
adj. 湿漉漉的

obligingly [əˈblaɪdʒɪŋli]
adv. 热情地

vex [veks]
v. 使烦恼

grievance [ˈgriːvəns]
n. 委屈

stiffen [ˈstɪfn]
v.（身体）变僵硬

recollection [ˌrekəˈlekʃn]
n. 回忆

resentment [rɪˈzentmənt]
n. 怨恨

laughable as its cause, was in no **whit allayed** and softened by time seemingly. She hated Gilbert Blythe! She would never forgive him!

whit [wɪt]
n. 一点点;丝毫
allay [əˈleɪ]
v. 减轻

"No," she said coldly, "I shall never be friends with you, Gilbert Blythe; and I don't want to be!"

"All right!" Gilbert sprang into his skiff with an angry color in his cheeks. "I'll never ask you to be friends again, Anne Shirley. And I don't care either!"

He pulled away with swift **defiant** strokes, and Anne went up the steep, ferny little path under the maples. She held her head very high, but she was conscious of an odd feeling of regret. She almost wished she had answered Gilbert differently. Of course, he had insulted her terribly, but still—! Altogether, Anne rather thought it would be a relief to sit down and have a good cry. She was really quite **unstrung**, for the reaction from her fright and cramped clinging was making itself felt.

defiant [dɪˈfaɪənt]
adj. 反抗的

unstrung [ʌnˈstrʌŋ]
adj. 情绪上紧张不安的

Halfway up the path she met Jane and Diana rushing back to the pond in a state narrowly removed from positive **frenzy**. They had found nobody at Orchard Slope, both Mr. and Mrs. Barry being away. Here Ruby Gillis had **succumbed** to hysterics, and was left to recover from them as best she might, while Jane and Diana flew through the Haunted Wood and across the brook to Green Gables. There they had found nobody either, for Marilla had gone to Carmody and Matthew was making hay in the back field.

frenzy [ˈfrenzi]
n. 疯狂

succumb [səˈkʌm]
v. 屈服

"Oh, Anne," gasped Diana, fairly falling on the former's neck and weeping with relief and delight, "oh, Anne—we thought—you were—drowned—and we felt like murderers—because we had made—you be—Elaine. And Ruby is in hysterics—oh, Anne, how did you escape?"

"I climbed up on one of the piles," explained Anne **wearily**,

wearily [ˈwɪərəli]
adv. 疲倦地

"and Gilbert Blythe came along in Mr. Andrews's dory and brought me to land."

"Oh, Anne, how splendid of him! Why, it's so romantic!" said Jane, finding breath enough for **utterance** at last. "Of course, you'll speak to him after this."

"Of course, I won't," flashed Anne, with a momentary return of her old spirit. "And I don't want ever to hear the word 'romantic' again, Jane Andrews. I'm awfully sorry you were so frightened, girls. It is all my fault. I feel sure I was born under an unlucky star. Everything I do gets me or my dearest friends into a **scrape**. We've gone and lost your father's flat, Diana, and I have a **presentiment** that we'll not be allowed to row on the pond anymore."

Anne's presentiment proved more trustworthy than presentiments are **apt** to do. Great was the **consternation** in the Barry and Cuthbert households when the events of the afternoon became known.

"Will you ever have any sense, Anne?" groaned Marilla.

"Oh, yes, I think I will, Marilla," returned Anne optimistically. A good cry, **indulged** in the grateful **solitude** of the east gable, had soothed her nerves and restored her to her wonted cheerfulness. "I think my prospects of becoming sensible are brighter now than ever."

"I don't see how," said Marilla.

"Well," explained Anne, "I've learned a new and valuable lesson today. Ever since I came to Green Gables, I've been making mistakes, and each mistake has helped to cure me of some great shortcoming. The affair of the amethyst brooch cured me of meddling with things that didn't belong to me. The Haunted Wood mistake cured me of letting my imagination run away with me. The liniment cake mistake cured me of carelessness in cooking. Dyeing my hair cured me of vanity. I never think about my hair and nose now—at least, very seldom.

utterance [ˈʌtərəns]
n. 说话

scrape [skreɪp]
n. 困境
presentiment
[prɪˈzentɪmənt]
n. 预感

apt [æpt]
adj. 易于……
consternation
[ˌkɒnstəˈneɪʃn]
n. 惊慌失措

indulge [ɪnˈdʌldʒ]
v. 沉溺
solitude [ˈsɒlətjuːd]
n. 独处

And today's mistake is going to **cure** me of being too romantic. I have come to the conclusion that it is no use trying to be romantic in Avonlea. It was probably easy enough in towered Camelot hundreds of years ago, but romance is not appreciated now. I feel quite sure that you will soon see a great improvement in me in this respect, Marilla."

"I'm sure I hope so," said Marilla skeptically.

But Matthew, who had been sitting **mutely** in his corner, laid a hand on Anne's shoulder when Marilla had gone out.

"Don't give up all your romance, Anne," he whispered shyly, "a little of it is a good thing—not too much, of course—but keep a little of it, Anne, keep a little of it."

CHAPTER XXIX

An **Epoch** in Anne's Life

Anne was bringing the cows home from the back pasture by way of Lover's Lane. It was a September evening and all the gaps and clearings in the woods were **brimmed** up with ruby sunset light. Here and there the lane was splashed with it, but for the most part it was already quite shadowy beneath the maples, and the spaces under the firs were filled with a clear violet **dusk** like airy wine. The winds were out in their tops, and there is no sweeter music on earth than that which the wind makes in the fir trees at evening.

The cows **swung placidly** down the lane, and Anne followed them **dreamily**, repeating aloud the battle **canto** from marmion—which had also been part of their English course the preceding winter and which Miss Stacy had made them learn off by heart—and **exulting** in its rushing lines and the clash of **spears** in its imagery. When she came to the lines

The stubborn spearsmen still made good

cure [kjʊə(r)]
v. 治疗

mutely [ˈmjuːtli]
adv. 无言地

epoch [ˈiːpɒk]
n. 时代

brim [brɪm]
v. 充满

dusk [dʌsk]
n. 黄昏

swing [swɪŋ]
v. 摆动
placidly [ˈplæsɪdli]
adv. 满足地
dreamily [ˈdriːmɪli]
adv. 心不在焉地
canto [ˈkæntəʊ]
n. 篇，章
exult [ɪgˈzʌlt]
v. 兴高采烈
spear [spɪə(r)]
n. 矛

Their dark **impenetrable** wood,

she stopped in ecstasy to shut her eyes that she might the better fancy herself one of that heroic ring. When she opened them again it was to behold Diana coming through the gate that led into the Barry field and looking so important that Anne instantly divined there was news to be told. But betray too eager curiosity she would not.

"Isn't this evening just like a purple dream, Diana? It makes me so glad to be alive. In the mornings I always think the mornings are best; but when evening comes, I think it's lovelier still."

"It's a very fine evening," said Diana, "but oh, I have such news, Anne. Guess. You can have three guesses."

"Charlotte Gillis is going to be married in the church after all and Mrs. Allan wants us to decorate it," cried Anne.

"No. Charlotte's beau won't agree to that, because nobody ever has been married in the church yet, and he thinks it would seem too much like a funeral. It's too mean, because it would be such fun. Guess again."

"Jane's mother is going to let her have a birthday party?"

Diana shook her head, her black eyes dancing with **merriment**.

"I can't think what it can be," said Anne in despair, "unless it's that Moody Spurgeon MacPherson saw you home from prayer meeting last night. Did he?"

"I should think not," exclaimed Diana indignantly. "I wouldn't be likely to **boast** of it if he did, the horrid creature! I knew you couldn't guess it. Mother had a letter from Aunt Josephine today, and Aunt Josephine wants you and me to go to town next Tuesday and stop with her for the Exhibition. There!"

"Oh, Diana," whispered Anne, finding it necessary to lean up against a maple tree for support, "do you really mean it? But I'm

impenetrable [ɪm'penɪtrəbl] *adj.* 无法穿过的

merriment ['merimənt] *n.* 欢乐

boast [bəʊst] *v.* 自夸

afraid Marilla won't let me go. She will say that she can't encourage **gadding** about. That was what she said last week when Jane invited me to go with them in their double-seated **buggy** to the American concert at the White Sands Hotel. I wanted to go, but Marilla said I'd be better at home learning my lessons and so would Jane. I was bitterly disappointed, Diana. I felt so heartbroken that I wouldn't say my prayers when I went to bed. But I repented of that and got up in the middle of the night and said them."

gad [gæd] *v.* 闲逛
buggy ['bʌgi] *n.* 专用小汽车

"I'll tell you," said Diana, "we'll get mother to ask Marilla. She'll be more likely to let you go then; and if she does, we'll have the time of our lives, Anne. I've never been to an exhibition, and it's so **aggravating** to hear the other girls talking about their trips. Jane and Ruby have been twice, and they're going this year again."

aggravating ['ægrəveɪtɪŋ] *adj.* 恼人的，令人生气的

"I'm not going to think about it at all until I know whether I can go or not," said Anne resolutely. "If I did and then was disappointed, it would be more than I could bear. But in case I do go I'm very glad my new coat will be ready by that time. Marilla didn't think I needed a new coat. She said my old one would do very well for another winter and that I ought to be satisfied with having a new dress. The dress is very pretty, Diana—navy blue and made so fashionably. Marilla always makes my dresses fashionably now, because she says she doesn't intend to have Matthew going to Mrs. Lynde to make them. I'm so glad. It is ever so much easier to be good if your clothes are fashionable. At least, it is easier for me. I suppose it doesn't make such a difference to naturally good people. But Matthew said I must have a new coat, so Marilla bought a lovely piece of blue **broad-cloth**, and it's being made by a real dressmaker over at Carmody. It's to be done Saturday night, and I'm trying not to imagine myself walking up the church aisle on Sunday in my new suit and cap, because

broadcloth ['brɔːdklɒθ] *n.* 细平布

I'm afraid it isn't right to imagine such things. But it just slips into my mind in spite of me. My cap is so pretty. Matthew bought it for me the day we were over at Carmody. It is one of those little blue velvet ones that are **all the rage**, with gold cord and tassels. Your new hat is elegant, Diana, and so becoming. When I saw you come into church last Sunday my heart **swelled** with pride to think you were my dearest friend. Do you suppose it's wrong for us to think so much about our clothes? Marilla says it is very sinful. But it is such an interesting subject, isn't it?"

all the rage
十分流行;风靡一时

swell [swel]
v. 充满

Marilla agreed to let Anne go to town, and it was arranged that Mr. Barry should take the girls in on the following Tuesday. As Charlottetown was thirty miles away and Mr. Barry wished to go and return the same day, it was necessary to make a very early start. But Anne counted it all joy, and was up before sunrise on Tuesday morning. A glance from her window assured her that the day would be fine, for the eastern sky behind the firs of the Haunted Wood was all silvery and cloudless. Through the gap in the trees a light was shining in the western gable of Orchard Slope, a token that Diana was also up.

Anne was dressed by the time Matthew had the fire on and had the breakfast ready when Marilla came down, but for her own part was much too excited to eat. After breakfast the jaunty new cap and jacket were **donned**, and Anne **hastened** over the brook and up through the firs to Orchard Slope. Mr. Barry and Diana were waiting for her, and they were soon on the road.

don [dɒn]
v. 戴上
hasten [ˈheɪsn]
v. 急忙做

It was a long drive, but Anne and Diana enjoyed every minute of it. It was delightful to **rattle** along over the moist roads in the early red sunlight that was **creeping** across the shorn harvest fields. The air was fresh and crisp, and little smoke-blue mists curled through the valleys and floated off from the hills. Sometimes the road went through

rattle [ˈrætl]
v. 发出咔嗒的声音
creep [kriːp]
v. 弥漫

woods where maples were beginning to hang out scarlet banners; sometimes it crossed rivers on bridges that made Anne's **flesh** cringe with the old, half-delightful fear; sometimes it wound along a harbor shore and passed by a little cluster of weather-gray fishing huts; again it mounted to hills whence a far sweep of curving **upland** or misty-blue sky could be seen; but wherever it went there was much of interest to discuss. It was almost noon when they reached town and found their way to "Beechwood". It was quite a fine old mansion, set back from the street in a **seclusion** of green **elms** and branching beeches. Miss Barry met them at the door with a twinkle in her sharp black eyes.

flesh [fleʃ]
n. 肉

upland [ˈʌplənd]
n. 高地

seclusion [sɪˈkluːʒn]
n. 与世隔绝

elm [elm]
n. 榆树

"So you've come to see me at last, you Anne-girl," she said. "Mercy, child, how you have grown! You're taller than I am, I declare. And you're ever so much better looking than you used to be, too. But I dare say you know that without being told."

"Indeed I didn't," said Anne **radiantly**. "I know I'm not so freckled as I used to be, so I've much to be thankful for, but I really hadn't dared to hope there was any other improvement. I'm so glad you think there is, Miss Barry." Miss Barry's house was furnished with "great **magnificence**", as Anne told Marilla afterward. The two little country girls were rather **abashed** by the splendor of the parlor where Miss Barry left them when she went to see about dinner.

radiantly [ˈreɪdiəntli]
adv. 喜气洋洋地

magnificence [mægˈnɪfɪsns]
n. 宏伟

abashed [əˈbæʃt]
adj. 羞愧的

"Isn't it just like a palace?" whispered Diana. "I never was in Aunt Josephine's house before, and I'd no idea it was so grand. I just wish Julia Bell could see this—she puts on such airs about her mother's parlor."

"Velvet carpet," sighed Anne luxuriously, "and silk curtains! I've dreamed of such things, Diana. But do you know I don't believe I feel very comfortable with them after all. There are so many things in this room and all so splendid that there is no scope for imagination. That is one consolation when you are poor—there are so many more things you can imagine about."

Their sojourn in town was something that Anne and Diana dated from for years. From first to last it was crowded with delights.

On Wednesday Miss Barry took them to the Exhibition grounds and kept them there all day.

"It was splendid," Anne related to Marilla later on. "I never imagined anything so interesting. I don't really know which department was the most interesting. I think I liked the horses and the flowers and the **fancywork** best. Josie Pye took first prize for **knitted** lace. I was real glad she did. And I was glad that I felt glad, for it shows I'm improving, don't you think, Marilla, when I can **rejoice** in Josie's success? Mr. Harmon Andrews took second prize for Gravenstein apples and Mr. Bell took first prize for a pig. Diana said she thought it was ridiculous for a Sunday-school superintendent to take a prize in pigs, but I don't see why. Do you? She said she would always think of it after this when he was praying so solemnly. Clara Louise MacPherson took a prize for painting, and Mrs. Lynde got first prize for homemade butter and cheese. So Avonlea was pretty well **represented**, wasn't it? Mrs. Lynde was there that day, and I never knew how much I really liked her until I saw her familiar face among all those strangers. There were thousands of people there, Marilla. It made me feel dreadfully insignificant. And Miss Barry took us up to the **grandstand** to see the horse races. Mrs. Lynde wouldn't go; she said horse racing was an **abomination** and, she being a church member, thought it her **bounden** duty to set a good example by staying away. But there were so many there I don't believe Mrs. Lynde's absence would ever be noticed. I don't think, though, that I ought to go very often to horse

fancywork [ˈfænsɪwɜːk] *n.* 刺绣品
knit [nɪt] *v.* 编织
rejoice [rɪˈdʒɔɪs] *v.* 非常高兴

represent [reprɪˈzent] *v.* 代表

grandstand [ˈɡrænstænd] *n.* 大看台
abomination [əˌbɒmɪˈneɪʃn] *n.* 可恶的东西
bounden [ˈbaʊndən] *adj.* 有责任感的

races, because they are awfully fascinating. Diana got so excited that she offered to bet me ten cents that the red horse would win. I didn't believe he would, but I refused to bet, because I wanted to tell Mrs. Allan all about everything, and I felt sure it wouldn't do to tell her that. It's always wrong to do anything you can't tell the minister's wife. It's as good as an extra conscience to have a minister's wife for your friend. And I was very glad I didn't bet, because the red horse did win, and I would have lost ten cents. So you see that virtue was its own reward. We saw a man go up in a balloon. I'd love to go up in a balloon, Marilla; it would be simply thrilling; and we saw a man selling fortunes. You paid him ten cents and a little bird picked out your fortune for you. Miss Barry gave Diana and me ten cents each to have our fortunes told. Mine was that I would marry a dark-**complected** man who was very wealthy, and I would go across water to live. I looked carefully at all the dark men I saw after that, but I didn't care much for any of them, and anyhow I suppose it's too early to be looking out for him yet. Oh, it was a never-to-be-forgotten day, Marilla. I was so tired I couldn't sleep at night. Miss Barry put us in the spare room, according to promise. It was an elegant room, Marilla, but somehow sleeping in a spare room isn't what I used to think it was. That's the worst of growing up, and I'm beginning to realize it. The things you wanted so much when you were a child don't seem half so wonderful to you when you get them."

complected [kəm'plektɪd] *adj.* 肤色……的

Thursday the girls had a drive in the park, and in the evening Miss Barry took them to a concert in the Academy of Music, where a **noted prima donna** was to sing. To Anne the evening was a glittering vision of delight.

noted ['nəʊtɪd] *adj.* 以……闻名
prima donna [priːmə'dɒnə] *n.* 首席女歌手

"Oh, Marilla, it was beyond description. I was so excited I couldn't even talk, so you may know what it was like. I just sat in

enraptured silence. Madame Selitsky was perfectly beautiful, and wore white satin and diamonds. But when she began to sing, I never thought about anything else. Oh, I can't tell you how I felt. But it seemed to me that it could never be hard to be good any more. I felt like I do when I look up to the stars. Tears came into my eyes, but, oh, they were such happy tears. I was so sorry when it was all over, and I told Miss Barry I didn't see how I was ever to return to common life again. She said she thought if we went over to the restaurant across the street and had an ice cream it might help me. That sounded so **prosaic**; but to my surprise I found it true. The ice cream was delicious, Marilla, and it was so lovely and **dissipated** to be sitting there eating it at eleven o'clock at night. Diana said she believed she was born for city life. Miss Barry asked me what my opinion was, but I said I would have to think it over very seriously before I could tell her what I really thought. So I thought it over after I went to bed. That is the best time to think things out. And I came to the conclusion, Marilla, that I wasn't born for city life and that I was glad of it. It's nice to be eating ice cream at brilliant restaurants at eleven o'clock at night once in a while; but as a regular thing I'd rather be in the east gable at eleven, sound asleep, but kind of knowing even in my sleep that the stars were shining outside and that the wind was blowing in the firs across the brook. I told Miss Barry so at breakfast the next morning and she laughed. Miss Barry generally laughed at anything I said, even when I said the most solemn things. I don't think I liked it, Marilla, because I wasn't trying to be funny. But she is a most hospitable lady and treated us royally."

Friday brought going-home time, and Mr. Barry drove in for the girls.

"Well, I hope you've enjoyed yourselves," said Miss Barry, as

enraptured [ɪnˈræptʃəd] *adj.* 狂喜的

prosaic [prəˈzeɪɪk] *adj.* 平庸的

dissipated [ˈdɪsɪpeɪtɪd] *adj.* 放纵的

she bade them good-bye.

"Indeed we have," said Diana.

"And you, Anne-girl?"

"I've enjoyed every minute of the time," said Anne, throwing her arms **impulsively** about the old woman's neck and kissing her wrinkled cheek. Diana would never have dared to do such a thing and felt rather **aghast** at Anne's freedom. But Miss Barry was pleased, and she stood on her **veranda** and watched the buggy out of sight. Then she went back into her big house with a sigh. It seemed very lonely, lacking those fresh young lives. Miss Barry was a rather selfish old lady, if the truth must be told, and had never cared much for anybody but herself. She valued people only as they were of service to her or amused her. Anne had amused her, and consequently stood high in the old lady's good graces. But Miss Barry found herself thinking less about Anne's **quaint** speeches than of her fresh enthusiasms, her **transparent** emotions, her little winning ways, and the sweetness of her eyes and lips.

"I thought Marilla Cuthbert was an old fool when I heard she'd adopted a girl out of an orphan asylum," she said to herself, "but I guess she didn't make much of a mistake after all. If I'd a childlike Anne in the house all the time I'd be a better and happier woman."

Anne and Diana found the drive home as pleasant as the drive in—pleasanter, indeed, since there was the delightful consciousness of home waiting at the end of it. It was sunset when they passed through White Sands and turned into the shore road. Beyond, the Avonlea hills came out darkly against the **saffron** sky. Behind them the moon was rising out of the sea that grew all **radiant** and **transfigured** in her light. Every little cove along the curving road was a **marvel** of dancing ripples. The waves broke with a soft swish on the rocks below

impulsively [ɪm'pʌlsɪvli] *adv.* 易冲动地
aghsat [ə'gɑːst] *adj.* 惊恐的
veranda [və'rændə] *n.* 走廊

quaint [kweɪnt] *adj.* 新奇有趣的
transparent [træns'pærənt] *adj.* 显而易见的

saffron ['sæfrən] *n.* 藏红花
radiant ['reɪdiənt] *adj.* 容光焕发
transfigure [træns'fɪgə(r)] *v.* 使改观
marvel ['mɑːvl] *n.* 奇迹

them, and the tang of the sea was in the strong, fresh air.

"Oh, but it's good to be alive and to be going home," breathed Anne.

When she crossed the log bridge over the brook the kitchen light of Green Gables winked her a friendly welcome back, and through the open door shone the **hearth** fire, sending out its warm red glow **athwart** the chilly autumn night. Anne ran **blithely** up the hill and into the kitchen, where a hot supper was waiting on the table.

hearth [hɑːθ]
n. 壁炉前的地面
athwart [ə'θwɔːt]
prep. 横跨
blithely ['blaɪðli]
adv. 快乐地

"So you've got back?" said Marilla, folding up her knitting.

"Yes, and oh, it's so good to be back," said Anne joyously. "I could kiss everything, even to the clock. Marilla, a broiled chicken! You don't mean to say you cooked that for me!"

"Yes, I did," said Marilla. "I thought you'd be hungry after such a drive and need something real **appetizing**. Hurry and take off your things, and we'll have supper as soon as Matthew comes in. I'm glad you've got back, I must say. It's been fearful lonesome here without you, and I never put in four longer days."

appetizing ['æpɪtaɪzɪŋ]
adj. 开胃的

After supper Anne sat before the fire between Matthew and Marilla, and gave them a full account of her visit.

"I've had a splendid time," she concluded happily, "and I feel that it marks an epoch in my life. But the best of it all was the coming home."

CHAPTER XXX

The Queens Class Is Organized

Marilla laid her knitting on her lap and leaned back in her chair. Her eyes were tired, and she thought **vaguely** that she must see about having her glasses changed the next time she went to town, for her eyes had grown tired very often of late.

vaguely ['veɪgli]
adv. 含糊地

It was nearly dark, for the full November twilight had fallen around Green Gables, and the only light in the kitchen came from the dancing red flames in the stove.

Anne was curled up Turk-fashion on the **hearthrug**, gazing into that joyous glow where the sunshine of a hundred summers was being **distilled** from the maple **cordwood**. She had been reading, but her book had slipped to the floor, and now she was dreaming, with a smile on her parted lips. Glittering castles in Spain were shaping themselves out of the mists and rainbows of her lively fancy; adventures wonderful and **enthralling** were happening to her in cloudland—adventures that always turned out **triumphantly** and never involved her in scrapes like those of actual life.

Marilla looked at her with a tenderness that would never have been suffered to **reveal** itself in any clearer light than that soft **mingling** of fireshine and shadow. The lesson of a love that should display itself easily in spoken word and open look was one Marilla could never learn. But she had learned to love this slim, gray-eyed girl with an **affection** all the deeper and stronger from its very **undemonstrativeness**. Her love made her afraid of being **unduly indulgent,** indeed. She had an uneasy feeling that it was rather sinful to set one's heart so intensely on any human creature as she had set hers on Anne, and perhaps she performed a sort of unconscious **penance** for this by being stricter and more critical than if the girl had been less dear to her. Certainly Anne herself had no idea how Marilla loved her. She sometimes thought wistfully that Marilla was very hard to please and distinctly lacking in sympathy and understanding. But she always checked the thought **reproachfully**, remembering what she owed to Marilla.

"Anne," said Marilla abruptly, "Miss Stacy was here this after-

hearthrug [ˈhɑːθrʌg]
n. 壁炉前的地毯
distill [dɪˈstɪl]
v. 蒸馏
cordwood [ˈkɔːdwʊd]
n. 四英尺长的木材

enthralling [ɪnˈθrɔːlɪŋ]
adj. 迷人的
triumphantly [traɪˈʌmfəntli]
adv. 得意扬扬地

reveal [rɪˈviːl]
v. 披露
mingle [ˈmɪŋgl]
v. 使混合

affection [əˈfekʃn]
n. 喜爱
undemonstrative [ʌndɪˈmɒnstrətɪv]
adj. 含蓄的，感情不外露的
unduly [ʌnˈdjuːli]
adv. 过分地
indulgent [ɪnˈdʌldʒənt]
adj. 纵容的
penance [ˈpenəns]
n. 忏悔

reproachfully [rɪˈprəʊtʃfəli]
adv. 责备地

noon when you were out with Diana."

Anne came back from her other world with a start and a sigh.

"Was she? Oh, I'm so sorry I wasn't in. Why didn't you call me, Marilla? Diana and I were only over in the Haunted Wood. It's lovely in the woods now. All the little wood things—the ferns and the satin leaves and the crackerberries—have gone to sleep, just as if somebody had **tucked** them away until spring under a blanket of leaves. I think it was a little gray fairy with a rainbow scarf that came tiptoeing along the last moonlight night and did it. Diana wouldn't say much about that, though. Diana has never forgotten the scolding her mother gave her about imagining ghosts into the Haunted Wood. It had a very bad effect on Diana's imagination. It blighted it. Mrs. Lynde says Myrtle Bell is a blighted being. I asked Ruby Gillis why Myrtle was **blighted**, and Ruby said she guessed it was because her young man had gone back on her. Ruby Gillis thinks of nothing but young men, and the older she gets the worse she is. Young men are all very well in their place, but it doesn't do to drag them into everything, does it? Diana and I are thinking seriously of promising each other that we will never marry but be nice old maids and live together forever. Diana hasn't quite made up her mind though, because she thinks perhaps it would be nobler to marry some wild, dashing, wicked young man and reform him. Diana and I talk a great deal about serious subjects now, you know. We feel that we are so much older than we used to be that it isn't becoming to talk of childish matters. It's such a solemn thing to be almost fourteen, Marilla. Miss Stacy took all us girls who are in our teens down to the brook last Wednesday, and talked to us about it. She said we couldn't be too careful what habits we formed and what ideals we acquired in our teens, because by the time we were twenty our characters would be developed and the foundation laid for our whole

tuck [tʌk]
v. 卷起,塞进

blight [blaɪt]
v. 损害

future life. And she said if the foundation was **shaky**, we could never build anything really worth while on it. Diana and I talked the matter over coming home from school. We felt extremely solemn, Marilla. And we decided that we would try to be very careful indeed and form respectable habits and learn all we could and be as sensible as possible, so that by the time we were twenty our characters would be properly developed. It's perfectly **appalling** to think of being twenty, Marilla. It sounds so fearfully old and grown up. But why was Miss Stacy here this afternoon?"

"That is what I want to tell you, Anne, if you'll ever give me a chance to get a word in edgewise. She was talking about you."

"About me?" Anne looked rather scared. Then she flushed and exclaimed:

"Oh, I know what she was saying. I meant to tell you, Marilla, honestly I did, but I forgot. Miss Stacy caught me reading Ben Hur in school yesterday afternoon when I should have been studying my Canadian history. Jane Andrews lent it to me. I was reading it at dinner hour, and I had just got to the **chariot** race when school went in. I was simply wild to know how it turned out—although I felt sure Ben Hur must win, because it wouldn't be **poetical** justice if he didn't—so I spread the history open on my desk lid and then tucked Ben Hur between the desk and my knee. I just looked as if I were studying Canadian history, you know, while all the while I was reveling in Ben Hur. I was so interested in it that I never noticed Miss Stacy coming down the aisle until all at once I just looked up and there she was looking down at me, so reproachful-like. I can't tell you how ashamed I felt, Marilla, especially when I heard Josie Pye giggling. Miss Stacy took Ben Hur away, but she never said a word then. She kept me in at **recess** and talked to me. She said I had done very wrong in two re-

shaky [ˈʃeɪki] *adj.* 颤抖的

appalling [əˈpɔːlɪŋ] *adj.* 令人震惊的

chariot [ˈtʃæriət] *n.* 敞篷马车

poetic [pəʊˈetɪk] *adj.* 诗歌的

recess [ˈriːses] *n.* 课间休息

spects. First, I was wasting the time I ought to have put on my studies; and secondly, I was **deceiving** my teacher in trying to make it appear I was reading a history when it was a storybook instead. I had never realized until that moment, Marilla, that what I was doing was deceitful. I was shocked. I cried bitterly, and asked Miss Stacy to forgive me and I'd never do such a thing again; and I offered to do penance by never so much as looking at Ben Hur for a whole week, not even to see how the chariot race turned out. But Miss Stacy said she wouldn't require that, and she forgave me freely. So I think it wasn't very kind of her to come up here to you about it after all."

deceive [dɪ'siːv]
v. 欺骗

"Miss Stacy never mentioned such a thing to me, Anne, and its only your guilty conscience that's the matter with you. You have no business to be taking storybooks to school. You read too many novels anyhow. When I was a girl I wasn't so much as allowed to look at a novel."

"Oh, how can you call Ben Hur a novel when it's really such a religious book?" protested Anne. "Of course, it's a little too exciting to be proper reading for Sunday, and I only read it on weekdays. And I never read any book now unless either Miss Stacy or Mrs. Allan thinks it is a proper book for a girl thirteen and three-quarters to read. Miss Stacy made me promise that. She found me reading a book one day called, *The Lurid Mystery of the Haunted Hall*. It was one Ruby Gillis had lent me, and, oh, Marilla, it was so fascinating and **creepy**. It just **curdled** the blood in my veins. But Miss Stacy said it was a very silly, unwholesome book, and she asked me not to read any more of it or any like it. I didn't mind promising not to read any more like it, but it was agonizing to give back that book without knowing how it turned out. But my love for Miss Stacy stood the test and I did. It's really wonderful, Marilla, what you can do when you're truly anxious to

creepy ['kriːpi]
adj. 令人毛骨悚然的
curdle ['kɜːdl]
v. (使)凝结

please a certain person."

"Well, I guess I'll light the lamp and get to work," said Marilla. "I see **plainly** that you don't want to hear what Miss Stacy had to say. You're more interested in the sound of your own tongue than in anything else."

plainly ['pleɪnli] *adv.* 明显地

"Oh, indeed, Marilla, I do want to hear it," cried Anne **contritely**. "I won't say another word—not one. I know I talk too much, but I am really trying to overcome it, and although I say far too much, yet if you only knew how many things I want to say and don't, you'd give me some credit for it. Please tell me, Marilla."

contritely [kən'traɪtli] *adv.* 懊悔地

"Well, Miss Stacy wants to organize a class among her advanced students who mean to study for the entrance examination into Queen's. She intends to give them extra lessons for an hour after school. And she came to ask Matthew and me if we would like to have you join it. What do you think about it yourself, Anne? Would you like to go to Queen's and pass for a teacher?"

"Oh, Marilla!" Anne straightened to her knees and clasped her hands. "It's been the dream of my life—that is, for the last six months, ever since Ruby and Jane began to talk of studying for the Entrance. But I didn't say anything about it, because I supposed it would be perfectly useless. I'd love to be a teacher. But won't it be dreadfully expensive? Mr. Andrews says it cost him one hundred and fifty dollars to put Prissy through, and Prissy wasn't a dunce in **geometry**."

geometry [dʒi'ɒmətri] *n.* 几何(学)

"I guess you needn't worry about that part of it. When Matthew and I took you to bring up we resolved we would do the best we could for you and give you a good education. I believe in a girl being fitted to earn her own living whether she ever has to or not. You'll always have a home at Green Gables as long as Matthew and I are here, but nobody knows what is going to happen in this uncertain world, and it's just as well to be prepared. So you can join the Queen's class if you like, Anne."

"Oh, Marilla, thank you." Anne flung her arms about Marilla's **waist** and looked up earnestly into her face. "I'm extremely grateful to you and Matthew. And I'll study as hard as I can and do my very best to be a credit to you. I warn you not to expect much in geometry, but I think I can hold my own in anything else if I work hard."

waist [weɪst]
n. 腰

"I dare say you'll get along well enough. Miss Stacy says you are bright and diligent." Not for worlds would Marilla have told Anne just what Miss Stacy had said about her; that would have been to **pamper** vanity. "You needn't rush to any extreme of killing yourself over your books. There is no hurry. You won't be ready to try the Entrance for a year and a half yet. But it's well to begin in time and be thoroughly grounded, Miss Stacy says."

pamper ['pæmpə(r)]
v. 纵容,娇惯

"I shall take more interest than ever in my studies now," said Anne **blissfully**, "because I have a purpose in life. Mr. Allan says everybody should have a purpose in life and pursue it faithfully. Only he says we must first make sure that it is a worthy purpose. I would call it a worthy purpose to want to be a teacher like Miss Stacy, wouldn't you, Marilla? I think it's a very noble profession."

blissfully ['blɪsfəli]
adv. 幸福地

The Queen's class was organized in due time. Gilbert Blythe, Anne Shirley, Ruby Gillis, Jane Andrews, Josie Pye, Charlie Sloane, and Moody Spurgeon MacPherson joined it. Diana Barry did not, as her parents did not intend to send her to Queen's. This seemed nothing short of a **calamity** to Anne. Never, since the night on which Minnie May had had the croup, had she and Diana been separated in anything. On the evening when the Queen's class first remained in school for the extra lessons and Anne saw Diana go slowly out with the oth-

calamity [kə'læməti]
n. 灾难

ers, to walk home alone through the Birch Path and Violet Vale, it was all the former could do to keep her seat and **refrain** from rushing impulsively after her chum. A lump came into her throat, and she **hastily** retired behind the pages of her uplifted Latin grammar to hide the tears in her eyes. Not for worlds would Anne have had Gilbert Blythe or Josie Pye see those tears.

refrain [rɪ'freɪn] v. 避免
hastily ['heɪstɪli] adv. 匆忙地

"But, oh, Marilla, I really felt that I had tasted the bitterness of death, as Mr. Allan said in his **sermon** last Sunday, when I saw Diana go out alone," she said mournfully that night. "I thought how splendid it would have been if Diana had only been going to study for the Entrance, too. But we can't have things perfect in this imperfect world, as Mrs. Lynde says. Mrs. Lynde isn't exactly a comforting person sometimes, but there's no doubt she says a great many very true things. And I think the Queen's class is going to be extremely interesting. Jane and Ruby are just going to study to be teachers. That is the height of their ambition. Ruby says she will only teach for two years after she gets through, and then she intends to be married. Jane says she will devote her whole life to teaching, and never, never marry, because you are paid a salary for teaching, but a husband won't pay you anything, and **growls** if you ask for a share in the egg and butter money. I expect Jane speaks from mournful experience, for Mrs. Lynde says that her father is a perfect old **crank**, and **meaner** than second skimmings. Josie Pye says she is just going to college for education's sake, because she won't have to earn her own living; she says of course it is different with orphans who are living on charity—they have to **hustle**. Moody Spurgeon is going to be a minister. Mrs. Lynde says he couldn't be anything else with a name like that to live up to. I hope it isn't **wicked** of me, Marilla, but really the thought of Moody Spurgeon being a minister makes me laugh. He's such a

sermon ['sɜːmən] n. 布道
growl [graʊl] n. 咆哮
crank [kræŋk] n. 脾气坏的人
mean [miːn] adj. 刻薄的
hustle ['hʌsl] v. 匆忙做事,推搡
wicked ['wɪkɪd] adj. 邪恶的

funny-looking boy with that big fat face, and his little blue eyes, and his ears **sticking** out like flaps. But perhaps he will be more intellectual looking when he grows up. Charlie Sloane says he's going to go into politics and be a member of Parliament, but Mrs. Lynde says he'll never succeed at that, because the Sloanes are all honest people, and it's only **rascals** that get on in politics nowadays."

"What is Gilbert Blythe going to be?" queried Marilla, seeing that Anne was opening her Caesar.

"I don't happen to know what Gilbert Blythe's ambition in life is—if he has any," said Anne scornfully.

There was open **rivalry** between Gilbert and Anne now. Previously the rivalry had been rather onesided, but there was no longer any doubt that Gilbert was as determined to be first in class as Anne was. He was a foeman worthy of her steel. The other members of the class **tacitly** acknowledged their superiority, and never dreamed of trying to compete with them.

Since the day by the pond when she had refused to listen to his plea for forgiveness, Gilbert, save for the **aforesaid** determined rivalry, had **evinced** no recognition whatever of the existence of Anne Shirley. He talked and **jested** with the other girls, exchanged books and puzzles with them, discussed lessons and plans, sometimes walked home with one or the other of them from prayer meeting or Debating Club. But Anne Shirley he simply ignored, and Anne found out that it is not pleasant to be ignored. It was in vain that she told herself with a toss of her head that she did not care. Deep down in her wayward, feminine little heart she knew that she did care, and that if she had that chance of the Lake of Shining Waters again, she would answer very differently. All at once, as it seemed, and to her secret **dismay**, she found that the old resentment she had cherished against him was

stick [stɪk]
v. 突出，伸出

rascal [ˈrɑːskl]
n. 坏蛋

rivalry [ˈraɪvlri]
n. 较量

tacitly [ˈtæsɪtli]
adv. 肃静地

aforesaid [əˈfɔːsɛd]
adj. 前述的

evince [ɪˈvɪns]
v. 表明

jest [dʒest]
v. 开玩笑

dismay [dɪsˈmeɪ]
n. 沮丧

gone—gone just when she most needed its sustaining power. It was in vain that she recalled every incident and emotion of that memorable occasion and tried to feel the old satisfying anger. That day by the pond had witnessed its last **spasmodic flicker**. Anne realized that she had forgiven and forgotten without knowing it. But it was too late.

spasmodic [spæz'mɒdɪk]
adj. 间歇的,断断续续的
flicker ['flɪkə(r)]
n. 闪烁

And at least neither Gilbert nor anybody else, not even Diana, should ever **suspect** how sorry she was and how much she wished she hadn't been so proud and horrid! She determined to "**shroud** her feelings in deepest **oblivion**", and it may be stated here and now that she did it, so successfully that Gilbert, who possibly was not quite so indifferent as he seemed, could not **console** himself with any belief that Anne felt his **retaliatory** scorn. The only poor comfort he had was that she **snubbed** Charlie Sloane, unmercifully, continually, and undeservedly.

suspect [sə'spekt]
v. 怀疑
shroud [ʃraʊd]
v. 隐藏
oblivion [ə'blɪviən]
n. 被遗忘
console [kən'səʊl]
v. 安慰
retaliatory [rɪ'tæliətri]
adj. 报复的
snub [snʌb]
v. 冷落

Otherwise the winter passed away in a round of pleasant duties and studies. For Anne the days slipped by like golden beads on the necklace of the year. She was happy, eager, interested; there were lessons to be learned and honor to be won; delightful books to read; new pieces to be practiced for the Sunday-school choir; pleasant Saturday afternoons at the manse with Mrs. Allan; and then, almost before Anne realized it, spring had come again to Green Gables and all the world was abloom once more.

Studies palled just a wee bit then; the Queen's class, left behind in school while the others scattered to green lanes and **leafy** wood cuts and meadow byways, looked wistfully out of the windows and discovered that Latin verbs and French exercises had somehow lost the tang and zest they had possessed in the crisp winter months. Even Anne and Gilbert **lagged** and grew indifferent. Teacher and taught were alike glad when the term was ended and the glad vacation days

leafy ['liːfi]
adj. 多叶的
lag [læg]
v. 落后于

stretched rosily before them.

"But you' ve done good work this past year," Miss Stacy told them on the last evening, "and you deserve a good, jolly vacation. Have the best time you can in the out-of-door world and lay in a good stock of health and vitality and ambition to carry you through next year. It will be the tug of war, you know—the last year before the Entrance."

"Are you going to be back next year, Miss Stacy?" asked Josie Pye.

Josie Pye never scrupled to ask questions; in this **instance** the rest of the class felt grateful to her; none of them would have dared to ask it of Miss Stacy, but all wanted to, for there had been **alarming** rumors running at large through the school for some time that Miss Stacy was not coming back the next year—that she had been offered a position in the grade school of her own home district and meant to accept. The Queen's class listened in breathless **suspense** for her answer.

"Yes, I think I will," said Miss Stacy. "I thought of taking another school, but I have decided to come back to Avonlea. To tell the truth, I' ve grown so interested in my pupils here that I found I couldn' t leave them. So I' ll stay and see you through."

"Hurrah!" said Moody Spurgeon. Moody Spurgeon had never been so carried away by his feelings before, and he **blushed** uncomfortably every time he thought about it for a week.

"Oh, I' m so glad," said Anne, with shining eyes. "Dear Stacy, it would be perfectly dreadful if you didn' t come back. I don' t believe I could have the heart to go on with my studies at all if another teacher came here."

When Anne got home that night, she **stacked** all her textbooks away in an old trunk in the **attic**, locked it, and threw the key into the blanket box.

instance [ˈɪnstəns]
n. 例子

alarming [əˈlɑːmɪŋ]
adj. 令人惊慌的

suspense [səˈspens]
n. 悬念

blush [blʌʃ]
v. 脸红；惭愧

stacked [stækt]
v. 使放成整齐的一叠

attic [ˈætɪk]
n. 阁楼

"I'm not even going to look at a schoolbook in vacation," she told Marilla. "I've studied as hard all the term as I possibly could and I've pored over that geometry until I know every proposition in the first book off by heart, even when the letters are changed. I just feel tired of everything sensible and I'm going to let my imagination run riot for the summer. Oh, you needn't be alarmed, Marilla. I'll only let it run **riot** within reasonable limits. But I want to have a real good jolly time this summer, for maybe it's the last summer I'll be a little girl. Mrs. Lynde says that if I keep stretching out next year as I've done this. I'll have to put on longer skirts. She says I'm all running to legs and eyes. And when I put on longer skirts, I shall feel that I have to live up to them and be very dignified. It won't even do to believe in fairies then, I'm afraid; so I'm going to believe in them with all my whole heart this summer. I think we're going to have a very gay vacation. Ruby Gillis is going to have a birthday party soon and there's the Sunday school picnic and the missionary concert next month. And Mrs. Barry says that some evening he'll take Diana and me over to the White Sands Hotel and have dinner there. They have dinner there in the evening, you know. Jane Andrews was over once last summer and she says it was a dazzling sight to see the electric lights and the flowers and all the lady guests in such beautiful dresses. Jane says it was her first glimpse into high life and she'll never forget it to her dying day."

riot [ˈraɪət] *n.* 暴乱

Mrs. Lynde came up the next afternoon to find out why Marilla had not been at the Aid meeting on Thursday. When Marilla was not at Aid meeting people knew there was something wrong at Green Gables.

"Matthew had a bad **spell** with his heart Thursday," Marilla explained, "and I didn't feel like leaving him. Oh, yes, he's all right again now, but he takes them spells oftener than he used to and I'm

spell [spel] *n.* 咒语

anxious about him. The doctor says he must be careful to avoid excitement. That's easy enough, for Matthew doesn't go about looking for excitement by any means and never did, but he's not to do any very heavy work either and you might as well tell Matthew not to breathe as not to work. Come and lay off your things, Rachel. You'll stay to tea?

"Well, seeing you're so pressing, perhaps I might as well, stay, " said Mrs. Rachel, who had not the slightest intention of doing anything else.

Mrs. Rachel and Marilla sat comfortably in the parlor while Anne got the tea and made hot biscuits that were light and white enough to **defy** even Mrs. Rachel's criticism.

defy [dɪˈfaɪ]
v. 违抗

"I must say Anne has turned out a real smart girl," admitted Mrs. Rachel, as Marilla accompanied her to the end of the lane at sunset. "She must be a great help to you."

"She is," said Marilla, "and she's real steady and reliable now. I used to be afraid she'd never get over her **featherbrained** ways, but she has and I wouldn't be afraid to trust her in anything now."

featherbrained
[ˈfeðəbreɪnd]
adj. 非常愚蠢的

"I never would have thought she'd have turned out so well that first day I was here three years ago," said Mrs. Rachel. "Lawful heart, shall I ever forget that **tantrum** of hers! When I went home that night I says to Thomas, says I, 'Mark my words, Thomas, Marilla Cuthbert'll live to rue the step she's took'. But I was mistaken and I'm real glad of it. I ain't one of those kinds of people, Marilla, as can never be brought to own up that they've made a mistake. No, that never was my way, thank goodness. I did make a mistake in judging Anne, but it wasn't no wonder, for an odder, unexpecteder **witch** of a child there never was in this world, that's what. There was no ciphering her out by the rules that worked with other children. It's nothing

tantrum [ˈtæntrəm]
n. 发脾气

witch [wɪtʃ]
n. 巫婆

short of wonderful how she's improved these three years, but especially in looks. She's a real pretty girl got to be, though I can't say I'm overly partial to that pale, big-eyed style myself. I like more snap and color, like Diana Barry has or Ruby Gillis. Ruby Gillis's looks are really showy. But somehow—I don't know how it is but when Anne and them are together, though she ain't half as handsome, she makes them look kind of common and **overdone**—something like them white June lilies she calls **narcissus** alongside of the big, red **peonies**, that's what."

overdo [ˌəʊvəˈduː] *v.* 做得过分
narcissus [nɑːˈsɪsəs] *n.* 水仙
peony [ˈpiːəni] *n.* 牡丹；芍药

CHAPTER XXXI

Where the Brook and River Meet

Anne had her "good" summer and enjoyed it wholeheartedly. She and Diana fairly lived outdoors, reveling in all the delights that Lover's Lane and the Dryad's Bubble and Willowmere and Victoria Island afforded. Marilla offered no objections to Anne's gypsyings. The Spencervale doctor who had come the night Minnie May had the **croup** met Anne at the house of a patient one afternoon early in vacation, looked her over sharply, screwed up his mouth, shook his head, and sent a message to Marilla Cuthbert by another person. It was:

croup [kruːp] *n.* 哮吼

"Keep that redheaded girl of yours in the open air all summer and don't let her read books until she gets more spring into her step."

This message frightened Marilla **wholesomely**. She read Anne's death warrant by **consumption** in it unless it was **scrupulously** obeyed. As a result, Anne had the golden summer of her life as far as freedom and frolic went. She walked, rowed, **berried**, and dreamed to her heart's content; and when September came, she was bright-eyed and alert, with a step that would have satisfied the Spencervale doctor and a heart full of ambition and zest once more.

wholesomely [ˈhəʊls(ə)mli] *adv.* 有益健康地
consumption [kənˈsʌmpʃn] *n.* 传染病
scrupulous [ˈskruːpjələs] *adj.* 细致的
berry [ˈberi] *v.* 采集浆果

"I feel just like studying with might and main," she declared as she brought her books down from the attic. "Oh, you good old friends, I' m glad to see your honest faces once more—yes, even you, geometry. I' ve had a perfectly beautiful summer, Marilla, and now I' m **rejoicing** as a strong man to run a race, as Mr. Allan said last Sunday. Doesn' t Mr. Allan preach magnificent **sermons**? Mrs. Lynde says he is improving every day and the first thing we know some city church will gobble him up and then we' ll be left and have to turn to and break in another green preacher. But I don' t see the use of meeting trouble halfway, do you, Marilla? I think it would be better just to enjoy Mr. Allan while we have him. If I were a man I think I' d be a minister. They can have such an influence for good, if their theology is sound; and it must be thrilling to preach splendid sermons and stir your hearers' hearts. Why can' t women be ministers, Marilla? I asked Mrs. Lynde that and she was shocked and said it would be a **scandalous** thing. She said there might be female ministers in the States and she believed there was, but thank goodness we hadn' t got to that stage in Canada yet and she hoped we never would. But I don' t see why. I think women would make splendid ministers. When there is a social to be got up or a church tea or anything else to raise money the women have to turn to and do the work. I' m sure Mrs. Lynde can pray every bit as well as Superintendent Bell and I' ve no doubt she could preach too with a little practice."

rejoice [rɪ'dʒɔɪs]
v. 非常高兴
sermon ['sɜːmən]
n. 布道

scandalous
['skændələs]
adj. 不可原谅的

"Yes, I believe she could," said Marilla dryly. "She does plenty of unofficial preaching as it is. Nobody has much of a chance to go wrong in Avonlea with Rachel to **oversee** them."

oversee [ˌəʊvə'siː]
v. 监管

"Marilla," said Anne in a burst of confidence, "I want to tell you something and ask you what you think about it. It has worried me terribly—on Sunday afternoons, that is, when I think specially about such matters. I do really want to be good; and when I'm with you or Mrs. Allan or Miss Stacy,, I want it more than ever and I want to do just what would please you and what you would approve of. But mostly when I'm with Mrs. Lynde I feel desperately wicked and as if I wanted to go and do the very thing, she tells me I oughtn't to do. I feel irresistibly **tempted** to do it. Now, what do you think is the reason I feel like that? Do you think it's because I'm really bad and **unregenerate**?"

Marilla looked dubious for a moment. Then she laughed.

"If you are I guess I am too, Anne, for Rachel often has that very effect on me. I sometimes think she'd have more of an influence for good, as you say yourself, if she didn't keep **nagging** people to do right. There should have been a special **commandment** against nagging. But there, I shouldn't talk so. Rachel is a good Christian woman and she means well. There isn't a kinder soul in Avonlea and she never shirks her share of work."

"I'm very glad you feel the same," said Anne decidedly. "It's so encouraging. I shan't worry so much over that after this. But I dare say there'll be other things to worry me. They keep coming up new all the time—things to **perplex** you, you know. You settle one question and there's another right after. There are so many things to be thought over and decided when you're beginning to grow up. It keeps me busy all the time thinking them over and deciding what is right. It's a serious thing to grow up, isn't it, Marilla? But when I have such good friends as you and Matthew and Mrs. Allan and Miss Stacy I ought to grow up successfully, and I'm sure it will be my own fault if I don't. I feel it's a great responsibility because I have only the one chance. If I don't grow up right I can't go back and begin over again. I've grown two inches this summer, Marilla. Mr. Gillis measured me at Ruby's

tempt [tempt]
v. 引诱
unregenerate
[ˌʌnrɪˈdʒenərət]
adj. 不悔改的

nag [næg]
v. 唠叨
commandment
[kəˈmaːndmənt]
n. 诫条

perplex [pəˈpleks]
v. 使困惑

party. I'm so glad you made my new dresses longer. That dark-green one is so pretty and it was sweet of you to put on the **flounce**. Of course, I know it wasn't really necessary, but flounces are so stylish this fall and Josie Pye has flounces on all her dresses. I know I'll be able to study better because of mine. I shall have such a comfortable feeling deep down in my mind about that flounce."

flounce [flaʊns]
n. (衣、裙的)荷叶边

"It's worth something to have that," admitted Marilla.

Miss Stacy came back to Avonlea school and found all her pupils eager for work once more. Especially did the Queen's class gird up their loins for the **fray**, for at the end of the coming year, **dimly** shadowing their pathway already, loomed up that fateful thing known as "the Entrance", at the thought of which one and all felt their hearts sink into their very shoes. Suppose they did not pass! That thought was **doomed** to haunt Anne through the waking hours of that winter, Sunday afternoons inclusive, to the almost entire exclusion of moral and theological problems. When Anne had bad dreams, she found herself staring miserably at pass lists of the Entrance exams, where Gilbert Blythe's name was **blazoned** at the top and in which hers did not appear at all.

fray [freɪ]
n. 争论
dim [dɪm]
adj. 暗淡的

doom [duːm]
v. 使注定……失败

blazon ['bleɪzn]
v. 生动展示

But it was a jolly, busy, happy swift-flying winter. Schoolwork was as interesting, class rivalry as absorbing, as of yore. New worlds of thought, feeling, and ambition, fresh, fascinating fields of unexplored knowledge seemed to be opening out before Anne's eager eyes.

"Hills peeped o'er hill and Alps on Alps arose."

Much of all this was due to Miss Stacy's **tactful**, careful, broad-minded guidance. She led her class to think and explore and discover for themselves and encouraged **straying** from the old beaten paths to a degree that quite shocked Mrs. Lynde and the school **trustees**, who viewed all innovations on established methods rather dubiously.

tactful ['tæktfl]
adj. 得体的

stray [streɪ]
v. 走失
trustee [trʌ'stiː]
n. (财产的)受托人

Apart from her studies Anne expanded socially, for Marilla, mindful of the Spencervale doctor's **dictum**, no longer vetoed occasional outings. The Debating Club **flourished** and gave several concerts; there were one or two parties almost verging on grown-up affairs; there were **sleigh** drives and skating **frolics galore**.

Betweentimes Anne grew, shooting up so rapidly that Marilla was astonished one day, when they were standing side by side, to find the girl was taller than herself.

"Why, Anne, how you've grown!" she said, almost unbelievingly. A sigh followed on the words. Marilla felt a queer regret over Anne's inches. The child she had learned to love had vanished somehow and here was this tall, serious-eyed girl of fifteen, with the thoughtful brows and the proudly poised little head, in her place. Marilla loved the girl as much as she had loved the child, but she was conscious of a queer sorrowful sense of loss. And that night, when Anne had gone to prayer meeting with Diana, Marilla sat alone in the wintry twilight and indulged in the weakness of a cry. Matthew, coming in with a lantern, caught her at it and gazed at her in such **consternation** that Marilla had to laugh through her tears.

"I was thinking about Anne," she explained. "She's got to be such a big girl—and she'll probably be away from us next winter. I'll miss her terrible."

"She'll be able to come home often," comforted Matthew, to whom Anne was as yet and always would be the little, eager girl he had brought home from Bright River on that June evening four years before. "The branch railroad will be built to Carmody by that time."

"It won't be the same thing as having her here all the time," sighed Marilla gloomily, determined to enjoy her luxury of grief uncomforted. "But there—men can't understand these things!"

dictum [ˈdɪktəm]
n. 格言
flourish [ˈflʌrɪʃ]
v. 繁荣
sleigh [sleɪ]
n. 雪橇
frolic [ˈfrɒlɪk]
n. 欢乐的活动
galore [ɡəˈlɔː(r)]
adj. 大量的

consternation
[ˌkɒnstəˈneɪʃn]
n. 惊愕

There were other changes in Anne no less real than the physical change. For one thing, she became much quieter. Perhaps she thought all the more and dreamed as much as ever, but she certainly talked less. Marilla noticed and commented on this also.

"You don't chatter half as much as you used to, Anne, nor use half as many big words. What has come over you?"

Anne colored and laughed a little, as she dropped her book and looked dreamily out of the window, where big fat red buds were bursting out on the creeper in response to the lure of the spring sunshine.

"I don't know—I don't want to talk as much," she said, **denting** her chin thoughtfully with her **forefinger**. "It's nicer to think dear, pretty thoughts and keep them in one's heart, like treasures. I don't like to have them laughed at or wondered over. And somehow I don't want to use big words any more. It's almost a pity, isn't it, now that I'm really growing big enough to say them if I did want to. It's fun to be almost grown up in some ways, but it's not the kind of fun I expected, Marilla. There's so much to learn and do and think that there isn't time for big words. Besides, Miss Stacy says the short ones are much stronger and better. She makes us write all our essays as simply as possible. It was hard at first. I was so used to crowding in all the fine big words I could think of—and I thought of any number of them. But I've got used to it now and I see it's so much better."

"What has become of your story club? I haven't heard you speak of it for a long time."

"The story club isn't in existence any longer. We hadn't time for it—and anyhow I think we had got tired of it. It was silly to be writing about love and murder and elopements and mysteries. Miss Stacy sometimes has us write a story for training in composition, but she won't let us write anything but what might happen in Avonlea in our

dent [dent]
v. 使产生凹痕
forefinger
['fɔːfɪŋgə(r)]
n. 食指

own lives, and she criticizes it very sharply and makes us criticize our own too. I never thought my compositions had so many faults until I began to look for them myself. I felt so ashamed I wanted to give up altogether, but Miss Stacy said I could learn to write well if I only trained myself to be my own severest critic. And so I am trying to."

"You've only two more months before the Entrance," said Marilla. "Do you think you'll be able to get through?"

Anne shivered.

"I don't know. Sometimes I think I'll be all right—and then I get horribly afraid. We've studied hard and Miss Stacy has **drilled** us thoroughly, but we mayn't get through for all that. We've each got a **stumbling block**. Mine is geometry of course, and Jane's is Latin, and Ruby and Charlie's is algebra, and Josie's is arithmetic. Moody Spurgeon says he feels it in his bones that he is going to fail in English history. Miss Stacy is going to give us examinations in June just as hard as we'll have at the Entrance and mark us just as strictly, so we'll have some idea. I wish it was all over, Marilla. It **haunts** me. Sometimes I wake up in the night and wonder what I'll do if I don't pass."

"Why, go to school next year and try again," said Marilla unconcernedly.

"Oh, I don't believe I'd have the heart for it. It would be such a disgrace to fail, especially if Gil—if the others passed. And I get so nervous in an examination that I'm likely to make a mess of it. I wish I had nerves like Jane Andrews. Nothing rattles her."

Anne sighed and, **dragging** her eyes from the **witcheries** of the spring world, the **beckoning** day of breeze and blue, and the green things upspringing in the garden, buried herself resolutely in her book. There would be other springs, but if she did not succeed in passing the

drill [drɪl]
v. 训练

stumble block
障碍物；绊脚石

haunt [hɔːnt]
v. (不快的事情)萦绕于脑际

drag [dræg]
v. 拖
witchery [ˈwɪtʃ(ə)ri]
n. 巫术
beckon [ˈbekən]
v. 吸引，招手示意

Entrance, Anne felt convinced that she would never recover sufficiently to enjoy them.

CHAPTER XXXII

The Pass List Is Out

With the end of June came the close of the term and the close of Miss Stacy's rule in Avonlea school. Anne and Diana walked home that evening feeling very **sober** indeed. Red eyes and damp handkerchiefs bore convincing **testimony** to the fact that Miss Stacy's farewell words must have been quite as touching as Mr. Phillips's had been under similar circumstances three years before. Diana looked back at the schoolhouse from the foot of the spruce hill and sighed deeply.

sober [ˈsəʊbə(r)] *adj.* 认真的,严肃的
testimony [ˈtestɪməni] *n.* 证据,证明

"It does seem as if it was the end of everything, doesn't it?" she said **dismally**.

dismally [ˈdɪzməli] *adv.* 沉闷地

"You oughtn't to feel half as badly as I do," said Anne, hunting vainly for a dry spot on her handkerchief. "You'll be back again next winter, but I suppose I've left the dear old school forever—if I have good luck, that is."

"It won't be a bit the same. Miss Stacy won't be there, nor you nor Jane nor Ruby probably. I shall have to sit all alone, for I couldn't bear to have another deskmate after you. Oh, we have had **jolly** times, haven't we, Anne? It's **dreadful** to think they're all over."

jolly [ˈdʒɒli] *adj.* 愉快的
dreadful [ˈdredfl] *adj.* 可怕的

Two big tears rolled down by Diana's nose.

"If you would stop crying I could," said Anne **imploringly**. "Just as soon as I put away my **hanky** I see you brimming up and that starts me off again. As Mrs. Lynde says, 'If you can't be cheerful, be as cheerful as you can.' After all, I dare say I'll be back next year. This is one of the times I know I'm not going to pass. They're getting

imploringly [ɪmˈplɔːrɪŋli] *adv.* 恳求地
hanky [ˈhæŋki] *n.* 手帕

alarmingly frequent."

"Why, you came out splendidly in the exams Miss Stacy gave."

"Yes, but those exams didn't make me nervous. When I think of the real thing you can't imagine what a horrid cold fluttery feeling comes round my heart. And then my number is thirteen and Josie Pye says it's so unlucky. I am not **superstitious** and I know it can make no difference. But still I wish it wasn't thirteen."

superstitious [ˌsuːpəˈstɪʃəs] *adj.* 迷信的

"I do wish I was going in with you," said Diana. "Wouldn't we have a perfectly elegant time? But I suppose you'll have to cram in the evenings."

"No, Miss Stacy has made us promise not to open a book at all. She says it would only tire and confuse us and we are to go out walking and not think about the exams at all and go to bed early. It's good advice, but I expect it will be hard to follow; good advice is apt to be, I think. Prissy Andrews told me that she sat up half the night every night of her Entrance week and **crammed** for dear life; and I had determined to sit up at least as long as she did. It was so kind of your Aunt Josephine to ask me to stay at Beechwood while I'm in town."

cram [kræm] *v.* 死记硬背,临时抱佛脚

"You'll write to me while you're in, won't you?"

"I'll write Tuesday night and tell you how the first day goes," promised Anne.

"I'll be **haunting** the post office Wednesday," vowed Diana.

haunt [ˈhɔːnt] *v.* 出没

Anne went to town the following Monday and on Wednesday Diana haunted the post office, as agreed, and got her letter.

"Dearest Diana' (wrote Anne)

"Here it is Tuesday night and I'm writing this in the library at Beechwood. Last night I was horribly **lonesome** all alone in my room and wished so much you were with me. I couldn't 'cram' because I'd promised Miss Stacy not to, but it was as hard to keep from

lonesome [ˈləʊnsəm] *adj.* 孤单的

opening my history as it used to be to keep from reading a story before my lessons were learned."

"This morning Miss Stacy came for me and we went to the Academy, calling for Jane and Ruby and Josie on our way. Ruby asked me to feel her hands and they were as cold as ice. Josie said I looked as if I hadn't slept a wink and she didn't believe I was strong enough to stand the **grind** of the teacher's course even if I did get through. There are times and seasons even yet when I don't feel that I've made any great headway in learning to like Josie Pye!"

grind [graɪnd] n. 苦差事

"When we reached the Academy there were scores of students there from all over the Island. The first person we saw was Moody Spurgeon sitting on the steps and muttering away to himself. Jane asked him what on earth he was doing and he said he was repeating the **multiplication table** over and over to steady his nerves and for pity's sake not to interrupt him, because if he stopped for a moment he got frightened and forgot everything he ever knew, but the multiplication table kept all his facts firmly in their proper place!"

multiplication table 乘法表

"When we were assigned to our rooms Miss Stacy had to leave us. Jane and I sat together and Jane was so composed that I envied her. No need of the multiplication table for good, steady, sensible Jane! I wondered if I looked as I felt and if they could hear my heart **thumping** clear across the room. Then a man came in and began **distributing** the English examination sheets. My hands grew cold then and my head fairly whirled around as I picked it up. Just one awful moment—Diana, I felt exactly as I did four years ago when I asked Marilla if I might stay at Green Gables—and then everything cleared up in my mind and my heart began beating again—I forgot to say that it had stopped altogether!—for I knew I could do something with that paper anyhow."

thump [θʌmp] v. 强有力地跳动

distribute [dɪˈstrɪbjuːt] v. 分发;分配

"At noon we went home for dinner and then back again for history in the afternoon. The history was a pretty hard paper and I got dreadfully mixed up in the dates. Still, I think I did fairly well today. But oh, Diana, tomorrow the geometry exam comes off and when I think of it, it takes every bit of determination I possess to keep from opening my Euclid. If I thought the multiplication table would help me any I would recite it from now till tomorrow morning."

"I went down to see the other girls this evening. On my way I met Moody Spurgeon **wandering** distractedly around. He said he knew he had failed in history and he was born to be a disappointment to his parents and he was going home on the morning train; and it would be easier to be a **carpenter** than a **minister**, anyhow. I cheered him up and persuaded him to stay to the end because it would be unfair to Miss Stacy if he didn't. Sometimes I have wished I was born a boy, but when I see Moody Spurgeon I'm always glad I'm a girl and not his sister."

"Ruby was **in hysterics** when I reached their boardinghouse; she had just discovered a fearful mistake she had made in her English paper. When she recovered we went uptown and had an ice cream. How we wished you had been with us."

"Oh, Diana, if only the geometry examination were over! But there, as Mrs. Lynde would say, the sun will go on rising and setting whether I fail in geometry or not. That is true but not especially comforting. I think I'd rather it didn't go on if I failed!"

"Yours devotedly, Anne"

The geometry examination and all the others were over in due time and Anne arrived home on Friday evening, rather tired but with an air of **chastened triumph** about her. Diana was over at Green Gables when she arrived and they met as if they had been parted for years.

wander [ˈwɒndə(r)] *v.* 徘徊；漫步

carpenter [ˈkɑːpəntə(r)] *n.* 木匠

minister [ˈmɪnɪstə(r)] *n.* 牧师

in hysterics 歇斯底里

chasten [ˈtʃeɪsn] *v.* 磨炼

triumph [ˈtraɪʌmf] *n.* 伟大胜利

"You old darling, it's perfectly splendid to see you back again. It seems like an age since you went to town and oh, Anne, how did you get along?"

"Pretty well, I think, in everything but the geometry. I don't know whether I passed in it or not and I have a **creepy**, crawly **presentiment** that I didn't. Oh, how good it is to be back! Green Gables is the dearest, loveliest spot in the world."

creepy [ˈkriːpi]
adj. 令人毛骨悚然的
presentiment
[prɪˈzentɪmənt]
n. (尤指不详的)预感

"How did the others do?"

"The girls say they know they didn't pass, but I think they did pretty well. Josie says the geometry was so easy a child of ten could do it! Moody Spurgeon still thinks he failed in history and Charlie says he failed in algebra. But we don't really know anything about it and won't until the pass list is out. That won't be for a **fortnight**. Fancy living a fortnight **in** such **suspense**! I wish I could go to sleep and never wake up until it is over."

fortnight [ˈfɔːtnaɪt]
n. 两周
in suspense
处于悬念中

Diana knew it would be useless to ask how Gilbert Blythe had fared, so she merely said:

"Oh, you'll pass all right. Don't worry."

"I'd rather not pass at all than not come out pretty well up on the list," flashed Anne, by which she meant—and Diana knew she meant—that success would be incomplete and bitter if she did not come out ahead of Gilbert Blythe.

With this end in view Anne had strained every nerve during the examinations. So had Gilbert. They had met and passed each other on the street a dozen times without any sign of recognition and every time Anne had held her head a little higher and wished a little more earnestly that she had made friends with Gilbert when he asked her, and vowed a little more determinedly to **surpass** him in the examination. She knew that all Avonlea junior was wondering which would come

surpass [səˈpɑːs]
v. 超过

out first; she even knew that Jimmy Glover and Ned Wright had a bet on the question and that Josie Pye had said there was no doubt in the world that Gilbert would be first; and she felt that her **humiliation** would be **unbearable** if she failed.

humiliation [hjuːˌmɪli'eɪʃn] n. 耻辱，蒙羞
unbearable [ʌn'beərəbl] adj. 难以忍受的

But she had another and nobler motive for wishing to do well. She wanted to "pass high" for the sake of Matthew and Marilla—especially Matthew. Matthew had declared to her his **conviction** that she "would beat the whole Island". That, Anne felt, was something it would be foolish to hope for even in the wildest dreams. But she did hope fervently that she would be among the first ten at least, so that she might see Matthew's kindly brown eyes gleam with pride in her achievement. That, she felt, would be a sweet reward indeed for all her hard work and patient **grubbing** among unimaginative **equations** and **conjugations**.

conviction [kən'vɪkʃn] n. 坚定的信仰（主张）

grubbing [grʌbɪŋ] n. 搜索，搜寻
equation [ɪ'kweɪʒn] n. 方程式，等式
conjugation [ˌkɒndʒu'geɪʃn] n. 动词的变化形式

At the end of the fortnight Anne took to "haunting" the post office also, in the distracted company of Jane, Ruby, and Josie, opening the Charlottetown dailies with shaking hands and cold, sink away feelings as bad as any experienced during the Entrance week. Charlie and Gilbert were not above doing this too, but Moody Spurgeon stayed **resolutely** away.

resolutely ['rezəluːtli] adv. 坚决地

"I haven't got the **grit** to go there and look at a paper in cold blood," he told Anne. "I'm just going to wait until somebody comes and tells me suddenly whether I've passed or not."

grit [grɪt] n. 勇气

When three weeks had gone by without the pass list appearing Anne began to feel that she really couldn't stand the strain much longer. Her appetite failed and her interest in Avonlea doings **languished**. Mrs. Lynde wanted to know what else you could expect with a Tory **superintendent** of education at the head of affairs, and Matthew, noting Anne's paleness and indifference and the **lagging**

languish ['læŋgwɪʃ] v. 变得衰弱
superintendent [ˌsuːpərɪn'tendənt] n. 负责人
lag [læg] v. 滞后

steps that bore her home from the post office every afternoon, began seriously to wonder if he hadn't better vote Grit at the next election.

But one evening the news came. Anne was sitting at her open window, for the time forgetful of the **woes** of examinations and the cares of the world, as she drank in the beauty of the summer dusk, sweet-scented with flower breaths from the garden below and **sibilant** and rustling from the stir of poplars. The eastern sky above the firs was flushed faintly pink from the reflection of the west, and Anne was wondering dreamily if the spirit of color looked like that, when she saw Diana come flying down through the firs, over the log bridge, and up the **slope**, with a fluttering newspaper in her hand.

woe [wəʊ]
n. 悲伤;痛苦

sibilant ['sɪbɪlənt]
adj. 发咝咝声的

slope [sləʊp]
n. 斜坡

Anne **sprang** to her feet, knowing at once what that paper contained. The pass list was out! Her head **whirled** and her heart beat until it hurt her. She could not move a step. It seemed an hour to her before Diana came rushing along the hall and burst into the room without even knocking, so great was her excitement.

spring [sprɪŋ]
v. 跳
whirl [wɜːl]
v. (使)旋转

"Anne, you've passed," she cried, "passed the very first—you and Gilbert both—you're ties—but your name is first. Oh, I'm so proud!"

Diana **flung** the paper on the table and herself on Anne's bed, utterly breathless and incapable of further speech. Anne lighted the lamp, **oversetting** the match safe and using up half a dozen matches before her shaking hands could accomplish the task. Then she **snatched** up the paper. Yes, she had passed—there was her name at the very top of a list of two hundred! That moment was worth living for.

fling [flɪŋ]
v. 掷,抛

overset [əʊvə'set]
v. 打翻

snatch [snætʃ]
一把抓起;抢夺

"You did just splendidly, Anne," puffed Diana, recovering sufficiently to sit up and speak, for Anne, starry eyed and **rapt**, had not **uttered** a word. "Father brought the paper home from Bright River not ten minutes ago—it came out on the afternoon train, you know,

rapt [ræpt]
adj. 专心致志的
utter ['ʌtə(r)]
v. 说

and won't be here till tomorrow by mail—and when I saw the pass list I just rushed over like a wild thing. You've all passed, every one of you, Moody Spurgeon and all, although he'**s conditioned in** history. Jane and Ruby did pretty well—they're halfway up— and so did Charlie. Josie just **scraped through** with three marks to spare, but you'll see she'll put on as many airs as if she'd led. Won't Miss Stacy be delighted? Oh, Anne, what does it feel like to see your name at the head of a pass list like that? If it were me I know I'd go crazy with joy. I am pretty near crazy as it is, but you're as calm and cool as a spring evening."

be conditioned in 需要补考

scrape[skreɪp]through 勉强通过

"I'm just **dazzled** inside," said Anne. "I want to say a hundred things, and I can't find words to say them in. I never dreamed of this—yes, I did too, just once! I let myself think once, 'What if I should come out first?' **quakingly**, you know, for it seemed so vain and **presumptuous** to think I could lead the Island. Excuse me a minute, Diana. I must run right out to the field to tell Matthew. Then we'll go up the road and tell the good news to the others."

dazzled [ˈdæzld] *adj.* 眼花缭乱的

quakingly [kweɪkɪŋli] *adv.* 颤抖地

presumptuous [prɪˈzʌmptʃuəs] *adj.* 自负;冒昧

They hurried to the hayfield below the barn where Matthew was **coiling** hay, and, as luck would have it, Mrs. Lynde was talking to Marilla at the lane fence.

coil [kɔɪl] *v.* 盘绕

"Oh, Matthew," exclaimed Anne, "I've passed and I'm first—or one of the first! I'm not vain, but I'm thankful."

"Well now, I always said it," said Matthew, gazing at the pass list delightedly. "I knew you could beat them all easy."

"You've done pretty well, I must say, Anne," said Marilla, trying to hide her extreme pride in Anne from Mrs. Rachel's critical eye. But that good soul said **heartily**:

heartily [ˈhɑːtɪli] *adv.* 尽情地;坚定地

"I just guess she has done well, and far be it from me to be backward in saying it. You're a credit to your friends, Anne, that's what, and we're all proud of you."

That night Anne, who had wound up the delightful evening with a serious little talk with Mrs. Allan at the **manse**, knelt sweetly by her open window in a great sheen of moonshine and **murmured** a prayer of gratitude and aspiration that came straight from her heart. There was in it thankfulness for the past and **reverent petition** for the future; and when she slept on her white pillow her dreams were as fair and bright and beautiful as **maidenhood** might desire.

manse [mæns]
n. 牧师住宅
murmur ['mɜːmə(r)]
v. 低语
reverent ['revərənt]
adj. 虔诚的
petition [pə'tɪʃn]
n. 祈求
maidenhood ['meɪdnhʊd]
n. 少女时期

CHAPTER XXXIII

The Hotel Concert

"Put on your white organdy, by all means, Anne," advised Diana decidedly.

They were together in the east gable chamber; outside it was only twilight—a lovely yellowish-green twilight with a clear-blue cloudless sky. A big round moon, slowly deepening from her **pallid** luster into **burnished** silver, hung over the Haunted Wood; the air was full of sweet summer sounds—sleepy birds twittering, **freakish** breezes, faraway voices and laughter. But in Anne's room the blind was drawn and the lamp lighted, for an important toilet was being made.

pallid ['pælɪd]
adj. 暗淡的
burnished ['bɜːnɪʃt]
adj. 光亮的
freakish ['friːkɪʃ]
adj. 反常的

The east gable was a very different place from what it had been on that night four years before, when Anne had felt its bareness **penetrate** to the marrow of her spirit with its **inhospitable** chill. Changes had **crept in**, Marilla conniving at them resignedly, until it was as sweet and dainty a nest as a young girl could desire.

The **velvet** carpet with the pink roses and the pink silk curtains of Anne's early visions had certainly never materialized; but her dreams had kept pace with her growth, and it is not probable she **lamented** them. The floor was covered with a pretty **matting**, and

penetrate ['penətreɪt]
v. 刺穿,渗入
inhospitable [ˌɪnhɒ'spɪtəbl]
adj. 不好客的
creep [kriːp] in
不知不觉发生
velvet ['velvɪt]
n. 天鹅绒
lament [lə'ment]
v. 痛惜
matting ['mætɪŋ]
n. 编垫子的材料

the curtains that softened the high window and **fluttered** in the **vagrant** breezes were of pale-green art muslin. The walls, hung not with gold and silver brocade tapestry, but with a dainty apple-blossom paper, were adorned with a few good pictures given Anne by Mrs. Allan. Miss Stacy's photograph occupied the place of honor, and Anne made a **sentimental** point of keeping fresh flowers on the bracket under it. Tonight a spike of white lilies faintly perfumed the room like the dream of a fragrance. There was no "**mahogany** furniture", but there was a white-painted bookcase filled with books, a cushioned wicker rocker, a toilet table **befrilled with** white muslin, a quaint, gilt-framed mirror with chubby pink Cupids and purple grapes painted over its **arched** top, that used to hang in the spare room, and a low white bed.

Anne was dressing for a concert at the White Sands Hotel. The guests had got it up **in aid of** the Charlottetown hospital, and had hunted out all the available amateur talent in the surrounding districts to help it along. Bertha Sampson and Pearl Clay of the White Sands Baptist choir had been asked to sing a duet; Milton Clark of Newbridge was to give a violin solo; Winnie Adella Blair of Carmody was to sing a Scotch ballad; and Laura Spencer of Spencervale and Anne Shirley of Avonlea were to recite.

As Anne would have said at one time, it was "an **epoch in** her life", and she was deliciously **athrill** with the excitement of it. Matthew was in the seventh heaven of gratified pride over the honor conferred on his Anne and Marilla was not far behind, although she would have died rather than admit it, and said she didn't think it was very proper for a lot of young folks to be **gadding** over to the hotel without any responsible person with them.

Anne and Diana were to drive over with Jane Andrews and her

flutter [ˈflʌtə(r)]
v. (使)飘动
vagrant [ˈveɪgrənt]
adj. 游移不定的

sentimental [ˌsentɪˈmentl]
adj. 多愁善感的
mahogany [məˈhɒgəni]
n. 红木

befrilled with
镶嵌着

arched [ɑːtʃt]
adj. 拱形的

in aid of
为帮助

epoch [ˈiːpɒk]
n. 纪元
athrill [əˈθril]
adj. 兴奋的

gad [gæd]
v. 闲逛

brother Billy in their double-seated **buggy**; and several other Avonlea girls and boys were going too. There was a party of visitors expected out from town, and after the concert a supper was to be given to the performers.

buggy [ˈbʌgi] *n.* 双排座马车

"Do you really think the organdy will be best?" queried Anne anxiously. "I don't think it's as pretty as my blue-flowered muslin—and it certainly isn't so fashionable."

"But it suits you ever so much better," said Diana. "It's so soft and **frilly** and **clinging**. The muslin is stiff, and makes you look too dressed up. But the organdy seems as if it grew on you."

frilly [ˈfrɪli] *adj.* 多褶边的
clinging [ˈklɪŋɪŋ] *adj.* 贴身的

Anne sighed and **yielded**. Diana was beginning to have a reputation for notable taste in dressing, and her advice on such subjects was much sought after. She was looking very pretty herself on this particular night in a dress of the lovely wild-rose pink, from which Anne was forever **debarred**; but she was not to take any part in the concert, so her appearance was of minor importance. All her pains were **bestowed** upon Anne, who, she vowed, must, for the credit of Avonlea, be dressed and combed and **adorned** to the Queen's taste.

yield [jiːld] *v.* 屈服
debar [dɪˈbɑː(r)] *v.* 阻止
bestow [bɪˈstəʊ] *v.* 给予,献给
adorn [əˈdɔːn] *v.* 装饰;打扮

"Pull out that frill a little more—so; here, let me tie your sash; now for your slippers. I'm going to braid your hair in two thick braids, and tie them halfway up with big white bows—no, don't pull out a single curl over your forehead—just have the soft part. There is no way you do your hair suits you so well, Anne, and Mrs. Allan says you look like a Madonna when you part it so. I shall fasten this little white house rose just behind your ear. There was just one on my bush, and I saved it for you."

"Shall I put my pearl beads on?" asked Anne. "Matthew brought me a string from town last week, and I know he'd like to see them on me."

Diana **pursed up** her lips, put her black head on one side critically, and finally pronounced in favor of the beads, which were thereupon tied around Anne's slim milk-white throat.

purse [pɜːs] up
噘起

"There's something so **stylish** about you, Anne," said Diana, with unenvious admiration. "You hold your head with such an air. I suppose it's your figure. I am just a dumpling. I've always been afraid of it, and now I know it is so. Well, I suppose I shall just have to **resign** myself to it."

stylish [ˈstaɪlɪʃ]
adj. 时髦的

resign oneself to
使听从于

"But you have such dimples," said Anne, smiling affectionately into the pretty, **vivacious** face so near her own. "Lovely dimples, like little dents in cream. I have given up all hope of dimples. My dimple-dream will never come true; but so many of my dreams have that I mustn't complain. Am I all ready now?"

vivacious [vɪˈveɪʃəs]
adj. 生动活泼的

"All ready," assured Diana, as Marilla appeared in the doorway, a **gaunt** figure with grayer hair than of yore and no fewer angles, but with a much softer face. "Come right in and look at our **elocutionist**, Marilla. Doesn't she look lovely?"

gaunt [gɔːnt]
adj. 憔悴的

elocutionist
[ˌeləˈkjuːʃnist]
n. 朗诵家

Marilla emitted a sound between a sniff and a grunt.

"She looks neat and proper. I like that way of fixing her hair. But I expect she'll ruin that dress driving over there in the dust and dew with it, and it looks most too thin for these damp nights. Organdy's the most unserviceable stuff in the world anyhow, and I told Matthew so when he got it. But there is no use in saying anything to Matthew nowadays. Time was when he would take my advice, but now he just buys things for Anne regardless, and the **clerks** at Carmody know they can palm anything off on him. Just let them tell him a thing is pretty and fashionable, and Matthew **plunks** his money down for it. Mind you keep your skirt clear of the wheel, Anne, and put your warm jacket on."

clerk [klɑːk]
n. 职员

plunk [plʌŋk] one's money down
掏钱

Then Marilla **stalked** downstairs, thinking proudly how sweet Anne looked, with that "One moonbeam from the forehead to the crown" and regretting that she could not go to the concert herself to hear her girl recite.

stalk [stɔːk]
v. 偷偷接近

"I wonder if it is too **damp** for my dress," said Anne anxiously.

damp [dæmp]
adj. 潮湿的

"Not a bit of it," said Diana, pulling up the window blind. "It's a perfect night, and there won't be any **dew**. Look at the moonlight."

dew [djuː]
n. 露水

"I'm so glad my window looks east into the sunrising," said Anne, going over to Diana. "It's so splendid to see the morning coming up over those long hills and glowing through those sharp fir tops. It's new every morning, and I feel as if I washed my very soul in that bath of earliest sunshine. Oh, Diana, I love this little room so dearly. I don't know how I'll get along without it when I go to town next month."

"Don't speak of your going away tonight," begged Diana. "I don't want to think of it, it makes me so miserable, and I do want to have a good time this evening. What are you going to recite, Anne? And are you nervous?"

"Not a bit. I've recited so often in public I don't mind at all now. I've decided to give 'The Maiden's Vow'. It's so pathetic. Laura Spencer is going to give a comic recitation, but I'd rather make people cry than laugh."

"What will you recite if they **encore** you?"

encore ['ɒŋkɔː(r)]
v. 加演的节目

"They won't dream of encoring me," scoffed Anne, who was not without her own secret hopes that they would, and already visioned herself telling Matthew all about it at the next morning's breakfast table. "There are Billy and Jane now—I hear the wheels. Come on."

Billy Andrews insisted that Anne should ride on the front seat with him, so she unwillingly climbed up. She would have much preferred to sit back with the girls, where she could have laughed and chattered to her heart's content. There was not much of either laughter or chatter in Billy. He was a big, fat, **stolid** youth of twenty, with a round, expressionless face, and a painful lack of conversational gifts. But he admired Anne immensely, and was **puffed up with** pride over the prospect of driving to White Sands with that slim, upright figure beside him.

stolid [ˈstɒlɪd] *adj.* 不易激动的，喜怒不形于色的

puffed up with pride 趾高气扬

Anne, **by dint of** talking over her shoulder to the girls and occasionally passing a sop of civility to Billy—who grinned and chuckled and never could think of any reply until it was too late—**contrived** to enjoy the drive in spite of all. It was a night for enjoyment. The road was full of buggies, all bound for the hotel, and laughter, silver clear, echoed and reechoed along it. When they reached the hotel it was a blaze of light from top to bottom. They were met by the ladies of the concert committee, one of whom took Anne off to the performers' dressing room which was filled with the members of a Charlottetown Symphony Club, among whom Anne felt suddenly shy and frightened and **countrified**. Her dress, which, in the east gable, had seemed so **dainty** and pretty, now seemed simple and plain—too simple and plain, she thought, among all the silks and laces that glistened and rustled around her. What were her pearl beads compared to the diamonds of the big, handsome lady near her? And how poor her one wee white rose must look beside all the hothouse flowers the others wore! Anne laid her hat and jacket away, and shrank miserably into a corner. She wished herself back in the white room at Green Gables.

by dint [dɪnt] of 凭借

contrive [kənˈtraɪv] *v.* 设法做到

countrified [ˈkʌntrifaɪd] *adj.* 土里土气的

dainty [ˈdeɪnti] *adj.* 精致的

It was still worse on the platform of the big concert hall of the hotel, where she presently found herself. The electric lights dazzled her eyes, the perfume and hum bewildered her. She wished she were sitting down in the audience with Diana and Jane, who seemed to be having a splendid time away at the back. She **was wedged in** between a **stout** lady in pink silk and a tall, scornful-looking girl in a white-lace dress. The stout lady occasionally turned her head squarely around and surveyed Anne through her eyeglasses until Anne, acutely sensitive of being so **scrutinized**, felt that she must scream aloud; and the white-lace girl kept talking **audibly** to her next neighbor about the "country bumpkins" and "rustic belles" in the audience, **languidly** anticipating "such fun" from the displays of local talent on the program. Anne believed that she would hate that white-lace girl to the end of life.

be wedged [wedʒ] in
被夹在中间
stout [staʊt]
adj. 高大结实的

scrutinize [ˈskruːtənaɪz]
v. 仔细检查
audibly [ˈɔːdəbli]
adv. 可听见地
languidly [ˈlæŋgwɪdli]
adv. 无精打采地

Unfortunately for Anne, a professional elocutionist was staying at the hotel and had **consented** to recite. She was a lithe, dark-eyed woman in a wonderful gown of **shimmering** gray stuff like woven moonbeams with gems on her neck and in her dark hair. She had a marvelously flexible voice and wonderful power of expression; the audience went wild over her selection. Anne, forgetting all about herself and her troubles for the time, listened with rapt and shining eyes; but when the recitation ended she suddenly put her hands over her face. She could never get up and recite after that—never. Had she ever thought she could recite? Oh, if she were only back at Green Gables!

consent [kənˈsent]
v. 同意
shimmer [ˈʃɪmə(r)]
v. 闪烁

At this **unpropitious** moment her name was called. Somehow Anne—who did not notice the rather guilty little start of surprise the white-lace girl gave, and would not have understood the subtle **compliment** implied therein if she had—got on her feet, and moved dizzily out to the front. She was so pale that Diana and Jane, down in the audience, clasped each other's hands in nervous sympathy.

unpropitious
[ʌnprəˈpɪʃəs]
adj. 不(吉)利的
compliment
[ˈkɒmplɪmənt]
n. 赞美

Anne was the victim of an overwhelming attack of **stage fright**. Often as she had recited in public, she had never before faced such an audience as this, and the sight of it paralyzed her energies completely. Everything was so strange, so brilliant, so bewildering—the rows of la-

stage fright
怯场

dies in evening dress, the critical faces, the whole atmosphere of wealth and culture about her. Very different this from the plain benches at the Debating Club, filled with the homely, sympathetic faces of friends and neighbors. These people, she thought, would be merciless critics. Perhaps, like the white-lace girl, they anticipated amusement from her "rustic" efforts. She felt hopelessly, helplessly ashamed and miserable. Her knees trembled, her heart fluttered, a horrible faintness came over her; not a word could she utter, and the next moment she would have fled from the platform despite the humiliation which, she felt, must ever after be her **portion** if she did so.

But suddenly, as her **dilated**, frightened eyes gazed out over the audience, she saw Gilbert Blythe away at the back of the room, bending forward with a smile on his face—a smile which seemed to Anne at once **triumphant** and **taunting**. In reality it was nothing of the kind. Gilbert was merely smiling with appreciation of the whole affair in general and of the effect produced by Anne's slender white form and spiritual face against a background of palms in particular. Josie Pye, whom he had driven over, sat beside him, and her face certainly was both triumphant and taunting. But Anne did not see Josie, and would not have cared if she had. She drew a long breath and flung her head up proudly, courage and determination **tingling over** her like an electric shock. She would not fail before Gilbert Blythe—he should never be able to laugh at her, never, never! Her fright and nervousness vanished; and she began her recitation, her clear, sweet voice reaching to the farthest corner of the room without a **tremor** or a break. Self-possession was fully restored to her, and in the reaction from that horrible moment of powerlessness she recited as she had never done before. When she finished there were bursts of honest applause. Anne, stepping back to her seat, blushing with shyness and delight, found her

portion [ˈpɔːʃn] *n.* 部分，份额
dilated [daɪˈleɪtɪd] *adj.* 扩大的

triumphant [traɪˈʌmfənt] *adj.* 得意扬扬的
taunting [ˈtɔːntɪŋ] *adj.* 戏弄的

tingle [ˈtɪŋgl] over 震颤

tremor [ˈtremə(r)] *n.* 颤抖

hand vigorously clasped and shaken by the stout lady in pink silk.

"My dear, you did splendidly," she puffed. "I've been crying like a baby, actually I have. There, they're encoring you—they're bound to have you back!"

"Oh, I can't go," said Anne confusedly. "But yet—I must, or Matthew will be disappointed. He said they would encore me."

"Then don't disappoint Matthew," said the pink lady, laughing.

Smiling, blushing, limpid eyed, Anne tripped back and gave a quaint, funny little selection that captivated her audience still further. The rest of the evening was quite a little triumph for her.

When the concert was over, the stout, pink lady—who was the wife of an American millionaire—took her under her wing, and introduced her to everybody; and everybody was very nice to her. The professional elocutionist, Mrs. Evans, came and chatted with her, telling her that she had a charming voice and "interpreted" her selections beautifully. Even the white-lace girl paid her a languid little compliment. They had supper in the big, beautifully decorated dining room; Diana and Jane were invited to **partake** of this, also, since they had come with Anne, but Billy was nowhere to be found, having **decamped** in mortal fear of some such invitation. He was in waiting for them, with the team, however, when it was all over, and the three girls came merrily out into the calm, white moonshine radiance. Anne breathed deeply, and looked into the clear sky beyond the dark **boughs** of the firs.

partake [pɑːˈteɪk]
v. 参加
decamp [dɪˈkæmp]
v. 匆忙离去,搬离

bough [baʊ]
n. 大树枝

Oh, it was good to be out again in the purity and silence of the night! How great and still and wonderful everything was, with the murmur of the sea sounding through it and the darkling cliffs beyond like grim giants guarding **enchanted** coasts.

enchanted [ɪnˈtʃɑːntɪd]
adj. 施过魔法的

"Hasn't it been a perfectly splendid time?" sighed Jane, as they drove away. "I just wish I was a rich American and could spend my summer at a hotel and wear jewels and low-necked dresses and have ice cream and chicken salad every blessed day. I'm sure it would be ever so much more fun than teaching school. Anne, your recitation was simply great, although I thought at first you were never going to begin. I think it was better than Mrs. Evans's."

"Oh, no, don't say things like that, Jane," said Anne quickly, "because it sounds silly. It couldn't be better than Mrs. Evans's, you know, for she is a professional, and I'm only a schoolgirl, with a little **knack** of reciting. I'm quite satisfied if the people just liked mine pretty well."

knack [næk] *n.* 技能；本领

"I've a **compliment** for you, Anne," said Diana. "At least I think it must be a compliment because of the tone he said it in. Part of it was anyhow. There was an American sitting behind Jane and me—such a romantic-looking man, with coal-black hair and eyes. Josie Pye says he is a **distinguished** artist, and that her mother's cousin in Boston is married to a man that used to go to school with him. Well, we heard him say—didn't we, Jane?—'Who is that girl on the platform with the splendid Titian hair? She has a face I should like to paint.' There now, Anne. But what does Titian hair mean?"

compliment [ˈkɒmplɪmənt] *n.* 表扬，恭维

distinguished [dɪˈstɪŋgwɪʃt] *adj.* 卓越的

"Being interpreted it means plain red, I guess," laughed Anne. "Titian was a very famous artist who liked to paint red-haired women."

"Did you see all the diamonds those ladies wore?" sighed Jane. "They were simply dazzling. Wouldn't you just love to be rich, girls?"

"We are rich," said Anne **staunchly**. "Why, we have sixteen years to our credit, and we're happy as queens, and we've all got imaginations, more or less. Look at that sea, girls—all silver and shadow and vision of things not seen. We couldn't enjoy its loveliness

staunchly [stɔːntʃli] *adv.* 坚定地

any more if we had millions of dollars and ropes of diamonds. You wouldn't change into any of those women if you could. Would you want to be that white-lace girl and wear a sour look all your life, as if you'd been born turning up your nose at the world? Or the pink lady, kind and nice as she is, so stout and short that you'd really no figure at all? Or even Mrs. Evans, with that sad, sad look in her eyes? She must have been dreadfully unhappy sometime to have such a look. You know you wouldn't, Jane Andrews!"

"I don't know—exactly," said Jane unconvinced. "I think diamonds would comfort a person for a good deal."

"Well, I don't want to be anyone but myself, even if I go uncomforted by diamonds all my life," declared Anne. "I'm quite content to be Anne of Green Gables, with my string of pearl **bead**s. I know Matthew gave me as much love with them as ever went with Madame the Pink Lady's jewels."

bead [biːd]
n. 珠子，串珠

CHAPTER XXXIV

A Queen's Girl

The next three weeks were busy ones at Green Gables, for Anne was getting ready to go to Queen's, and there was much **sewing** to be done, and many things to be talked over and arranged. Anne's outfit was **ample** and pretty, for Matthew saw to that, and Marilla for once made no objections whatever to anything he purchased or suggested. More—one evening she went up to the east gable with her arms full of a delicate pale green material.

sewing [ˈsəʊɪŋ]
n. 缝纫

ample [ˈæmpəl]
adj. 充足的

"Anne, here's something for a nice light dress for you. I don't suppose you really need it; you've plenty of pretty waists; but I thought maybe you'd like something real dressy to wear if you were asked out anywhere of an evening in town, to a party or anything like that. I hear that Jane and Ruby and Josie have got 'evening dresses,' as they call them, and I don't mean you shall be behind them. I got Mrs. Allan to help me pick it in town last week, and we'll get Emily Gillis to make it for you. Emily has got taste, and her fits aren't to be equaled."

"Oh, Marilla, it's just lovely," said Anne. "Thank you so much. I don't believe you ought to be so kind to me—it's making it harder every day for me to go away."

The green dress was made up with as many tucks and frills and **shirrings** as Emily's taste permitted. Anne put it on one evening for Matthew's and Marilla's benefit, and recited "The Maiden's Vow" for them in the kitchen. As Marilla watched the bright, **animated** face and graceful motions her thoughts went back to the evening Anne had arrived at Green Gables, and memory recalled a vivid picture of the odd, frightened child in her **preposterous** yellowish-brown **wincey** dress, the heartbreak looking out of her tearful eyes. Something in the memory brought tears to Marilla's own eyes.

"I declare, my recitation has made you cry, Marilla," said Anne **gaily stooping** over Marilla's chair to drop a butterfly kiss on that lady's cheek. "Now, I call that a positive triumph."

"No, I wasn't crying over your piece," said Marilla, who would have scorned to be betrayed into such weakness by any poetry stuff. "I just couldn't help thinking of the little girl you used to be, Anne. And I was wishing you could have stayed a little girl, even with all your queer ways. You've grown up now and you're going away; and you look so tall and stylish and so—so—different altogether in that dress—as if you didn't belong in Avonlea at all—and I just got lonesome thinking it all over."

"Marilla!" Anne sat down on Marilla's gingham lap, took

shirring [ˈʃɜːrɪŋ]
n. 装饰性的褶带

animated [ˈænɪmeɪtɪd]
adj. 活泼的

preposterous
[prɪˈpɒstərəs]
adj. 荒谬的
wincey [ˈwinsi]
n. 棉绒

gaily [ˈgeɪli]
adv. 快乐地
stoop [ˈstuːp]
v. 弯腰，俯身

Marilla's lined face between her hands, and looked gravely and tenderly into Marilla's eyes. "I'm not a bit changed—not really. I'm only just **pruned** down and branched out. The real me—back here—is just the same. It won't make a bit of difference where I go or how much I change **outwardly**; at heart I shall always be your little Anne, who will love you and Matthew and dear Green Gables more and better every day of her life."

prune [pruːn]
v. 修剪,修整

outwardly ['aʊtwədli]
adv. 表面上

Anne laid her fresh young cheek against Marilla's faded one, and reached out a hand to pat Matthew's shoulder. Marilla would have given much just then to have possessed Anne's power of putting her feelings into words; but nature and habit had willed it otherwise, and she could only put her arms close about her girl and hold her tenderly to her heart, wishing that she need never let her go.

Matthew, with a suspicious **moisture** in his eyes, got up and went out-of-doors. Under the stars of the blue summer night he walked **agitatedly** across the yard to the gate under the poplars.

moisture ['mɔɪstʃə(r)]
n. 湿气,水分

agitatedly ['ædʒɪteɪtɪdli]
adv. 焦急地

"Well now, I guess she ain't been much spoiled," he muttered, proudly. "I guess my putting in my oar occasional never did much harm after all. She's smart and pretty, and loving, too, which is better than all the rest. She's been a blessing to us, and there never was a luckier mistake than what Mrs. Spencer made—if it was luck. I don't believe it was any such thing. It was **providence**, because the almighty saw we needed her, I reckon."

providence ['prɒvɪdəns]
n. 上帝;苍天

The day finally came when Anne must go to town. She and Matthew drove in one fine September morning, after a tearful parting with Diana and an untearful practical one—on Marilla's side at least—with Marilla. But when Anne had gone Diana dried her tears and went to a beach picnic at White Sands with some of her Carmody cousins, where she contrived to enjoy herself tolerably well; while Marilla plunged fiercely into unnecessary work and kept at it all day long with the bitterest kind of heartache—the ache that burns and **gnaws** and cannot wash itself away in ready tears. But that night, when Marilla went to bed, acutely and miserably conscious that the little gable room at the end of the hall was **untenanted** by any vivid young life and unstirred by any soft breathing, she buried her face in her pillow, and wept for her girl in a passion of sobs that appalled her when she grew calm enough to reflect how very wicked it must be to take on so about a sinful fellow creature.

gnaw [nɔː]
v. 啃噬，侵蚀

untenanted [ʌn'tɛnəntɪd]
adj. 无人居住的

Anne and the rest of the Avonlea scholars reached town just in time to hurry off to the Academy. That first day passed pleasantly enough in a **whirl** of excitement, meeting all the new students, learning to know the professors by sight and being assorted and organized into classes. Anne intended taking up the Second Year work being advised to do so by Miss Stacy; Gilbert Blythe elected to do the same. This meant getting a First Class teacher's license in one year instead of two, if they were successful; but it also meant much more and harder work. Jane, Ruby, Josie, Charlie, and Moody Spurgeon, not being troubled with the stirrings of ambition, were content to take up the Second Class work. Anne was conscious of a **pang** of loneliness when she found herself in a room with fifty other students, not one of whom she knew, except the tall, brown-haired boy across the room; and knowing him in the fashion she did, did not help her much, as she reflected pessimistically. Yet she was undeniably glad that they were in the same class; the old rivalry could still be carried on, and Anne would hardly have known what to do if it had been lacking.

whirl [wɜːl]
n. (使)旋转

pang [pæŋ]
n. 突然的疼痛

"I wouldn't feel comfortable without it," she thought. "Gilbert looks awfully determined. I suppose he's making up his mind, here and now, to win the medal. What a splendid **chin** he has! I never no-

chin [tʃɪn]
n. 下巴

ticed it before. I do wish Jane and Ruby had gone in for First Class, too. I suppose I won't feel so much like a cat in a strange **garret** when I get acquainted, though. I wonder which of the girls here are going to be my friends. It's really an interesting speculation. Of course I promised Diana that no Queen's girl, no matter how much I liked her, should ever be as dear to me as she is; but I've lots of second-best affections to **bestow**. I like the look of that girl with the brown eyes and the crimson waist. She looks vivid and red-rosy; there's that pale, fair one gazing out of the window. She has lovely hair, and looks as if she knew a thing or two about dreams. I'd like to know them both—know them well—well enough to walk with my arm about their waists, and call them nicknames. But just now I don't know them and they don't know me, and probably don't want to know me particularly. Oh, it's lonesome!"

garret [ˈgærət]
n. 顶楼小屋，阁楼

bestow [bɪˈstəʊ]
v. 赐予，授予

It was lonesome still when Anne found herself alone in her hall bedroom that night at **twilight**. She was not to board with the other girls, who all had relatives in town to take pity on them. Miss Josephine Barry would have liked to board her, but Beechwood was so far from the Academy that it was out of the question; so Miss Barry hunted up a boarding-house, assuring Matthew and Marilla that it was the very place for Anne.

twilight [ˈtwaɪlaɪt]
n. 黄昏，暮色

"The lady who keeps it is a reduced gentlewoman," explained Miss Barry. "Her husband was a British officer, and she is very careful what sort of boarders she takes. Anne will not meet with any **objectionable** persons under her roof. The table is good, and the house is near the Academy, in a quiet neighborhood."

objectionable
[əbˈdʒekʃənəbl]
adj. 令人不悦的

All this might be quite true, and indeed, proved to be so, but it did not materially help Anne in the first agony of homesickness that seized upon her. She looked dismally about her narrow little room, with its dull-papered, pictureless walls, its small iron **bedstead** and empty book-case; and a horrible choke came into her throat as she thought of her own white room at Green Gables, where she would have the pleasant consciousness of a great green still outdoors, of sweet peas growing in the garden, and moonlight falling on the orchard, of the brook below the slope and the spruce boughs tossing in the night wind beyond it, of a vast starry sky, and the light from Diana's window shining out through the gap in the trees. Here there was nothing of this; Anne knew that outside of her window was a hard street, with a network of telephone wires shutting out the sky, the **tramp** of alien feet, and a thousand lights gleaming on stranger faces. She knew that she was going to cry, and fought against it.

bedstead [ˈbedsted] *n.* 床架

tramp [træmp] *n.* 沉重的脚步声

"I won't cry. It's silly—and weak—there's the third tear **splashing** down by my nose. There are more coming! I must think of something funny to stop them. But there's nothing funny except what is connected with Avonlea, and that only makes things worse—four—five—I'm going home next Friday, but that seems a hundred years away. Oh, Matthew is nearly home by now—and Marilla is at the gate, looking down the lane for him—six—seven—eight—oh, there's no use in counting them! They're coming in a flood presently. I can't cheer up—I don't want to cheer up. It's nicer to be miserable!"

splash [splæʃ] *v.* 液体溅落

The flood of tears would have come, no doubt, had not Josie Pye appeared at that moment. In the joy of seeing a familiar face Anne forgot that there had never been much love lost between her and Josie. As a part of Avonlea life even a Pye was welcome.

"I'm so glad you came up," Anne said sincerely.

"You've been crying," remarked Josie, with **aggravating** pity. "I suppose you're homesick—some people have so little self-control in that respect. I've no intention of being homesick, I can tell you.

aggravate [ˈæɡrəveɪt] *v.* 激怒，使严重

Town's too **jolly** after that poky old Avonlea. I wonder how I ever existed there so long. You shouldn't cry, Anne; it isn't becoming, for your nose and eyes get red, and then you seem all red. I'd a perfectly scrumptious time in the Academy today. Our French professor is simply a duck. His moustache would give you kerwollowps of the heart. Have you anything eatable around, Anne? I'm literally starving. Ah, I guessed likely Marilla'd load you up with cake. That's why I **called round**. Otherwise I'd have gone to the park to hear the band play with Frank Stockley. He boards same place as I do, and he's a sport. He noticed you in class today, and asked me who the red-headed girl was. I told him you were an orphan that the Cuthberts had **adopted**, and nobody knew very much about what you'd been before that."

Anne was wondering if, after all, **solitude** and tears were not more satisfactory than Josie Pye's companionship when Jane and Ruby appeared, each with an inch of Queen's color ribbon—purple and scarlet—pinned proudly to her coat. As Josie was not "speaking" to Jane just then she had to subside into comparative harmlessness.

"Well," said Jane with a sigh, "I feel as if I'd lived many moons since the morning. I ought to be home studying my Virgil—that horrid old professor gave us twenty lines to start in on tomorrow. But I simply couldn't settle down to study tonight. Anne, **methinks** I see the traces of tears. If you've been crying do own up. It will restore my self-respect, for I was **shedding** tears freely before Ruby came along. I don't mind being a goose so much if somebody else is **goosey**, too. Cake? You'll give me a teeny piece, won't you? Thank you. It has the real Avonlea flavor."

Ruby, perceiving the Queen's calendar lying on the table, wanted to know if Anne meant to try for the gold medal.

Anne blushed and admitted she was thinking of it.

jolly ['dʒɒli] *adj.* 愉快的

call round 拜访

adopt [ə'dɒpt] *v.* 领养

solitude ['sɒlətjuːd] *n.* 独处,孤独

methinks [mɪ'θɪŋks] *v.* 我认为

shed [ʃed] *v.* 落泪

goosey ['guːsi] *adj.* 愚蠢的

"Oh, that reminds me," said Josie, "Queen's is to get one of the Avery scholarships after all. The word came today. Frank Stockley told me—his uncle is one of the board of governors, you know. It will be announced in the Academy tomorrow."

An Avery scholarship! Anne felt her heart beat more quickly, and the horizons of her ambition shifted and broadened as if by magic. Before Josie had told the news Anne's highest **pinnacle** of aspiration had been a teacher's provincial license, First Class, at the end of the year, and perhaps the medal! But now in one moment Anne saw herself winning the Avery scholarship, taking an Arts course at Redmond College, and graduating in a gown and **mortar board**, before the echo of Josie's words had died away. For the Avery scholarship was in English, and Anne felt that here her foot was on native **heath**.

pinnacle [ˈpɪnəkl] *n.* 顶点，极点

mortar board 学位帽

heath [hiːθ] *n.* 荒野

A wealthy manufacturer of New Brunswick had died and left part of his fortune to **endow** a large number of scholarships to be distributed among the various high schools and academies of the Maritime Provinces, according to their **respective** standings. There had been much doubt whether one would be allotted to Queen's, but the matter was settled at last, and at the end of the year the graduate who made the highest mark in English and English Literature would win the scholarship—two hundred and fifty dollars a year for four years at Redmond College. No wonder that Anne went to bed that night with tingling cheeks!

endow [ɪnˈdaʊ] *v.* 捐赠

respective [rɪˈspektɪv] *adj.* 分别的

"I'll win that scholarship if hard work can do it," she resolved. "Wouldn't Matthew be proud if I got to be a B.A.? Oh, it's delightful to have ambitions. I'm so glad I have such a lot. And there never seems to be any end to them—that's the best of it. Just as soon as you attain to one ambition you see another one glittering higher up still. It does make life so interesting."

CHAPTER XXXV

The Winter at Queen's

Anne's homesickness wore off, greatly helped in the wearing by her weekend visits home. As long as the open weather lasted the Avonlea students went out to Carmody on the new branch railway every Friday night. Diana and several other Avonlea young folks were generally on hand to meet them and they all walked over to Avonlea in a merry party. Anne thought those Friday evening gypsyings over the autumnal hills in the crisp golden air, with the homelights of Avonlea twinkling beyond, were the best and dearest hours in the whole week.

Gilbert Blythe nearly always walked with Ruby Gillis and carried her **satchel** for her. Ruby was a very handsome young lady, now thinking herself quite as grown up as she really was; she wore her skirts as long as her mother would let her and did her hair up in town, though she had to take it down when she went home. She had large, bright-blue eyes, a brilliant **complexion**, and a plump **showy** figure. She laughed a great deal, was cheerful and good-tempered, and enjoyed the pleasant things of life frankly.

satchel ['sætʃəl] *n.* 书包,背包

complexion [kəm'plekʃn] *n.* 面色,肤色

showy ['ʃəʊi] *adj.* 华丽的

"But I shouldn't think she was the sort of girl Gilbert would like," whispered Jane to Anne. Anne did not think so either, but she would not have said so for the Avery scholarship. She could not help thinking, too, that it would be very pleasant to have such a friend as Gilbert to jest and chatter with and exchange ideas about books and studies and ambitions. Gilbert had ambitions, she knew, and Ruby Gillis did not seem the sort of person with whom such could be profitably discussed.

There was no silly sentiment in Anne's ideas concerning Gilbert. Boys were to her, when she thought about them at all, merely possible good **comrades**. If she and Gilbert had been friends she would not have cared how many other friends he had nor with whom he walked. She had a **genius** for friendship; girl friends she had in plenty; but she had a **vague** consciousness that masculine friendship might also be a good thing to round out one's conceptions of companionship and **furnish** broader standpoints of judgment and comparison. Not that Anne could have put her feelings on the matter into just such clear definition. But she thought that if Gilbert had ever walked home with her from the train, over the crisp fields and along the ferny byways, they might have had many and merry and interesting conversations about the new world that was opening around them and their hopes and ambitions therein. Gilbert was a clever young fellow, with his own thoughts about things and a determination to get the best out of life and put the best into it. Ruby Gillis told Jane Andrews that she didn't understand half the things Gilbert Blythe said; he talked just like Anne Shirley did when she had a thoughtful fit on and for her part she didn't think it any fun to be bothering about books and that sort of thing when you didn't have to. Frank Stockley had lots more dash and go, but then he wasn't half as good-looking as Gilbert and she really couldn't decide which she liked best!

comrade [ˈkɒmreɪd]
n. 同志，伙伴

genius [ˈdʒiːniəs]
n. 天赋，天才

vague [veɪɡ]
adj. 模糊的

furnish [ˈfɜːnɪʃ]
v. 提供，供应

In the Academy Anne gradually drew a little circle of friends about her, thoughtful, imaginative, ambitious students like herself. With the "rose-red" girl, Stella Maynard, and the "dream girl", Priscilla Grant, she soon became intimate, finding the latter pale spiritual-looking maiden to be full to the brim of mischief and **pranks** and fun, while the vivid, black-eyed Stella had a heartful of wistful dreams and fancies, as aerial and rainbow-like as Anne's own.

prank [præŋk]
n. 恶作剧

After the Christmas holidays the Avonlea students gave up going home on Fridays and settled down to hard work. By this time all the

Queen's scholars had gravitated into their own places in the ranks and the various classes had assumed distinct and settled shadings of individuality. Certain facts had become generally accepted. It was admitted that the medal contestants had practically narrowed down to three—Gilbert Blythe, Anne Shirley, and Lewis Wilson; the Avery scholarship was more doubtful, any one of a certain six being a possible winner. The bronze medal for mathematics was considered as good as won by a fat, funny little up-country boy with a **bumpy** forehead and a patched coat.

bumpy [ˈbʌmpi]
adj. 颠簸的

Ruby Gillis was the handsomest girl of the year at the Academy; in the Second Year classes Stella Maynard carried off the palm for beauty, with small but critical minority in favor of Anne Shirley. Ethel Marr was admitted by all competent judges to have the most stylish modes of hair-dressing, and Jane Andrews—plain, **plodding**, conscientious Jane—carried off the honors in the domestic science course. Even Josie Pye attained a certain **preeminence** as the sharpest-tongued young lady in attendance at Queen's. So it may be fairly stated that Miss Stacy's old pupil's held their own in the wider arena of the academical course.

plodding [ˈplɒdɪŋ]
adj. 做事慎重而呆板的

preeminence [ˌpriːˈemɪnəns]
n. 卓越，杰出

Anne worked hard and steadily. Her **rivalry** with Gilbert was as intense as it had ever been in Avonlea school, although it was not known in the class at large, but somehow the **bitterness** had gone out of it. Anne no longer wished to win for the sake of defeating Gilbert; rather, for the proud consciousness of a well-won victory over a worthy **foeman**. It would be worthwhile to win, but she no longer thought life would be insupportable if she did not.

rivalry [ˈraɪvlri]
n. 竞争，对抗

bitterness [ˈbɪtənəs]
n. 苦涩，怨恨

foeman [ˈfəʊmən]
n. 敌人，对手

In spite of lessons the students found opportunities for pleasant times. Anne spent many of her spare hours at Beechwood and generally ate her Sunday dinners there and went to church with Miss Barry.

The latter was, as she admitted, growing old, but her black eyes were not dim nor the **vigor** of her tongue in the least **abated**. But she never sharpened the latter on Anne, who continued to be a prime favorite with the critical old lady.

vigor [ˈvɪgə] *n.* 精力，活力
abate [əˈbeɪt] *v.* 减轻，减弱

"That Anne-girl improves all the time," she said. "I get tired of other girls—there is such a provoking and eternal sameness about them. Anne has as many shades as a rainbow and every shade is the prettiest while it lasts. I don't know that she is as amusing as she was when she was a child, but she makes me love her and I like people who make me love them. It saves me so much trouble in making myself love them."

Then, almost before anybody realized it, spring had come; out in Avonlea the Mayflowers were peeping pinkly out on the **sere barrens** where snow-wreaths lingered; and the "mist of green" was on the woods and in the valleys. But in Charlottetown **harassed** Queen's students thought and talked only of examinations.

sere [sɪə] *adj.* 干枯的
barren [ˈbærən] *n.* 荒地，荒野
harass [ˈhærəs] *v.* 骚扰，烦扰

"It doesn't seem possible that the term is nearly over," said Anne. "Why, last fall it seemed so long to look forward to—a whole winter of studies and classes. And here we are, with the exams looming up next week. Girls, sometimes I feel as if those exams meant everything, but when I look at the big **buds** swelling on those chestnut trees and the **misty** blue air at the end of the streets they don't seem half so important."

bud [bʌd] *n.* 芽；蓓蕾
misty [ˈmɪsti] *adj.* 雾蒙蒙的

Jane and Ruby and Josie, who had dropped in, did not take this view of it. To them the coming examinations were constantly very important indeed—far more important than chestnut buds or Maytime hazes. It was all very well for Anne, who was sure of passing at least, to have her moments of **belittling** them, but when your whole future depended on them—as the girls truly thought theirs did—you

belittle [bɪˈlɪtl] *v.* 贬低，轻视

could not regard them philosophically.

"I' ve lost seven pounds in the last two weeks," **sighed** Jane. "It' s no use to say don' t worry. I will worry. Worrying helps you some—it seems as if you were doing something when you' re worrying. It would be dreadful if I failed to get my license after going to Queen' s all winter and spending so much money."

sigh [saɪ]
v. 叹息

"I don' t care," said Josie Pye. "If I don' t pass this year I' m coming back next. My father can afford to send me. Anne, Frank Stockley says that Professor Tremaine said Gilbert Blythe was sure to get the medal and that Emily Clay would likely win the Avery scholarship."

"That may make me feel badly tomorrow, Josie," laughed Anne, "but just now I honestly feel that as long as I know the violets are coming out all purple down in the hollow below Green Gables and that little ferns are poking their heads up in Lovers' Lane, it' s not a great deal of difference whether I win the Avery or not. I' ve done my best and I begin to understand what is meant by the 'joy of the strife'. Next to trying and winning, the best thing is trying and failing. Girls, don' t talk about exams! Look at that **arch** of pale green sky over those houses and picture to yourself what it must look like over the purply-dark beech-woods back of Avonlea."

arch [ɑːtʃ]
n. 拱门

"What are you going to wear for commencement, Jane?" asked Ruby practically.

Jane and Josie both answered at once and the chatter drifted into a side **eddy** of fashions. But Anne, with her elbows on the window sill, her soft cheek laid against her clasped hands, and her eyes filled with visions, looked out unheedingly across city roof and spire to that glorious dome of sunset sky and wove her dreams of a possible future from the golden tissue of youth' s own optimism. All the Beyond was

eddy ['edi]
n. 漩涡

hers with its possibilities lurking **rosily** in the oncoming years—each year a rose of promise to be woven into an immortal **chaplet**.

rosily ['rəʊzɪli] *adv.* 充满希望地
chaplet ['ʃæplət] *n.* 花环，花冠

CHAPTER XXXVI

The Glory and the Dream

On the morning when the final results of all the examinations were to be posted on the bulletin board at Queen's, Anne and Jane walked down the street together. Jane was smiling and happy; examinations were over and she was comfortably sure she had made a pass at least; further considerations troubled Jane not at all; she had no soaring ambitions and consequently was not affected with the **unrest** attendant thereon. For we pay a price for everything we get or take in this world; and although ambitions are well worth having, they are not to be cheaply won, but exact their dues of work and self-denial, anxiety and discouragement. Anne was pale and quiet; in ten more minutes she would know who had won the medal and who the Avery. Beyond those ten minutes there did not seem, just then, to be anything worth being called Time.

unrest [ʌn'rest] *n.* 不安，动荡

"Of course you'll win one of them anyhow," said Jane, who couldn't understand how the faculty could be so unfair as to order it otherwise.

"I have not hope of the Avery," said Anne. "Everybody says Emily Clay will win it. And I'm not going to **march up** to that bulletin board and look at it before everybody. I haven't the moral courage. I'm going straight to the girls' dressing room. You must read the announcements and then come and tell me, Jane. And I **implore** you in the name of our old friendship to do it as quickly as possible. If I have failed just say so, without trying to break it gently; and whatever you do don't sympathize with me. Promise me this, Jane."

march up 往上方走

implore [ɪm'plɔː(r)] *v.* 恳求

Jane promised solemnly; but, as it happened, there was no necessity for such a promise. When they went up the entrance steps of Queen's they found the hall full of boys who were carrying Gilbert Blythe around on their shoulders and yelling at the tops of their voices, "Hurrah for Blythe, Medalist!"

For a moment Anne felt one **sickening** pang of defeat and disappointment. So she had failed and Gilbert had won! Well, Matthew would be sorry—he had been so sure she would win.

sickening ['sɪkənɪŋ] *adj.* 令人厌恶的

And then!

Somebody called out:

"Three cheers for Miss Shirley, winner of the Avery!"

"Oh, Anne," gasped Jane, as they fled to the girls' dressing room amid hearty cheers. "Oh, Anne I'm so proud! Isn't it splendid?"

And then the girls were around them and Anne was the center of a laughing, congratulating group. Her shoulders were thumped and her hands shaken vigorously. She was pushed and pulled and hugged and among it all she managed to whisper to Jane:

"Oh, won't Matthew and Marilla be pleased! I must write the news home right away."

Commencement was the next important happening. The exercises were held in the big assembly hall of the Academy. Addresses were given, essays read, songs sung, the public award of diplomas, prizes and medals made.

Matthew and Marilla were there, with eyes and ears for only one student on the platform—a tall girl in pale green, with faintly flushed cheeks and starry eyes, who read the best essay and was pointed out and whispered about as the Avery winner.

"Reckon you're glad we kept her, Marilla?" whispered Matthew, speaking for the first time since he had entered the hall, when

Anne had finished her essay.

"It's not the first time I've been glad," **retorted** Marilla. "You do like to **rub** things **in**, Matthew Cuthbert."

Miss Barry, who was sitting behind them, leaned forward and poked Marilla in the back with her parasol.

"Aren't you proud of that Anne-girl? I am," she said.

Anne went home to Avonlea with Matthew and Marilla that evening. She had not been home since April and she felt that she could not wait another day. The apple blossoms were out and the world was fresh and young. Diana was at Green Gables to meet her. In her own white room, where Marilla had set a flowering house rose on the window sill, Anne looked about her and drew a long breath of happiness.

"Oh, Diana, it's so good to be back again. It's so good to see those pointed firs coming out against the pink sky—and that white orchard and the old Snow Queen. Isn't the breath of the mint delicious? And that tea rose—why, it's a song and a hope and a prayer **all in one**. And it's good to see you again, Diana!"

"I thought you like that Stella Maynard better than me," said Diana **reproachfully**. "Josie Pye told me you did. Josie said you were infatuated with her."

Anne laughed and **pelted** Diana with the faded "June lilies" of her **bouquet**.

"Stella Maynard is the dearest girl in the world except one and you are that one, Diana," she said. "I love you more than ever—and I've so many things to tell you. But just now I feel as if it were joy enough to sit here and look at you. I'm tired, I think—tired of being studious and ambitious. I mean to spend at least two hours tomorrow lying out in the orchard grass, thinking of absolutely nothing."

"You've done splendidly, Anne. I suppose you won't be teaching

retort [rɪˈtɔːt]
v. 反驳，回嘴
rub in
不断提及（某人不愿记住的事）

all in one
多合一

reproachfully [rɪˈprəʊtʃfəli]
adv. 责备地
pelt [pelt]
v. 扔，投掷
bouquet [buˈkeɪ]
n. 花束

now that you've won the Avery?"

"No. I'm going to Redmond in September. Doesn't it seem wonderful? I'll have a brand new **stock** of ambition laid in by that time after three glorious, golden months of vacation. Jane and Ruby are going to teach. Isn't it splendid to think we all got through even to Moody Spurgeon and Josie Pye?"

"The Newbridge trustees have offered Jane their school already," said Diana. "Gilbert Blythe is going to teach, too. He has to. His father can't afford to send him to college next year, after all, so he means to earn his own way through. I expect he'll get the school here if Miss Ames decides to leave."

Anne felt a queer little sensation of **dismayed** surprise. She had not known this; she had expected that Gilbert would be going to Redmond also. What would she do without their inspiring rivalry? Would not work, even at a **co-educational** college with a real degree in prospect, be rather flat without her friend the enemy?

The next morning at breakfast it suddenly struck Anne that Matthew was not looking well. Surely he was much grayer than he had been a year before.

"Marilla," she said hesitatingly when he had gone out, "is Matthew quite well?"

"No, he isn't," said Marilla in a troubled tone. "He's had some real bad spells with his heart this spring and he won't spare himself **a mite**. I've been really worried about him, but he's some better this while back and we've got a good hired man, so I'm hoping he'll kind of rest and pick up. Maybe he will now you're home. You always cheer him up."

Anne leaned across the table and took Marilla's face in her hands.

"You are not looking as well yourself as I'd like to see you,

stock [stɒk]
n. 存货，货物

dismayed [dɪsˈmeɪd]
adj. 惊愕的

co-educational
[ˌkəʊˌedʒuˈkeɪʃənl]
adj. 男女合校的

a mite
一点

Marilla. You look tired. I'm afraid you've been working too hard. You must take a rest, now that I'm home. I'm just going to take this one day off to visit all the dear old spots and hunt up my old dreams, and then it will be your turn to be lazy while I do the work."

Marilla smiled affectionately at her girl.

"It's not the work—it's my head. I've got a pain so often now—behind my eyes. Doctor Spencer's been fussing with glasses, but they don't do me any good. There is a distinguished **oculist** coming to the Island the last of June and the doctor says I must see him. I guess I'll have to. I can't read or sew with any comfort now. Well, Anne, you've done real well at Queen's I must say. To take First Class License in one year and win the Avery scholarship—well, well, Mrs. Lynde says pride goes before a fall and she doesn't believe in the higher education of women at all; she says it unfits them for woman's true sphere. I don't believe a word of it. Speaking of Rachel reminds me—did you hear anything about the Abbey Bank lately, Anne?"

oculist [ˈɒkjəlɪst] *n.* 眼科医生

"I heard it was shaky," answered Anne. "Why?"

"That is what Rachel said. She was up here one day last week and said there was some talk about it. Matthew felt really worried. All we have saved is in that bank—every penny. I wanted Matthew to put it in the Savings Bank in the first place, but old Mr. Abbey was a great friend of father's and he'd always banked with him. Matthew said any bank with him at the head of it was good enough for anybody."

"I think he has only been its **nominal** head for many years," said Anne. "He is a very old man; his nephews are really at the head of the institution."

nominal [ˈnɒmɪnəl] *adj.* 名义上的

"Well, when Rachel told us that, I wanted Matthew to draw our money right out and he said he'd think of it. But Mr. Russell told him yesterday that the bank was all right."

Anne had her good day in the companionship of the outdoor world. She never forgot that day; it was so bright and golden and fair, so free from shadow and so **lavish** of blossom. Anne spent some of its rich hours in the orchard; she went to the Dryad's Bubble and Willowmere and Violet Vale; she called at the manse and had a satisfying talk with Mrs. Allan; and finally in the evening she went with Matthew for the cows, through Lovers' Lane to the back pasture. The woods were all gloried through with sunset and the warm splendor of it streamed down through the hill gaps in the west. Matthew walked slowly with bent head; Anne, tall and **erect**, suited her springing step to his.

lavish [ˈlævɪʃ] *adj.* 大量的

erect [ɪˈrekt] *adj.* 挺拔的

"You've been working too hard today, Matthew," she said reproachfully. "Why won't you take things easier?"

"Well now, I can't seem to," said Matthew, as he opened the yard gate to let the cows through. "It's only that I'm getting old, Anne, and keep forgetting it. Well, well, I've always worked pretty hard and I'd rather drop in **harness**."

harness [ˈhɑːnɪs] *n.* 马具

"If I had been the boy you sent for," said Anne wistfully, "I'd be able to help you so much now and spare you in a hundred ways. I could find it in my heart to wish I had been, just for that."

"Well now, I'd rather have you than a dozen boys, Anne," said Matthew patting her hand. "Just mind you that—rather than a dozen boys. Well now, I guess it wasn't a boy that took the Avery scholarship, was it? It was a girl—my girl—my girl that I'm proud of."

He smiled his shy smile at her as he went into the yard. Anne took the memory of it with her when she went to her room that night and sat for a long while at her open window, thinking of the past and dreaming of the future. Outside the Snow Queen was mistily white in the moonshine; the frogs were singing in the marsh beyond Orchard Slope. Anne always remembered the silvery, peaceful beauty and fragrant calm of that night. It was the last night before sorrow touched her life; and no life is ever quite the same again when once that cold, **sanctifying** touch has been laid upon it.

sanctify [ˈsæŋktɪfaɪ] *v.* 使神圣化

CHAPTER XXXVII

The Reaper Whose Name Is Death

"Matthew—Matthew—what is the matter? Matthew, are you sick?"

It was Marilla who spoke, alarm in every jerky word. Anne came through the hall, her hands full of white narcissus—it was long before Anne could love the sight or odor of white narcissus again—in time to hear her and to see Matthew standing in the porch doorway, a folded paper in his hand, and his face strangely drawn and gray. Anne dropped her flowers and sprang across the kitchen to him at the same moment as Marilla. They were both too late; before they could reach him Matthew had fallen across the threshold.

"He's fainted," gasped Marilla. "Anne, run for Martin—quick, quick! He's at the barn."

Martin, the hired man, who had just driven home from the post office, started at once for the doctor, calling at Orchard Slope on his way to send Mr. and Mrs. Barry over. Mrs. Lynde, who was there on an errand, came too. They found Anne and Marilla distractedly trying to restore Matthew to consciousness.

Mrs. Lynde pushed them gently aside, tried his **pulse**, and then laid her ear over his heart. She looked at their anxious faces sorrowfully and the tears came into her eyes.

pulse [pʌls] *n.* 脉搏

"Oh, Marilla," she said gravely. "I don't think—we can do anything for him."

"Mrs. Lynde, you don't think—you can't think Matthew is—

is—" Anne could not say the dreadful word; she turned sick and pallid.

"Child, yes, I'm afraid of it. Look at his face. When you've seen that look as often as I have you'll know what it means."

Anne looked at the still face and there **beheld** the seal of the Great Presence.

behold [bɪˈhəuld]
v. 见到，看到

When the doctor came, he said that death had been instantaneous and probably painless, caused in all likelihood by some sudden shock. The secret of the shock was discovered to be in the paper Matthew had held and which Martin had brought from the office that morning. It contained an account of the failure of the Abbey Bank.

The news spread quickly through Avonlea, and all day friends and neighbors thronged Green Gables and came and went on **errands** of kindness for the dead and living. For the first time shy, quiet Matthew Cuthbert was a person of central importance; the white majesty of death had fallen on him and set him apart as one crowned.

errand [ˈerənd]
n. 差事，使命

When the calm night came softly down over Green Gables the old house was hushed and **tranquil**. In the parlor lay Matthew Cuthbert in his coffin, his long gray hair framing his placid face on which there was a little kindly smile as if he but slept, dreaming pleasant dreams. There were flowers about him—sweet old-fashioned flowers which his mother had planted in the **homestead** garden in her **bridal** days and for which Matthew had always had a secret, wordless love. Anne had gathered them and brought them to him, her **anguished**, tearless eyes burning in her white face. It was the last thing she could do for him.

tranquil [ˈtræŋkwɪl]
adj. 安静的，宁静的

homestead [ˈhəumsted]
n. 宅地，农庄
bridal [ˈbraɪdl]
adj. 新婚的，婚礼的
anguished [ˈæŋgwɪʃt]
adj. 感到极其痛苦的

The Barrys and Mrs. Lynde stayed with them that night. Diana, going to the east gable, where Anne was standing at her window, said gently:

"Anne dear, would you like to have me sleep with you tonight?"

"Thank you, Diana." Anne looked earnestly into her friend's face. "I think you won't misunderstand me when I say I want to be alone. I'm not afraid. I haven't been alone one minute since it happened—and I want to be. I want to be quite silent and quiet and try to realize it. I can't realize it. Half the time it seems to me that Matthew can't be dead; and the other half it seems as if he must have been dead for a long time and I've had this horrible dull ache ever since."

Diana did not quite understand. Marilla's impassioned grief, breaking all the bounds of natural reserve and lifelong habit in its stormy rush, she could comprehend better than Anne's tearless **agony**. But she went away kindly, leaving Anne alone to keep her first **vigil** with sorrow.

agony ['ægəni] n. 极度的痛苦，苦恼
vigil ['vɪdʒɪl] n. 守夜，守夜祈祷

Anne hoped that the tears would come in solitude. It seemed to her a terrible thing that she could not shed a tear for Matthew, whom she had loved so much and who had been so kind to her, Matthew who had walked with her last evening at sunset and was now lying in the dim room below with that awful peace on his brow. But no tears came at first, even when she knelt by her window in the darkness and prayed, looking up to the stars beyond the hills—no tears, only the same horrible dull ache of misery that kept on aching until she fell asleep, worn out with the day's pain and excitement.

In the night she awakened, with the **stillness** and the darkness about her, and the recollection of the day came over her like a wave of sorrow. She could see Matthew's face smiling at her as he had smiled when they parted at the gate that last evening—she could hear his voice saying, "My girl—my girl that I'm proud of." Then the tears came and Anne wept her heart out. Marilla heard her and **crept in** to comfort her.

stillness ['stɪlnəs] n. 平静；寂静

creep [kriːp] in 悄悄混进

"There—there—don't cry so, dearie. It can't bring him back.

It—it—isn't right to cry so. I knew that today, but I couldn't help it then. He'd always been such a good, kind brother to me—but God knows best."

"Oh, just let me cry, Marilla," sobbed Anne. "The tears don't hurt me like that ache did. Stay here for a little while with me and keep your arm round me—so. I couldn't have Diana stay, she's good and kind and sweet—but it's not her sorrow—she's outside of it and she couldn't come close enough to my heart to help me. It's our sorrow—yours and mine. Oh, Marilla, what will we do without him?"

"We've got each other, Anne. I don't know what I'd do if you weren't here—if you'd never come. Oh, Anne, I know I've been kind of strict and harsh with you maybe—but you mustn't think I didn't love you as well as Matthew did, for all that. I want to tell you now when I can. It's never been easy for me to say things out of my heart, but at times like this it's easier. I love you as dear as if you were my own flesh and blood and you've been my joy and comfort ever since you came to Green Gables."

Two days afterwards they carried Matthew Cuthbert over his homestead threshold and away from the fields he had tilled and the orchards he had loved and the trees he had planted; and then Avonlea settled back to its usual **placidity** and even at Green Gables affairs slipped into their old groove and work was done and duties fulfilled with regularity as before, although always with the aching sense of "loss in all familiar things". Anne, new to grief, thought it almost sad that it could be so—that they could go on in the old way without Matthew. She felt something like shame and **remorse** when she discovered that the sunrises behind the firs and the pale pink buds opening in the garden gave her the old inrush of gladness when she saw them—that Diana's visits were pleasant to her and that Diana's merry words

placidity [plə'sɪdəti] *n.* 宁静，平静

remorse [rɪ'mɔːs] *n.* 懊悔，自责

and ways moved her to laughter and smiles—that, in brief, the beautiful world of blossom and love and friendship had lost none of its power to please her fancy and thrill her heart, that life still called to her with many insistent voices.

"It seems like disloyalty to Matthew, somehow, to find pleasure in these things now that he has gone," she said wistfully to Mrs. Allan one evening when they were together in the manse garden. "I miss him so much—all the time—and yet, Mrs. Allan, the world and life seem very beautiful and interesting to me for all. Today Diana said something funny and I found myself laughing. I thought when it happened I could never laugh again. And it somehow seems as if I oughtn't to."

"When Matthew was here he liked to hear you laugh and he liked to know that you found pleasure in the pleasant things around you," said Mrs. Allan gently. "He is just away now; and he likes to know it just the same. I am sure we should not shut our hearts against the healing influences that nature offers us. But I can understand your feeling. I think we all experience the same thing. We **resent** the thought that anything can please us when someone we love is no longer here to share the pleasure with us, and we almost feel as if we were unfaithful to our sorrow when we find our interest in life returning to us."

resent [rɪ'zent] *v.* 怨恨,愤怒

"I was down to the **graveyard** to plant a rosebush on Matthew's grave this afternoon," said Anne dreamily. "I took a slip of the little white Scotch rosebush his mother brought out from Scotland long ago; Matthew always liked those roses the best—they were so small and sweet on their **thorny** stems. It made me feel glad that I could plant it by his grave—as if I were doing something that must please him in taking it there to be near him. I hope he has roses like them in heaven. Perhaps the souls of all those little white roses that he has

graveyard ['greɪvjɑːd] *n.* 墓地,坟场

thorny ['θɔːni] *adj.* 棘手的

loved so many summers were all there to meet him. I must go home now. Marilla is all alone and she gets lonely at twilight."

"She will be lonelier still, I fear, when you go away again to college," said Mrs. Allan.

Anne did not reply; she said good night and went slowly back to green Gables. Marilla was sitting on the front door-steps and Anne sat down beside her. The door was open behind them, held back by a big pink **conch** shell with hints of sea sunsets in its smooth inner **convolutions**.

conch [kɒntʃ]
n. 螺壳,海螺壳
convolution
[ˌkɒnvəˈluːʃn]
n. 盘绕,弯曲

Anne gathered some sprays of pale-yellow honeysuckle and put them in her hair. She liked the delicious hint of fragrance, as some aerial **benediction**, above her every time she moved.

benediction
[ˌbenɪˈdɪkʃn]
n. 祝福

"Doctor Spencer was here while you were away," Marilla said. "He says that the specialist will be in town tomorrow and he insists that I must go in and have my eyes examined. I suppose I'd better go and have it over. I'll be more than thankful if the man can give me the right kind of glasses to suit my eyes. You won't mind staying here alone while I'm away, will you? Martin will have to drive me in and there's **ironing** and baking to do."

ironing [ˈaɪənɪŋ]
n. 熨烫

"I shall be all right. Diana will come over for company for me. I shall attend to the ironing and baking beautifully—you needn't fear that I'll **starch** the handkerchiefs or flavor the cake with **liniment**."

starch [stɑːtʃ]
v. 给……上浆
liniment [ˈlɪnəmənt]
n. 擦剂，涂抹油

Marilla laughed.

"What a girl you were for making mistakes in them days, Anne. You were always **getting into scrapes**. I did use to think you were possessed. Do you mind the time you dyed your hair?"

get into scrapes
陷入困境

"Yes, indeed. I shall never forget it," smiled Anne, touching the heavy braid of hair that was wound about her shapely head. "I laugh a little now sometimes when I think what a worry my hair used to be to me—but I don't laugh much, because it was a very real trouble then. I did suffer terribly over my hair and my freckles. My freckles are really gone; and people are nice enough to tell me my hair is auburn now—all but Josie Pye. She informed me yesterday that she really thought it was redder than ever, or at least my black dress made it look redder, and she asked me if people who had red hair ever got used to having it. Marilla, I've almost decided to give up trying to like Josie Pye. I've made what I would once have called a heroic effort to like her, but Josie Pye won't be liked."

"Josie is a Pye," said Marilla sharply, "so she can't help being disagreeable. I suppose people of that kind serve some useful purpose in society, but I must say I don't know what it is any more than I know the use of **thistles**. Is Josie going to teach?"

thistle ['θɪsl] *n.* 蓟

"No, she is going back to Queen's next year. So are Moody Spurgeon and Charlie Sloane. Jane and Ruby are going to teach and they have both got schools—Jane at Newbridge and Ruby at some place up west."

"Gilbert Blythe is going to teach too, isn't he?"

"Yes"—briefly.

"What a nice-looking fellow he is," said Marilla absently. "I saw him in church last Sunday and he seemed so tall and manly. He looks a lot like his father did at the same age. John Blythe was a nice boy. We used to be real good friends, he and I. People called him my beau."

Anne looked up with swift interest.

"Oh, Marilla—and what happened?—why didn't you—"

"We had a quarrel. I wouldn't forgive him when he asked me to. I meant to, after awhile—but I was **sulky** and angry and I wanted to punish him first. He never came back—the Blythes were all mighty independent. But I always felt—rather sorry. I've always kind of wished

sulky ['sʌlki] *adj.* 生闷气的

I'd forgiven him when I had the chance."

"So you've had a bit of romance in your life, too," said Anne softly.

"Yes, I suppose you might call it that. You wouldn't think so to look at me, would you? But you never can tell about people from their outsides. Everybody has forgot about me and John. I'd forgotten myself. But it all came back to me when I saw Gilbert last Sunday."

CHAPTER XXXVIII

The Bend in the Road

Marilla went to town the next day and returned in the evening. Anne had gone over to Orchard Slope with Diana and came back to find Marilla in the kitchen, sitting by the table with her head leaning on her hand. Something in her **dejected** attitude struck a chill to Anne's heart. She had never seen Marilla sit **limply inert** like that.

"Are you very tired, Marilla?"

"Yes—no—I don't know," said Marilla wearily, looking up. "I suppose I am tired but I haven't thought about it. It's not that."

"Did you see the oculist? What did he say?" asked Anne anxiously.

"Yes, I saw him. He examined my eyes. He says that if I give up all reading and sewing entirely and any kind of work that strains the eyes, and if I'm careful not to cry, and if I wear the glasses he's given me he thinks my eyes may not get any worse and my headaches will be cured. But if I don't, he says I'll certainly be **stone-blind** in six months. Blind! Anne, just think of it!"

For a minute Anne, after her first quick exclamation of **dismay**, was silent. It seemed to her that she could not speak. Then she said bravely, but with a **catch** in her voice:

dejected [dɪˈdʒektɪd] *adj.* 沮丧的

limply [ˈlɪmpli] *adv.* 无力地,软弱地

inert [ɪˈnɜːt] *adj.* 不活泼的

stone-blind [ˈstəunˈblaɪnd] *adj.* 盲目的

dismay [dɪsˈmeɪ] *n.* 惊愕,沮丧

catch [kætʃ] *n.* 突然停顿,哽咽

"Marilla, don't think of it. You know he has given you hope. If you are careful, you won't lose your sight altogether; and if his glasses cure your headaches it will be a great thing."

"I don't call it much hope," said Marilla bitterly. "What am I to live for if I can't read or sew or do anything like that? I might as well be blind—or dead. And as for crying, I can't help that when I get lonesome. But there, it's no good talking about it. If you'll get me a cup of tea I'll be thankful. I'm about done out. Don't say anything about this to any one for a spell yet, anyway. I can't bear that **folks** should come here to question and sympathize and talk about it."

folk [fəʊk] *n.* 人们

When Marilla had eaten her lunch Anne persuaded her to go to bed. Then Anne went herself to the east gable and sat down by her window in the darkness alone with her tears and her heaviness of heart. How sadly things had changed since she had sat there the night after coming home! Then she had been full of hope and joy and the future had looked rosy with promise. Anne felt as if she had lived years since then, but before she went to bed there was a smile on her lips and peace in her heart. She had looked her duty courageously in the face and found it a friend—as duty ever is when we meet it frankly.

One afternoon a few days later Marilla came slowly in from the front yard where she had been talking to a caller—a man whom Anne knew by sight as Sadler from Carmody. Anne wondered what he could have been saying to bring that look to Marilla's face.

"What did Mr. Sadler want, Marilla?"

Marilla sat down by the window and looked at Anne. There were tears in her eyes **in defiance of** the oculist's prohibition and her voice broke as she said:

in defiance of 不顾，无视

"He heard that I was going to sell Green Gables and he wants to buy it."

"Buy it! Buy Green Gables?" Anne wondered if she had heard aright. "Oh, Marilla, you don't mean to sell Green Gables!"

"Anne, I don't know what else is to be done. I've thought it all over. If my eyes were strong I could stay here and make out to look after things and manage, with a good hired man. But as it is I can't. I may lose my sight altogether; and anyway I'll not be fit to run things. Oh, I never thought I'd live to see the day when I'd have to sell my home. But things would only go behind worse and worse all the time, till nobody would want to buy it. Every cent of our money went in that bank; and there's some notes Matthew gave last fall to pay. Mrs. Lynde advises me to sell the farm and board somewhere—with her I suppose. It won't bring much— it's small and the buildings are old. But it'll be enough for me to live on I reckon. I'm thankful you're provided for with that scholarship, Anne. I'm sorry you won't have a home to come to in your vacations, that's all, but I suppose you'll manage somehow."

Marilla broke down and wept bitterly.

"You mustn't sell Green Gables," said Anne resolutely.

"Oh, Anne, I wish I didn't have to. But you can see for yourself. I can't stay here alone. I'd go crazy with trouble and loneliness. And my sight would go—I know it would."

"You won't have to stay here alone, Marilla. I'll be with you. I'm not going to Redmond."

"Not going to Redmond!" Marilla lifted her worn face from her hands and looked at Anne. "Why, what do you mean?"

"Just what I say. I'm not going to take the scholarship. I decided so the night after you came home from town. You surely don't think I could leave you alone in your trouble, Marilla, after all you've done for me. I've been thinking and planning. Let me tell you my plans.

Mr. Barry wants to rent the farm for next year. So you won't have any bother over that. And I'm going to teach. I've applied for the school here—but I don't expect to get it for I understand the trustees have promised it to Gilbert Blythe. But I can have the Carmody school—Mr. Blair told me so last night at the store. Of course that won't be quite as nice or convenient as if I had the Avonlea school. But I can **board** home and drive myself over to Carmody and back, in the warm weather at least. And even in winter I can come home Fridays. We'll keep a horse for that. Oh, I have it all planned out, Marilla. And I'll read to you and keep you cheered up. You sha'n't be dull or lonesome. And we'll be real **cozy** and happy here together, you and I."

board [bɔːd]
v. 寄宿

cozy [ˈkəʊzi]
adj. 舒适的,温馨的

Marilla had listened like a woman in a dream.

"Oh, Anne, I could get on real well if you were here, I know. But I can't let you sacrifice yourself so for me. It would be terrible."

"Nonsense!" Anne laughed merrily. "There is no sacrifice. Nothing could be worse than giving up Green Gables—nothing could hurt me more. We must keep the dear old place. My mind is quite made up, Marilla. I'm not going to Redmond; and I am going to stay here and teach. Don't you worry about me a bit."

"But your ambitions—and—"

"I'm just as ambitious as ever. Only, I've changed the object of my ambitions. I'm going to be a good teacher—and I'm going to save your eyesight. Besides, I mean to study at home here and take a little college course all by myself. Oh, I've dozens of plans, Marilla. I've been thinking them out for a week. I shall give life here my best, and I believe it will give its best to me in return. When I left Queen's my future seemed to **stretch out** before me like a straight road. I thought I could see along it for many a milestone. Now there is a **bend** in it. I don't know what lies around the bend, but I'm going to believe that

stretch [stretʃ] out
伸手
bend [bend]
n. 弯曲

the best does. It has a fascination of its own, that bend, Marilla. I wonder how the road beyond it goes—what there is of green glory and soft, **checkered** light and shadows—what new landscapes—what new beauties—what curves and hills and valleys further on."

checkered [ˈtʃekəd] *adj.* 多变的

"I don't feel as if I ought to let you give it up," said Marilla, referring to the scholarship.

"But you can't prevent me. I'm sixteen and a half, '**obstinate** as a mule', as Mrs. Lynde once told me," laughed Anne. "Oh, Marilla, don't you go pitying me. I don't like to be pitied, and there is no need for it. I'm heart glad over the very thought of staying at dear Green Gables. Nobody could love it as you and I do—so we must keep it."

obstinate [ˈɒbstɪnət] *adj.* 固执的

"You blessed girl!" said Marilla, yielding. "I feel as if you'd given me new life. I guess I ought to stick out and make you go to college—but I know I can't, so I ain't going to try. I'll make it up to you though, Anne."

When it became noised abroad in Avonlea that Anne Shirley had given up the idea of going to college and intended to stay home and teach there was a good deal of discussion over it. Most of the good folks, not knowing about Marilla's eyes, thought she was foolish. Mrs. Allan did not. She told Anne so in approving words that brought tears of pleasure to the girl's eyes. Neither did good Mrs. Lynde. She came up one evening and found Anne and Marilla sitting at the front door in the warm, **scented** summer dusk. They liked to sit there when the twilight came down and the white moths flew about in the garden and the odor of mint filled the dewy air.

scented [ˈsentɪd] *adj.* 有香味的

Mrs. Rachel **deposited** her substantial person upon the stone bench by the door, behind which grew a row of tall pink and yellow **hollyhocks**, with a long breath of mingled **weariness** and relief.

deposit [dɪˈpɒzɪt] *v.* 存放
hollyhock [ˈhɒlihɒk] *n.* 蜀葵
weariness [ˈwɪərinəs] *n.* 疲倦

"I declare I'm getting glad to sit down. I've been on my feet all day, and two hundred pounds is a good bit for two feet to carry round. It's a great blessing not to be fat, Marilla. I hope you appreciate it. Well, Anne, I hear you've given up your notion of going to college. I was really glad to hear it. You've got as much education now as a woman can be comfortable with. I don't believe in girls going to college with the men and **cramming** their heads full of Latin and Greek and all that nonsense."

cram [kræm] *v.* 死记硬背

"But I'm going to study Latin and Greek just the same, Mrs. Lynde," said Anne laughing. "I'm going to take my Arts course right here at Green Gables, and study everything that I would at college."

Mrs. Lynde lifted her hands in holy horror.

"Anne Shirley, you'll kill yourself."

"Not a bit of it. I shall thrive on it. Oh, I'm not going to overdo things. As 'Josiah Allen's wife', says, I shall be 'mejum'. But I'll have lots of spare time in the long winter evenings, and I've no vocation for fancy work. I'm going to teach over at Carmody, you know."

"I don't know it. I guess you're going to teach right here in Avonlea. The trustees have decided to give you the school."

"Mrs. Lynde!" cried Anne, springing to her feet in her surprise. "Why, I thought they had promised it to Gilbert Blythe!"

"So they did. But as soon as Gilbert heard that you had applied for it he went to them—they had a business meeting at the school last night, you know—and told them that he withdrew his application, and suggested that they accept yours. He said he was going to teach at White Sands. Of course he knew how much you wanted to stay with Marilla, and I must say I think it was real kind and **thoughtful** in him, that's what. Real self-sacrificing, too, for he'll have his board to pay at White Sands, and everybody knows he's got to earn his own way through college. So the trustees decided to take you. I was

thoughtful [ˈθɔːtfl] *adj.* 关切的

tickled to death when Thomas came home and told me."

"I don't feel that I ought to take it," murmured Anne. "I mean—I don't think I ought to let Gilbert make such a sacrifice for—for me."

"I guess you can't prevent him now. He's signed papers with the White Sands trustees. So it wouldn't do him any good now if you were to refuse. Of course you'll take the school. You'll get along all right, now that there are no Pyes going. Josie was the last of them, and a good thing she was, that's what. There's been some Pye or other going to Avonlea school for the last twenty years, and I guess their mission in life was to keep school teachers reminded that earth isn't their home. Bless my heart! What does all that winking and blinking at the Barry gable mean?"

"Diana is signaling for me to go over," laughed Anne. "You know we keep up the old custom. Excuse me while I run over and see what she wants."

Anne ran down the clover slope like a deer, and disappeared in the firry shadows of the Haunted Wood. Mrs. Lynde looked after her indulgently.

"There's a good deal of the child about her yet in some ways."

"There's a good deal more of the woman about her in others," retorted Marilla, with a momentary return of her old crispness.

But crispness was no longer Marilla's distinguishing characteristic. As Mrs. Lynde told her Thomas that night.

"Marilla Cuthbert has got **mellow**. That's what."

Anne went to the little Avonlea graveyard the next evening to put fresh flowers on Matthew's grave and water the Scotch rosebush. She lingered there until dusk, liking the peace and calm of the little place, with its poplars whose rustle was like low, friendly speech, and its whispering grasses growing at will among the graves. When she fi-

tickle ['tɪkl]
v. 高兴

mellow ['meləʊ]
adj. 成熟的

nally left it and walked down the long hill that sloped to the Lake of Shining Waters it was past sunset and all Avonlea lay before her in a dreamlike **afterlight**— "a **haunt** of ancient peace". There was a freshness in the air as of a wind that had blown over honey-sweet fields of clover. Home lights twinkled out here and there among the homestead trees. Beyond lay the sea, misty and purple, with its haunting, unceasing murmur. The west was a glory of soft mingled hues, and the pond reflected them all in still softer shadings. The beauty of it all thrilled Anne's heart, and she gratefully opened the gates of her soul to it.

afterlight [ˈɑːftəlaɪt]
n. 死后（灵魂的）生活
haunt [hɔːnt]
n. 常去的场所

"Dear old world," she murmured, "you are very lovely, and I am glad to be alive in you."

Halfway down the hill a tall lad came whistling out of a gate before the Blythe homestead. It was Gilbert, and the whistle died on his lips as he recognized Anne. He lifted his cap **courteously**, but he would have passed on in silence, if Anne had not stopped and held out her hand.

courteously [ˈkɜːtiəsli]
adv. 彬彬有礼地

"Gilbert," she said, with scarlet cheeks, "I want to thank you for giving up the school for me. It was very good of you—and I want you to know that I appreciate it."

Gilbert took the offered hand eagerly.

"It wasn't particularly good of me at all, Anne. I was pleased to be able to do you some small service. Are we going to be friends after this? Have you really forgiven me my old fault?"

Anne laughed and tried unsuccessfully to withdraw her hand.

"I forgave you that day by the pond landing, although I didn't know it. What a stubborn little goose I was. I've been—I may as well make a complete confession—I've been sorry ever since."

"We are going to be the best of friends," said Gilbert, **jubilantly**.

jubilantly [ˈdʒuːbɪləntli]
adv. 欢欣鼓舞地

"We were born to be good friends, Anne. You' ve **thwarted** destiny enough. I know we can help each other in many ways. You are going to keep up your studies, aren' t you? So am I. Come, I' m going to walk home with you."

thwart [θwɔːt]
v. 受挫

Marilla looked curiously at Anne when the latter entered the kitchen.

"Who was that came up the lane with you, Anne?"

"Gilbert Blythe," answered Anne, **vexed** to find herself blushing. "I met him on Barry' s hill."

vexed [vekst]
adj. 伤脑筋的

"I didn' t think you and Gilbert Blythe were such good friends that you' d stand for half an hour at the gate talking to him," said Marilla with a dry smile.

"We haven' t been—we' ve been good enemies. But we have decided that it will be much more sensible to be good friends in the future. Were we really there half an hour? It seemed just a few minutes. But, you see, we have five years' lost conversations to catch up with, Marilla."

Anne sat long at her window that night companioned by a glad content. The wind **purred** softly in the cherry boughs, and the **mint** breaths came up to her. The stars twinkled over the pointed firs in the hollow and Diana' s light gleamed through the old gap.

purr [pɜː(r)]
v. 咕噜咕噜叫
mint [mɪnt]
n. 薄荷

Anne' s horizons had closed in since the night she had sat there after coming home from Queen' s; but if the path set before her feet was to be narrow she knew that flowers of quiet happiness would bloom along it. The joy of sincere work and worthy aspiration and **congenial** friendship were to be hers; nothing could rob her of her birthright of fancy or her ideal world of dreams. And there was always the bend in the road!

congenial [kən'dʒiːniəl]
adj. 意气相投的

"God' s in his heaven, all' s right with the world," whispered Anne softly.

Section C

Answer Key

Answer Key

Unit One

Text 1

Ⅰ.

1—5 TTFTF

Ⅱ.

1. The study examined how watching images and videos of cute animals for 30 minutes affects blood pressure, heart rate and anxiety.

2. The video is a 30-minute cute critters put together by montage, including some kittens, puppies, baby gorillas, and quokkas.

3. The sessions he chose were conducted in December 2019, involved 19 subjects—15 students and four staff—and were intentionally timed during winter exams, a time when stress is at a significantly high level, particularly for medical students.

4. We can use the State-Trait Anxiety Inventory to measure our anxiety level, a self-assessment method often used in clinical settings to diagnose anxiety.

Ⅲ. Answers vary.

Text 2

Ⅰ.

1. When his leg hurting got worse, to the point where he was limping and having problems walking, he paid a visit to the doctor and went through some tests.

2. He wanted to give kids in the hospital hope and let them know that they were not alone. He used pipe cleaners to make figurines he called "stick men" to hand out to other kids.

3. North Texas Giving Day is on Sept. 17.

4. He thinks Jaxon is such an incredible trooper, and an incredible young man . He's got an infectious smile and everything he does to make people feel good around him really covers such powerful and personal stories that he's been through.

Ⅱ.

1.Her voice was shaking despite all her efforts to control it.

2.If you have an umbrella, please share it with you.

3.People just don't stop to think about the consequences.

4.He is a person who always considers others.

Ⅲ. Answers vary.

Text 3

Ⅰ.

1.opposite, to

2.out

3.while

4.to

5.out

Ⅱ.

1.talk to oneself

2.bubble up to the surface

3.feelings of loneliness

4.tell a story

Ⅲ. Answers vary.

Text 4

Ⅰ.

1.Because the many stresses of higher education wear on students. This stress can incite new mental health concerns and worsen existing ones.

2. Sleep-deprived students will have trouble staying awake, and have trouble completing tasks. They may also be irritable or easily angered. Significant and frequent sleep disturbances are linked to depression.

3.Georgia Tech, is encouraging students to move into single dorms in an attempt to prevent the spread of COVID-19.

4.They can take advantage of green space in good weather to get natural light, which can offer vitamin D and receive light therapy in the colder months.

Ⅱ.

1.I have trouble reading her handwriting.

2.All living things depend on the sun for their growth.

3.He flipped through the post without opening any of it.

4.He takes advantage of the good weather to go for a walk.

Ⅲ. Answers vary.

Text 5

Ⅰ.

1—5 TFFTT

Ⅱ.

1.Many people come to the zoo just to catch a glimpse of the pandas.

2.The question has been lingering in my mind since I saw the film last night.

3.If we had realized the problem earlier, we would have done it differently.

4.We embarked on an urgent mission with the aim of achieving an ambitious goal.

5.This paper probes into a series of issues, including language expression, literary accomplishment, stylistic style and so on.

Ⅲ. Answers vary.

Unit Two

Text 1

Ⅰ.

1.Because of her aspirations and latest projects that could change the world for future generations.

2.Because she wants to be known for solving large problems facing our world, leaving the planet a better place and improving the lives of all people.

3.Their curiosity about the world.

4.By staying true to her scientific pursuit.

Ⅱ.

1.endeavors

2.take control of

3.aspired to

4.a sense of responsibility

5.serve as

6.undo the damage

7.curious about

8.contributed to

Ⅲ. Answers vary.

Text 2

Ⅰ.

1—5 FFFTT

Ⅱ.

1. In addition to improving children' s job prospects in later life, learning another language can boost their self-esteem.

2.The gallery has a range of modern artworks which can satisfy all kinds of visitors.

3.It can be difficult to carve out a niche in the fashion industry.

4.One of the concerns that people have is the side effects of the treatment.

Ⅲ. Answers vary.

Text 3

Ⅰ.

1. 虽然这些"智能"缝合线在美国可能有所帮助,但昂贵的工具可能不太适用于发展中国家的人,因为在发展中国家,互联网的接连和移动技术有时比较欠缺。

2. 着眼于全球卫生的公平性,她希望,改变颜色的缝合线有朝一日能帮助患者尽早发现手术感染部位,以便在影响最大时就医。

3. 我认为,这位年轻的高中科学家受到启发,致力于解决这一问题,这真是令人惊奇。

4. 回顾科学博览会的经历,泰勒最想感谢卡罗琳·沃林鼓励她参加科学博览会。

Ⅱ.

1—6 cdafbe

Ⅲ. Answers vary.

Text 4

Ⅰ.

1. To introduce the topic

2. 9/11 and Covid-19

3. Necessity

4. Increasing the use of robots doesn't necessarily have to mean that jobs disappear. Instead, it means a redeployment of human workers to the intellectual rather than mechanical tasks that humans excel at.

Ⅱ.

1.Recent business news has been littered with stories of companies failing.

2.It should come as no surprise that cycling builds leg strength.

3.He seemed to take it for granted that he should speak as a representative.

4.Having this disease does not necessarily mean that you will die young.

Ⅲ. Answers vary.

Text 5

Ⅰ.

1. 在极度的焦急不安中,我拿起身边各种激活生命所需要的仪器,准备给躺在我脚下的躯体注入生命。

2. 已经是凌晨一点了;雨滴打在玻璃上,发出凄厉的声音,我的蜡烛几乎要熄灭了,这时,在半灭的微光下,我看到了那只生物的暗黄色眼睛睁开了。它喘着粗气,抽搐的动作刺激着它的四肢。

3.我以一种远超适度的热情渴望它;但现在我已经完成了,梦想的美丽消失了,令人窒息的恐惧和厌恶充满了我的心。

4.终于,我之前忍受的骚动接二连三地疲倦了;我穿着衣服扑倒在床上,努力寻找片刻的遗忘。

5.我既高兴又惊讶,拥抱了她;但是当我在她的唇上印下第一个吻时,他们因死亡的色调而变得铁青;她的容貌似乎发生了变化,我以为我怀里抱着死去的母亲的尸体;一件裹尸布包裹着她的身躯,我看到那些蠕虫在法兰绒的褶皱中爬行。

6.没有什么能比得上看到克莱瓦尔的喜悦了;他的出现让我想起了我的父亲伊丽莎白,以及我记忆中如此珍贵的所有家乡场景。我握住他的手,一瞬间忘记了我的恐惧和不幸。

Ⅱ.

1.At length, the roses bloomed, and the tomatoes ripened.

2.There are various reasons that impel me to that conclusion.

3.We have endeavoured to make the vehicle environmentally friendly.

4.Scientific research permitted me to undertake a voyage of discovery to the land of knowledge

Ⅲ. Answers vary.

Unit Three

Text 1

Ⅰ.

1—4 ACBA

Ⅱ.

1—7 egcbdfa

Ⅲ. Answers vary.

Text 2

Ⅰ.

1. By dying.

2. Pontius Pilate wanted to let Jesus go.

3. The soldiers put a crown of thorns on Jesus's head, nailed him to a cross, put him into a tomb and used a big rock to block the entrance.

4. Because Jesus already took our punishment.

Ⅱ.

1.Tom doesn't dare to speak in public because he is afraid of being made fun of.

2.Anyone who breaks the school rules deserves punishment.

3.Michael was the first to spot the danger in the expedition.

4.With the joint efforts of several doctors, he finally came back to life.

Ⅲ. Answers vary.

Text 3

Ⅰ.

1—5 FFTFT

Ⅱ.

1—5 cebad

Ⅲ. Answers vary.

Text 4

Ⅰ.

1. British people felt offended by a video posted by an American on TikTok showing how to make hot tea.

2. He made a video of how Americans make coffee in an improper way to fight back.

3. Answers vary.

Ⅱ.

1—5 aebdc

Ⅲ. Answers vary.

Text 5

Ⅰ.

1—5 CACCA

Ⅱ.

1—6 daefcb

Ⅲ. Answers vary.

Unit Four

Text 1

Ⅰ.

1. Human trafficking.
2. That her article had inspired more efforts.
3. A grade 10 student at North Grenville District High School.
4. Knowing who her articles have inspired and seeing them sharing their knowledge with others is the most valuable to her.

Ⅱ.

1. I have reached a point in my life where I can make my own decision.
2. My grandfather inspired me with enthusiasm and passion for life.
3. The proposals are expected to spark heated debate.
4. His painstaking efforts contributed to the success in his career.

Ⅲ. Answers vary.

Text 2

Ⅰ.

1—5 TFTFT

Ⅱ.

1.What I'm going to do in this lecture is focus on something very specific.

2.Technology has a powerful influence on our lives, whether it's good or bad.

3.What mattered most was the students' physical health and mental status.

4.When caught cheating in the exam, he begged for the teacher's pardon and tried to escape punishment.

Ⅲ. Answers vary.

Text 3

Ⅰ.

1—4 FTFF

Ⅱ.

1. a person's child or children
2. a person regarded as a representative symbol
3. bad
4. strange

Ⅲ. Answers vary.

Text 4

Ⅰ.

1.Listen to and report on

2.Be similar to

3.Expect

4.Handle or control

5.Must or have to

6.Give away her personal photos

7.Be unrelated to

8.Make use of our weak points

Ⅱ.

1.We found fossils that old which bear remarkable resemblance to the tree.

2.If you don't drive carefully, we will be obliged to revoke your license.

3.All this wealth would be irrelevant to their survival if the island had few resources such as food, clean air and water.

4.Along with his strength, he had an uncanny ability to spot and exploit any weaknesses in an opponent.

Ⅲ. Answers vary.

Text 5

Ⅰ.

1—5 FTFFT

Ⅱ.

1.She stumbled upon a delicate vase in the yard sale of her neighborhood.

2.He had to rack his brains to figure out the problem.

3.Obsessed with mobile games, he spends hours daily, affecting both academics and social life.

4.He is determined to take action and put an end to this unpleasant disagreement.

5.The amusing video he shared began to go viral within a few hours, quickly gaining a number of views.

Ⅲ. Answers vary.

Unit Five

Text 1

Ⅰ.

1.Four.

2.It is headquarted in Silver Spring, Maryland.

3.They often consult NWS forecast maps and weather warnings.

4.We can know water-related hazards, including winds, rip currents, wave heights and flow rates.

Ⅱ.

1.She is not only an actress but also a good mother.

2.He began to focus on this topic.

3.The doctor monitored his blood pressure regularly.

4.I am familiar with this city.

Ⅲ. Answers vary.

Text 2

Ⅰ.

1—5 FTFTF

Ⅱ.

1. Moreover, they are often able to deduce much information about events that have never been recorded before.

2. In particular, he should enlist the help of those who study the fossilized remains of extinct species of plants and animals.

3. Our inferences may be wrong, just as we often misunderstand nature and the meaning of observed phenomena in nature.

4. Buried coins somehow tell us the reign of a certain Roman emperor.

Ⅲ. Answers vary.

Text 3

Ⅰ.

1.to; explain

2.or; arriving

3.shade; for; for

4.demonstrates; titled; on

Ⅱ.

1.stand for

2.run through

3.point north

4.be located at

Ⅲ. Answers vary.

Text 4

Ⅰ.

1.Eight.

2.The temperature gets warmer.

3.Rainfall is common throughout the year.

4.No, it doesn't.

Ⅱ.

1.The United States borders on Canada.

2.The prices range from 20 to 198 yuan.

3.The books in the library are classified by subject.

4.Geography is a subject that needs to be practiced

Ⅲ. Answers vary.

Text 5

Ⅰ.

1—4 BAAA

Ⅱ.

1.is made up of

2.keep track of

3.have been carried away

4.fell straight back

5.blend in with

6.throw off

7.shot out

8.stands for

9.is located on

10.solidify

Ⅲ. Answers vary.